D1612294

Cinema and radio in Britain and America, 1920–60

Manchester University Press

STUDIES IN
POPULAR
CULTURE
General editor: Professor Jeffrey Richards

Already published

Cinema and radio in Britain and America, 1920–60

JEFFREY RICHARDS

Manchester University Press

Manchester and New York

distributed in the United States exclusively by
Palgrave Macmillan

Published by Manchester University Press
Oxford Road, Manchester M13 9NR, UK
and Room 400, 175 Fifth Avenue, New York, NY 10010, USA
www.manchesteruniversitypress.co.uk

Distributed in the United States exclusively by
Palgrave Macmillan, 175 Fifth Avenue, New York,
NY 10010, USA

Distributed in Canada exclusively by
UBC Press, University of British Columbia, 2029 West Mall,
Vancouver, BC, Canada V6T 1Z2

British Library Cataloguing-in-Publication Data
A catalogue record for this book is available from the British Library

Library of Congress Cataloging-in-Publication Data applied for

ISBN 978 0 7190 8166 8 *hardback*

First published 2010

Edited and typeset
by Frances Hackeson Freelance Publishing Services, Brinscall, Lancs
Printed in Great Britain
by TJ International Ltd, Padstow

STUDIES IN POPULAR CULTURE

There has in recent years been an explosion of interest in culture and cultural studies. The impetus has come from two directions and out of two different traditions. On the one hand, cultural history has grown out of social history to become a distinct and identifiable school of historical investigation. On the other hand, cultural studies has grown out of English literature and has concerned itself to a large extent with contemporary issues. Nevertheless, there is a shared project, its aim, to elucidate the meanings and values implicit and explicit in the art, literature, learning, institutions and everyday behaviour within a given society. Both the cultural historian and the cultural studies scholar seek to explore the ways in which a culture is imagined, represented and received, how it interacts with social processes, how it contributes to individual and collective identities and world views, to stability and change, to social, political and economic activities and programmes. This series aims to provide an arena for the cross-fertilisation of the discipline, so that the work of the cultural historian can take advantage of the most useful and illuminating of the theoretical developments and the cultural studies scholars can extend the purely historical underpinnings of their investigations. The ultimate objective of the series is to provide a range of books which will explain in a readable and accessible way where we are now socially and culturally and how we got to where we are. This should enable people to be better informed, promote an interdisciplinary approach to cultural issues and encourage deeper thought about the issues, attitudes and institutions of popular culture.

Jeffrey Richards

For
Mary Cadogan
Brian Sibley
Norman Wright

Contents

Preface

The importance of films in the cultural and social life of both Britain and the United States has long been recognized. Only recently has the equally significant role of radio in both countries begun to be explored in detail, even though as early as 1939 Basil Maine wrote in *The BBC and Its Audience*: 'Of the external forms that are helping to shape human life and behaviour, none I should say is more ubiquitous and permeating than radio'. What has been almost entirely overlooked is the symbiotic relationship that developed between the two media in their heyday. That is the subject of the present book. It covers the period from the 1920s when radio emerged as a major cultural force to 25 November 1960 which has been retrospectively dubbed 'the day radio drama died' in the United States though not in Britain. It was on that date that CBS simultaneously cancelled its four remaining radio soap operas, effectively completing the process by which television had been gradually supplanting radio during the 1950s, taking over comedy and dramatic shows and performers wholesale and leaving the radio networks only with news and music. Although radio survived in Britain more or less intact, by 1960 it too had taken second place to television as the prime domestic medium.

The book begins by analysing the very different relationships between cinema and radio that emerged in Britain and the United States. It moves on to examine the ways in which cinema adapted radio programmes in the fields of comedy and detective fiction and then how radio dramatized films. There are chapters on the radio studio as a performance space and the role of film and radio in politics and war. The book ends with a look in detail at the ways in which the two media have dealt with three popular fictional characters, the Scarlet Pimpernel, Tarzan and Sherlock Holmes.

The Leverhulme Foundation generously funded the hiring of a teaching replacement for me in 2007–08 to enable me to complete research for the project. Progress was hampered by a broken right wrist sustained at Christmas

2007 and I am grateful to my surgeon Mr Ho for repairing my damaged arm and facilitating my return to the project. I am grateful to the staffs of Lancaster University Library, the British Film Institute and the BBC for their assistance. The following individuals have aided me in various ways and I extend my deep gratitude to them all for helping to make this book possible: Liz Anstee, David Ashford, Robert R. Barrett, Roger Bickerton, Mary Cadogan, Simon Callow, Steve Chibnall, Peter Coke, Stephen Constantine, Barbara Coulson, David Stuart Davies, Bob Dillon, Ernest Dudley, Christine Dundas, Sir Christopher Frayling, Mark Glancy, Marijke Good, Tom Hamilton, J.A. Hilton, Joel Hockey, Ian Horsfall, Toby Horton, Bernard Hrusa-Marlow, David Jacobs, Lynda Kelly, Tim O'Sullivan, Linda Persson, Karl Phillips, Jon Rolph, Joy Shelton, Brian Sibley, Anthony Slide, Keith Soothill, Andrew Spicer, Susan Stranks, Enyd Williams, Helen Williams, Deborah Williamson, Roger Wood and Norman Wright. I am indebted to James Deboo for compiling the index. The book is dedicated to Mary Cadogan, Brian Sibley and Norman Wright in token of many years of valued friendship.

Jeffrey Richards

Hollywood and radio: the creative nexus

It has long been recognized that films played a vital role in the social and cultural lives of the people of the United States and the United Kingdom in the first half of the twentieth century. But the power of films in the imaginative lives of audiences can only be properly understood when films are located within the wider cinema culture, which comprised fan magazines, cigarette cards, postcards, cheap biographies, the book of the film, the sheet music of the film and above all radio.

When radio first took off in the United States in the late 1920s, it was regarded by the film industry as a rival, something to keep people at home and away from the cinema. But during the 1930s, Hollywood began to appreciate the value of radio in publicizing and promoting its films. It discovered that radio complemented films rather than substituted for them and a richly symbiotic relationship developed between Hollywood and radio. For radio, unlike television, is a fundamentally different medium from film, being aural rather than visual. It uses words and sound effects to tell its stories, convey information and create atmosphere. Radio is experienced in the home as part of the domestic routine: cinema you go out to and it is part of the leisure pattern. Radio listening was a unique experience. Susan Douglas has perceptively identified three different types of listening: flat listening for information (the news), dimensional listening in which the listeners create their own mental images (drama) and associational listening which activates memories (music).[1]

For three decades in both the United Kingdom and the United States from the 1930s to the late 1950s radio was the dominant medium for the daily domestic consumption of news, music and drama. Then in the United States not only was its dominance ended by the rise of television but in the field of drama and story-telling it became virtually extinct. A different fate awaited it in the United Kingdom where television came similarly to dominate but because of the existence of the publicly funded BBC, as opposed to the largely commercial American radio, the medium not only survived but came to flourish in all its forms.

In the United States the fate of dramatic radio resembles that of silent films. Silent cinema, which died at the end of the 1920s, was an entirely visual medium, telling its stories pictorially and with a form of mime acting that became increasingly sophisticated. The form had reached a peak of achievement when the emergence of sound destroyed it and replaced it with what initially was a hybrid of theatre and film but soon developed into a distinctive new medium – the talkies. Dramatic radio, which was entirely aural, similarly reached a peak of accomplishment in the 1950s just as it was overtaken by television.

The first radio broadcast in the United States took place in 1920 and initiated a communications and media revolution. Within two years, there were 550 different radio stations and 1.5 million wireless sets. Unlike the United Kingdom where broadcasting developed under a monopolistic public corporation, the BBC, American radio was from the first a commercial operation. Most programmes came to be sponsored by commercial enterprises and to be used to advertise their products. This meant that the greatest power in American broadcasting was exercised by the advertising agencies who handled the accounts of the sponsoring companies. Initially programming centred on news bulletins, talks and recorded music. In the 1920s 60% of all broadcasting was music. But the first radio drama was broadcast in 1922, the first football match commentary also in 1922 and the first comedy series in 1925. During the 1930s, all the elements of programming that were to become broadcasting staples developed rapidly from these tentative beginnings.

The major structural development in the 1920s was the emergence of national networks: the National Broadcasting Company (NBC), initially two networks, Red and Blue, in 1926 and the Columbia Broadcasting System (CBS) in 1927. They were joined by a fourth network, Mutual, in 1934 and in 1943 the Federal Communications Commission and the United States Supreme Court compelled NBC to sell its Blue Network, to prevent the development of a monopoly. Under new ownership, it became the American Broadcasting Company (ABC). By the late 1920s therefore a major entertainment rival to Hollywood had come into existence.

Hollywood's reaction to this new rival was a divided one. There were those who saw radio as the deadly enemy of films, keeping people at home, threatening the cinema-going habit, and providing the same kind of entertainment as the movies but much more cheaply. This was particularly the view of cinema-owners and exhibitors and some studio heads. But there was an alternative view within the film industry which saw radio as a positive asset, a ready-made means of promoting and publicizing films and stars and a potential source of new talent for the movies. This was the view of David Sarnoff, the visionary president of the Radio Corporation of America (RCA). He envisaged a cross-fertilizing, all-embracing media empire which would take in films, radio, vaudeville, gramophone records and even television. RCA already controlled the NBC radio network and in 1928 Sarnoff presided over the acquisition of the Keith-Albee-Orpheum vaudeville circuit and the small FBO Studio in Hollywood. The resulting corporation named Radio-Keith-Orpheum (RKO) was headed by Sarnoff. Its movie-making wing was christened Radio Pictures (from 1936 RKO Radio Pictures) and its films were to be preceded by the logo of a radio tower emitting its signal. Sarnoff envisaged a totally symbiotic relationship between films and radio. Within months, the new corporation had launched the *RKO Hour* on NBC to promote its films and at the same time began to build feature films around popular radio performers such as Amos 'n' Andy (*Check and Double Check*, 1930) and 'Seth Parker' (*Way Back Home*, 1932). But RKO was not the only studio to get involved in radio. Paramount Pictures bought a substantial stake in CBS and launched the *Paramount Publix Hour* on the network to publicize its films. MGM laid plans to set up its own radio network.

But Paramount and the other studios pulled back from involvement in radio after an initial burst of enthusiasm. Fears of anti-trust suits against potential entertainment monopolies, enhanced by the passing of the Radio Act in 1927 to regulate the industry, and the costs of re-equipping studios and cinemas for sound following the arrival of the talkies had deterred them. They also found that many of their stars were reluctant to perform on radio, regarding it as an inferior medium but also in some cases being terrified of appearing live before the microphone. Then as cinema-going declined in the early years of the Depression, the pressure from cinema-owners increased to the extent that in 1932 all the studios apart from RKO banned their contract artists from appearing on radio. Within six months, however, the ban had collapsed as the studios increasingly appreciated the value of radio publicity and sponsors were pressing the networks for Hollywood-based product. The demand was the result of perceived audience tastes as charted by the increasingly sophisticated ratings of listener approval of radio programmes. They were known successively as the Crossley Ratings (1929), the Hooper Ratings (1935) and the Nielsen Ratings (1949).

The cinema-owners remained implacably opposed and waged a campaign against radio throughout the 1930s through their organization the Motion Picture Theatre Owners of America (MPTOA). As a result of the pressure, Will H. Hays, President of the Motion Picture Producers and Distributors of

America (MPPDA), set up a committee in 1936 to investigate the threat from radio. Its report, circulated to studio chiefs but not made public, concluded that radio publicity for current cinema releases boosted box office takings but that over-exposure of film stars on radio (Eddie Cantor, Jimmy Durante, Maurice Chevalier for instance) could adversely affect their box-office takings. The report allayed the fears of studio chiefs and from the mid-1930s onwards the relationship between radio and Hollywood strengthened and deepened.

Hollywood had direct input into radio in three main areas. First there were the Hollywood gossip and news programmes. Perhaps the most famous was *Hollywood Hotel*, hosted by the celebrated Hearst newspaper columnist Louella Parsons. It ran on CBS from 1934 to 1938 and was the first major network show to be broadcast from the West Coast. It featured studio news, star interviews and scenes from new movies acted in the radio studio. It was enormously influential and was credited with improving the box-office takings of the films featured. It even inspired a musical feature film, *Hollywood Hotel*, produced in 1938 by Warner Brothers starring Dick Powell and featuring Louella Parsons as herself. No one who appeared in the radio show was paid, even the actors playing in the scenes from films specially staged as a promotional exercise. This eventually ended the show, for in 1938 the Radio Guild banned so-called 'free broadcasting'. But Parsons was not without her rivals. Her principal newspaper competitor Hedda Hopper had various shows on various networks between 1939 and 1951. From 1930 to 1957 newspaperman Walter Winchell, broadcasting from New York, dispensed Hollywood gossip in his distinctive staccato delivery, beginning 'Good Evening, Mr and Mrs North America'. Jimmy Fidler, 'the Hollywood Reporter', delivered news and gossip on a variety of networks from 1934 to 1950. The sum total of all these programmes was free publicity for Hollywood and its stars.

The second source of Hollywood promotion was straight radio adaptations of hit films. The giant in this field was the *Lux Radio Theatre* (1934–55), described by radio historian J. Fred MacDonald as 'the greatest broadcasting vehicle for Hollywood stars'.[2] But the crucial fact to note here is that in 1936 the *Lux Radio Theatre* transferred its operations from New York, where the bulk of radio programming had been hitherto produced, to Hollywood. Within a year, 90% of radio programmes were being made in Hollywood, vastly improving the access by the radio networks to the studios and their stars and vice versa. In 1935 NBC built a new radio studio in Hollywood next door to RKO Radio Studios. This move by the radio industry made it possible for stars to pursue both film and radio careers, and the prestige and popularity of the *Lux Radio Theatre* – among other programmes – helped them overcome their initial disdain for the medium. The success of the Lux format inspired a host of imitations, half-hour and hour-long programmes presenting adaptations of famous films, *Screen Guild Theatre* (1939–52), *Screen Directors' Playhouse* (1949–51), *Dreft Star Playhouse* (1943–45), *Hollywood Startime* (1946–47), *MGM Theatre of the Air* (1949–52) and *Hollywood Soundstage* (1951–52).

Such was the hunger for movie adaptations that when Orson Welles' innovative *Mercury Theatre on the Air*, which had earned notoriety with its broadcast of *The War of the Worlds*, 'the broadcast that terrified America', acquired a sponsor (Campbell's Soup) and became *The Campbell Playhouse* (1938–41), it was compelled to abandon its previous policy of dramatizing classic novels and embark on a series of movie adaptations, all of them starring Orson Welles with a different Hollywood co-star guesting each week.

Once the production base for radio shifted to Hollywood, a third form of product was possible, the dramatic anthology series featuring a different star each week. Two of the most notable and longlasting of these were *The Cavalcade of America* (1935–55) and *Suspense* (1942–62). *Cavalcade*, sponsored by Dupont and broadcast first on CBS and later NBC, consisted of dramatized episodes from American history and attracted the cream of Hollywood talent to play the leading roles. *Suspense*, produced initially by William Spier, who was dubbed 'the Hitchcock of the Air Waves', delivered a succession of spine-tingling dramas with top star names in the lead. Some of the stories so gripped audiences that repeat productions were demanded. The record was held by *Sorry, Wrong Number* starring Agnes Moorehead as the bedridden invalid who overhears on the telephone the plans for her murder. It was repeated seven times after its first production in 1943 and repeat in this case meant fresh production as this was before the introduction of tape. Its success with the radio public meant that it was turned into a Hollywood film with Barbara Stanwyck in 1948. There were many similar dramatic anthologies (*Hollywood Playhouse* 1937–40, *Silver Theatre* 1937–47, *Ford Theatre* 1947–49, *Hallmark Playhouse* 1948–55 and so forth). One novelty was the short-lived *Four-Star Playhouse* (1949) in which four stars (Fred MacMurray, Loretta Young, Rosalind Russell and Robert Cummings) appeared each in turn once a month in a story adapted from *Cosmopolitan* magazine.

Hollywood was quick to see the potential of making film versions of radio shows, depending on the proven success of certain shows and the curiosity of audiences to see their sound favourites. One problem was that there was no guarantee that the actors looked anything like their radio roles. So radio roles were regularly recast on film to ensure they conformed to the appropriate appearance.

RKO Radio Pictures and Paramount were the Hollywood companies who made the most use of radio shows and radio performers for films. Paramount paraded a series of popular radio personalities in a succession of all-star vehicles, *The Big Broadcast* (1932), *The Big Broadcast of 1936* (1935), *The Big Broadcast of 1937* (1936) and *The Big Broadcast of 1938* (1937). George Burns and Gracie Allen starred in the first three and Bing Crosby, Jack Benny and Bob Hope all turned up in individual films. Crosby, Hope and Benny all developed significant and substantial film careers on the basis of their radio stardom.

RKO Radio Pictures teamed Fibber McGee and Molly with the popular ventriloquist Edgar Bergen and his cheeky dummy Charlie McCarthy, whose top-rated variety show ran on radio from 1937 to 1956, in two films *Look Who's Laughing* (1941) and *Here We Go Again* (1942). Both were box office successes despite the surreal feature of an animated dummy as leading man in a comedy with topical overtones. Fibber McGee and Molly starred alone in *Heavenly Days* (1944) but this Capraesque tale of Fibber going to Washington as representative of the Average Man failed at the box office and terminated their film career.

Just as *The Thin Man*, *The Falcon* and *Philo Vance* film series inspired follow-up radio series, so popular radio series *The Whistler* (1942–55), *Crime Doctor* (1940–47), *Doctor Christian* (1937–54), *Inner Sanctum* (1941–52) and *The Great Gildersleeve* (1941–57) inspired follow-up film series. There were eight *Whistler* films between 1944 and 1948; ten *Crime Doctor* films between 1943 and 1949; six *Doctor Christian* films between 1939 and 1941; six *Inner Sanctum* films between 1943 and 1945; and four *Gildersleeve* films between 1942 and 1944.

Where cinema was preoccupied with getting the visuals right, radio required sound design to create an aural texture. This involved balancing foreground and background sounds, arranging words, music and sound effects and determining rhythm and pace. Music played a similar role in radio to that in films. The same principles outlined by Claudia Gorbman in her definition of the classical film score can be applied to radio. First, it should not be heard consciously but should subordinate itself to the dialogue and narrative, which are the primary means of telling the story. Second, it should set the moods and emphasize the emotions integral to the story being told. Third, it should provide referential and narrative cues for the audience, indicating for instance the historical and geographical setting of the story, identifying individual characters, establishing and shading atmosphere, integrating and illustrating what is going on. Finally, it should unify the work by repetition and variation of the basic themes it has established.[3]

The specifically aural nature of radio meant that sound effects and sound-effects men were essential to good radio. The first permanent sound-effects team on radio were Arthur and Ora Nicols, who after twenty-three years supplying sound effects for vaudeville and silent films, found their work drying up as those media disappeared. In 1928 they were invited to apply their talents to radio and after several years of freelancing were taken on by CBS as permanent sound-effects staff. Soon all the networks had permanent and expanding sound staffs.

In the studio, the sound-effects man would have basic tools such as a portable door for slamming, a variety of knockers and doorbells, special boards and gravel trays for footsteps, coconut shells for horses' hooves and guns with blank cartridges. Many other sounds (cars, trains, aeroplanes, etc.) would be on records and soundmen had to be masters of split-second timing, often operating several turntables simultaneously. The basic repertoire of sound effects was added to by ingenious inventions. Stuart McQuade of NBC invented the rain machine, speed-controlled wagon wheels and a thunder screen.

Some sound-effects demands were more elaborate than others. Robert L. Mott, who had a forty-year career in sound in radio and television, wrote:

> The sound-effects demands on a soap were for the most part uninspired and pre-dictable. In addition to the phone bells, door buzzers, and bing-bong doorbells, we opened and closed a lot of doors, rang a lot of phones, opened and closed ice-boxes, set off oven timers, poured coffee, whistled tea kettles, put ice cubes (really camera flash bulbs) into endless glasses of lemonade, clinked dishes and silverware, washed dishes and silverware … and so it went.[4]

Rather more inventiveness was required in providing the sound effects for horror stories, such as Arch Oboler's *Lights Out* series. This involved creating 'the sound of a man frying in the electric chair (sizzling bacon), bones being snapped (spareribs or Life Savers crushed between teeth), heads being severed (chopped cabbages), a knife slicing through a man's body (a slab of pork cut in two), and, most grisly of all, somebody eating human flesh (wet noodles squished with a bathroom plunger) … The series' most celebrated studio effect – a man being turned inside out – was achieved by turning a watery rubber glove inside out to the accompaniment of crushed berry baskets, to simulate broken bones'.[5]

One of the features in many films set in radio studios was a scene showing the sound-effects men in action. As the years passed, the sound patterns, as they came to be called, became more and more sophisticated and were an essential part of the radio experience. Orson Welles developed the idea of layers of sound for his radio shows and experimented tirelessly to get the right sounds. To get the right echoing sound for the sewers of Paris in *Les Misérables* he had the scenes performed in the studio toilets. Many subsequent directors followed Welles in creating layers of sound. Welles took his expertise with sound to Hollywood and applied the same principles to his film soundtracks. The introduction of tape in 1946 made the life of the sound men much easier and long-running shows like *Dragnet* and *Gunsmoke* had taped libraries of sound effects.

Radio acting too was a distinctive art form. The voice was all the actor had and this was played like a musical instrument, with shadings, colourings, intonations and modulations. Stage actors used to projecting to the back of the stalls were often hopeless on radio and some film actors such as Gary Cooper and Clark Gable, used to playing to the camera, had to be coached in microphone technique to convey everything with the voice. Some stars remained terrified of live radio, notably Joan Crawford, Norma Shearer, Humphrey Bogart and James Cagney.

Veteran radio actor Parley Baer, who played Chester in the longrunning Western series *Gunsmoke* among many other roles, defined the essence of good radio acting:

> I don't know of a radio actor who, at the first reading or whatever, could not see the character he was playing. Maybe the actor didn't see him as you did, but that was the beautiful part of radio. If there were five million people listening, you were giving five million different performances. If there was a word of technique involved in that sort of thing it would be *belief*. You had to believe what you were saying; you had to be just as concerned with what you were saying even though some people said you only had to read it. That's why actors used to hyperventilate sometimes when they were climbing mountains that weren't there … The ability to fade in, fade out, or drop the voice was tantamount to an entrance or exit (on the stage). Shadings and colourings were our makeup, they were our wardrobe in many instances. It's much like a musician modulating and modifying tones.[6]

Many of the long-running radio shows functioned like repertory companies with the same actors working together week after week and developing an ensemble feel. Listening to a run of shows from the beginning, it is possible to hear the actors growing into the parts, interacting with each other and deepening their interpretations as they go on.

Since the voice was what counted and not the appearance, actors who were accomplished dialecticians could play several different roles in the same show (Hans Conreid was renowned for this) and actors and actresses could play roles for which they sounded but did not necessarily look right: old men could play young men, young women could play old women. In 1951 Janet Gaynor and Charles Farrell, then in their late forties and long retired from films, played the young lovers in *Seventh Heaven* as they had in the 1927 silent film which had been broadcast as the first *Lux Radio Theatre* play in 1934. Similarly Al Jolson was too old to play himself in the hit films *The Jolson Story* and *Jolson Sings Again* – Larry Parks played Jolson – but Jolson did play himself in the *Lux Radio Theatre* adaptations of the films. The actress Peggy Webber who was younger than actor Jack Webb aged her voice to play his mother in *Dragnet*. Thirteen-year-old Miriam Wolfe played a 100-year-old witch in the supernatural series *The Witch's Tale*. English actor Ben Wright played Chinese waiter Hey Boy in the Western series *Have Gun, Will Travel*. Amos and Andy, the archetypal black men, were played by white performers; Beulah, the black maid in *Fibber McGee and Molly*, was played by a white man. Typical of what occurred when the visual medium supplanted the aural, when the hit radio show *Gunsmoke* transferred to television in 1955, the radio cast were tested for the leading roles and all rejected because they did not look right. All four leading roles were recast for television; but the radio series continued alongside the television version with its original radio performers until 1961.

In the United Kingdom, fruity-voiced humorist Arthur Marshall played Nurse Dugdale in two series of *Calling Nurse Dugdale* in the 1940s. Jimmy Clitheroe, a forty-year-old dwarf, played a cheeky schoolboy in the popular comedy series, *The Clitheroe Kid*, on BBC between 1958 and 1972. When they attempted to transfer it to television the reality was cruelly exposed. Mabel Constanduros played all the members of the Buggins family in the eponymous longrunning BBC sitcom while in the United States Jimmy Scribner played all the roles in the daily soap opera *The Johnson Family*. Perhaps the most bizarre of all audio phenomena was the popularity in both the United States and the United Kingdom of ventriloquists' dummies on radio: Edgar Bergen and Charlie McCarthy in the United States, Peter Brough and Archie Andrews in the United Kingdom.

Most of the early radio shows featured anonymous radio actors, some of whom spent their whole careers in radio. It was not until the late 1940s that the names of the supporting casts in radio shows were even announced. It was also in the late 1940s that radio turned wholesale to Hollywood star names to ensure success for their shows. Edward G. Robinson in *Big Town* (1937) and Basil Rathbone and Nigel Bruce in *Sherlock Holmes* (1939) pioneered the trend. But in their wake and particularly after the war, most of the major Hollywood stars had their own dramatic or comedy series:

> Dana Andrews, *I Was a Communist for the F.B.I.* (1952–54)
> Lucille Ball, *My Favourite Husband* (1948–51)
> Joan Blondell, *Miss Pinkerton Inc.* (1952)
> Humphrey Bogart and Lauren Bacall, *Bold Venture* (1951–52)

Errol Flynn, *Modern Adventures of Casanova* (1952)

Glenn Ford, *Adventures of Christopher London* (1950)

Ronald Colman and Benita Hume, *Halls of Ivy* (1950–52)

Marlene Dietrich, *Café Istanbul* (1952)

Brian Donlevy, *Dangerous Assignment* (1949–53)

Cary Grant and Betsy Drake, *Mr and Mrs Blandings* (1951)

Sir Cedric Hardwicke, *Bulldog Drummond* (1954)

Rex Harrison, *The Private Files of Rex Saunders* (1951)

Alan Ladd, *Box 13* (1948–49)

Herbert Marshall, *The Man Called X* (1944–52)

Ilona Massey, *Top Secret* (1950)

Joel McCrea, *Tales of the Texas Rangers* (1950–52)

Dick Powell, *Richard Diamond, Private Detective* (1949–53)

Tyrone Power, *Freedom USA* (1952)

Vincent Price, *The Saint* (1947–51)

Edward G. Robinson and Claire Trevor, *Big Town* (1937–42)

Frank Sinatra, *Rocky Fortune* (1953–54)

Ann Sothern, *Maisie* (1945–52)

James Stewart, *The Six-Shooter* (1953–54)

The fact that more male stars than female stars had their own series is a reflection of the dominance of detective, mystery and adventure shows in the schedules in the late 1940s and early 1950s and that the long-running soap operas, aimed at women, featured well-established radio performers rather than film stars.

Many of the star-based series were deliberately constructed to fit the existing screen images of the stars. Cary Grant and Betsy Drake's series *Mr and Mrs Blandings* was based on the popular film comedy *Mr Blandings Builds His Dream House* (1948), in which Grant had co-starred with Myrna Loy. Bogart and Bacall's series *Bold Venture*, in which he ran a hotel and boat in Havana and she was his 'ward', was based directly on *To Have and Have Not* (1944). MGM deliberately revived several of its popular film series as radio series in the late 1940s, usually with their original stars: *Doctor Kildare* (1949–52) starred Lew Ayres and Lionel Barrymore in their original screen roles, a partnership interrupted during the war when MGM had dropped Ayres because he was a conscientious objector; *The Hardy Family* (1949–53) with Mickey Rooney and Lewis Stone; and *Maisie* (1945–52) with Ann Sothern. The passage of time made no difference on radio as long as the voices conveyed the appropriate age. The way in which film stars were taking over on radio is epitomized by the story of *Rocky Jordan*, a series clearly modelled on *Casablanca* in which an American expatriate ran the Café

Tambourine in Cairo and encountered adventures. It ran from 1948 to 1950 with radio actor Jack Moyles in the lead. But in 1951 George Raft became available and replaced Moyles as Rocky.

What is now forgotten is that many actors who went on to become top Hollywood stars started out on radio and were often 'discovered' directly from radio, though they usually had to have photogenic looks to go with the microphone-friendly voice. Among the film stars who had busy radio careers before breaking into Hollywood were Richard Widmark, Richard Crenna, Jeff Chandler, Alan Ladd, John Hodiak, Orson Welles, Howard Duff, Frank Lovejoy, Paul Douglas, Mercedes McCambridge, Shirley Booth, Macdonald Carey, Gary Merrill, Dane Clark and Don Ameche. Some notable character actors also made their names on radio and later brought their talents to films, among them John McIntire, Jeanette Nolan, William Conrad, John Dehner and Agnes Moorehead. But for those actors and actresses whose faces did not match their voices, the radio remained a continuing source of employment.

The same qualities that ensured radio stardom in the United States also applied in the United Kingdom but there was much less overlap between the cinema and radio in terms of personnel. In the United Kingdom stars remained radio stars and rarely made the transition to the screen. Val Gielgud, the BBC Head of Drama, writing in 1957, recorded that the ability to broadcast was not given to all but that the BBC had produced a range of actors who had mastered the technique – Gladys Young, Mary O'Farrell, Belle Chrystall, Mary Wimbush, Norman Shelley, Carleton Hobbs, Valentine Dyall, James McKechnie, Laidman Browne, Cyril Shaps and David Kossoff.

> Such mastery consisted of personality in the voice itself; of variety of characterization combined with the most absolute sincerity; of understanding of the effects to be achieved, the slightest changes of inflection, the value of the significant pause, the immediate response to light- or hand-cues. It was motivated by comprehension of the relation of the actors to the mechanical aspects of Radio production, and of the peculiarly intimate approach required to an audience made up of individuals or small groups. It was marked – to any interested onlooker – by what seemed a curiously effortless technique – short steps to and fro, slight movements of the head and body, a stylised holding of the script – combined with extreme concentration. It had become, in short, professional accomplishment of a high order, born of study and experience.[7]

The actor Martin Jarvis observed one of the greatest exponents of radio acting in performance:

> I was particularly impressed with a small, bun-shaped, grey-haired woman who danced up to the microphone with phenomenal energy. It was always specially

lowered to accommodate her four foot ten inches. I watched her all one afternoon as, script in hand, she created, out of the air, a whole world of sophistication, of heady romance and well-heeled humour. Her voice – oh so charming, so feminine, so all-knowing and full of wit – swept and soared and dived into the mike, and out again, nationwide, to fire the ready imagination of her listening fans. This elderly bundle of vocal genius was Marjorie Westbury … Really she could do anything, *be* anyone she wanted, within the radius of the microphone. She knew, *we* knew, the moment she approached its attentive ear, that she *was* Elvira in *Blithe Spirit*, or Paul Temple's witty young wife in the Durbridge mystery serials … Watching from the sidelines, having completed my own part as a lumpy detective sergeant, I was spellbound by her skill. Her imaginative technique, harnessed to her understanding of character and situation, was breathtaking. The precision and delicacy of her movements around the microphone, her knowledge of just how much difference a retreat or an approach would make to the depth of the sound-picture, was the start of my radio education. Such sonic choreography was entertaining enough to watch. When you closed your eyes and *listened*, it was dazzling[8]

Anna Massey, who has a wide experience of all media, expressed in her autobiography, her love of radio:

All my life I have loved working on the radio. The microphone has for me all the intimacy of the camera, and the two mediums of filming and recording have many similarities. Theatre demands vocal projection, and thus intimacy is harder to achieve. There is a sense of freedom at a microphone and before a camera, and the merest whisper can effortlessly convey your innermost thought. Live audiences show their anger or appreciation audibly and immediately. Their mood is constant, whereas the microphone and the camera are silent recorders, and therefore constant and non-judgemental, at least at the time of the performance. I have always felt that radio is an extremely visual medium. When recording a radio play, you must bring the listener into the world of the action with the utmost subtlety and detail, and all you have at your disposal in this medium is your voice. This instrument must convey everything, the heartbeat of your character. The microphone picks up in an instant anything that is false. It is like a complicated lie detector. Over the years I have moved physically closer to the microphone, for in this way you can attain the greatest truth with the minimum effort.[9]

It is a commonplace of film history that the cinema both reflected and constructed a view of contemporary American society. But there are two opposed views of the effect of radio on American society. The first, articulated by J. Fred MacDonald, is that radio increased national homogeneity by creating programmes and personalities that were listened to nationwide and disseminating values that cut across difference of gender, race and locality. MacDonald argues:

Network radio increased the similarity among Americans because it communicated the same stimuli throughout the nation. It developed as a national constituency for its programs and commercials. In doing so it had to avoid offending sectional or regional differences. Forced to find the common denominator among all groups within the United States, radio became the thread that tied together all people. More than print or film, politics or laws, radio united the nation. When by the late 1940s more than 90 per cent of the homes in America had radio receivers, it seems clear that the homogeneous passage of broadcasting was heard and appreciated. In a single stroke network radio standardized, entertained, informed and educated its mass audience. In this function it bound together the American people as had no single communications medium since the printing press.[10]

By the mid-twentieth century radio listening was ranked second only to sleeping as the major leisure activity of the American people. By the late 1930s Americans spent an average five hours a day listening to the radio. Because radio was listened to every day, it consequently had a greater continuous impact than films, which might be visited only once or twice a week. But the symbiosis between radio and cinema reinforced the messages and images that were coming out of Hollywood.

Michele Hilmes, by contrast, argues that rather than 'a naturally arising, consensus-shaped, and unproblematic reflection of a pluralistic society', radio should be seen as 'the conflicting, tension-ridden site of the ruthless exercise of cultural hegemony, often demonstrating in its very efforts to exert control the power and diversity of the alternative popular constructions that oppose and resist it'.[11] She agrees that radio unified the nation physically, linguistically and culturally, that it created 'an imagined community'. However, she argues that radio helped to preserve the 'cultural otherness' of blacks and that the role of women as the chief purchasers of household goods set up conflict between radio's role as a masculine public sphere and its feminized commercial base. The majority of radio's listeners were female, 55–60% in the evening, 70% during the day. But the majority of writers, producers, performers and critics were male.

In evaluating these interpretations, certain facts need to be taken into consideration. First, strict censorship rules existed which paralleled those existing in films. They set up the parameters within which programme makers had to operate. The federal government did not censor radio, in conformation with the constitutional requirement for free speech. The Federal Radio Commission (set up in 1927 and absorbed into the Federal Communications Commission in 1934) was permitted only to ban 'obscene, indecent or profane language' under the 1927 Radio Act. There was, however, a voluntary system of censorship instituted by the broadcasters themselves. The National Association of Broadcasters adopted a code of ethics which amounted to self-censorship. This prescribed that:

  i No program shall offend public taste or common decency.

  ii No program shall be planned as an attack on the United States government, its officers or otherwise constituted authorities of its fundamental principles.

  iii No program shall be conceived or presented for the purpose of deliberately offending the racial, religious or otherwise socially-conscious groups of the community.[12]

This was usually interpreted as avoiding all controversial issues and dramatizing what were perceived as commonly held beliefs: patriotism, family values, law and order and so forth. This directly paralleled the censorship code under which Hollywood films operated, enabling each medium to reinforce the other's world-view.

Second, there is the obvious fact that American radio was a commercial operation. The programmes were there to sell the products of their sponsors and therefore the sponsors would not back programmes which made audiences unhappy or disaffected. There were periodic bids by the networks to establish their credentials as cultural leaders: Mutual putting out Orson Welles' serialization of *Les Miserables* in 1937, NBC establishing in 1937 its NBC Symphony Orchestra under Arturo Toscanini, and CBS also in 1937 running a summer series of Shakespeare plays, though sugaring the pill by casting Hollywood stars in the lead: Burgess Meredith as Hamlet, Edward G. Robinson as Petruchio, Thomas Mitchell as King Lear and in *Henry IV* Walter Huston as the King, Brian Aherne as Hal and Humphrey Bogart as Hotspur. These were not dissimilar to Hollywood's periodic prestige cultural projects, such as Walt Disney's *Fantasia*, Warner Brothers' *A Midsummer Night's Dream* with James Cagney and MGM's *Romeo and Juliet* with Norma Shearer and Leslie Howard. The networks also developed a number of what were called 'sustaining programmes', which had no sponsors but were funded by the networks themselves to fulfil a public service obligation.

But as in Hollywood, so too in radio, box-office returns decided the fate of programmes and stars. The public was not the passive recipient of cultural dictation. The ratings were minutely studied and programmes were ruthlessly terminated if they failed to make the grade in listening figures. What is remarkable and suggests a persistent homogeneity of audience taste and attitude is that give or take the odd new entry, the top ten programmes in the popularity ratings remained remarkably stable for the enduring favourites. In 1950, there were 108 programmes that had been on the air for ten years and twelve that had been on the air for twenty.[13] The top ten programmes annually between 1937 and 1953 were:

October 1937–April 1938

1 Edgar Bergen – Charlie McCarthy
2 Jack Benny
3 Bing Crosby
4 *Lux Radio Theatre*
5 Eddie Cantor
6 George Burns and Gracie Allen
7 Major Bowes
8 Rudy Vallee
9 Fred Allen
10 Al Jolson

April 1943

1 *Fibber McGee and Molly*
2 Bob Hope
3 Edgar Bergen – Charlie McCarthy
4 *Lux Radio Theatre*
5 *The Aldrich Family*
6 Walter Winchell
7 Fannie Brice
8 *Mr District Attorney*
9 Jack Benny
10 Rudy Vallee

April 1948

1 *Fibber McGee and Molly*
2 Jack Benny
3 Amos 'n' Andy
4 *Lux Radio Theatre*
5 Walter Winchell
6 Fred Allen
7 Bob Hope
8 Phil Harris, Alice Faye
9 Edgar Bergen – Charlie McCarthy
10 Arthur Godfrey

April 1953

1 Amos 'n' Andy
2 Jack Benny

3 *Lux Radio Theatre*
4 Edgar Bergen – Charlie McCarthy
5 *You Bet Your Life*
6 *My Little Margie*
7 Bob Hawk
8 *Fibber McGee and Molly*
9 *My Friend Irma*
10 *Mr and Mrs North*

In addition, surveys taken by CBS and NBC indicated that there was no significant difference in listening tastes between different income groups.

Hilmes argues that to please advertisers, the networks created a classless,
raceless, rigidly gendered world of the 'typical American family' in sitcoms and
established a distinction between daytime programming, aimed exclusively at
women, and evening programming, directed at the family as a whole. But this
reflected the reality that women were at home during the day and formed the
bulk of the audience.[14] The daytime serials, broadcast daily in fifteen-minute
episodes, were dubbed soap operas, because many of them were sponsored by
soap companies, and they became the staple listening during the day. In this
sphere, women were prominent as creators and writers of long-running soaps
(Irna Phillips, Anne Hummert, Jane Cruisinberry). The content of soaps centred
on women's lives, family relationships, marriage, child-rearing, with the running
theme of tension between marriage and career which was almost always resolved
in favour of domesticity. Soaps dramatized 'the pursuit of happiness' and this
happiness was generally to be found supporting husband, rearing family, making
a home and doing good in the community.

Hilmes claims that the 'daytime serials both addressed and helped to create
an explicitly feminine subaltern counterpublic, reinforcing and acknowledg-
ing the difference between men and women's lives within the hierarchy of
American culture and providing ways to envision changes, negotiations and
oppositions'. But she admits that 'few serials endorsed a specifically feminist
agenda, and indeed most took very conservative positions when called upon to
do so'.[15]

The single exception to the conservative run of shows was *The Story of Mary
Marlin*, one of the highest rated daytime serials between 1937 and 1943, which
featured a woman US senator. But the staple fare was much more domestic and
as with evening radio, many of the shows retained their loyal followings for
decades. On 25 November 1960, CBS broadcast the last of its daytime serials
for the final time. Four of them had survived to that date. *Ma Perkins*, which

began in 1933 had lasted until 1960, with the same actress Virginia Payne in the title role. She was twenty-three when she began playing sixty-year-old Ma and she did it for 7,065 performances. She was billed as 'America's mother of the air', was a widow with three grown-up children and she ran a lumber yard in Rushville Center (population 4,000). *The Right to Happiness* (1939–60) centred on Carolyn Allen who got through four husbands during the run of the serial. *Young Doctor Malone* (1939–60) focused on the title character and his family in the small town of Three Oaks. *The Second Mrs Burton* (1949–60) featured Terry Burton and her husband and family in the small town of Dickson. The soaps were cheap to make, featured casts of radio actors and not Hollywood stars and developed faithful followings as they presented stylized versions of everyday experiences resolved by the central female characters in such a way as to endorse the values of family, morality and community.

Some soaps took their basic premises from popular Hollywood films with women's themes. *Stella Dallas* (1937–55), 'the true-to-life story of mother love and sacrifice', was inspired by the novel of Olive Higgins Prouty and the two hit films based on it (1925, 1937). *David Harum* (1936–51) was about a folksy banker in Homeville who solves the problems in his community. It was based on a 1934 Will Rogers film inspired by the 1898 novel by Edward Royes Westcott. *Mrs Wiggs of the Cabbage Patch* (1935–38) was based on the novel by Alice Hegan Rice which featured a woman supporting her family in a shanty town. It inspired two popular film versions (1919, 1934). But these were the exceptions. Most soaps were created directly for the radio.

In parallel with developments in films which reflected the greater responsibility and social change in the status of women produced by the war, some new soaps in the 1940s focused on female professionals, such as lawyers (*Portia Faces Life*, 1940–51), doctors (*Joyce Jordan M.D.*, 1945–48, 1951–52, 1955) and nurses (*Women in White* 1938–42, 1944–48). But these tended to fade in popularity after the war when there was pressure on women to return to home and family. During the war, the soaps were used to put over important messages, instructions and propaganda about the war effort and to explain 'why we fight'. The Office of War Information issued radio writers with pamphlets explaining government wartime measures which could be incorporated into scripts.

The basic ideological question which needs to be asked about the structures, values and images to be found in all kinds of radio programmes is this: is the world-view embodied in radio a view imposed from above or does it arise from below as a reflection of widely-held views? Scholars have argued for both interpretations over the years. But what explains the extraordinary duration of the popularity of particular shows and performers through the very different circumstance of the 1930s, 1940s and 1950s? This is perhaps the strongest argument for the homogeneity of a society bound together by its film going and radio listening. Radio historian Gerald Nachman records: 'From this small box with the diagonal speaker slots I learned much of what I knew about honor, romance, justice, evil, humor, manhood, motherhood, marriage, women, law and order, history, sports and families. I was told how life was meant to unfold and what America was all about'.[16]

During the war, radio like the movies came under the oversight of the Office of War Information and radio programmes were encouraged to promote support for the war effort and the war aims of the allies. But the networks and the sponsors were anxious to be seen to be patriotic and chose to introduce strongly pro-American and pro-war themes into their programmes, reinforcing the message from other media and ensuring a national consensus behind the war effort.[17]

Until the late 1940s, all radio was done live – though many live broadcasts were recorded on disc as they were going out, which is why so many of them have survived. The networks insisted on live broadcasts because they believed the resulting broadcasts were more spontaneous. The move to audiotape came about almost entirely because of the persistence and box-office clout of one man – Bing Crosby. Crosby had heard of the German development of audiotape and realized that if he could pre-record his shows it would give him more flexibility in his career. He could record as and when it suited him. His network (NBC) and sponsors (Kraft) were adamantly opposed, Crosby walked out and a court case ensued. The settlement allowed Crosby once he had completed his current run of the *Kraft Music Hall*, to pursue the option of taping. He was able to find a network (ABC) and sponsor (Philco Radios) willing to meet his terms and so from 1946 Crosby's radio show was taped – or transcribed as the jargon of the time had it. The content and appeal of his shows remained the same, the audience remained loyal, and so more and more shows went over to pre-recording. This also had the effect of allaying the nerves of stars like Humphrey Bogart who hated doing live radio. Pre-recording allowed for retakes and also permitted the recording of shows in batches. So Bogart and Bacall did *Bold Venture* as a pre-recorded dramatic show. Dramatic shows were not normally performed live. The *Lux Radio Theatre* and other film adaptation shows did, however, have audiences. So did *Sherlock Holmes*. Edward G. Robinson had insisted on an audience for his series *Big Town* in which he played a tough newspaper editor. Orson Welles specifically banned audiences from *The Mercury Theatre on the Air* to preserve the magic and mystique of the aural experience in its pure form. Comedy shows invariably had audiences whose reactions to the antics before the microphone were part of the appeal of the shows.

Between 1948 and 1952 television began to replace radio as the major entertainment medium. In 1948 there were only 172,000 television receivers in the United States; by 1952 there were seventeen million sets. The falling radio ratings informed the sponsors about the relative status of the two domestic media with the public. The networks began to channel their radio profits into developing television programmes. As the television habit grew, radio audiences fell by 40%.

In the comedy field, the leading stars were reluctant to transfer to television, and when they did many of them continued to appear on radio until well into the 1950s, despite falling audiences. Television took longer to do than radio, scripts had to be learned instead of read and the nature of the humour inevitably changed to incorporate the visual. The established radio stars were forced to move to television or risk being eclipsed by the emergence of a generation of new, specifically television stars like Milton Berle, Jackie Gleason and Sid Caesar, recruited from Broadway, vaudeville and nightclubs. Jack Benny, Bing Crosby, Bob Hope, George Burns and Gracie Allen all moved to television. Jack Benny's show on television was to run from 1950 to 1965. Fred Allen, whose radio show ended in 1949, detested television and he made only sporadic appearances before his death in 1956. Some shows were tried on television and failed, remaining exclusively on radio, among them *Fibber McGee and Molly* and *The Great Gildersleeve*, whose surreal sound effects and larger than life characters did not suit the more naturalistic mode of television.

But television was the perfect medium for the half-hour domestic sitcom and the cream of the radio sitcoms transferred effortlessly to television, often enjoying long runs and renewed popularity. *The Adventures of Ozzie and Harriet, The Aldrich Family, The Goldbergs, The Life of Riley, Our Miss Brooks* all moved to television. *Father Knows Best* ran on television from 1954 to 1963. The greatest success was *I Love Lucy*, which took over characters, situation, format and often dialogue from the radio show *My Favourite Husband*, and recasting Desi Arnaz, Lucille Ball's real-life husband, as her television husband created a series that ran from 1951 to 1961.

Many drama and mystery shows went directly to television, either without their original film star leads who would not appear on television (which was a much more direct rival to Hollywood than radio) or because shooting a television series could not be accommodated in filming schedules. If the radio lead had been a radio actor, he was often not cast for the television because he did not look right. *Dangerous Assignment, Box 13, Tales of the Texas Rangers, Halls of Ivy* and *Richard Diamond* all moved successfully to television. But perhaps the greatest television success was enjoyed by *Dragnet* which ran on television from 1951 to 1959 with its original star Jack Webb and *Gunsmoke* which ran from 1955 to 1975 with an entirely new television cast. Nothing could more graphically illustrate the demise of dramatic radio.[18]

Radio proved to be an invaluable training ground both for writers and performers anxious to make the transition to films. As has already been mentioned, many notable film stars started out in radio. Screen actors if they had good voices could act on radio and radio actors if their faces suited the camera could act on screen. The easiest transition from medium to medium was that of writers. Many writers who learned their craft (dramatic construction, dialogue-writing, narrative flow, character-drawing) working in radio effortlessly transferred these skills to the screen.

Such familiar names among screenwriters as Edmund Beloin, True Boardman, Richard Breen, Mel Dinelli, Gil Doud, Blake Edwards, Melvin Frank, Larry Gelbart, Robert Hardy Andrews, Hal Kanter, Ernest Kinoy, Millard Lampell, Arthur Laurents, Robert Libott, Ranald MacDougall, E. Jack Neuman, Norman Panama, Abraham Polonsky, Jack Rose and Bernard Schoenfeld began their writing careers on radio. The great American playwright Arthur Miller who later in his career wrote several screenplays, notably *The Misfits* (1960) and *The Crucible* (1996), served his apprenticeship on radio in the 1940s. He was a regular contributor to the historical drama series *Cavalcade of America*, notably writing a verse play *Juarez: Thunder from the Hills*, broadcast in 1942 with Orson Welles in the lead role.[19] The two longest serving scriptwriters on *Lux Radio Theatre*, George Wells (1934–43) and Sanford H. Barnett (1944–54) both went into films and won Oscars, Wells for *Designing Women* in 1957 and Barnett for *Father Goose* in 1964.

Two writers in particular graduated spectacularly from radio to cinema: Howard Koch and John Michael Hayes. Howard Koch was a young, unknown playwright when he was taken on in 1938 by John Houseman and Orson Welles to write the scripts for the *Mercury Theatre on the Air*. Although Welles was billed as writer of the show as well as director and star, it is now well established that the first few programmes were jointly written by Welles and Houseman; Houseman wrote the remainder of the scripts in the first series but thereafter the *Mercury* scripts were written by other, uncredited writers. In his generous foreword to Koch's autobiography, John Houseman recalled that he and Welles could not handle everything themselves on the show and Koch was brought in and successfully adapted *Hell on Ice*, *Seventeen* and *Around the World in 80 Days* for *Mercury*.[20] It was Koch who scripted the most celebrated *Mercury* show, *The War of the Worlds*, 'the broadcast that panicked America'. The sensation created by the broadcast led to Welles and the Mercury company of actors acquiring a sponsor and becoming *The Campbell Playhouse* before being transported to Hollywood where they made *Citizen Kane*, *The Magnificent Ambersons* and *Journey into Fear*. Koch did not go with them to RKO but having written many of the *Campbell Playhouse* scripts, he was snapped up by Warner Bros where during the 1940s he wrote or co-wrote such notable films as *The Sea Hawk* (1940), *The Letter* (1940), *Sergeant York* (1941), *Casablanca* (1943), *Mission to Moscow* (1943) and *Rhapsody in Blue* (1945). Although Oscar-nominated for *Sergeant York* and a winner for *Casablanca*, Koch's Hollywood career was abruptly terminated by the McCarthyite purge of Hollywood. It forced Koch and his wife Anne to relocate to the United Kingdom where they both worked under pseudonyms in television and 'B' pictures. When the blacklist was abolished, he was able to return to big screen scriptwriting in major British films, *The Greengage Summer* (1961), *The War Lover* (1962) and *The Fox* (1967).[21]

John Michael Hayes, who was described by one journalist as looking 'like a Hollywood scriptwriter as played by a Hollywood star in a Hollywood film about Hollywood' had a similarly successful transition from radio to cinema.[22] He embarked on a career as radio writer following army service during the war and earned a reputation for being 'the fastest writer in Hollywood' and had over 1,500 scripts to his credit by the time he graduated to films in 1951. On radio he had worked on such hit shows as *Suspense*, *Amos 'n' Andy*, *Yours Truly, Johnny Dollar*, *Nightbeat* and *Richard Diamond, Private Eye* among them. But he became best known for the snappy dialogue and wisecracking banter of his scripts for *The Adventures of Sam Spade*.

Hayes was recruited by Alfred Hitchcock to script *Rear Window* (1954) which decisively re-established Hitchcock as a box-office winner after a series of commercial failures. Hayes earned an Oscar nomination. He went on to script for Hitchcock *To Catch a Thief* (1955), *The Trouble With Harry* (1955) and *The Man Who Knew Too Much* (1956). They fell out when Hayes contested Hitchcock's desire to give his old friend Angus MacPhail a co-writing credit on *The Man Who Knew Too Much*. Hayes contended that MacPhail had worked on plot construction but that the script was his work alone. The Writers Guild of America upheld Hayes' view and he was given the sole scriptwriting credit. Hitchcock dropped Hayes, pointedly employing MacPhail on his next film *The Wrong Man*. He later sought to downplay Hayes' contribution, telling François

Truffaut that Hayes was 'a radio writer and he wrote the dialogue', nothing more. However, Hayes went on to script *Peyton Place* (1957), winning another Oscar nomination, *The Carpetbaggers* (1963), *The Chalk Garden* (1964), *Harlow* (1965) and *Nevada Smith* (1966) before turning to television. He ended his career as professor of film studies and screenwriting at Dartmouth College.[23]

Radio directors were conspicuously less successful in switching media than writers. The three greatest creative talents in the heyday of radio were by common consent Norman Corwin, Arch Oboler and Orson Welles. All three understood and exploited to the full the potentialities of the medium. They became so well known that their names alone were enough to carry programmes, for example, *Columbia Presents Corwin, Arch Oboler's Plays, Orson Welles' Almanac*. Oboler and Corwin were writer-directors; Welles was director, sometimes writer but always the star. Only Welles made a completely successful transition from radio to films. But all three, overtly left/liberal in their politics, found their careers blighted by McCarthyism and the blacklist.

Corwin perfected the form of the radio documentary which in his hands was personal, poetic, passionate, and political. His biographer LeRoy Bannerman recorded:

> He gave the Golden Age of Radio a greatness, a grasp of aesthetic principles, a promise of intellectual substance … Corwin brought not only talent to radio and the arts, he also brought pride, a personification of gentlemanly altruism. He was, Gilbert Seldes observed, 'an admirable carrier of the liberal-patriotic ideals of the time, an admirer of the New Deal, a mature anti-fascist, with a poetic sense of dignity and worth of the individual life'. Central to Corwin's character has been a concern for others … He popularized the Common Man. Such solicitude often embraced the conflicts and problems of the world. He constantly attacked the existence of war, of tyranny and injustice, always in sharp, literate, often lyrical prose. His finest hours celebrated the dignity of mankind.[24]

Erik Barnouw called him quite simply 'America's unofficial poet laureate'.[25] His talents came into their own during the war and can be seen at their best in his justly famed wartime documentaries, beginning with his celebration of The Bill of Rights, *We Hold These Truths*, broadcast over all four networks, just eight days after Pearl Harbor. This was followed by the powerful and moving series *This is War* and *An American in England* and the special shows on the occasion of President Roosevelt's re-election (*The Roosevelt Special*), the United Nations San Francisco Conference (*Word from the People*) and VE Day (*On a Note of Triumph*). However, the post-war climate became increasingly hostile to Corwin's approach. The rise of television and the gathering pace of the anti-Communist witch hunt drove radio to pursue ratings popularity on reduced budgets at the expense of grand, committed public service projects. Corwin left CBS in 1949 to take up a part-time post as Chief of Special Projects at the United Nations where he made radio documentaries promoting world peace which in some quarters were denounced as Communist propaganda and which were met with increasing lack of interest. He made his last UN programme in association with the BBC in 1955. In the meantime he had sought to develop a Hollywood career. His radio documentaries had no cinematic counterpart and in Hollywood he became merely a hired hand, scriptwriting but never directing. His screenplays for *The Blue Veil* (1951), *Scandal at Scourie* (1953), *Lust for Life* (1956), *The Naked Maja* (1959) and *The Story of Ruth* (1960) were, as might be expected, civilized and humane but had none of the uniqueness of his radio work. His day had passed with the passing of radio as a dominant medium.

Arch Oboler experienced something similar. He has been described as radio's 'greatest exponent of using sound effects to maximise drama'.[26] He realized when he first came to radio in the 1930s the possibilities of the medium:

> Radio in those days was an imitation of motion pictures, and an echo of the stage. No one had really used it as a theatre of the mind, had realized that a few words, a sound effect, a bit of music, could transport – in the mind of the listeners – one to any corner of the world, evoke emotions that were deep in the consciousness of the listener.[27]

Oboler came to specialize in 'internal dramas, plays which took the listener into the minds of the protagonists', and he perfected a stream of consciousness technique to convey this.[28] He made his name in horror radio, taking over in 1936 the spine-chilling series *Lights Out*, created in 1934 by Wyllis Cooper and since then written and directed by him. In 1936 Cooper departed for Hollywood, where his only notable script was *Son of Frankenstein* (1939) and from where he returned to horror radio in 1947 with a new series *Quiet Please*.[29] Oboler took over from him on *Lights Out* writing and directing one hundred shows between 1936 and 1938. He learned early on the effect he could create by his combination of first person narration and imaginative sound effects. His very first *Lights Out* story, *Burial Services*, featured the burial alive of a sixteen-year-old girl. Oboler later recalled:

> That broadcast taught me two things: the tremendous impact of radio – because of its intimacy, an impact far greater than any other medium we've ever had and ever will have – and the responsibility of the people doing radio. I had forgotten that in that tremendous audience there were many people who had buried their children. I remember one letter in particular … It was written on a ragged piece of paper, a woman's handwriting. It said 'I buried my sixteen-year-old last week. Remember that, Arch Oboler. Don't forget'. I've never forgotten it.[30]

Lights Out had been produced in Chicago but in 1938 Oboler left the show and moved to New York to produce adult dramas on current political issues, particularly the rise of fascism. He scripted and directed 800 shows between 1938 and 1948 and suffered a similar eclipse to Corwin, with whom he was often bracketed. In 1948 he abandoned radio, denouncing deteriorating standards in the medium, the tyranny of the sponsors and the low wages paid to radio writers. Detesting television, he sought to make a career in films. He made a promising start in films as writer-director. *Bewitched* (1945) was based on his radio play *Alter Ego* which had been such a sensation when broadcast that MGM signed its author-director to recreate it for the screen. It is a superb thriller about a murderess with multiple personalities which are in conflict with one another and are gradually uncovered by a psychiatrist. It contained excellent performances from Phyllis Thaxter as the woman, Edmund Gwenn as the psychiatrist and Audrey Totter as the voice of the evil personality. Oboler followed this up with *The Arnelo Affair* (1947), a moody and atmospheric *film noir* starring John Hodiak, George Murphy and Frances Gifford, about a manipulative Chicago nightclub owner who hypnotizes a lawyer's wife into carrying out his will, including murder.

However, he left MGM and embarked on a series of independent film productions which were basically gimmicks. *Five* (1951) was an anti-nuclear warning about five survivors of a nuclear holocaust, reduced eventually to two, a man and a woman who have to start a new world together. *Bwana Devil* (1953) was the first feature film in the short-lived 3D process and concerned an American engineer who has to deal with killer lions impeding the construction of an African railway. *The Twonky* (1953) was a heavy-handed anti-television satire in which a television takes over the life of a philosophy professor. *One Plus One* (1961) was a misguided and unsuccessful attempt to dramatize episodes from the Kinsey Report. Like Corwin, Oboler's is a career that having been central to radio becomes marginal in cinema.

Orson Welles is today widely regarded as one of the world's greatest film directors, a true master of the cinematic medium. But this reputation is based on a dozen films made between 1941 and 1973; a further four remained uncompleted at the time of his death. What is much less frequently acknowledged is that he was also a master of radio. As Paul Heyer justly observes in the only book-length study of Welles' radio work to date, 'Welles had an impact on broadcast radio as great as the one he exerted on film and theater'.[31] In films he achieved the double feat of raising pulp thrillers (*The Lady from Shanghai*, *The Stranger*, *Touch of Evil*) to the level of high art and of bringing Shakespeare to the masses (*Macbeth*, *Othello*, *Chimes at Midnight*). Both these enterprises began with his work on stage and on radio. As early as 1934 he had co-edited with his former headmaster Roger Hill, *Everybody's Shakespeare*, a series of volumes giving the texts of three plays with essays on their relevance and how to stage them: *Twelfth Night*, *The Merchant of Venice* and *Julius Caesar*. After Welles became famous, they were reissued in a single volume, retitled *The Mercury Shakespeare* and accompanied by performances of the plays on gramophone records with Welles in the starring roles. By this time Welles had already starred in radio versions of *Hamlet*, *Macbeth* and *Twelfth Night* on CBS.[32]

Radio was ideal for Welles, as both actor and director. He did a prodigious amount of radio work, much of it of the highest quality. While he could endlessly delay completing his films, the deadlines for live radio broadcasts were inflexible. He had to be before the microphone ready to broadcast at the moment the green light went on. As his producing partner John Houseman wrote:

> For Orson, as an actor, radio was a heaven-sent medium. With a vocal instrument of abnormal resonance and flexibility, uninhibited by that neurotic preoccupation with his own physical appearance that affected his stage performances, he was capable of expressing an almost unlimited range of moods and emotions. Entirely through his voice and the dramatic tensions it enabled him to create, he projected a personality on the air that soon made him one of the radio stars of his day.[33]

In his *Mercury Theatre on the Air* productions Welles, as well as narrating, regularly played several roles; Dr Seward and Count Dracula in *Dracula*, Dr Manette and Sydney Carton in *A Tale of Two Cities*, Marmaduke Jopley and Richard Hannay in *The 39 Steps*, for example. He excelled in radio plays which crucially depended on one person utilising multiple voices. His performances in *The Dark Tower*, *The Magnificent Barastro* and *Donovan's Brain*, all for the *Suspense* series, were vocal tours de force.

But Welles was equally creative as a radio director, drawing on his inventive, spontaneous, improvisatory imagination to conjure up whole worlds by sound alone. William Alland, one of his regular troupe of radio actors, recalled that what he brought to radio was an ensemble style of performance, the idea of an integrated musical score and a fascination with sound effects and the creation of sound patterns. Sound effects engineer Cliff Thorsness compared him to the conductor of a symphony orchestra who stood on a podium and directed all the elements of the radio show.[34] As Paul Heyer has pointed out, Welles' 'greatness as an artist lay in adaptation, in interpreting the work of others. With his Mercury cohorts he would transform one type of theatre into another; on radio he made novels and short stories come alive'.[35]

Welles, in partnership with John Houseman, famously electrified the American stage with a series of revolutionary productions for the Federal Theatre project and their own Mercury Theatre Company: the all-black voodoo *Macbeth*, the modern-dress, Fascist *Julius Caesar*, the radical pro-labour musical play *The Cradle Will Rock* and a version of *Doctor Faustus* full of dazzling stage magic tricks.

Already in demand as a radio actor on such series as *Cavalcade of America*, *CBS Workshop* and *The March of Time*, for which he impersonated Emperor Haile Salassie, Leopold Stokowski, Sigmund Freud and Fiorello La Guardia, Welles' theatrical success led to his being cast as the crime-fighting super-sleuth Lamont Cranston in the 1937–38 season of the Mutual Broadcasting Company's series *The Shadow*. Welles' identity was kept secret until the final episode of the season, *The White Legion*, was broadcast on 20 March 1938. At the end of the programme, Welles was introduced as 'the most distinguished figure in the theatre today … Mr Welles, still a very young man, is making for himself a unique place in the field of dramatic art'. For Welles the bonus of starring in *The Shadow* was that he persuaded Mutual to allow him in the summer of 1937 to write, direct, narrate and star in a seven-part adaptation of *Les Miserables*, for which he brought together the nucleus of his radio acting company (Martin Gabel, Ray Collins, Agnes Moorhead, William Alland, Richard Wilson, Everett Sloane) and began to develop his unique approach to sound effects.

Then in 1938 CBS offered Welles a budget of $50,000 to write, produce, present and star in nine hour-long programmes to replace the *Lux Radio Theatre* during its summer break. The show was to be called *First Person Singular* but it rapidly became known by its subtitle *The Mercury Theatre on the Air*. Welles brought in John Houseman who became essential to the success of the show and his radio repertory company augmented by members of his theatrical company (George Coulouris, Erskine Sanford, Edgar Barrier, Eustace Wyatt). He also acquired the services of the CBS orchestra under Bernard Herrmann, a character as volatile and unpredictable as Welles himself but with a serious approach to scoring for radio. Herrmann regularly composed the scores for the show which became an integral part of the sound mix and the story-telling.[36]

The CBS announcer declared at the start of the first programme in the series:

> The Columbia network is proud to give Orson Welles the opportunity to bring to the air those same qualities of vitality and imagination that have made him the most talked about theatrical director in America today. And it is this project which Columbia brings you this summer; the first time in its history that radio has ever extended such an invitation to an entire theatrical company.

The opening programme, Bram Stoker's *Dracula*, was a superbly atmospheric version of the Gothic classic and it was followed by equally impressive and lovingly crafted versions of *Treasure Island*, *A Tale of Two Cities*, *The 39 Steps* and *The Count of Monte Cristo*. The remaining programmes were a triple bill of short stories by Carl Ewald, Saki and Sherwood Anderson (*My Little Boy*, *The Open Window*, *I'm a Fool*), two plays (Arthur Schnitzler's *The Affairs of Anatol* and John Drinkwater's *Abraham Lincoln*) and a Welles favourite, G.K. Chesterton's *The Man Who Was Thursday*. The series had been sufficiently popular with audiences and critics for CBS to renew its contract, moving the programme from 9.00 p.m. on Mondays (to which slot *The Lux Radio Theatre* now returned) to 8.00 p.m. on Sundays. The new season began with an hour-long version of *Julius Caesar*, adapted from the Mercury stage production, and this was followed by *Jane Eyre*, *Sherlock Holmes*, *Oliver Twist*, *Hell on Ice*, Booth Tarkington's *Seventeen* and *Around the World in 80 Days*. The seventeenth Mercury production was H.G. Wells' *The War of the Worlds*, broadcast on 30 October 1938. The story, transposed from Edwardian Home Counties England to Grovers Mill in contemporary New Jersey, was done as a series of news bulletins and radio addresses and was leant a further immediacy by actor Frank Readick basing his reporter's commentary on the landing of the Martians on Herbert Morrison's celebrated reporting of the burning of the airship *Hindenburg* and Kenneth Delmar delivering an address by the unnamed Secretary of State in the tones of President Roosevelt. It created a sensation as people fled from their homes to avoid the invasion from Mars.[37] It made Welles a nationwide celebrity and led to some people believing that reports of the Japanese attack on Pearl Harbor in 1941 was another Welles hoax. This is alluded to in two wartime films, *Air Force* and *To the Shores of Tripoli*. It also led to the series acquiring a sponsor (Campbell's Soup), a new name (*The Campbell Playhouse*) and a new remit, adaptations of hit films with Welles playing the lead opposite a different guest star each week. This enabled him to star in *A Farewell to Arms* with Katharine Hepburn, *Arrowsmith* with Helen Hayes, *The Green Goddess* with Madeleine Carroll, *Beau Geste* with Laurence Olivier, *The Patriot* with Anna May Wong, *The Hurricane* with Mary Astor and *Algiers* with Paulette Goddard, among many others.

Although the fiction was maintained that Welles wrote, produced, directed and starred in all the programmes, in fact Houseman wrote most of the early shows and managed the Mercury company until Howard Koch was taken on as writer for *Hell on Ice* and thereafter wrote regularly. Paul Stewart, a radio actor and aspiring director became associate producer. Welles was initially preoccupied with preparing his latest Broadway shows *Too Much Johnson* and *Danton's Death*.

Then after his notoriety earned him a film contract at RKO, he relocated to Hollywood, flying every week to New York to appear in *The Campbell Playhouse* until CBS were persuaded in November 1940 to shift production of the show to Hollywood. The show continued until 31 March 1940, when the final production, a new version of *Jane Eyre* went out. But by this time Houseman and Welles had quarrelled bitterly and Houseman had left the show and returned to New York.

Houseman invaluably recalled the process by which the Mercury and then the Campbell shows came into being:

> Even with our augmented staff everyone was perpetually over-worked and we rarely managed to get even a half-jump ahead of ourselves. Shows were created week after week under conditions of soul – and health – destroying pressure. But between us we had gradually worked out a system – a sort of chaotic routine which was supposed to survive the eccentricities of our leader. As general editor of the series I chose the material with Welles and when possible, discussed the tone and general form of the show and its casting possibilities. I then laid it out roughly and turned it over to Koch and Annie (Froelich, the script typist) who would have a first draft ready by Wednesday night, when Orson was supposed to read it but seldom did … On Thursday Paul would put the show through its first paces, rehearsing all day with a skeleton cast while Koch and I made whatever adjustments and changes seemed needed in the script after we had heard it spoken. Late in the afternoon, without music and with only rudimentary sound, we would make an acetate recording of the show. From this record, played back late … that night, Orson would give us his reactions and revisions, which we would accept or dispute. In the next thirty-six hours the script would be reshaped and rewritten, sometimes drastically. Saturday afternoon, there was another rehearsal, with sound – with or without Welles. It was not until the last day that Orson really took over.[38]

The show went out live at 8.00 p.m. and in the early afternoon the cast and the orchestra under Bernard Herrmann assembled in Studio One at CBS. Welles now took over:

> Sweating, howling, dishevelled and single-handed he wrestled with chaos and time – always conveying an effect of being alone, traduced by his collaborators, surrounded by treachery, ignorance, sloth, indifference, incompetence – and – more often than not – downright sabotage. Every Sunday it was touch and go. As the hands of the clock moved relentlessly toward air time the crisis grew more extreme, the peril more desperate … Scripts and scores flew through the air, doors were slammed, batons smashed. Scheduled for six – but usually nearer seven – there was a dress rehearsal, a thing of wild improvisations and irrevocable catastrophes. After that, with only a few minutes to go, there was a final frenzy of correction and reparation, of utter confusion and absolute horror, aggravated by the gobbling of sandwiches and the bolting of oversize milkshakes. By now it was less than a minute

to air time. At that instant, quite regularly week after week, with not one second to spare, the buffoonery stopped. Suddenly out of chaos, the show emerged – delicately poised, meticulously executed, precise as clockwork, smooth as satin, what Orson accomplished each week in those eight terrible hours was quite extraordinary.[39]

After Welles' unique RKO contract resulted in a succession of box-office failures, *Citizen Kane* (1941), *The Magnificent Ambersons* (1942) and *Journey into Fear* (1942), he was not to direct again until *The Stranger* (1946), *The Lady from Shanghai* (1947) and *Macbeth* (1948), after which he retreated to Europe, taking years to complete and sometimes failing to complete his film projects, which he frequently funded out of what he earned acting in other directors' films. He made one return to Hollywood, producing a masterpiece *Touch of Evil* before he returned to the piecemeal business of putting films together in Europe without adequate resources. His departure from the United States was partly a result of the McCarthyite purge of the film industry but also partly that his reputation for box-office failure closed the major studios to him.

However throughout the 1940s, while his film work was intermittent, he was continually on the radio, starring in his own shows, *The Orson Welles Show, The Orson Welles Almanac, Hello Americans, This is My Best, Orson Welles Commentaries* and guesting in other shows, both dramatic (*Lux Radio Theatre, Inner Sanctum, Suspense*) and comic (the Fred Allen, Bob Hope and Rudy Vallee shows). For five weeks he stood in for an indisposed Jack Benny, hosting his weekly show. He even revived the Mercury Theatre for CBS in June 1946 for a series called *Mercury Summer Theatre* in which he remade some of the programmes from the original series and interspersed them with new productions.

This work inevitably tailed off when he relocated to Europe, where he was from 1949–51 starring in a succession of major films, *Black Magic, The Third Man, The Prince of Foxes* and *The Black Rose*, while trying to set up and start work on his own production of *Othello*. It was while he was in London in 1951 that he made his last major radio series for producer Harry Alan Towers. He recreated his film role of Harry Lime in a hugely entertaining 52-part thriller series *The Third Man; The Lives of Harry Lime*, writing half a dozen of the scripts himself. The series was syndicated in the United States and played on the BBC in Britain. For Towers he also narrated a 28-part series *The Black Museum* which featured dramatized versions of some of Scotland Yard's most famous cases.[40]

The influence of his radio years can be found throughout Welles' film work. He began by transporting his Mercury Radio Theatre company to Hollywood for *Citizen Kane*. None of them had appeared in films before and he supplemented his usual company with Ruth Warrick, also recruited from New York radio, to play the first Mrs Kane. Welles collaborated on the script with Herman J. Mankiewicz, who had scripted several of the *Campbell Playhouse* broadcasts (*The Murder of Roger Ackroyd*, *The Garden of Allah*, *Vanity Fair* and *Huckleberry Finn*). The script adopted the structure of multiple perspectives used in *Dracula*. *The Magnificent Ambersons* was even more strongly rooted in the radio. Welles had produced it on *The Campbell Playhouse* on 29 October 1939, narrating and playing George Amberson Minafer with guest star Walter Huston as Eugene Morgan. It was a favourite novel of Welles' and he adapted it himself for the radio. He persuaded RKO studio chief George Schaefer to authorize production of the film by playing him the discs of the radio show and he played it constantly during the production of the film, which is why surviving versions of the show now sound so scratchy and hissy. He narrated the film but cast Tim Holt as George with other Mercury regulars in important roles. He originally had the idea of prerecording the entire film and getting the actors to lip-synch their parts but this proved impractical. He paid particular attention to the film's soundtrack. His RKO films are remembered for their 'deep focus' photography but should also be recalled for what Rick Altman has dubbed 'deep focus sound',[41] a layering of sounds Welles had learned on radio and which characterized his Hollywood films. As Charles Higham has written: 'Aurally, the American films are as exciting as they are visually captivating. The tracks leap and fizz like loose electric wires, full of screams, shouts, hisses and explosions of music, designed by a man in love with sound'.[42] Time and again he turned back to radio for his performers and his film project ideas. His original plan for his RKO film contract was to film Joseph Conrad's *Heart of Darkness*, which he had done as a radio show. It was abandoned when the proposed budget exceeded one million dollars. When he played Edward Rochester in the 20th Century Fox film of *Jane Eyre* (1943) directed by Robert Stevenson, he prepared by playing over and over the records of his first radio version of the novel. Indeed he played them so much that they are now irrevocably damaged and cannot be heard at all. Altogether he did *Jane Eyre* four times on radio. When casting *Macbeth*, he chose Jeanette Nolan, an experienced radio actress with whom he had performed on *Cavalcade of America*, to play Lady Macbeth and a supporting cast included many of his radio regulars. He cast an unknown American actor Robert Arden as the hero of *Confidential Report* after working with him on *The Third Man* radio series. He developed two full film scripts from the half-hour plays he had contributed to *The Third Man*. The episode *Man of Mystery* became the basis for *Confidential Report*, with many of the lines of the radio script reproduced verbatim. Another *Third Man* script *Buzzo Gospel* was reworked as *V.I.P.* and intended for filming by Alexander

Korda but Korda's death in 1956 terminated the project.

Around the World in 80 Days, which Welles did twice on radio, once playing the intrepid traveller Phileas Fogg and on the other occasion Detective Fix, became the basis of a massive stage show *Around the World* with filmed inserts and a Cole Porter score. It failed, partly because Welles' producing partner Mike Todd ran out of money. Welles tried to make a film version for Korda but failed. Mike Todd did succeed in producing a lavish film version in 1956 with David Niven as Phileas Fogg and a cast of fifty guest stars but with no role for Welles.

Welles performed *Julius Caesar* on stage, radio and gramophone records, succeeding in playing all three leading roles, Brutus, Cassius and Antony, over the years. But plans to film a modern-dress version of the play in Europe were scotched by the successful 1953 MGM production of John Houseman which starred Marlon Brando, James Mason and John Gielgud. *Treasure Island*, which had been the second Mercury production, remained part of Welles schedule for years and he planned to follow *Chimes at Midnight* with a version made in Spain and featuring some of the cast from *Chimes*. Eventually he did get to play Long John Silver in a film version he co-scripted under the pseudonym O.W. Jeeves and which was produced in Spain with an international cast in 1972 by his old radio producer Harry Alan Towers and directed by John Hough. Welles never ceased to regret the demise of dramatic radio and there can be little doubt that it gave him some of the finest acting and producing opportunities of his career. As Simon Callow writes of *The Mercury Theatre on the Air* shows in his brilliant biography of Welles:

> They exploit the medium fully, but without a trace of self-consciousness. The Mercury Theatre of the Air programmes embody everyone's ideal of radio drama, projecting larger-than-life images onto our mental screens, plundering our own memories to tell the story. The most radical medium devised by man … its decline in the latter half of the twentieth century (with the honourable exception of the BBC) into a mere carrier of music and news is a shameful waste. Welles' and his collaborators' work in radio … is a great memorial to an exceptional art form one whose influence remained central to his output.[43]

Of the many other outstanding and innovative American radio producers, William Spier, William Robson, Elliot Lewis and Norman MacDonnell notably, none made the move from radio into films and remained with their original medium to the end.

In the United Kingdom the most spectacular failure to make the transition was Martyn C. Webster, doyen of radio thriller producers. In 1953 he directed the film version of Francis Durbridge's first television serial, *The Broken Horseshoe*.

But Peter Coke, radio's Paul Temple who was playing a Scotland Yard inspector in the film, recalled him being notably ill at ease in the new medium and turning regularly to Coke, an experienced film actor, for advice. Webster never made another film and stayed in radio for the remainder of his career.[44]

Notes

1 Susan Douglas, *Listening In: Radio and the American Imagination*, Minneapolis: University of Minnesota Press, 2004, p. 33.
2 J. Fred MacDonald, *Don't Touch That Dial: Radio Programming in American Life from 1920 to 1960*, Chicago: Nelson-Hall, 1996, p. 51.
3 Claudia Gorbman, *Unheard Melodies*, London: BFI, 1987, pp. 73–91.
4 Robert Mott, *Radio Sound Effects*, Jefferson, NC: McFarland, 1993, p. 187. On sound effects, see also Leonard Maltin, *The Great American Broadcast*, New York: Dutton, 1997, pp. 87–112.
5 Gerald Nachman, *Raised on Radio*, Berkeley: University of California Press, 2000, p. 313.
6 Maltin, *The Great American Broadcast*, pp. 119–20.
7 Val Gielgud, *British Radio Drama 1922–1956*, London: George G. Harrap, 1957, p. 123.
8 Martin Jarvis, *Acting Strangely*, London: Methuen, 1999, pp. 168–9.
9 Anna Massey, *Telling Some Tales*, London: Hutchinson, 2006, p. 139.
10 MacDonald, *Don't Touch That Dial*, p. 37.
11 Michele Hilmes, *Radio Voices: American Broadcasting, 1922–1952*, Minneapolis: University of Minnesota Press, 1997, p. xvii.
12 Hadley Cantril and Gordon W. Allport, *The Psychology of Radio*, New York: Harper and Bros., 1935, p. 53.
13 MacDonald, *Don't Touch That Dial*, p. 80.
14 Hilmes, *Radio Voices*, pp. 151–2.
15 Hilmes, *Radio Voices*, p. 174.
16 Nachman, *Raised on Radio*, p. 4.
17 Gerd Horten, *Radio Goes to War*, Berkeley: University of California Press, 2002; Howard Blue, *Words at War*, Lanham, MD: Scarecrow Press, 2002.
18 On the last years of network radio see Jim Cox, *Say Goodnight, Gracie: The Last Years of Network Radio*, Jefferson, NC: McFarland, 2002.
19 Christopher Bigsby, *Arthur Miller*, London: Weidenfeld and Nicolson, 2008, pp. 153–6, 183–4, 194–211.
20 Howard Koch, *As Time Goes By*, New York: Harcourt Brace Jovanovich, 1979, p. xiii.
21 Koch, *As Time Goes By*, covers his film career.
22 Steven de Rosa, *Writing With Hitchcock*, London: Faber and Faber, 2001, p. xiii.
23 de Rosa, *Writing With Hitchcock*, tells the full story of the Hayes–Hitchcock collaboration. Hitchcock's comments on Hayes are in François Truffaut, *Hitchcock*, London: Panther, 1969, p. 274.

24 R. LeRoy Bannerman, *On a Note of Triumph: Norman Corwin and the Golden Years of Radio*, New York: Carol Publishing Group, 1986, p. 11.

25 Bannerman, *On a Note of Triumph*, p. ix.

26 MacDonald, *Don't Touch That Dial*, p. 57.

27 MacDonald, *Don't Touch That Dial*, p. 56.

28 MacDonald, *Don't Touch That Dial*, p. 57.

29 On horror radio see Richard J. Hand, *Horror on the Air! Horror Radio in America, 1931–1952*, Jefferson, NC: McFarland, 2006.

30 Maltin, *The Great American Broadcast*, p. 49.

31 Paul Heyer, *The Medium and the Magician: Orson Welles, the Radio Years*, Lanham, MD: Rowman and Littlefield, 2005, p. xiv.

32 On Welles' Shakespeare work see Michael Anderegg, *Orson Welles, Shakespeare and Popular Culture*, New York: Columbia University Press, 1999.

33 John Houseman, *Run-Through*, New York: Touchstone, 1980, p. 362.

34 William Alland and Cliff Thorsness interviews, *Theatre of the Imagination: Radio Stories by Orson Welles and the Mercury Theatre*, Santa Monica, CA: Voyager, 1988, audio collection.

35 Heyer, *The Medium and the Magician*, p. 11.

36 On Bernard Herrmann's contribution to *Mercury Theatre* and other radio programmes see Steven C. Smith, *A Heart at Fire's Center: The Life and Music of Bernard Herrmann*, Berkeley: University of California Press, 1991, pp. 42–70.

37 On *The War of the Worlds* story see Houseman, *Run-Through*, pp. 390–406; Heyer, *The Medium and the Magician*, pp. 81–112; Hadley Cantril, *The Invasion from Mars: A Study in the Psychology of Panic*, Princeton, NJ: Princeton University Press, 1940; Howard Koch, *The Panic Broadcast*, New York: Avon, 1970 (includes the complete script).

38 Houseman, *Run-Through*, pp. 390–1.

39 Houseman, *Run-Through*, pp. 391–2.

40 *The Third Man* episodes are listed in Martin Grams Jr, *Radio Drama*, Jefferson, NC: McFarland, 2000, p. 290.

41 Heyer, *The Medium and the Magician,* p. 158.

42 Charles Higham, *The Films of Orson Welles*, Berkeley: University of California Press, 1970, p. 3, where he gives a series of good examples of Welles' use of sound. On the influence of radio drama on *Citizen Kane*, see Evan William Cameron (ed.), *Sound and the Cinema*, Pleasantville, NY: Redgrave Publishing Company, 1980, pp. 202–16.

43 Simon Callow, *Orson Welles: The Road to Xanadu*, London: Vintage, 1996, p. 389.

44 Author's interview with Peter Coke, 20 May 1998.

2

British radio and cinema:
the creative tension

The British broadcasting service was set up in 1922 with a monopoly and finance from a licence fee following negotiations between the Post Office, which controlled the air waves, and the radio industry, which manufactured the equipment. The Post Office was anxious to avoid what it saw as the chaos of unregulated broadcasting in the United States and was concerned with the function of broadcasting as a public utility. But it had no philosophy, no overall vision. That was provided by John Reith, Director-General of the BBC from 1923 to 1938. He provided a manifesto for public service broadcasting in his book *Broadcast Over Britain*, published in 1924. It is passionate, romantic, idealistic, evangelical. It is almost a Bible of broadcasting with Reith as its prophet. He outlines a firm set of principles – one is almost tempted to call them commandments: the maintenance of high standards; a unified and centralized policy towards the whole service; the preservation of a high moral tone; the spreading of culture, knowledge and education and not just entertainment; the promotion of inter-class harmony and national cohesion; the promotion of religion; the creation of an informed and enlightened public. Such was the power of John Reith's vision and his personality that the BBC in the inter-war years embodied precisely these ideals. Reith's detractors dubbed him the 'Czar of Savoy Hill' and there was undoubtedly a stern Calvinist rigour about his attitude to people, policy and programmes. But it would be wrong to suggest that he did not believe in democracy. His definition of democracy, however, was freedom of access rather than freedom of choice.

It was both a matter of temperament and of strategy that led him to see what he called 'the brute force of monopoly' as the best means of implementing his programme. So Reith worked for, advocated and achieved in 1927 the transformation of the British Broadcasting Company into the British Broadcasting Corporation, with a charter, a board of governors and a commitment to public service. As Paddy Scannell and David Cardiff point out in their social history of

British broadcasting, the BBC was one of the great achievements of an essentially middle-class, Victorian cultural ideal – public service.[1] This ideal comprised several dominant themes in Victorian thought: the desire to raise the general cultural level of the population, to incorporate the newly enfranchised working classes into the existing social and political order, and to educate the population for participation in mass democracy, something that was only fully established in the United Kingdom after the First World War, when women finally got the vote. Radio was uniquely placed in the inter-war years to undertake the implementation of these ideals and sought consistently to do so during the Reith regime: by providing access for all to the best in music, drama and literature; by creating a sense of community through the broadcasting of the great public events and ceremonies in the national calendar – royal, imperial, religious, sporting, political; by creating a wider knowledge and understanding of public affairs and a lively and active sense of participatory citizenship. It is a measure of Reith's vision and idealism that these three objectives remain continuing strands in the philosophy of public service broadcasting.

The structural means by which Reith sought to achieve his ends were the creation of a national programme universally available, the centralization of decision-making and a policy of mixed programming, aimed at the general audience. But in fulfilling each of his aims, Reith and the BBC faced major struggles and uncovered fundamental tensions that remain unresolved to this day. In seeking to promote political awareness and democratic participation, the BBC immediately encountered the question of bias. From 1923 onwards there have been complaints in press and Parliament and by members of the public that the BBC has been guilty of bias for and against the government of the day, for and against the opposition. Initially the Post Office imposed a crippling 'no controversy' rule but after extensive lobbying this was replaced in 1928 by the requirement for balance in comment and reporting. There was bitter rivalry with the newspapers over access to news. Initially the BBC was not allowed to broadcast news before 7.00 p.m. and even then was required to use Reuters news bulletins. It was not until 1934 that the BBC was able to set up its own News Department but it was afflicted by the difficulty of getting access to official sources of information, technological limitations and political pressure. The government remained suspicious about an institution it did not control directly. As early as 1923 Reith had made plans for broadcasting parliament, believing that people should have direct access to the deliberation of their legislators, but this was ruled out completely by the government and was not to be accomplished until 1978.

Despite this many latterday commentators are uncomfortable with Reith and his world-view. One of their main narrative thrusts is the bureaucratization and centralization of the institution, which they see as deadening debate. Their heroes are the 'progressives' of the Talks Department and Regional broadcasting, chiefly in the north. They argue that from 1927 to 1935 the Talks Department was one of the most exciting areas of broadcasting, strongly committed to the social importance of the medium, to relevance and topicality, and regularly employing the finest left-wing thinkers of the day – Wells, Shaw, Huxley, Keynes, Beveridge and the Webbs. Scannell and Cardiff see radio talks as part of that key inter-war phenomenon of providing the public with facts generally from a progressive standpoint and this ranks the BBC Talks Department under Hilda Matheson and Charles Siepmann alongside the Left Book Club, Mass Observation, *Picture Post* and the British documentary movement, whose leading figure, John Grierson, strongly resembled Reith. But in 1935 with the charter renewal approaching and increasing criticism of left-wing bias, the corporation decided to play safe by appointing the former British Minister in Kabul, Sir Richard Maconachie, Head of Talks and ensured its transformation almost overnight from the liveliest to the dullest department in the BBC.[2]

In the Northern Region, the director of programmes, Archie Harding, and pioneer producers D.G. Bridson and Olive Shapley shared the view that broadcasting should reflect the lives and opinions of ordinary people and made programmes that were accessible, relevant and demotic. Olive Shapley took advantage of the possibilities provided by location sound recording on disc to bring 'the voices of the people to the people'. But Grace Wyndham Goldie, then radio critic of *The Listener*, put this into perspective when she highlighted the difference between London and the regions: 'In London the search is for the best possible play, feature, actor, talk or entertainment and to provide it for listeners. But in the regions there is something else. For it is the business of regional broadcasting to be expressive of … the everyday life of the region, its daily work, its past, its attitude of mind, and above all the quality of the people'.[3] In paying their well-deserved tribute to regional broadcasting, Scannell and Cardiff perhaps undervalue that search for excellence that was the hallmark of the centre.[4]

It was one of Reith's most cherished principles. 'Our responsibility is to carry into the greatest possible number of homes everything that is best in every department of human knowledge, endeavour and achievement', he said. He also believed 'it is better to overestimate the mentality of the public than to underestimate it'.[5] Reith's critics then and since have regularly accused him of being paternalist and patronising. Paternalist he certainly was. But then Reith was a Victorian, his mental universe akin to those of Ruskin and Matthew Arnold. It is unrealistic to expect him to have endorsed or implemented what have subsequently come to be seen as desirable broadcasting goals: informality, public participation, interaction between broadcaster and audience. Patronising is another matter. There is nothing inherently patronising about wanting to share with people the great works of music and literature or a knowledge of public affairs. In fact it is Reith perhaps more than anyone else in broadcasting history, who has been retrospectively subjected to what E.P. Thompson called 'the enormous condescension of posterity', the 'politically correct' view that the present has a monopoly of wisdom and that the past and its great figures are benighted, retrograde and ultimately laughable.

In the same spirit the story of broadcasting is often written in terms of a stuffy, high-culture monopoly being breached by the rise of variety and greater attention being paid to audience preference. But this is overly one-dimensional. There was a continuing debate both inside and outside the BBC, between those who sought to raise public taste and those who desired to follow the wishes of the public. For the BBC the question was getting the balance right.

The BBC monopoly was challenged directly by the growth of commercial broadcasting. The pioneer here was Captain Leonard Plugge, who set up in 1930 the International Broadcasting Company (IBC). It cheekily established studios in Portland Place, a stone's throw from Broadcasting House. There programmes could be pre-recorded and shipped out to the Continent for transmission by Radio Luxembourg (transmitting from 1933 to 1939), Radio Normandy (1924 to 1939), Radio Lyons (1924 to 1939) and Radio Toulouse (1928 to 1938), among others. Overseas transmission circumvented the BBC's monopoly control of transmission in the United Kingdom. The J. Walter Thompson Advertising Agency also produced programmes from its up-to-date studios in Bush House. The commercial stations were modelled directly on American broadcasting with the programmes sponsored by companies such as Rinso, Horlicks, Lux Toilet Soap and Rizla Cigarettes, as part of their promotional strategies for their products. The success of the stations can be measured by the amounts spent by the companies on purchasing airtime. It rose from £30,000 in 1934 to £315,000 in 1935 to £630,000 in 1936.[6]

The British press refused to publish the commercial stations' programme listings, regarding them as pirates, so IBC launched its own magazine *Radio Pictorial* in 1934, which contained listings for all the commercial stations. Popular music and variety were the staple products of the stations with Radio Luxembourg's *The Ovaltineys Concert Party of the Air*, aimed at young people, becoming a particular favourite. It would run from 1934 to 1957, excluding the war years. There were no news or religious programmes. As Sean Street has argued in his masterly study of commercial radio: 'The commercial stations deliberately set out to satisfy the audience most neglected by the BBC, that is to say the young and the working class who felt disenfranchised by the Corporation's Sunday policy'.[7]

Battle was joined between the BBC and the commercial stations over Sunday broadcasting. The Corporation's Sunday policy was devised and strictly enforced by Sir John Reith. Its programme consisted of religious services and programmes, classical music and learned talks. In 1935 the Radio Manufacturers' Association submitted a memorandum to the BBC complaining that the dullness of its programmes was affecting wireless sales and recommending more variety shows and more American-style programmes. Radio Normandy responded to the BBC Sunday by putting out programmes featuring Jessie Matthews, Tommy Handley and Harry Roy and his band. The mass audience turned gratefully to the commercial stations to brighten their Sundays. IBC research demonstrated that 70.3% of radio sets working after noon on Sundays were tuned to commercial stations. All the commercial stations except for Radio Toulouse had their highest listening figures on Sundays.[8]

Despite the reluctance of Reith, who did not want programmes dictated by audience preference lest the corporation's output went downmarket, the BBC eventually set up an Audience Research Department in 1936 under Robert Silvey, a statistician working for the London Press Exchange, one of the larger British advertising agents, but a firm believer in public service broadcasting.

Silvey's research revealed the popular preference for variety (93%), theatre and cinema organs (82%), military bands (72%), musical comedy (69%), dance music (68%), plays (68%), and light music (65%). Apart from plays, the survey reveals the overwhelming desire for variety and music. At the other end of the scale, came grand opera (21%), violin recitals (19%), serial readings (12%) and chamber music (8%).[9]

The listening figures certainly provided ammunition inside the corporation for debates about the extent to which the BBC should be influenced by American practices. The BBC did not shun the United States. The corporation arranged 120 relays from the United States in 1937, which included dance bands, political talks, sports commentaries and items by film stars.[10] Alistair Cooke was broadcasting talks on American popular music, though his celebrated *Letter from America* did not begin until the war. The BBC borrowed and anglicized *Amateurs Hour*, a popular showcase for non-professional performers, heard in the United States from 1934 and in the United Kingdom from 1936. It also picked up the craze for Spelling Bees, justifying it on educational grounds. First heard in the United States in 1937, they reached the United Kingdom in 1938. *The Times* (14 August 1934) lamented: 'Like syncopated dance music, Hollywood humour and Hollywood drama are foreign to the British temperament, but the fact remains that they are in fashion, and we are not likely to be able to beat the Americans at their own game'.[11]

Within the BBC, there were enthusiastic Americanizers like Eric Maschwitz, the head of Variety, and Maurice Gorham, editor of *Radio Times*.[12] But Cecil Graves, Controller of Programmes, urged the development of 'a truly British type of light entertainment'.[13] Peter Eckersley, BBC chief engineer, who was later to change his mind, after his first visit to the United States in 1924 complained that Americans went for quantity rather than quality, mocked the soaps and concluded that America had nothing to teach the United Kingdom.[14] R.S. Lambert, editor of *The Listener*, sought to articulate a middle way: 'Dislike of the blatancy and commercialism of much of U.S. broadcasting should not blind one to its virtues: speed, slickness, freshness and topicality. There is less departmentalism, less censorship, less red-tape – all because there is more competition. For monopoly works as insidiously as an anaesthetic upon those who possess it. The BBC's programmes possess the virtues of being wholesome and edifying but lack adequate safeguards against dullness, against the inclusion of material, not on its intrinsic merit as broadcast entertainment, but for irrelevant reasons such as the need to propitiate established interests, or to collaborate with Government policies'.[15]

The BBC took its role as cultural arbiter with the utmost seriousness. It rapidly became the largest single employer of musicians and the most powerful patron of music in the United Kingdom. The Music Department was the largest programme department at the BBC with a staff of fifty-four in 1937. It was headed by Dr Adrian Boult who was also permanent conductor of the BBC Symphony Orchestra, created in 1930 with the clear aim of becoming one of the world's greatest orchestras. In 1927 the BBC took over Sir Henry Wood's Promenade Concerts and the Proms became the embodiment of the Corporation's musical philosophy.

In the 1930s the BBC divided music into 'serious' and 'light', aiming to provide the best in both, and in 1932 the BBC set up its own Dance Orchestra under Henry Hall which rapidly became a national favourite. A *Radio Times* editorial in 1935 declared that the BBC wanted listeners who 'were not only tolerant but eclectic in their taste – who can listen to and enjoy either Bach or Henry Hall'.[16] *Punch* (10 February 1932) satirized the BBC's aspirations with a cartoon of two working-class men listening to the wireless and one saying to the other 'The *Pizzicato* for the double basses in the coda seems to me to want body, Alf'. The Listener Research report, which revealed that 68% of those questioned liked dance band music compared to only 21% liking grand opera and a mere 8% chamber music, suggests that there was polarization between 'high brow' and 'low brow' music. But this should not be overstated. For there was a substantial middle ground of people who liked tuneful, tasteful music, the dance bands, the brass bands, light classics and Victorian ballads, which also featured in BBC output.[17]

But for all the popularity of broadcast music, what the 1939 survey revealed was that 93% of the audience enjoyed variety shows. This considerably strengthened the hand of the Variety Department, established in 1933, to provide more of what the public wanted. The combination of Listener Research, press campaigns against alleged BBC stuffiness and competition from the commercial Radio Luxembourg led the BBC to eliminate public chamber concerts, reduce the number of weekly adult education talks, allow dance band music on a Sunday and extend the output of variety. A *Punch* (24 February 1937) cartoon at the time showed two ladies seated by the wireless and one saying to the other: 'What I says is, Mrs Jones, there's too much of this 'ere variety and most of it's all the same'. But the extent to which this took the BBC downmarket can be exaggerated. For instance, the BBC experimented with a wide variety of entertainment shows: the comic character monologue, the stand-up comedian, the concert party, the radio revue and it proved an ideal medium for the humour of language – puns, parodies, pastiches, surreal verbal narratives.

What people wanted, among other things, was to belong. Radio variety made them feel that and so did the BBC's fulfilment of its third great aim – the promotion of inter-class harmony and national cohesion. As Sir Michael Swann, chairman of the BBC Board of Governors, told the Annan Committee in 1977: 'an enormous amount of the BBC's work was in fact social cement … Royal occasions, religious services, sports coverage and police series, all reinforced the sense of belonging to our country, being involved in its celebrations and accepting what it stands for'. The Annan Report endorsed this view, describing the BBC as 'the natural interpreter of great national events to the nation as a whole'.[18] The first royal wedding – between the Duke of Kent and Princess Marina of Greece – was broadcast in 1934. King Edward VIII made his abdication speech on radio. The Silver Jubilee celebrations of 1935 and the coronation of King George VI were broadcast. The Boat Race, the Cup Final, Wimbledon and Derby Day became part of the broadcast fabric of the national year. In the inter-war years too the

BBC was active in the promotion of a sense of pride and participation in the Empire, with Reith describing the broadcasting of the opening of the Empire Exhibition at Wembley in 1924 as 'the biggest thing we have yet done'.[19] There were annual broadcast celebrations of Empire Day and regular documentaries on imperial themes. But nothing symbolises the role of the BBC as national unifier more than the King's Christmas Day broadcast, which began in 1932, brought the voice of the sovereign into the home and rapidly became the central feature of the national Christmas Day. By 1934 more than half the population had access to a radio and by 1939 three-quarters of British households had the radio. Social surveys stressed the role of the radio in promoting domesticity. The primacy of home and family had been one of the key elements of the Victorian world-view; home as bulwark against the outside temptation and distraction. Wireless provided a potent means of keeping people at home and there providing education and entertainment. The promotion of the concept of the royal family, the recurrence of the idea of empire and nation as one great family epitomized by the King's Christmas Broadcast, the development of what were later to be called soap operas and sitcoms with their focus on the family and the introduction of *Children's Hour* presenters addressed as aunties and uncles all fostered the ideas of home and family as essential to national well-being. The BBC saw its audience, as Scannell and Cardiff put it, as 'a constellation of individuals positioned within families'[20] and its function as linking their private world to the public world, broadening horizons of understanding of current affairs, culture and knowledge of all kinds. Nothing is more symbolic of the integration of radio into the fabric of British life than the fact that in 1914 the declaration of war was read about in the newspapers and in 1939 it was listened to on the radio. During the war the wireless enjoyed perhaps its finest hour as a purveyor of information and entertainment, as maintainer of morale and enhancer of national unity. But after the war the division into Home, Light and Third Programmes and subsequently Radios 1, 2, 3, 4 and 5 conceded the existence of a variety of audiences which Reithians would never have accepted. Ironically television remained truer to the Reithian concept of general programming but with its emphasis on the visual was never able to match the creative use of language or appeal to the imagination that are the strengths of pure radio.

Paddy Scannell and David Cardiff in their social history of the BBC see the fundamental contribution of the BBC to social relations in modern society as the change in the ethos of communication, from a distanced, paternalist, authoritarian mode to a more relaxed, informal and interactive system, a trend which has reflected and enhanced the eclipse of social deference by greater egalitarianism.

But that is more a product of post-Second World War, indeed post-1960s, developments. The BBC in the 1930s, with its dinner-jacketed announcers, upper middle-class voice, and benign paternalism remained part of the Establishment but an Establishment animated by a high sense of social and cultural responsibility and responsive – up to a point – to the desires of the audience. My own view is that the fundamental achievement of the BBC in the 1930s was the development and extension of a national culture, a middle-brow rather than a middle-class culture. Listener Research revealed a remarkable unanimity of national taste, with hardly any regional difference, little distinction between rural and urban listeners, comparatively few differences between men and women and some, but not marked difference between working-class and middle-class listeners, and between youthful and elderly listeners. In assessing this phenomenon, it is necessary to read, alongside Scannell and Cardiff, D.L. Le Mahieu's important book *A Culture for Democracy*. Le Mahieu argues convincingly for the emergence in the inter-war years of a genuinely national culture, a shared experience transcending class and social boundaries without diminishing their importance. He sees this national culture embodied in the popular press, with its emphasis on human interest stories, accessible style and regular columnists, in the cinema with its favourite stars, genres and themes, and in BBC Radio once it had broadened its mix of education and entertainment. The common values expressed in this culture were patriotism, religion, the family, a belief in law and order, self-discipline and the gentlemanly ethic.[21] On the wireless this middle-brow culture overlapped with the high-brow culture of the intelligentsia and the non-literary unofficial culture of the working classes, defined by Orwell as 'the pub, the football match, the back garden, the fireside and the "nice cup of tea"'. Le Mahieu underestimates the extent to which the basic elements of this common culture had emerged by the latter part of the nineteenth century when the mass media first developed and when the railway network bound the country together, facilitating the exchange of tastes and ideas. But it was nevertheless deepened and strengthened by the technological advances of the inter-war years. Winifred Gill and Hilda Jennings, surveying radio use in the United Kingdom in 1939, concluded: 'The prevalent habit of daily listening to the news, the opportunities for cultural enjoyments such as music and drama, which were formerly denied to the poorer sections of the population, the increased familiarity with standardised diction and a greater vocabulary, tend to do away with those class barriers which are the result of paucity of common interests. Broadcasting is thus an equalising and unifying factor in national life'.[22]

Orwell clearly saw the wireless as a vital element in preserving national stability at a testing time for the social fabric: a time of recession and unemployment at home, of wars and rumours of wars abroad. Created at a time of considerable concern about the destabilisation of society in the wake of the Great War, and very real fears of revolution following the overthrow of the Czarist regime in Russia by the Bolsheviks, the BBC became a vital vehicle in the maintenance of consensus and continuity. In so doing it was in tune with the wishes of the majority of the population who during the 1930s voted for the election and re-election of a largely Conservative National Government. To consensus and continuity, Reith added culture to complete a trio of structuring ideals that can be seen to underpin the programming of the corporation in the inter-war years.

However much the BBC has changed since the Second World War – and in part this has been a response to changes in the wider world – it has retained a commitment to broadcasting as a public service. Broadcasting has come under attack in recent years with the rise of ideas about the paramountcy of the market, the supremacy of consumer choice and the questioning of notions of cultural authority. But the commitment to public service which Reith outlined in his valedictory speech on leaving the BBC in 1938 remains part of the BBC's philosophy, however much of the corporation's output Reith would now find incompatible with his vision.

> That broadcasting should be merely a vehicle for light entertainment was a limitation of its functions which we declined to accept. It has been our endeavour to give a conscious, social purpose to the exploitation of this medium. Not that we underrated the importance of wholesome entertainment or failed to give it due place; but that we realised in the stewardship vested in us the responsibility of contributing consistently and cumulatively to the intellectual and moral happiness of the community. … We have tried to found a tradition of public service, and to dedicate the service of broadcasting to the service of humanity in its fullest sense. We believe that a new national asset has been created … the asset referred to is of the moral and not of the material order – that which, down the years, brings the compound interest of happier homes, broader culture and truer citizenship.[23]

When the war broke out in 1939, television, which had just begun, was closed down for the duration. The Second World War became a radio war. Initially the BBC put out a scratch programme in anticipation of saturation bombing. It consisted of news bulletins, gramophone records and ministerial talks. After several weeks of this, *The Sunday Pictorial* exploded: 'For God's sake how long is the BBC to be allowed to broadcast this travesty of a programme that goes under the name of entertainment'.[24]

The BBC soon got its act together, dispersing departments to prevent the immobilization of the service in the event of Broadcasting House being hit – Variety, for instance, was located in Bangor – and organizing a service which would meet the need for news, information and entertainment. It was subject, of course, to censorship restrictions, forbidden to broadcast anything that would give information to the enemy, cause alarm among the troops or alienate our allies.

The BBC rapidly became the Voice of Britain during the Second World War, expanding its operations massively. In 1939 the BBC had a staff of 4,233 and twenty-three transmitters: by 1945 it had a staff of 11,417 and 138 transmitters. It increased its foreign language broadcasting: by 1943 it was broadcasting in forty-seven languages as opposed to the eight in 1939. It became a source for news all over the world and the announcers, who were now obliged to give their names on the air to prevent impersonation by German propaganda stations, became national celebrities; men like Alvar Liddell, Frank Phillips, Bruce Belfrage, Stuart Hibberd and Joseph McLeod. Winston Churchill became a master of radio broadcasting, his radio addresses inspiring the nation.

The radio became a powerful proponent of the idea of 'The People's War' on every level: from J.B. Priestley's populist Postscripts to the first daily radio soap opera *The Robinsons*, billed as the story of a typical frontline family; it began in 1941. In plays, documentaries and talks, radio promoted the idea that the war was being fought to eliminate the evils of pre-war Britain: poverty, slums, unemployment. The people began to appear in radio much more than before.

In 1940 Ernest Bevin, the Minister of Labour, suggested a factory variety programme to keep up morale and so a variety show from the canteen of a factory was put on under the title *Workers' Playtime*, as well as *Works Wonders*, a canteen concert by the workers themselves billed as coming from a factory 'somewhere in England' (which became a popular catchphrase). Also there was, to encourage the workers, *Music While You Work*, continuous background music in factories, introduced by the signature tune 'Calling All Workers'. Music was now accepted as background noise in a way it never had been in the 1930s when listeners were encouraged to listen concentratedly to programmes. Industrial features set in factories highlighted the hard work, patriotism and sense of commitment of the workforce, particularly the popular *Billy Welcome* series, in which northern actor and personality Wilfred Pickles as Billy Welcome toured factories, interviewing the workers, introducing them in musical turns and leading at the end a communal singsong.

The Second World War led to a revolution too in the nature of radio entertainment. The National Programme was divided between the Forces Programme, mainly light entertainment, and the Home Service, which included music, talks, features, documentaries and some comedy. Before the war the BBC sought to avoid the routinization of listening as likely to make the listener lazy and unadventurous. But 1938 brought a new kind of variety show, *Monday Night at Seven*, a continuity show with a compendium of recurring features – *Puzzle Corner*, songs, comedians, and a weekly mystery *Inspector Hornleigh Investigates*. The formula was copied from the United States and allowed the build-up of a regular audience. The format next was applied to a pure comedy show that became the prototype radio comedy show *Band Waggon*, which exploited the surreal possibilities of radio.

Before the war the BBC banned the importation of American programmes but this was breached during the war with the import of the Bob Hope, Fred Allen, Edgar Bergen and Jack Benny radio programmes, shorn of their advertisements. The hit show *Hi Gang!* starring American film stars Bebe Daniels and Ben Lyon, who remained in the United Kingdom throughout the war, was closely modelled on the American comedy shows. The resistance to over-Americanization continued. R.A. Rendall, Assistant Controller (Overseas Service) wrote in 1944: 'In general I think we must be careful to see that we do not become an agent for American cultural propaganda'. William Haley, Editor-in-Chief of the BBC and later Director-General, also wrote in 1944: 'I do not feel we should remain satisfied with a state of affairs in which we have put regular American programmes into our home service because we have nothing better of our own. So long as this is the case … there is no room for the BBC to do brave things'. Basil Nicolls, the BBC Senior Controller of Programmes, issued a memorandum in December 1944 with instructions for post-war programming, stating: 'The programmes shall be firmly British in character … this implies in particular an effective resistance to the Americanisation of our entertainment'.[25] But the biggest hit show of the war was home-grown – *ITMA* (short for 'It's That Man Again', originally a newspaper reference to Hitler). Sixteen million people tuned in weekly to hear it, from the royal family in Buckingham Palace to the humblest home in the land. It poked fun at wartime restrictions and red tape, but also utilized tortuous verbal punning routines, catchphrases and regular characters.

But there was not just comedy. Reith had banned quizzes but they appeared after his departure, starting with spelling bees, but later including *Have A Go* and *Twenty Questions*. One of the surprise hits of the war was *The Brains Trust* (1941), which attracted 10–12 million listeners a week, and made celebrities of regular panel members Julian Huxley the zoologist, Professor Cyril Joad the philosopher and Commander A.B. Campbell, the naval officer and traveller,

answering questions like 'What is happiness?' It indicated a raised level of interest in intellectual enquiry. Radio reached its peak in the 1940s but after the
war television returned and by the mid-1950s was displacing radio as the major
broadcasting medium, just as in the United States.

   The situation regarding drama in the United Kingdom was completely different from that in the United States. The symbiosis was not between radio and
cinema but between radio and theatre. In this respect the most influential figure
was Val Gielgud, the BBC's head of drama from 1928 to 1963. His tastes and
attitudes were vital in shaping policy at the BBC. In his autobiographical volume
Years of the Locust (1947) he felt the need to defend himself against charges of
being too highbrow in his tastes.

> I must make one thing clear. I am not a highbrow. By which I mean that I am not
> a member of the self-conscious *intelligentsia*. The highbrow label has, on occasions,
> been affixed to my coat-tails by some of my colleagues, in circumstances of exaspera-
> tion both pardonable and easily comprehensible. It is true that I like Russian plays;
> that I prefer ballet and revue to music halls and musical comedy; ... and that I am
> regrettably allergic to the extremely successful stage pieces of Miss Dodie Smith and
> Miss Esther McCracken. But as far as films are concerned my tastes are essentially
> catholic. I like the Brothers Marx. I like Walt Disney. I like Miss Ginger Rogers and
> Miss Rita Hayworth. I like the work of Ernst Lubitsch. I liked the 'silents' of Fritz
> Lang. I liked *Potemkin*. I liked *Quai des Brumes*. I liked *Scarface* and *Stage-Coach*.
> I liked *Ninotchka*. I liked *The Road to Frisco* and *Under the Clock* and *The Congress
> Dances*. I like Garbo and Judy Garland, and Walter Pidgeon and Charles Coburn
> and Gene Tierney, and Charles Boyer, and Daniele Darrieux, and Michele Morgan,
> and Ann Sheridan, and Nazimova. I like most – but not all – French films. Most of
> all I like going to the cinema. Indeed, if put into a corner over it, I would confess
> that by and large I prefer going to the cinema to going to the theatre. I find, as a
> rule, that I get more fun out of it.[26]

Films then, for him, were fun but not art. As he wrote earlier in the same book:
'It would be astonishing ... were the films to take the lead in raising the level
of popular taste ... it is doubtful whether even now, looked at from the artistic
standpoint, the talking picture can demand the serious attention won by the
silent film at the climax of its achievement. "Going to the pictures" remains a
phrase tinged, however slightly, with contempt'.[27] He outlined how he saw his
own job:

> It was ... part of my professional business to see every play I could; to be acquainted
> with a wide range of authors, producers and actors; to read theatrical criticism,
> both significant and insignificant; to try to keep abreast of matters theatrical on
> the Continent and in the United States.[28]

Gielgud wrote twelve plays and published seventeen novels and also four books in collaboration with Eric Maschwitz but, no doubt to his frustration, was best known for his detective thrillers. He was a self-admitted failed actor ('the worst actor of my generation') and failed playwright ('That failure has been one of my bitterest disappointments'). This must have been all the more galling for someone whose brother, Sir John Gielgud, was one of the most acclaimed actors of the age.[29]

Theatre was to be the dominant theme of radio drama. The first dramatic broadcast from the BBC studios on Savoy Hill on 16 February 1923 was scenes from *Julius Caesar, Henry VIII* and *Much Ado About Nothing* featuring stage stars Robert Atkins, Arthur Bourchier, Basil Gill and Acton Bond. The first full-length play to be broadcast on 28 May 1923 was *Twelfth Night*. Gielgud noted 'Shakespeare remained the indispensable ballast of respectable output'.[30] This encapsulates the BBC vision of itself as the purveyor of all that was best in the national culture. This continued to inform its policy towards radio drama. For example, in 1948 it was possible to hear on the BBC productions of *Hamlet* with John Gielgud, *King Lear* with Donald Wolfit, *Romeo and Juliet* with Celia Johnson, Robert Eddison, Edith Evans and Marius Goring, *Macbeth* with Stephen Murray and Flora Robson, *Othello* with Jack Hawkins, Margaret Leighton, John Clements and Fay Compton, *Henry V* with Richard Burton and *The Merchant of Venice* with Laidman Browne.

There were also plays written specially for broadcasting, the first being Richard Hughes' *Danger*, which was set in a coalmine and was broadcast in 1924. There were experimental dramas like Lance Sieveking's *The First Kaleidoscope*, subtitled 'A Rhythm, representing the Life of Man from Cradle to Grave'. But Gielgud lamented: 'The original radio play had to compete with the innate conservatism of the listening audience, which thought of a play as something essentially written for the theatre and by an acknowledged playwright. The play which they recognized as having the prestige of theatrical performance behind it was more acceptable than the new work by the unknown author'.[31]

So it was to cater to this demand that the BBC's drama output regularly included half-hour excerpts from current West End plays, the latest stage musicals restaged for the microphone in the studio and where possible, actors recreating their roles in hit plays. Gielgud recalled the successes on pre-war radio in their original stage roles of Henry Ainley and Leon Quartermaine in *Hassan*, Ernest Milton in *Rope* and Malcolm Keen in *A Bill of Divorcement*.

Just as one of the selling points of the radio versions of films in the United States was the presence of the original stars recreating their screen roles, so the plays done on the BBC regularly announced that stage stars were returning to roles they had created in the theatre. For example, Ralph Richardson played the inspector in J.B. Priestley's *An Inspector Calls* in 1950, the role he had created at the Old Vic in 1946. In 1949 Eric Portman and Mary Ellis recreated their roles in the 1948 production of Terence Rattigan's *The Browning Version*. In 1948 Ivor Novello, Zena Dare and Fay Compton recreated on radio their roles from the 1934 production of Novello's *Murder in Mayfair* and in 1949 Novello and Mary Ellis recreated their roles in Novello's 1939 production *The Dancing Years*. In 1948 Joyce Barbour recreated her role in Gerald Savory's *George and Margaret* which had run for 799 performances after it opened at Wyndham's Theatre in 1937. Reaching even further back, in 1948 Franklyn Dyall, Arthur Hardy and Ronald Simpson returned to the roles in *The Limping Man* they had created in 1931.

A new development after the war was for the casts of current West End productions to come into the radio studio and perform audio versions of their plays. In 1949 Paul Scofield and Gwen Ffrangçon-Davies recorded a radio version of Terence Rattigan's *Adventure Story*, his drama about Alexander the Great. In 1948 Basil Radford and Wyndham Goldie starred in Patrick Hastings' *The Blind Goddess*, currently playing at the Apollo Theatre, and Jean Cadell and Selma Vaz Dias in Wynyard Browne's *Dark Summer*, then at the St Martins Theatre. In 1949 Wendy Hiller and Cyril Ritchard starred in H.G. Wells' *Ann Veronica*, then playing at the Lyric Theatre.

Eventually there were distinctive play seasons: *Saturday Night Theatre* (from 1943), *World Theatre* (from 1946) and *Curtain Up* (from 1946). *Saturday Night Theatre* rapidly became a much-loved national broadcasting institution. Howard Rose, celebrating its fourth anniversary in 1947, recorded an audience rise from two-and-a-half million when it began in 1943 to eleven million by 1945. Most of the plays, he revealed, were proven West End successes, with a leavening of new plays written specially for broadcasting. The largest audiences were achieved by the radio productions of *Love on the Dole*, *The Housemaster*, *Dangerous Corner*, *Murder on the Second Floor* and *Laburnum Grove*. Interestingly all five plays had been filmed but it was their stage success and not their cinematic incarnations which dictated their selection.[32] By 1955, *Saturday Night Theatre*'s audience had fallen back to six-and-three-quarter million, a result doubtless of the rise of television.[33]

Looking back in 1957 at the evolution of radio drama during his reign, Gielgud concluded:

It may, I think, be claimed without risking any undue indictment for pomposity that what had been established was a reasonably good substitute for a National Theatre … There was representation of the acknowledged classics of the International Theatre, from Aeschylus and Shakespeare to Rostand and Shaw … There was representation of the contemporary English theatre, popular – and not so popular. There were 'thrillers' for their own large and by no means contemptible public. There were productions of *Radio Theatre* for that undaunted and admirable minority who persisted in support of and interest in a fresh and fascinating medium for tellers of dramatic tales. To sum up, by the close of the War there was a regularly satisfied programme demand for between three and four hundred plays each year.[34]

Other than transposed stage plays, one of the mainstays of BBC radio became the classic serial based on an established literary work. The first was *The Count of Monte Cristo* in 1938. The bulk of the classic serials derived from nineteenth-century novels, many of which, having been published serially in periodicals, were ideally suited to radio serial adaptation. They usually ran for eight to ten weeks in hour-long or half-hour episodes and utilized as much as possible of the original dialogue.[35]

Just as Shakespeare was the foundation on which drama was built, so Dickens performed the same function in serials. The classic serial fulfilled Reith's belief in making the best of literature and culture available to all. Charles Kingsley's *Westward Ho!* was the first classic novel to be dramatized for radio in 1924, followed by Joseph Conrad's *Lord Jim* in 1925. There had been serial readings from Dickens and performances from Bransby Williams of Dickens' characters, based on his music hall acts, during the 1930s. But serial versions with full casts began in 1939 with *The Pickwick Papers* followed by *David Copperfield* (1940, 1951), *Oliver Twist* (1941), *The Mystery of Edwin Drood* (1941), *Nicholas Nickleby* (1942), *A Christmas Carol* (1943, 1947), *Bleak House* (1944), *The Old Curiosity Shop* (1945), *Dombey and Son* (1946), *Barnaby Rudge* (1948), *Our Mutual Friend* (1950), and *Martin Chuzzlewit* (1954). Jane Austen, Anthony Trollope, William Makepeace Thackeray, Thomas Hardy, Wilkie Collins, George Eliot and the Brontës also figured among serial adaptations, with twentieth-century writers John Galsworthy and Arnold Bennett. There was also a regular sequence of adventure novels starting with *The Prisoner of Zenda* and including *The Three Musketeers*, *Twenty Years After*, *The Tower of London*, *The Four Feathers*, *King Solomon's Mines*, *Treasure Island* and *Tom Sawyer*.

The writer Alan Sillitoe was born in 1928 into a very poor Nottingham family, his labourer father being frequently unemployed. But he testified to the importance of the BBC serials in his life and the life of the neighbourhood.

The BBC dramatized *The Cloister and the Hearth* by Charles Reade, and *The Count of Monte Cristo*, each doled out in twelve weekly half-hour parts. My father had acquired a wireless on the never-never, paying three shillings a week when he could, against the ten guinea total. These serials were popular with the neighbours, as well as Aunt Edith's house, and during each thrilling instalment, the whole family transfixed, there was nevertheless a strong undercurrent of anxiety that the shopkeeper might walk in to claim his set back before the entertainment was finished.[36]

Meanwhile the commercial stations' contribution to broadcast drama was dictated directly by their American counterparts. Radio Normandy put out as part of their daily afternoon schedules three fifteen-minute American soap operas (*Backstage Wife*, *Stella Dallas* and *Young Widow Jones*). These were not the American originals but anglicized British remakes. There was also a daily fifteen-minute crime thriller, *Mr Keen, Tracer of Lost Persons*, which in the United States ran variously on NBC and CBS from 1937 to 1955. For much of its run Bennett Kilpack played Mr Keen. Milton Rosmer took the role in the British version. Radio Luxembourg would run its own version of *Perry Mason* from 1951 to 1954. But before the war its major drama contribution was *Dr Fu Manchu*, a weekly serial based on Sax Rohmer's novels and described by one well-informed American observer as 'one of the most interesting dramatic programs for British listeners during the spring of 1937'.[37]

Val Gielgud wanted to create a radio operetta to match the radio drama he was pioneering and invited Eric Maschwitz, editor of *Radio Times* and later head of Variety, to help. Maschwitz had scripted the successful radio adaptation of Compton Mackenzie's *Carnival*, the story of an Edwardian chorus girl. Maschwitz as lyricist and scriptwriter teamed up with composer George Posford and they produced *Good Night, Vienna* which became the first successful radio operetta in 1932. Producer Herbert Wilcox heard the broadcast and immediately bought the film rights. Although Maschwitz wrote that the operetta 'included almost every sugary cliché imaginable' but was blessed with a 'fresh and tuneful score', it was turned into a big hit by Wilcox.[38] The film, starring Jack Buchanan and Anna Neagle, told the familiar story of an Austrian army officer who rejects his aristocratic fiancée for the love of a flower girl, who later becomes a successful opera singer. It ran for thirteen weeks at the Carlton cinema, Haymarket and became Wilcox's most profitable production to date.[39] It initiated a new genre of radio operettas. Another Maschwitz–Posford radio collaboration, *Invitation to the Waltz* was also sold to a British studio, British International Pictures, and successfully transferred to the screen in 1935 by director Paul Stein with Lillian Harvey, Carl Esmond and Richard Bird. It told a fictional tale of an English ballerina Jenny Peachey (Lillian Harvey), unrequitedly loved by her accompanist, the real-life composer Carl Maria von Weber (Richard Bird). She agrees to become the mistress of the Duke of Württemberg in order to get him to sign a treaty with England rather than with Napoleon. She eventually escapes with the man she really loves, young officer Karl Kerner (Carl Esmond). It was the usual Viennese confection of misunderstandings, mistaken identity and star-crossed lovers, beautifully photographed in a whirl of waltzing hussars and ballerinas against a background of wedding cake architecture.

In 1933 Maschwitz was made head of Variety at the BBC. One of his most successful creations was *Café Colette*, devised as a vehicle 'to present continental music as an alternative to American jazz'. It opened on 18 July 1933 and was an instant hit. Maschwitz recalled:

> Though *Café Colette* was actually staged in a basement, we attempted to reproduce the atmosphere of a noisy establishment abroad, with the popping of champagne corks and conversation in fluent French 'overheard' from members of the audience (we even employed a waiter from Soho to call supper orders down an imaginary lift-shaft to a non-existent kitchen). The whole effect was so realistic that for several weeks the French post office had to forward to us great batches of letters addressed to 'Café Colette, Paris, France'.[40]

This convincing atmosphere was deployed in a film *Café Colette* in 1937. Directed by Paul Stein and scripted by Eric Maschwitz, Val Gielgud, Katherine Strueby and Val Valentine, it used the café as the setting for an espionage plot in which a Russian spy tries to steal the formula of a new explosive. The film starred Paul Cavanagh, Greta Nissen and Sally Gray. In 1937 Maschwitz resigned as head of Variety and embarked on a successful career as lyricist ('These Foolish Things', 'A Nightingale Sang in Berkeley Square'), scenarist (*Goodbye, Mr Chips*) and musical book writer (*Balalaika, Paprika*). He was succeeded by John Watt.

Dramatizations of films came a very long way after the stage plays and classic novels. Sometimes a story would be dramatized on radio to capitalize on the publicity generated by a film version. In 1939 the BBC serialized A.E.W. Mason's *The Four Feathers* in eight episodes with Marius Goring in the leading role and Clive Baxter repeating the part he played in the 1939 Alexander Korda film, young Harry Faversham. The radio serial utilized sound effects from the film but stressed that its version was more faithful to the novel than the film.

When the BBC broadcast an adaptation of James Hilton's *Lost Horizon* on 2 August 1948 with Sebastian Shaw as Conway and Esme Percy as the High Lama, it was firmly described by *Radio Times* (30 July 1948) as 'not a radio version of the film'. Val Gielgud, previewing the production in *Radio Times* (23 July 1948), noted that when first produced fifteen years earlier it had been 'an astonishing success' with listeners. He explained it: 'I have always believed that a portion of this success has been due to the fact that they were enabled to build their own Shangri-La in their imaginations. When a film version of the story was made in Hollywood, this ideal dream city took the form of a grandiose mixture of Coney Island and Blackpool. It seemed inadequate.'

He took the same view of the superiority of radio to film when in 1948 the Light Programme broadcast a radio version of the 1946 Michael Powell and Emeric Pressburger film *A Matter of Life and Death*: 'Like most stories dealing with an imaginary other world, *A Matter of Life and Death* should transfer to the microphone with some advantage. The visual presentation of some people's conception of heaven, or even of some undefined purgatory, tends to be either vulgar or peculiar.' (*Radio Times*, 23 July 1948).

If radio drama was comparatively uninfluenced by cinema, British cinema was willing to cash in on the popularity of radio plays by producing cinematizations of pre-sold properties with name recognition. Philip Wade's romantic drama, *Wedding Group*, the story of a young Scottish girl who follows her army officer lover to the Crimea and becomes one of Florence Nightingale's nurses, reached the screen in 1936 within a year of its first broadcast. It starred Fay Compton as Florence Nightingale. Patrick Hamilton's *To the Public Danger*, an attack on drunk driving embodied in a tense thriller, had been 'sensationally effective' in Val Gielgud's 1939 radio production.[41] It became an equally effective film in 1948 in the hands of director Terence Fisher. Wheeler Winston Dixon, in his study of Fisher, calls it 'a harrowing, accomplished, thoroughly frightening film'.[42] It starred Dermot Walsh, Susan Shaw and Roy Plomley.

The boom period for film adaptations of radio plays came in the period 1948–53 when British B picture companies sought to capitalize in particular on the popularity of BBC thrillers. Butchers Films made screen versions of four of Francis Durbridge's *Paul Temple* serials (1946, 1948, 1950, 1952) and Vernon Harris's serial *There Was a Young Lady* (1953). Apex released a film version of Gerald Verner's serial *The Show Must Go On* as *Tread Softly* (1953). But it was Hammer who dominated the field with film versions of serials such as *Dick Barton – Special Agent* (1948), *Lady in the Fog* (1952), *The Lady Craved Excitement* (1950), *Return from Darkness* filmed as *Black Widow* (1951), series such as *Doctor Morelle* (1949), *The Man in Black* (1950) and *PC 49* (1951) and one-off plays such as *Room to Let* (1950) and *Spaceways* (1953). They were almost invariably inferior to the radio originals, suffering as they did from low budgets, indifferent acting and in the case of serials the necessity of compressing what had originally been six or eight half-hour episodes into a mere 70–80 minutes.

Rather more upmarket and more entertaining as film adaptations were *Valley of Song* and *The Oracle*. Associated British Pictures' *Valley of Song* (1953) was based on Cliff Gordon's radio play *Choir Practice*. It was a charming Welsh comedy about a village split by a feud over the choice of solo singer for a performance of *Messiah*, a feud which threatens – *Romeo and Juliet*-like – the romance of the children of the rival singers. It is all resolved by the intervention of the local minister. Clifford Evans as the choirmaster, Mervyn Johns as the minister and Rachel Thomas as soloist starred in the film. The radio play had been transmitted on the BBC on 7 March 1946, repeated on 6 August 1947. Ivor Novello played the choirmaster and Mervyn Johns and Rachel Thomas played the same roles they took in the film. Group 3 produced *The Oracle* (1953) (US title: *The Horse's Mouth*), based on Robert Barr's radio play *To Tell The Truth*. In this case, it was a whimsical Irish comedy about an English reporter holidaying on a remote Irish island who discovers that the village has an oracle at the bottom of a well which can foretell the future. The villagers use it only to find lost items, locate good catches of fish and tell the weather. But the reporter gets it to predict horse race winners, thus wholly ruining the racing industry, and predict future events, which causes widespread misery until the oracle is persuaded to migrate to avoid further disaster. Robert Beatty, Virginia McKenna and Michael Medwin starred and the voice of the bad-tempered oracle was provided by the famously irascible radio and television personality Gilbert Harding. By the mid-1950s Hammer had switched to making film versions of television series, notably the hugely popular *Quatermass* serials. This was a clear indication of the superseding of radio by television as the mass medium of choice.

Notes

1   Paddy Scannell and David Cardiff, *A Social History of British Broadcasting, vol. 1, 1922–1939*, Oxford: Blackwell, 1991, p. 9.
2   Scannell and Cardiff, *A Social History of British Broadcasting*, vol. 1, pp. 68–71.
3   *The Listener*, 6 March 1939.
4   Scannell and Cardiff, *A Social History of British Broadcasting*, vol. 1, pp. 333–55.
5   J.C.W. Reith, *Broadcast Over Britain*, London: Hodder and Stoughton, 1924, p. 34.
6   Sean Street, *Crossing the Ether: British Public Service Radio and Commercial Competition*, Eastleigh: John Libbey Publishing, 2004, p. 108.
7   Street, *Crossing the Ether*, p. 162.
8   Richard Nichols, *Radio Luxembourg: The Station of the Stars*, London: Comet, 1983, p. 47.
9   Robert E. Silvey, *Who's Listening?: The Story of BBC Audience Research*, London:

George Allen and Unwin, 1974, pp. 68–9.

10   Valeria Camporesi, *Mass Culture and National Traditions: the BBC and American Broadcasting 1922–1954*, Fucecchio, Italy: European Press Academic Publishing, 2000, p. 110.

11   Camporesi, *Mass Culture and National Traditions*, p. 134.

12   Maurice Gorham, *Sound and Fury: twenty one years in the BBC*, London: Percival Marshall, 1948, p. 38.

13   Camporesi, *Mass Culture and National Traditions*, p. 132.

14   P.P. Eckersley, *The Power Behind the Microphone*, London: Scientific Book Club, 1942, pp. 136–7.

15   R.S. Lambert, *Ariel and All His Quality*, London: Victor Gollancz, 1940, pp. 306–7.

16   Scannell and Cardiff, *A Social History of British Broadcasting*, vol. 1, p. 206.

17   On BBC music policy see Scannell and Cardiff, *A Social History of British Broadcasting*, vol. 1, pp. 181–227. On radio and popular music see also James J. Nott, *Music for the People: popular music and dance in inter-war Britain*, Oxford: Oxford University Press, 2002, pp. 58–85.

18   Scannell and Cardiff, *A Social History of British Broadcasting*, vol. 1, p. 10.

19   Scannell and Cardiff, *A Social History of British Broadcasting*, vol. 1, p. 281.

20   Scannell and Cardiff, *A Social History of British Broadcasting*, vol. 1, p. 14.

21   D.L. LeMahieu, *A Culture for Democracy*, Oxford: Clarendon Press, 1988.

22   Quoted in Mark Pegg, *Broadcasting and Society 1918–1939*, Beckenham: Croom Helm, 1983, p. 149.

23   J.C.W. Reith, *Into the Wind*, London: Hodder and Stoughton, 1949, p. 116.

24   On the BBC and the war see Sian Nicholas, *The Echo of War: Homefront Propaganda and the Wartime BBC, 1939–45*, Manchester: Manchester University Press, 1996, and Asa Briggs, *History of Broadcasting in the United Kingdom, vol. 3: The War of Words*, Oxford: Oxford University Press, 1970.

25   Camporesi, *Mass Culture and National Traditions*, pp. 165, 169.

26   Val Gielgud, *Years of the Locust*, London: Nicholson and Watson, 1947, pp. 126–7.

27   Gielgud, *Years of the Locust*, p. 109.

28   Val Gielgud, *Years in a Mirror*, London: The Bodley Head, 1965, p. 157.

29   Gielgud, *Years in a Mirror*, pp. 147, 143.

30   Val Gielgud, *British Radio Drama 1922–1956*, London: George G. Harrap and Co., 1957, p. 19.

31   Gielgud, *British Radio Drama*, p. 49.

32   *Radio Times*, 28 March 1947.

33   Gielgud, *British Radio Drama*, p. 30.

34   Gielgud, *British Radio Drama*, p. 73. See also Roger Wood, 'Radio Drama at the Crossroads: The History and Contemporary Context of Radio Drama at the BBC', Ph.D. dissertation, De Montfort University, 2008.

35   On radio serials see Robert Giddings and Keith Selby, *The Classic Serial on Television and Radio*, Basingstoke: Palgrave, 2001 and H. Philip Bolton, *Dickens Dramatized*, London: Mansell, 1987.

36 Alan Sillitoe, *Life without Armour*, London: Harper Collins, 1995, p. 30.
37 Street, *Crossing the Ether*, p. 88.
38 Eric Maschwitz, *No Chip On My Shoulder*, London: Herbert Jenkins, 1957, p. 56.
39 Herbert Wilcox, *25,000 Sunsets*, London: The Bodley Head, 1967, p. 91.
40 Maschwitz, *No Chip On My Shoulder*, p. 69.
41 Gielgud, *British Radio Drama*, p. 67.
42 Wheeler Winston Dixon, *The Charm of Evil*, Metuchen, NJ and London: Scarecrow Press, 1991, p. 22.

3

Filming radio genres: i) comedy

Comedy was consistently the most popular genre of radio programme. In a 1946 US survey, 59% of respondents listed comedy as their favourite form of programme.[1] This is perhaps not surprising, given the background first of economic depression and later world war. People wanted to be cheered up. But radio imposed certain restrictions on comedy. Visual comedy such as slapstick was impossible. Comedy needed to be predominantly verbal and radio was the home of puns, catchphrases, malapropisms, spoonerisms, alliteration and one-liners, though the creative use of sound effects could produce comedic surrealism. The primacy of verbal comedy put paid to any radio career for Harpo Marx, who never spoke in the Marx Brothers' films. So on radio in shows like *Flywheel, Shyster and Flywheel* (1932–33) the Marx Brothers were reduced to two: Chico with his malapropisms and cod-Italian accent and Groucho with his quickfire gag routines.[2]

There was also strict censorship, with sex, politics, race, religion, profanity and bodily functions all banned. When Mae West and Don Ameche performed an Adam and Eve sketch on *The Edgar Bergen Show* in 1937, there was an outcry. The Catholic Church threatened a boycott of Chase and Sanborn Coffee, the programme's sponsor, and there was a formal investigation by the Federal Communications Commission. As a result Mae West was off the air for the next 37 years. Censorship was relaxed somewhat during the war when much of the humour revolved around topical issues such as rationing, war work, the draft, and it was possible to poke fun at the enemy. Sponsors were also very anxious to eliminate any criticism or satire at the expense of their product and any prospective customers.

Vaudeville, badly hit by the rise of the cinema, was in decline and many of its performers moved gratefully to radio. With their verbal, often pun-based, routines, their catchphrases, their stooges and a live audience, they took the air waves by storm. Ed Wynn in his character of 'The Fire Chief', Joe Penner with his catchphrase 'Wanna buy a duck', German dialect comedian Jack Pearl and Ziegfeld Follies' star Eddie Cantor became radio stars almost overnight. As their already old-fashioned material came to seem increasingly stale and repetitive, the popularity of most of them waned almost as rapidly as it had risen. Pearl and Wynn peaked in 1932–33 and Penner in 1933–35 and they never recaptured their early popularity.

The great exception was Eddie Cantor, whose radio show ran from 1931 to 1949. He studied radio and its needs intently and essentially created the radio variety show in the form it was to maintain throughout the history of American radio. It consisted of comic monologues, sketches, guest stars and musical in- terludes, all put over – in Cantor's case – with manic energy and pace. He kept the format fresh by introducing new talent (such as dialect comics Bert Gordon 'The Mad Russian' and Harry Einstein as the Greek Nick Parkyarkarkas), devel- oping audience participation and running gags – like his bid for the presidency. There were also regular references to his wife Ida and their five daughters. This helped to create the illusion of intimacy that was one of the distinctive charac- teristics of radio. Glimpses of the home life of the stars generated the sense that the performers were friends and was one of the enduring appeals of radio. The variety show format succeeded triumphantly both in the cases of Bing Crosby, whose radio show ran from 1936 to 1956 and Bob Hope, whose show ran from 1938 to 1955. Eddie Cantor was already a film star under contract to Samuel Goldwyn for whom in the early 1930s he starred in a succession of spectacu- lar musical comedies combining the clowning of Cantor with dance routines choreographed by Busby Berkeley, the glamour of the Goldwyn girls, and new songs by Hollywood's top songwriters: *Whoopee* (1930), *Palmy Days* (1931), *The Kid from Spain* (1932), *Roman Scandals* (1933), *Kid Millions* (1934) and *Strike Me Pink* (1936). But it was their radio success that led Paramount to sign both Hope and Crosby, producing individual films as vehicles for them and teaming them in the ever-popular *Road* films (1940–52).

Next to the variety show, the other comedy format that became a staple of radio was the situation comedy or sitcom. The prototype sitcom was one of the most remarkable shows on radio, *Amos 'n' Andy*. *Amos 'n' Andy* ran in various formats on American radio from 1928 to 1960. It charted the comic misadventures of Amos Jones and Andy Brown, Southern blacks who had migrated from Atlanta to Chicago and there lived and worked in the black community, running a taxi company. What was remarkable about the show was that Amos and Andy were played by two white men, Freeman Gosden and Charles Correll, who wrote the scripts and played all the parts in the show. The show, initially a daily fifteen-minute programme in serial form, was a huge hit. Amos and Andy's catchphrases became national currency. Presidents Coolidge and Hoover declared themselves fans. There were Amos 'n' Andy toys, comic strips, candy bars and records and they were so popular that cinemas had to halt their showings at 7.00 p.m. and pipe in the latest *Amos 'n' Andy* episode in order to keep their audiences.[3]

In 1943, their ratings were falling and so the show was revamped with new writers, a genuinely black supporting cast and a half-hour sitcom format. Listening figures doubled and the show continued on radio until 1960. Almost from the first, the show was denounced by black organizations as demeaning but it was defended by black newspapers and listened to by black audiences. It was not the only ethnically-based comedy show. The Jews featured in *The Goldbergs* (1929–34, 1936–45, 1949–50), created and written by and starring Gertrude Berg; and the Italians in *Life With Luigi* (1948–53).[4] The most popular ethnic programmes succeeded because they dealt with the universal issues of family life, work and community.

The fully formed sitcom was a weekly half-hour with a self-contained story, continuing characters and usually a family basis. They promoted family values and defined gender roles; they were generally middle-class in ethos and most often set in an idealized small-town America. There tended to be two models of marriage: one in which there was an impractical, incompetent but lovable and good-hearted husband and a shrewd, level-headed, supremely competent wife who actually ran things, and one in which there was a scatterbrained, lovable scheming wife and a patient and long-suffering husband who has to sort out her disasters.

The prototype of the first model was *Fibber McGee and Molly* (1935–56) which starred real-life husband and wife team Jim and Marion Jordan, who were veteran vaudevillians. By the 1940s, they had one of the four top-rated comedy shows on American radio, along with Bob Hope, Jack Benny and Edgar Bergen. Fibber McGee was a good-natured, day-dreaming incompetent with a penchant for boastful tall tales; his wife Molly was practical, sensible and managerial. Their home was in the small mid-Western town of Wistful Vista and the characters, their friends, relatives and fellow citizens. Such was the success of the series that it gave rise to two spin-offs, making it the first major radio series to generate its own offspring. Fibber's bombastic neighbour, Throckmorton P. Gildersleeve (Harold Peary), who had joined the cast in 1937, got his own series in 1941 *The Great Gildersleeve*. It ran until 1957, even though Peary, who had tired of the role, left in 1950 to be replaced for the duration of the run by Willard Waterman. The other popular character to get a series was the black maid Beulah, initially played by a white man Marlin Hurt. *Beulah* debuted in 1945 but Hurt died the following year. The series was revived in 1947 and ran until 1954 with Beulah this time played successively by black actresses Hattie McDaniel, Lillian Randolph and her sister Amanda Randolph. The cast of characters who became old friends, the running gags (such as McGee's overfilled closet that spilled its contents whenever the door was opened) and the catchphrases (such as Molly's 'Heavenly Days') all ensured the continuing appeal of *Fibber McGee and Molly*.[5]

The Hollywood agency MCA had several of the top radio comedy stars under contract and they wanted to put them into films. So they packaged several of their clients, provided a director (Allan Dwan) and sold the idea to RKO Radio Pictures who produced two films *Look Who's Laughing* (1941) and *Here We Go Again* (1942). Both were dire, depending on the established personalities of the radio performers and their catchphrases and involving them in some tired and unoriginal slapstick.

Look Who's Laughing, written by James V. Kern, opens at NBC studios with ventriloquist Edgar Bergen, whose lips are clearly moving, and his monocled, tophatted boy dummy Charlie McCarthy going through their act in the last show of the season. Then they fly off on holiday and land at Wistful Vista where they encounter Fibber McGee and Molly, and their neighbour Throckmorton P. Gildersleeve. Bergen and his assistant Julie (Lucille Ball) help Fibber, chairman of the local chamber of commerce, to acquire a disused airfield as a site for a new factory which will benefit the town economically. There are scenes of the dummy Charlie being cheeky, ogling girls and getting tipsy on milkshakes at the drug store, and slapstick scenes in which Fibber's new dishwasher goes berserk and Fibber causes havoc when he takes the controls of a plane.

In *Here We Go Again*, written by Paul Gerard Smith and Joe Bigelow, Fibber McGee and Molly go to a swish lodge to celebrate their twentieth wedding anniversary and become innocently involved in a scheme to swindle Bergen into buying a new synthetic fuel. It involves the McGees in familiar domestic sitcom situations and Bergen disguising as an Indian squaw and being chased by a bear. The films served only to demonstrate that the performers involved were best suited to radio. *Heavenly Days* (1944), directed and co-written by Howard Estabrook, featured Fibber McGee and Molly alone and attempted a kind of downmarket *Mr Smith Goes to Washington* as Fibber, identified as Mr Average Man in a Gallup Poll, gets to tell Congress how to sort out the country. It flopped.

The archetypal sitcom revolved around the white middle-class family living comfortably in an idealized mid-Western town, usually with a husband working in one of the professions, his housewife spouse and one or more teenage children. Classic versions of this format were *The Aldrich Family*, *The Adventures of Ozzie and Harriet* and *Father Knows Best*. *The Aldrich Family*, which ran on radio from 1939 to 1953, embodies the extraordinary and creative symbiosis of the mass media in the heyday of radio. It originated in a Broadway play, *What a Life*, by Clifford Goldsmith, which revolved around the misadventures of accident-prone sixteen-year-old Henry Aldrich of Central High School, Centerville. Author Goldsmith then developed the situation in comedy sketches for the Rudy Vallee and Kate Smith radio shows in 1938. Their success led to a thirteen-year run on radio for *The Aldrich Family*, a weekly half-hour sitcom, with Ezra Stone, who had played Henry on Broadway, repeating his characterization and the series including his lawyer father, housewife mother, teenage sister and best friend Homer Brown. It opened every week with mother calling 'Henry! Henry Aldrich!' and Henry replying 'Coming mother' and the episode would begin. But at the same time as *The Aldrich Family* was running on radio, there was a series of eleven films (1939–44) made for cinemas, beginning with *What a Life* and starring James Lydon as Henry Aldrich.

Father Knows Best (1949–53) starred Robert Young as insurance agent Jim Anderson in the small town of Springfield and featured his wife and three children. Fiction and reality overlapped in *The Adventures of Ozzie and Harriet* (1944–54) which starred bandleader Ozzie Nelson and his wife, singer Harriet Hilliard. The series had been developed by Ozzie Nelson and featured the adventures of 'America's favourite young couple', joined by their sons David and Ricky. Initially played by actors, David and Ricky were from 1949 played by the real-life sons David and Ricky Nelson. It was situations such as this that gave the series that sense of recognizable reality and promoted audience identification with the characters and situations. The series transferred effortlessly to television in 1952, running until 1966. There was also a big-screen version for Universal in 1952, *Here Come the Nelsons*, directed by Frederick De Cordova, co-written by Ozzie and co-starring Rock Hudson and Barbara Lawrence.

The popularity of the domestic sitcom format was such that it revitalized the radio careers of George Burns and Gracie Allen. Real-life husband and wife Burns and Allen had teamed up as a vaudeville cross-talk act in 1923, she as the zany, scatterbrained girlfriend and he as the longsuffering suitor. They had their own radio show from 1932. When ratings began to slip, they revamped the format as a domestic sitcom with themselves as husband and wife and involving a supporting cast of friends and neighbours. In its new format, it regained popularity and ran from 1941 to 1950, transferring effortlessly to television to run from

1950 to 1958 when Gracie Allen retired.

The prototype of these radio family sitcoms involving teenage sons was probably MGM's much-loved Hardy Family series, which spanned fifteen films and ran from 1937 to 1946 with Mickey Rooney as Andy Hardy and Lewis Stone as his father, Judge Hardy. It belatedly reached radio in 1949–50. The Hardy Family had its cinematic rivals in the Higgins Family films, with nine titles between 1938 and 1941, and the Jones Family films, with seventeen titles between 1936 and 1940.

A new development in the sitcom in the late 1940s found the focus of the action shifting from teenage son or daughter to the wife, a direct reflection of the increasing prominence of women in wartime cinema. *My Favourite Husband* (1948–51), billed as 'the story of two people who live together and like it', was a vehicle for Lucille Ball and was a classic example of the second type of domestic sitcom: scatterbrained wife and long-suffering husband. It originated as a summer replacement for *The Adventures of Ozzie and Harriet* and was scripted by the regular writers of that show. It was based on a novel by Isabel Scott Rorick, *Mr and Mrs Cugat*, a high society comedy about a sophisticated couple, a staid bank vice-president and his flighty and spendthrift wife. Paramount had filmed the Rorick novel in 1942 as *Are Husbands Necessary?* with Ray Milland and Betty Field and *Lux* had aired their radio version of the film with George Burns and Gracie Allen on 15 February 1943. The new radio show starred Lucille Ball and Richard Denning. It was popular enough with audiences for CBS to want to continue with it. They hired Jess Oppenheimer as head writer and later as producer-director. Oppenheimer made a number of significant changes which reflected his perception of the basic appeal of the sitcom. He changed the surname of leading characters George and Liz from the exotic sounding Cugat to the more homely Cooper, to make them more likely to gain universal identification. He made it clear that they were not rich and sophisticated but on an average wage and living in a small town (Sheridan Falls). He made Liz Cooper more dizzy, comic and scheming and to counterpoint the Coopers, he invented another couple, George's boss, bank president Rudolph Atterbury (Gale Gordon) and his wife Iris (Bea Benaderet), Liz Cooper's best friend. The model Oppenheimer seems to have had in mind was Burns and Allen. Certainly the changes worked, the show acquired a sponsor (General Foods' Jello) and it ran successfully until 1951. There were plans to transfer it to television but Lucille Ball was adamant that she wanted the role of her television husband to go to her real-life husband, Cuban bandleader Desi Arnaz. Oppenheimer devised a new format, with Lucille Ball and Desi Arnaz as husband and wife, two new best friends and often reworking material from *My Favourite Husband*, created one of TV's best-loved sitcoms *I Love Lucy* (1951–1956), whose roots were firmly in radio.[6]

Although most domestic sitcoms were middle-class, there was a blue-collar sitcom, *The Life of Riley*, which ran on NBC from 1944 to 1951. It starred William Bendix as Chester A. Riley, a stubborn but goodnatured and rather dim riveter in an aircraft factory, who had a sensible wife, two children and two best friends. A feature film of the series *The Life of Riley* was produced by Universal Pictures in 1949, directed and written by Irving Brecher, creator-producer of the radio show. An adaptation of the film version appeared on the *Lux Radio Theatre* on the rival CBS network on 8 May 1950. The radio series transferred to television where it ran from 1953 to 1958.

Half-way between the variety show and the sitcom was *The Jack Benny Programme*, which ran on radio from 1932 to 1955. Benny and his writers devised a new format for the radio show. Benny was a radio star who in the first half of the programme would be heard preparing his weekly show with his entourage and undertaking his domestic duties at his Beverly Hills home. In the second half of the show there would be a sketch from the radio show, often a movie parody (*The Lost Weekend* or *The Treasure of the Sierra Madre* for instance). Benny at the centre of the action was characterized as penny-pinching and vain and was the butt of many of the jokes. But as Gerald Nachman observes, the show's ingenuity derived in part from the fact that Benny was the ultimate audience identification figure, a 'middle-aged, middle-American, middle-class Everyman'.[7] For it was Benny's mid-Western origins (Waukegan, Illinois) rather than his Jewishness which the programme stressed. The fact that he and some of the cast acted under their own names, like Ozzie and Harriet, conveyed the sense of a stylized and comic version of reality. The entourage consisted of his 'girl Friday' Mary Livingstone (played by his real-life wife Sadie Marks), his long-suffering but acid-tongued black valet Rochester Van Jones (Eddie Anderson), the hard-drinking braggart bandleader Phil Harris (who was married in real life to movie star Alice Faye to whom he would often refer), the idiot boy singer Dennis Day who sang like an angel and was dominated by a fictional battleaxe mother, and announcer Don Wilson, constantly ribbed about his weight. From 1945 Ronald Colman and his wife Benita Hume joined the cast as semi-regulars playing Jack's high-toned next-door neighbours who detest him. References to real people and real events gave the whole thing comic credibility. When Vincent Price was first invited to dinner by the Colmans, he and his wife turned up at Jack Benny's believing that the Colmans genuinely lived next door, only to find they actually lived miles away.[8] Several of Jack Benny's films were based on aspects of the show:

Buck Benny Rides Again (1940) expanded a regular segment of the show, *Love Thy Neighbor* (1940) dramatized the Benny–Fred Allen 'feud' and *The Meanest Man in the World* (1943) focused on his legendary parsimony. Only one of his films, *To Be or Not to Be* (1942), proved memorable and longlasting. The series spawned two spin-offs, *A Day in the Life of Dennis Day* (1946–51) and *The Phil Harris/Alice Faye Show* (1945–54).[9]

One of the appeals of the series was running gags: Benny's taking in washing to make ends meet, keeping his money in a vault and refusing to replace an elderly car whose wheezing and whirring journeys were voiced by impressionist Mel Blanc, who also played Benny's tormented violin teacher Professor Le Blanc. One of the most popular running gags was Benny's feud with Fred Allen, one of a series of manufactured radio feuds which allowed the stars to trade insults over the air. Another was between columnist Walter Winchell and bandleader Ben Bernie which became the basis of a feature film, 20th Century Fox's *Wake Up and Live* (1937). Fred Allen, whose comedy shows, successively titled *Town Hall Tonight*, *The Fred Allen Show* and *Allen's Alley* ran from 1932 to 1949, originated in New York (Allen hated Hollywood), were scripted by Allen himself and had a supporting cast of vivid characters (Falstaff Openshaw, Pansy Nussbaum, Titus Moody, Senator Beauregard Claghorn) off whom Allen bounced his humour. Fred Allen's programmes were more sharply satirical and pointedly topical than other comedy shows. Allen was renowned for his ad libs and his fights with network censors and sponsors and on occasions was cut off in mid-show for insulting them.

Familiarity is the key to the success of the long-running comedy shows: characters, catchphrases, situations based on misunderstandings and human frailties (vanity, jealousy, greed, ambition), lines that audiences could anticipate and relish, and events which were comedic and stylized versions of their domestic experience. Interestingly only Bob Hope duplicated his radio success in the cinema with a long career in films, in which his vain, cowardly and lecherous radio persona transferred readily to the big screen. Particularly popular were the *Road* films which teamed him felicitously with crooner Bing Crosby and glamorous Dorothy Lamour. Fred Allen, Edgar Bergen and Charlie McCarthy, Fibber McGee and Molly, George Burns and Gracie Allen, Milton Berle and Jack Benny all tried films and there were one-off cinema versions of popular sitcoms like *The Life of Riley* and *The Adventures of Ozzie and Harriet* but none of the radio stars succeeded in establishing themselves as screen stars in the way that Hope did. Somehow they never matched up to the imaginary picture the radio audience had of them.

Just as vaudeville supplied some of the early comedy stars of American radio, so the music halls furnished ready-made comedy acts for British radio. Music hall had been the dominant cultural form of the second half of the nineteenth century, providing songs and sketches which allowed the audience to recognise and affirm their basic values, attitudes and aspirations. The subjects treated by the music hall were generally love (treated as romantic), marriage (seen as a trap and a disaster), work (and how to avoid it), city life, food and drink, clothes and holidays. The values celebrated were comradeship, a mild anti-authoritarianism, defined gender roles and the idea of an immutable social order. It was the music hall (or variety, the form into which it evolved in the twentieth century) which fed the twentieth century's new media – films, records and the wireless. Music hall provided the songs, the sketches and the stars for these new media.

Michael Standing, Head of BBC Variety, claiming that his department's remit was 'to amuse all and offend none' revealed in the *Radio Times* (25 February 1949) that his department produced one hundred programmes a week, sixty of them musical and the remainder scripted, twenty of them peak-hour comedy programmes. But he indicated that they were handicapped by a shortage of performers familiar with radio technique and first-class writers because of the demands of the medium, estimating that twenty comedy shows a week ate up something like three million words a year. He stressed the fact that 'Broadcasting is a highly specialised business and a training in stage and screen work, though often helpful, can sometimes be a positive disadvantage to an artist. In any event, it is in itself quite insufficient to equip him for the microphone. No artist can hope to achieve lasting success on the air unless he is ready to study and conform closely to the peculiar needs of the different medium. Too many of the occasional broadcasters are apt to be satisfied with a mild and inadequate adaptation of their stage material and technique'. As examples of artists who had mastered the medium he cited Tommy Handley (ITMA), Richard Murdoch and Kenneth Horne (*Much Binding in the Marsh*), Wilfred Pickles (*Have a Go*), Eric Barker (*Waterlogged Spa*) and Jimmy Edwards, Joy Nichols and Dick Bentley (*Take It From Here*).

One of the giants of British comedy in the first half of the twentieth century was Will Hay (1888–1949). His comic persona, whether schoolmaster, station-master or prison governor, was a quintessentially English archetype – the sly, shabby – genteel, pompous, blustering, fundamentally fraudulent professional man, claiming an education but ever revealing his abysmal ignorance, aspiring to authority but seeing it constantly subverted by his underlings. It was a character Hay evolved during years of touring the music halls, where in his celebrated 'schoolmaster' act in a much-reworked sketch 'the Fourth Form at St Michaels' he perfected an immaculate sense of timing, developed a classic line in punning exchanges and created his familiar trademarks (the adjustable pince-nez and the disapproving sniff). The secret of both his appeal and his success lay in the split-level response of the British audience, blended of a love of seeing petty authority exposed and deflated, the national mistrust of the intellectual and the affection for the genial incompetent who always muddles through.

Hay's film career, which stretched from 1934 to 1943 and embraced some eighteen films, saw him bringing his comic character to a peak of perfection. In three of his films (*Boys Will Be Boys*, *Good Morning, Boys* and *The Ghost of St Michaels*) he played a seedy schoolmaster in a third-rate public school, constantly challenged and outwitted by the boys. But his greatest successes came in the six films in which he was teamed with Moore Marriott and Graham Moffatt and in particular the sublime *Oh, Mr Porter* (1937) in which Hay was the stationmaster of a haunted, rundown station at Buggleskelly in Northern Ireland. The presence of Marriott and Moffatt gave a rich and subtle extra dimension to Hay's screen comedy. Marriott was the cranky, toothless old man who embodies an anarchy with its own relentless logic that Hay can never tame and is summed up by his immortal one-liner 'Next train's gone'. Moffatt, on the other hand, is the absolutely level-headed, down-to-earth boy who sees through all Hay's posturing pretences and is often responsible for saving him from the disastrous consequences of them. The two sidekicks became so popular that Hay came to feel that they were 'swamping him' and after *Where's That Fire* (1939) he broke up the team, left Gainsborough where he had made ten films and signed for Ealing where as a solo artist he made four more films.

Hay came late to radio, starring on the BBC in three series of *The Will Hay Programme* in 1944 and early 1945, which achieved considerable popularity. He was back with his beloved schoolmaster character, named now Dr Muffin, who in the first half of the show would be sweet-talking his landlady and in the second half presiding in his classroom at St Michaels. This involved him interacting with a grovelling swot D'Arcy (John Clark) and a disrespectful and aggressive Smart (Charles Hawtrey). 'Thank you, D'Arcy' became a popular catchphrase which when quoted in school was calculated to reduce any class of schoolboys to knowing laughter. The third series was abruptly terminated when Hay refused to perform the final two scripts, regarding them as substandard, and telling the *Daily Mail*: 'I won't risk broadcasting an inferior show. It took me twenty years to build up the reputation I have. It could be torn down in two broadcasts'.[10] However soon his performing career was over for good. He suffered a stroke in 1946 which forced him to retire and in 1949 he died following a second stroke.

Another symbol of authority defeated by incompetence and a much loved comic figure of the music hall, radio and films was Robb Wilton (1882–1957). He developed both his character and his delivery, slow and deliberate with a repertoire of mannerisms (tooth-sucking, brow-wiping, finger-chewing) on the halls in the 1920s as in a succession of sketches as police sergeant, fire chief, prison governor and magistrate he constantly sought and failed to do his duty by reason of a cosmic but good-hearted incompetence. These sketches were reproduced in short films, on gramophone records and on the wireless. Coincidentally they were the same professions adopted by Will Hay in his films.

Wilton's popular magistrate character was developed as the mainstay of a succession of radio series between 1937 and 1948. Mr Muddlecombe JP, principal magistrate of Nether Backwash, found himself generally at sea in attempting to fulfil his professional duties and at home was henpecked by a domineering wife. In wartime his character thrived on the popular perception of all authority as incompetent and heavy-handed. His series were performed without a studio audience to allow the slow-building pace of delivery to be uninterrupted.[11]

Authority was challenged in a different way by another veteran of the halls, Old Mother Riley. Played in drag by Arthur Lucan (1887–1954), Old Mother Riley was the central character in fourteen films made between 1937 and 1952. Cheaply produced on rudimentary sets with functional direction and dismal supporting casts, the films adopted a genuinely populist stance and provided a comic heroine of titanic dimensions, exaggerated admittedly but rooted in truth. Old Mother Riley, the Irish washerwoman with apron, shawl, old black dress and poke bonnet, was the inextinguishable life force of the slums, a veritable Brünnhilde of the backstreets. A garrulous malaprop, vituperative and combative, she had an unforgettable physical presence. She was a breast-beating, arm-waving, finger-pointing, hand-flourishing, elbow-stretching, knee-bending, sleeve-rolling, superanimated, rubber-limbed rag doll. Hers was truly a case of body language gone berserk, but it was an outward and visible sign of her refusal to be cowed or to conform.

Lucan was partnered by his wife, the wholly talentless Kitty McShane, who played Mother Riley's daughter Kitty. The characterizations were developed in a popular music hall sketch 'Bridget's Night Out' in which Lucan and McShane toured the halls in the 1930s. It featured an elderly Irish mother waiting for her daughter to return from a night out and led to a massive row culminating in the smashing of a kitchen full of crockery.

The character transferred to BBC radio in three series, *Old Mother Riley Takes the Air* (1941) and *Old Mother Riley and Her Daughter Kitty* series 1 (1942) and series 2 (1948). Lucan and McShane learned their parts, appeared in full costume and make-up and performed before a studio audience to give something of the flavour of the music hall act. Their visual familiarity from the films will have enabled audiences to envisage them but Mother Riley's verbal anarchy adapted easily to the air waves. Old Mother Riley would greet audiences with a high speed burst of 'Good evening blackguards, bodyguards, coalyards and fireguards. It's me, Mother Riley, just blown in for a breath of fresh air' and would proceed to mangle the language, rebuking her daughter for instance by declaring: 'It's disgusterating, disgraceful, delicious, delightful'.[12]

An altogether gentler working-class matriarch was portrayed by another drag act. Norman Evans (1901–62) was best known for his impersonation of an ample-bosomed Lancashire housewife, in the music hall sketch 'Over the Garden Wall'. Toothless, aproned, confidential, she would lean on the wall retelling local gossip and gleefully discussing family scandals and people's ailments. It is the comic evocation of the archetypal Lancashire housewife and was taken over and faithfully reproduced by Les Dawson and Roy Barraclough in their much-loved double act as Cissie and Ada.

Norman Evans made three films for Manchester-based Mancunian Films. In *Demobbed* (1944) he and a group of ex-soldiers were seeking work, eventually finding it in a scientific instrument factory where they are seen defying, sending up and bamboozling the management before they successfully foil a robbery. *Under New Management* (1946) had the same comic team trying to run a hotel. But *Over the Garden Wall* (1950), taking its title from Evans' well-loved sketch, was Norman Evans' celluloid apotheosis. Now he spent the whole film in drag as Fanny Lawton, in what was effectively a prototype sitcom, complete with husband (played by chainsmoking Jimmy James who got to perform his popular drunk act) and two lodgers (Dan Young and Alec Pleon). The plot, such as it was, had Fanny preventing the break-up of her daughter's marriage. But on this slender thread hung a succession of sketches based on everyday life: using the bathroom, having breakfast, washing up, going to bed, gossiping with neighbours. Similar material was to be found in three BBC radio series also called *Over the Garden Wall* (1948–50) where this time Evans was called Fanny Fairbottom. The programmes featured her interaction with her neighbour, Mrs Ethel Higginbottom.

Sir John Reith left the BBC in 1938 and it cannot be mere coincidence that in the same year the BBC developed its first great original comedy series, the variety show *Band Waggon*. Reith had opposed the introduction of audience research but when it was introduced in 1936 it revealed the overwhelming audience preference for variety shows. Reith had opposed regular weekly slots for programmes, wanting audiences to discover the full range of BBC offerings by serendipity. *Band Waggon* became the first regularly scheduled comedy programme with its own resident comedian, which allowed audiences to tune in every week at the same time. It was a comedy/variety show on the established American model. The stars were music hall and concert party artist Arthur Askey and musical comedy star Richard Murdoch. There were comedy sketches, dance band interludes, guest stars, a talent spot ('New Voices'), 'Chestnut Corner' (a shameless recycling of hoary old gags), a regular comic song from Arthur Askey. The chemistry between the diminutive, bustling, lower middle-class Liverpool-born comic Askey and the upper-class Charterhouse and Cambridge-educated Murdoch was excellent and their teaming one of the reasons for the series success.

It had an inauspicious start. The early scripts were poor and after three programmes, John Watt, the head of Variety, decided to terminate the show after six. In consequence, Askey and Murdoch were allowed to do more or less as they liked. So they created the fantasy of a flat on the roof of Broadcasting House, where they had a cleaner, Mrs Bagwash whose daughter, Nausea, was Arthur's fiancée and where they kept two pigeons, Basil and Lucy, and Lewis the goat. They developed this aspect of the fantasy; letting down a can of water into the board room to boil their eggs over the fire; secretly using the announcers' bathroom; polishing the pips in the morning. This surreal fantasy caught the popular fancy as it demystified the great monolith in Portland Place. Giving each other nicknames, 'Big' for Arthur (from 'Big-hearted') and 'Stinker' for Murdoch, they developed a range of catchphrases which Askey recalled soon 'were being used everywhere':[13] 'Aythangyew', 'Before your very eyes', 'Hello, playmates', 'proper 'umdrum'', 'Doesn't it make you want to spit?', 'You silly little man'. The use of catchphrases made people feel part of the show and when used in everyday conversation created a palpable feeling of a community with shared reference points. The show ran for three series, from 5 January 1938 to 25 November 1939, fifty-two programmes in all, a short run compared to other shows but as Askey recalled: 'the strain of finding new material every week was beginning to tell, and I would have hated our high standard to have dropped'.[14] The BBC wanted to keep them and the critics and public protested the show's demise.

But that shrewd showman, Jack Hylton, acquired the stage rights to *Band Waggon* and put together a show, which included his own band. They embarked on a triumphal provincial tour, culminating in a run at the London Palladium in summer 1939. During the Palladium run, Gainsborough Films signed Askey to a film contract with *Band Waggon* as the first project. The film was shot in

August and September 1939 and released in January 1940 after the radio series had finished its run.

The film, which purported to tell the story of how *Band Waggon* had come to radio, was in effect a filmed variety show with a tenuous and familiar plot-line – the apparently haunted castle which is really the headquarters of a gang of spies/crooks. It was used at least three times by Will Hay as well as Laurel and Hardy, Abbott and Costello and Bob Hope. The film opened with a visual recreation of the set-up familiar from the radio series, the flat on the roof of Broadcasting House, a washing line stretched between the aerials, Lewis the goat and two hens, and Askey and Murdoch, calling each other by their nicknames 'Big' and 'Stinker', discussing Mrs Bagwash and Nausea and delivering their catchphrases.

They are discovered by John Pilkington, the head of Music at the BBC, who is depicted as a stuffy, pompous, monocled establishment figure who actually hates music, a typical populist tilt at what was perceived as a BBC type. They explain they have been waiting three months for an audition but he evicts them. Leaving Broadcasting House they encounter the BBC's gardening expert, Mr C.H. Middleton and the first BBC commentator to do interviews with 'the man in the street', Michael Standing.

Jack Hylton, who had also found it impossible to get an audition from Pilking-ton, has broken glass spread on the road outside his roadhouse to stop Pilkington's car. Having secured his presence, he and the band with singers Pat Kirkwood and Bruce Trent and the dancing Sherman Fisher Girls perform a ballad 'I'm a simple melody maker' and a big production number 'On the good ship Saucy Jane'. Pilkington discovers the trick played on him and leaves in a fury.

Arthur and Dickie Murdoch now join forces with Jack Hylton and his band. They take over Droon Castle, discover the 'haunting' to be the work of the ancient caretaker (Moore Marriott), keeping people away from a group of commercial television makers using it as a studio. The television makers turn out to be German spies who depart, leaving the television equipment behind. So Arthur and Dickie decide on a pirate television broadcast to showcase their talents. They cut into the BBC television service where Jasmine Bligh is seen doing her announce-ments and they basically stage a television version of *Band Waggon* with 'Chestnut Corner', a comic song from Arthur, 'A pretty little bird am I', a romantic duet from Murdoch and Pat Kirkwood, 'The only one who's difficult is you', and a comic oratorio 'Old King Cole' with Murdoch, two fat sopranos and a fat tenor, sabotaged by Arthur. Arthur does a parody of 'The Dying Swan' ballet and there is a big band production number 'Boomps-a-daisy'. The spies return to blow up the television equipment but are captured. The police arrive to break up the television broadcast but a telegram arrives from the Director-General, Sir Angus MacBeath, to say that the pirate broadcast was a marvellous publicity gimmick and the show should be given a regular radio slot.

Apart from the inherent unlikelihood of Sir John Reith acting like his Scottish namesake in the film, this is a lively and entertaining cinematic reworking of the radio show, with all the familiar elements, the two stars on top form. *Band Waggon* was directed by Marcel Varnel, who had directed the Will Hay and Crazy Gang films at Gainsborough, and who Askey recalled as 'an excitable Frenchman … his great asset was his speed. He was paid a bonus which depended on how quickly he finished a film. His big catchphrase was "Vy are ve vaiting?" He used to sit under the camera waving his handkerchief during every shot, and when he was satisfied he always said, "Cut-print-give me a viewfinder – ooh, Christ". This was when he banged his head on the camera as he sprang up from his seat'.[15]

The 1940s became the great era of screen transcriptions of hit comedy shows, an extension of their role in morale-boosting during the war. Gainsborough next snapped up *Hi, Gang!* for the big screen. *Hi, Gang!* was the brainchild of American stars Bebe Daniels (1901–71) and Ben Lyon (1901–79). Married in 1930, they had both been Hollywood stars in the silent screen days, successfully making the transition to sound in hit films, Ben in *Hell's Angels* (1930) and Bebe in the musicals *Rio Rita* (1929) and *Forty-Second Street* (1932). As their Hollywood movie careers began to fade in the mid–1930s, they accepted an invitation to tour British music halls and stayed on in the United Kingdom, appearing on radio (both BBC and Radio Luxembourg) and the fledgling BBC television service and making several films. When war broke out, they came up with the idea of a morale-boosting comedy show. Enlisting the aid of their old friend, the comedian Vic Oliver, they devised *Hi, Gang!* As Ben outlined it to Vic, 'In this show … we all appear as ourselves, under our own names. I'll be the down-trodden one, you be the smart one, and Bebe will be on your side against me. We'll insult each other for all we're worth. It's bound to succeed'. Other features of the show would be a guest star who would fulfil a secret ambition and a new song to be premiered by Bebe.[16] Vic Oliver recorded the reaction of the BBC:

> When we approached the BBC they adopted the attitude I had anticipated. Our show was to be built on insults, and insults were un-British. To make it worse, we were not appearing in comic character *rôles*; we were appearing as ourselves … and the audience would lose their respect for us if they heard us constantly insulting each other. 'But it's been done in America for years', protested Ben. The official shrugged, 'Oh, America … ' he said, as if we had introduced a black-sheep relation whose name had become distasteful in the family circle.[17]

But eventually they persuaded the BBC to let them make a pilot programme; this blossomed into a six-part series and was continuously extended until it became the first BBC series to run for fifty-two weeks as well as the first BBC comedy series to go out on a Sunday. The shows were scripted by Bebe and Ben, included comedy sketches, musical interludes and the 'If I had a chance' guest spot, the first of which featured organist Sandy MacPherson seeking to fulfil his ambition to be a tapdancer. It was slick, fast-moving and transatlantic in style, its obvious models being the Jack Benny, Bob Hope and Fred Allen radio shows. It ran from 1940 to 1942, ending only when Ben joined the United States Army Airforce in December 1942 as a major. While the radio show was on the air, Ben and Bebe starred for forty-seven weeks at the London Palladium in a stage show, *Gangway*, and in the same year came the film version, directed like *Band Waggon* by Marcel Varnel.

Hi, Gang! (1941) revived the popular 1930s formula of the fast-moving, fast-talking comedy-thriller in which rival reporters, male and female, constantly sought to upstage each other over scoop stories. In this version set in New York, the rival reporters, Ben and Bebe, were married but working for rival broadcasting networks, he for the General Broadcasting Company (GBC) and she for the Liberty Broadcasting Company (LBC). The film consists of Bebe and Ben, aided and abetted by Vic Oliver, each trying to get the better of the other with stories. After various comic contretemps, Ben and Bebe adopt a British evacuee, who turns out to be a cabin boy (Graham Moffatt) accompanied by his uncle Jerry (Moore Marriott). Believing him to be the son of Lord Amersham, Bebe raises 50,000 dollars by a radio appeal to restore the bombed Amersham Castle. Bebe flies to England to present the cheque to Lord Amersham and with the help of the BBC arranges a variety show with guest artists George Arliss, David Niven, Robert Donat and Richard Tauber. Vic cancels the guests but Ben, Bebe and Vic manage to arrange a joint broadcast to the United States by LBC and GBC and for it stage what is in effect a potted version of *Hi, Gang!* with gags, cross-talk acts, musical interludes from Jay Wilbur and his orchestra, and songs from the Greene Sisters, Sam Browne and Bebe. However it ends with all three of the stars sacked when they inadvertently cause the ringing of the church bells which is the signal for invasion. But the radio show, the stage show and the film can be seen as an important means of cementing Anglo-American friendship in the early days of the war.[18]

After the war, Ben and Bebe returned to The United States, where Bebe wrote and produced a film *The Fabulous Joe* but in 1948 they returned to the United Kingdom when Ben was appointed London casting director for 20th Century

Fox. They revived *Hi, Gang!* for a season in 1949. But in 1950 they launched themselves into another and equally successful comedy direction – the sitcom – with *Life with the Lyons.*

A more traditional form of morale-boosting came in *The Happidrome,* a variety show broadcast live from the Grand Theatre, Llandudno, before an audience of war workers and service personnel. It ran on the BBC from 1941 to 1947 and featured virtually all the best-known variety artists at work in the United Kingdom during those years. The show was linked by sketches featuring the staff of the imaginary Happidrome Theatre: Harry Korris, as the large, grandiloquent, magnificently seedy impresario J. Sheridan Lovejoy, the suave Chesney-Allen type straight man Cecil Frederick as stage manager Ramsbottom and Robbie Vincent as the gormless North Country call boy with his much repeated catch-phrase 'Let me tell you'.

The film version, *The Happidrome,* directed by Phil Brandon and released in April 1943, was a variant on perennial plot favourite – 'Let's put the show on right here'. It begins with the three stars singing their celebrated song 'We three in Happidrome, working for the BBC, Ramsbottom and Enoch and me' and reminiscing about how they first met. Penniless but grandiloquent actor-manager Lovejoy arrives in Westhampton and claims to be recruiting new talent for a show to take to London. He stages a supposedly serious show, *Nero,* which is so funny that Mr Mossop, father of aspiring singer Bunty, agrees to finance the new show and so like *Band Waggon* and *Hi, Gang!,* the last half hour of the film is a potted version of the familiar radio format with the crosstalk act of the three stars, guest appearances by pianist 'Hutch' and the clowns, the Cairolis, a comic sketch sending up romantic historical drama 'Napoleon's Retreat' and a trio of cockney charwomen commenting on the action.

John Watt, the head of Variety, wanted a new show to follow up the success of *Band Waggon,* a show with a regular slot and a resident comedian. His choice of comedian was Tommy Handley (1894–1949), highly experienced in music hall as well as broadcasting. The first plan was a British equivalent of Burns and Allen with Handley partnered by Canadian actress Celia Eddy. But Handley disliked the scripts and script-writer Ted Kavanagh and producer Francis Worsley came up with a comedy format based on a radio cruise ship run by Handley with Celia Eddy as his secretary. The title, *It's That Man Again* (later shortened to *ITMA*) came from the headline the *Daily Express* used to report Hitler's latest demand. The show ran fortnightly from 12 July to 30 August 1939, its run being terminated by the declaration of war. The Variety Department was evacuated to Bristol and Kavanagh and Worsley came up with the format that the mature series was to maintain for the rest of its life. Handley would play an incompetent authority figure around whom a constellation of comic characters revolved and the action would be punctuated by a song and a number by the band. Kavanagh had a distinctive view of radio-writing:

> It was to use sound for all it was worth, the sound of different voices and accents, the use of catch-phrases, the impact of funny sounds in words, of grotesque effects to give atmosphere – every device to create the illusion of rather crazy or inverted reality.[19]

Kavanagh aimed to pack one hundred gags into the eighteen-and-a-half minutes of comedy contained in the half-hour show. So each script was a rapid stream of malapropisms, puns, comic dialects, catchphrases and sound effects, leavened with the inevitable wartime jokes about salvage, rationing and fire-watching.

Kavanagh worked in perfect harmony with Worsley and Handley. He wrote that Worsley was 'the ideal producer, unafraid of innovations, helpful, receptive and unfailingly understanding'.[20] Of Handley he wrote:

> His comedy sense amounted to genius … He was never difficult; he helped enormously once the script was written; he could suggest the pointing of a gag, the re-writing of a line, which lifted it right out of the rut. He was gifted with an uncanny ear for the *sound* of words. He was generous in letting others get the laughs, unselfish, dependable, and unfailingly hardworking.[21]

The show ran until 1949, chalking up 310 editions, ended only by Handley's death from a stroke halfway through the twelfth series. His death was regarded as a national tragedy as *ITMA* was seen as a major morale-booster during the war years.

When Handley died, Sir William Haley, Director-General of the BBC, broadcast a tribute in which he spoke for many:

> In affliction, in adversity, in triumph and in austerity, *Itma* typified the spirit of the British nation. And Tommy Handley, the man to whom everything happened, who had to suffer curmudgeons and cranks and clowns, who resourcefully came through every ordeal, whose cheerfulness and sanity never failed, was the man that we all of us in our inmost hearts felt ourselves to be … he was not only broadcasting's greatest but also its most natural comedian. He had that rare gift which few are born with and most never acquire of being able to broadcast sincerity. As you listened to him you felt you were receiving a personality as well as an act and the personality was that of an essentially friendly and good man. The sense of a friend being missing will be felt tonight in millions of homes … With his death something inestimable has been lost. (*Radio Times*, 21 January 1949)

Soon after Handley, also in 1949, producer Francis Worsley died at the early age of 47. *ITMA* had been kept fresh by regular changes of venue, with Tommy being cast successively as the Minister of Aggravation and Mysteries, the Mayor of Foaming-at-the-Mouth and the Governor of Tomtopia. The cast of characters and catchphrases were changed at periodic intervals, more than one hundred being invented and performed. The catchphrases entered the language. Kavanagh recalled:

> There was the letter from the head of a demolition squad. His men had been called to a house which had received a direct hit. He clambered over a pile of rubble which had once been a little home in Bath. 'Anyone there?' he called as he flashed his torch here and there. 'Yes', piped a small boy lying buried under the debris. 'Can you do me now, sir?' Doctors and nurses wrote of the victims of bombs who, knowing that death was coming, murmured T.T.F.N. (Ta-Ta-For-Now) as the last coherent thing they said. It was the commonplace joke of an indomitable people. Cecil and Claude's ultra-polite conversation and consideration for one another's convenience became a catchphrase with servicemen, Pilots of bombers queuing up over a target would shout it over the inter-com to one another as they manoeuvred for the bombing run.[22]

After a command performance of *ITMA* at Windsor Castle, the Queen expressed regret that the show would be coming off the air in the spring. Reassured that it would return, she replied in words of Ali Oop 'you go – you come back'.[23]

As with *Band Waggon*, Jack Hylton bought the stage and film rights and produced a stage version which went on a six-month provincial tour but Kavanagh records: 'although packed houses greeted the show everywhere, the tour could hardly have been called a success. It was an expensive production; it had colour, glamour and expert direction – but it just was not funny. In short, it was impossible to transfer the radio version which, for its success, depended on sound alone. In other words, the *ITMA* characters were designed to be heard and not seen. As far as Tommy was concerned, the difference between his stage and radio personality was very obvious – he did not appear to be the cheery carefree man of *ITMA* and his unerring instinct told him the stage version was wrong'.[24] Nevertheless, a film version followed the stage shows. It was Gainsborough again who undertook to bring *ITMA* to the screen in 1942. *It's That Man Again* was written by Ted Kavanagh and Howard Irving Young and directed by Walter Forde. The plot, such as it is, has Tommy Handley as the Mayor of Foaming-at-the-Mouth gambling away the town hall funds and ending up owning a blitzed theatre, the Olympian, in London. He is pursued by the town council and the unpaid actors from the theatre. He seeks to recoup his fortunes by stealing a play from a drunken playwright which is staged by impresario C.B. Cato. But the production is sabotaged by the out-of-work actors and Handley exits pursued by his creditors.

ITMA inevitably presented the same problem of translation from radio to screen as from radio to stage. It was predominantly and pre-eminently verbal. This was resolved first of all by having all the regular characters appear and deliver their catchphrases: Mrs Mopp the charlady ('Can I do you now, sir?'), Ali Oop the greasy Arab pedlar selling 'filthy postcards' ('I go – I come back'), the two bowler-hatted brokers' men ('After you, Claude', 'No, after you, Cecil'), Sam Scram, the bespectacled, loud-suited spiv ('Boss, boss, sump'n terrible's happened'), the commercial salesman ('Good morning, nice day'), the American gangster Lefty ('It's my noives'), Signor So-So with his appallingly mispronounced English and the voice of the German spy ('This is Funf speaking').

Second, there were sketches. Tommy impersonates Country and Western singer Big Bill Campbell (as Big Tom Handbell) and sings 'Riding the Kitchen Range'. Tommy cons a soldier out of drinks with a series of verbal tricks. Purely visual is the sabotaging of the show with collapsing sets, trap doors opening, characters swinging on wires and the regulars each getting in on the act as when Mrs Mopp and Signor So-So in full evening dress perform a romantic duet. The film gave the fans a chance to see as well as hear their favourites from the radio but the concentrated verbal anarchy of the original radio half-hour was inevitably diluted by the imposition of a plot and the introduction of two glamorous Gainsborough stars Greta Gynt and Jean Kent.

Most of the popular radio comedy series of the 1950s remained on radio and did not reach the cinema screen. This included such popular hits as *Take It From Here* (1948–60), *Ray's a Laugh* (1949–61), *Educating Archie* (1950–59), *The Goon Show* (1951–60), *Hancock's Half Hour* (1954–59), and *Beyond Our Ken* (1958–64). The single exception to this cinematic absence was sitcoms.

The comic domestic sitcom on British radio was the creation of the multi-talented Mabel Constanduros (1880–1957). She discovered while studying at the Central School of Speech Training a facility for writing and performing comic monologues. A friend encouraged her to apply to the BBC and following an audition she was engaged by the Radio Repertory Company and made her first broadcast in 1925. She created the Buggins Family of Halcyon Row, Walworth and initially she played all the parts: Grandma Buggins, Mrs Buggins, the three children, Alfie, Emma and Baby and Aunt Maria. They were featured in gently comic sketches in which the family visit the seaside and the zoo, have a party during which Grandma loses her teeth and panic when they think baby has swallowed a silk worm. Between 1928 and 1948 Mabel Constanduros wrote and performed in over 250 Buggins radio scripts. The Buggins family rapidly became multi-media, moving from radio to gramophone records, the variety stage, a book *The Bugginses* and films, where Mabel Constanduros made cameo appearances in such filmed revues as *Radio Parade* (1933) and *Stars on Parade* (1936) in her most popular role, the cantankerous Grandma Buggins. But as she stressed in the preface to the book, she was laughing with and not at the characters.[25] Initially, Father did not appear but in the early 1930s she teamed up with actor and writer Michael Hogan who played Father and collaborated on the scripts. He eventually moved to Hollywood to write the scripts for such romantic dramas as *Arabian Nights*, *The Fortunes of Captain Blood* and *Bride of Vengeance* and was replaced as Father and co-writer by John Rorke. The Buggins Family became great favourites with the radio audience. My mother, now 92, recalls that her family nicknamed her brother 'Our Alfie' and she can still recall lines from the sketches such as 'Our Alfie's put his hairbrush in the butter again'. During the war, the Ministry of Food capitalized on the popularity of Grandma Buggins by using her to broadcast recipes that would provide nutrition on the ration. Interestingly Mabel Constanduros always considered herself primarily a writer, producing a stream of stage plays, radio serial adaptations of classic novels and film scripts. It was in this capacity that Mabel and her nephew Denis, her regular writing partner by this time, created the Huggett family who featured in four popular post-war British films.

Radio picked up the series from the cinema and created *Meet the Huggetts*, a light-hearted family series which ran from 1952 to 1961 and starred Jack Warner and Kathleen Harrison as Joe and Ethel Huggett. Jack Warner had become a major star when he portrayed that icon of Englishness, P.C. George Dixon in *The Blue Lamp* (1949). The character was shot dead halfway through the film but was revived for a long-running BBC television series, *Dixon of Dock Green* in 1955. Warner starred in that series alongside his radio incarnation as Joe Huggett.

Joe Huggett first appeared with his family in the film *Holiday Camp* (1947). The Huggetts, Joe and Ethel, their three children and their cantankerous Grandma were such a hit with the public that they came back in their own series, *Here Come the Huggetts* (1948), *Vote for Huggett* (1949) and *The Huggetts Abroad* (1949). In terms of Jack Warner's role as the ideal working-class paterfamilias, it might also be noted that he did a summer season in Blackpool in a stage version of the long-running radio soap opera *The Archers*, playing Ambridge farmer Dan Archer. George Dixon, Joe Huggett, Dan Archer; if ever there was a roster of four-square, solid, decent Englishmen it is these and Jack Warner played them all.

The Huggetts are an all-purpose, upper-working/lower-middle class family and above all else the epitome of respectability. They live in a suburban semi with a car and a phone (not typical working-class possessions). Joe is a factory foreman, honest, industrious, decent. Ethel is his devoted, hardworking wife, who shops, cooks and cleans, calls everyone 'ducks', gossips over the garden wall and constantly makes 'the nice cup of tea' which George Orwell saw as symbolic of working-class culture.

The three films endorse established male/female roles, family life and sexual respectability. *Here Come the Huggetts* runs several plotlines that reinforce these. It details the havoc caused by the arrival of a blonde floozie cousin (Diana Dors). Ethel worries that Joe may be seduced by her. But Joe reassuringly tells her; 'There are two things in the world I can't abide – a pretty woman and a clever woman. And you're neither'. Ethel is delighted. Daughter Jane Huggett has a dilemma. Attracted to a Bohemian intellectual who does not believe in marriage, she settles in the end for the boy next door, an ex-airman and steady dependable type played by Jimmy Hanley. She marries him and they plan to emigrate to South Africa.

In *Vote for Huggett* Joe stands for the Council. He is a Progressive and stands against the Moderates; code for Labour and Conservative. He has proposed creating a lido as a war memorial and community facility, and has to deal with the machinations of corrupt property speculators and the class snobberies of other councillors at their golf club. But he overcomes all this and wins the election. The film celebrates local democracy, public service and government by decent men.

Then, in *The Huggetts Abroad* the couple decide to emigrate to South Africa, largely because of the weather. Ethel doesn't know the difference between South Africa and South America ('It's the same thing – natives and all that'). They go overland by lorry, passing through Algiers which Ethel thinks looks like Bournemouth, and cross the Sahara making cups of tea whenever their spirits need raising. They survive sandstorms and sabotage and are rescued by French troops, but refuse the celebratory champagne ('It's not quite my cuppa tea', says Joe). But Joe misses the pub, Ethel misses the queues and they decide to return home, leaving Jane and Jimmy to proceed to South Africa as the pioneers and settlers.

The film sees no contradiction between local communality (the pub, the youth club, family wedding, local election all form the background of the action), the nation (one important plot theme has the Huggetts sleeping in the street to witness the royal wedding of Princess Elizabeth and Prince Philip, which they describe as 'a family affair of the nation') and the Empire (to part of which they propose to emigrate). Here the multiple identities – London suburbs, British nation and British Empire – all interlock and are centred on permanent values: work, thrift, patriotism, family, loyalty, marriage. Moreover, the Huggett family structure and ethos is not an isolated phenomenon. It is part of a continuing cultural strand. The Huggetts are the direct successors of the Buggins family, the popular pre-war radio series, and the precursors of the first popular television soap opera family, the Groves, in the mid–1950s. They all endorsed the same basic values.

The structure of the radio family differed from the film family. In *Holiday Camp* Joe and Ethel had a sixteen year-old son Harry and a war-widowed daughter Joan. In the three other Huggett films, they had three daughters, Jane, Susan and Petula. On the radio there was a son Harry (in the forces), daughter Jane and son Bobby (living at home). But the ethos and values remained constant.

Where the Huggetts embodied a homely, slow-paced British domestic humour, *Life with the Lyons* was faster, slicker and more self-evidently influenced by American sitcoms like *Life With Father*. It ran from 1950 to 1961, written by Bebe Daniels with a succession of collaborators. It was built around Bebe and Ben and their real-life children Richard and Barbara with a permanent supporting cast of the Scottish cook Aggie, the neighbours and the local handyman. The two film spin-offs give a good idea of the flavour. *Life with the Lyons* (1953) and *The Lyons in Paris* (1954), featuring the cast of the radio shows, were produced by Hammer Films at Southall Studios and written and directed by Val Guest, who had co-written the film of *Hi, Gang!* The Lyons were billed as 'the world's most lovable family'. *Life with the Lyons* featured Ben as the harassed paterfamilias, Bebe as the scatterbrained wife, Richard as the eager beaver 'gee, Pop' teenage son and Barbara as the adolescent daughter, forever mooning over her latest romantic attachment: 'If he doesn't call, I'll die, I'll just die'. The supporting cast included three *ITMA* veterans: Mollie Weir as Aggie the cook, constantly threatening to leave; Horace Percival as the handyman Wimple and Hugh Morton, who played Ben's boss on the radio, here cast as the hapless householder trying to sell his house to the Lyons. Also featured was Doris Rogers as neighbour Florrie Wainwright, forever trading insults with Ben. The action centred on the comic mayhem surrounding the Lyon family's moving into a new house, Ben trying to build a rock garden and pool and the family having to deal with Barbara's desire to marry singing cowboy Slim Cassidy. *The Lyons in Paris* featured the chaos caused by calling in the decorators, Ben forgetting his wedding anniversary and a trip to Paris which resulted in a nightclub brawl, a duel and Ben suspected of having an affair with a French actress. The popularity of the radio series also led to a stage version at Blackpool and effortless transfers of the formula to television in 1955, 1957 and 1961. But in 1963 Bebe had a cerebral haemorrhage which terminated her acting and writing career, though she and Ben remained in London until her death in 1971.

The Navy Lark at eighteen-and-a-half years (1959–77) was the then longest-running sitcom on the BBC. The BBC's answer to ITV's *The Army Game*, it contained all the classic ingredients of the service farce: incompetent officers, scheming NCO's, bureaucratic blunders. It was written or co-written by Lawrie Wyman for the duration of the run and starred Stephen Murray (replacing Dennis Price after the first series) as the laidback Number One on *HMS Troutbridge*, Leslie Phillips as the 'silly ass' sub-lieutenant and Jon Pertwee as the fast-talking Chief Petty Officer, up to his ears in scams and rip-offs. Richard Caldicot played the harassed and exasperated Commander Povey and Heather Chasen his secretary and Leslie Phillips' girlfriend, Wren Chasen. Most of the other parts were played by a highly talented supporting cast who regularly undertook a variety of roles requiring different voices: Michael Bates, Ronnie Barker and Tenniel Evans.

The immediate success of the series led producer Herbert Wilcox to purchase the film rights and a feature-length comedy, *The Navy Lark*, directed by Gordon Parry, appeared in 1959. Although co-written by Wyman, it suffered the fate of many big screen transfers of radio shows. Most of the radio cast were replaced by better-known cinema stars. Only Leslie Phillips was retained in the same role. Cecil Parker replaced Stephen Murray, Ronald Shiner replaced Jon Pertwee, Elvi Hale replaced Heather Chasen and Gordon Jackson replaced Ronnie Barker. The narrative centred on the various stratagems launched by the crew of the minesweeper *Compton*, stationed in the Channel Islands, to avoid being de-commissioned and closed down. A broad, cheerful, service farce along familiar lines, it lacked the rich cast of supporting characters, regular catchphrases and warm familiarity engendered by the radio series which sailed on undisturbed to its broadcasting record while the film version rapidly fell unlamented into oblivion.

Leslie Phillips recalled: 'This comic saga of naval incompetence was to become a national institution … and over the next seventeen years, I recorded some 250 episodes. I didn't miss a single one, and such was my love of the show and my loyalty to it, that I once flew back from Rome, where I was making an Italian movie … to record an episode before flying straight back. My rather insubstantial BBC fee didn't cover even half the cost of the trip, but *The Navy Lark* was one of those jobs where the money was irrelevant'. [26] He makes no mention of the film.

Notes

1   J. Fred MacDonald, *Don't Touch That Dial: Radio Programming in American Life from 1920 to 1960*, Chicago: Nelson-Hall, 1996, p. 95.

2   On American radio comedy see in particular Arthur Frank Wertheim, *Radio Comedy*, New York: Oxford University Press, 1992.

3   On Eddie Cantor see Herbert Goldman, *Banjo Eyes*, New York: Oxford University Press, 1997; on Amos 'n' Andy see Melvin Patrick Ely, *The Adventures of Amos 'n' Andy: A Social History of an American Phenomenon*, New York: Free Press, 1991.

4   David and Susan Siegel, *Radio and the Jews*, Yorktown Heights, NY: Bokk Hunter Press, 2007.

5   Charles Stumpf and Tom Price, *Heavenly Days! The Story of Fibber McGee and Molly*, Waynesville, NC: The World of Yesterday, 1987.

6   On *My Favourite Husband* and its transition to *I Love Lucy* see Jess and Gregg Oppenheimer, *Laughs, Luck and Lucy*, Syracuse, NY: Syracuse University Press, 1999.

7   Gerald Nachman, *Raised on Radio*, Berkeley: University of California Press, 2000, p. 54.

8   Victoria Price, *Vincent Price*, London: Sidgwick and Jackson, 1999, p. 203.

9   On Jack Benny see Mary Livingstone Benny and Hilliard Marks with Marcia Borie, *Jack Benny*, London: Robson Books, 1978 and Milt Josefsberg, *The Jack Benny Show*, New Rochelle, NY: Arlington House, 1977.

10 Ray Seaton and Roy Martin, *Good Morning, Boys: Will Hay, Master of Comedy*, London: Barrie and Jenkins, 1978, p. 132. On Hay see also John Fisher, *Funny Way To Be A Hero*, St Albans: Paladin, 1976, pp. 45–54 and Eric Midwinter, *Make 'Em Laugh*, London: George Allen and Unwin, 1979, pp. 54–70. On British radio comedy, see Andy Foster and Steve Furst, *Radio Comedy 1938–1968*, London: Virgin, 1994.

11 On Robb Wilton, see Fisher, *Funny Way To Be A Hero*, pp. 111–21 and Midwinter, *Make 'Em Laugh*, pp. 74–86.

12 Fisher, *Funny Way To Be A Hero*, p. 80.

13 Arthur Askey, *Before Your Very Eyes*, London: Coronet Books, 1977, p. 95.

14 Askey, *Before Your Very Eyes*, p. 104.

15 Askey, *Before Your Very Eyes*, p. 110.

16 Vic Oliver, *Mr Showbusiness*, London: George G. Harrap and Co., 1954, pp. 133–4.

17 Oliver, *Mr Showbusiness*, p. 134.

18 Jill Allgood, *Bebe and Ben*, London: Robert Hale and Company, 1975.

19 Ted Kavanagh, *Tommy Handley*, London: Hodder and Stoughton, 1949, p. 107.

20 Kavanagh, *Tommy Handley*, p. 107.

21 Kavanagh, *Tommy Handley*, p. 109.

22 Kavanagh, *Tommy Handley*, pp. 148–9.

23 Kavanagh, *Tommy Handley*, p. 157.

24 Kavanagh, *Tommy Handley*, pp. 129–30. On *ITMA* see also Francis Worsley, *ITMA 1939–1948*, London: Vox Mundi, 1948 and Jack Train, *Up and Down the Line*, London: Odhams Press, 1956.

25 Mabel Constanduros and Michael Hogan, *The Bugginses*, London: Hutchinson, 1928, p. 8.

26 Leslie Phillips, *Hello*, London: Orion, 2006, p. 193.

4

Filming radio genres ii): detective stories

Detective stories were popular on radio: the suspense, the puzzle (pitting your wits against the detective), the exposition, all made for engaging radio drama. But crime stories in which the law always triumphed and evil was always exposed and punished provided audiences with a recurrent sense of reassurance in troubled times (the Depression, the wars, the Cold War). Where the sitcom affirmed the validity of family life and the timelessness of gender roles, the detective story underlined the moral that crime did not pay – as Philip Marlowe barked at the outset of every episode of *The Adventures of Philip Marlowe*, 'Get this and get it straight – crime is a sucker's road and those who travel it end up in the gutter, the prison or the grave' – and stressed the essential underlying soundness of society. Detective stories were on the whole much less costly to put on than comedy or variety. In 1945, it was estimated that four-and-a-half mystery and detective stories were broadcast on American radio every day of the year.[1] In 1950 *Variety* estimated that the weekly costs of the Jack Benny and Bing Crosby shows were $40,000; the average detective story came in for between $4,000 and $7,000 dollars.[2] This was helped by the fact that the detective series were initially done by inexpensive radio actors and not Hollywood stars and relied on the proven appeal of the fictional characters featured, who were often appearing simultaneously in Hollywood film series.

During the 1930s and early 1940s the emphasis was on realistic police and law enforcement dramas, catering to the need to allay the anxiety of the public about the threat to civil society from gangsters and racketeers. One of the most influential creator-producers of such shows was Phillips H. Lord, himself an early radio star in the role of homespun philosopher Seth Parker. Lord devised *Gangbusters* (1935–57), which was billed as 'the only national program that brings you authentic police case histories'. Radio historian John Dunning has called it 'the noisiest show on the air'.[3] It was a sound symphony of police whistles, gun shots, sirens, screaming tyres and breaking glass as it recounted its cases, beginning with those of such celebrated criminals as John Dillinger, 'Babyface' Nelson and 'Pretty Boy' Floyd. Added authenticity was provided by having real-life police chiefs introduce and narrate the programme. Universal's film serial *Gangbusters* (1942) starring Kent Taylor as Lt Bill Bannister, a character not in the radio series, retained only the narrated opening of the series. The narrative, far removed from the factual basis of the radio series, pitted the gangbusters against the League of Murdered Men, and their leader, sinister scientist Dr Mortis.

Lord went on to devise such shows as *Mr District Attorney* (1939–53), inspired by the career of Thomas E. Dewey, crusading New York District Attorney of the late 1930s, *Treasury Agent* (1947–49), *Police Woman* (1946–47) and *Counterspy* (1942–57). Republic Pictures produced a trio of *Mr District Attorney* films in the early 1940s. On the radio the district attorney had no name, so Republic christened him P. Cadwallader Jones. He was played successively by Dennis O'Keefe, James Ellison and John Hubbard. *Mr District Attorney* (1941) had Jones and reporter Terry Parker (Florence Rice) looking for a missing politician (Peter Lorre). *Mr District Attorney in the Carter Case* (UK title: *The Carter Case*) involved Jones and Terry Parker (Virginia Gilmore) investigating the murder of a fashion magazine publisher. In *Secrets of the Underground* (1943) Jones and Terry Parker (Virginia Grey) help smash a Nazi counterfeiting racket in the United States.

Columbia Pictures produced their own *Mr District Attorney* (1947) with District Attorney Craig Warren (Adolphe Menjou) and his radio assistants (absent from the Republic films), investigator Harrington and secretary Miss Miller. But the film effectively sidelined the District Attorney to focus in what was essentially a *film noir* melodrama on his deputy, Steve Bennett (Dennis O'Keefe) and his infatuation with a beautiful ruthless murderess (Marguerite Chapman), who eventually falls to her death while trying to kill him.

Columbia also made a couple of slick fast-moving programmers inspired by the *Counterspy* series. *David Harding, Counterspy* (1950) had Harding (Howard St John) telling in flashback the story of a wartime operation in which the counterspies uncover a gang of Nazi agents working in a top-secret torpedo plant. *Counterspy Meets Scotland Yard* (1950) had Harding, aided by a Scotland Yard detective, tracking down the killer of one of his agents at a guided missile plant. National security was the linking theme of the films and the radio series. Aiming for a similar combination of authenticity and drama were *True Detective Mysteries* (1929–31, 1936–39, 1944–58), based on stories in *True Detective* magazine. Two of the most popular series of the 1940s were *The FBI in Peace and War* (1944–58) and *This is Your FBI* (1945–53), the latter of which had the full cooperation and backing of FBI chief J. Edgar Hoover.

Alongside the realistic docudramas were a series of detective stories derived from pulp fiction. One of the most celebrated series on American radio was *The Shadow* (1930–54). He was as much superhero as detective, using his mysterious powers to fight crime in the seamy underworld of Depression-era America. The character emerged from the creative relationship in the 1930s and 1940s between pulp fiction and radio. The pulps were mass-circulation thrillers of 50–60,000 words churned out monthly by an army of overworked, underpaid hacks and decorated with eye-catchingly vivid, not to say lurid, covers to tempt would-be readers to part with their cash for the chance of sampling the thrills and sensations contained within. Their nickname derived from the wood pulp from which their cheap paper was manufactured but also carried the onomatopoeic ring of a savage beating which appropriately signified the world of crime fiction. The battle against crime was a staple of the pulps, reflecting the widespread public concern at the level of organized crime in 1930s United States. To combat this, it sometimes seemed that a man with supernatural powers was needed. The pulps produced that man in the person of The Shadow.

The leading pulp publishers were Street and Smith and they had a weekly mystery show on radio in which their thriller stories were dramatized. The programme was introduced and narrated by a mysterious figure with a sinister laugh known only as The Shadow. The character became so popular with radio audiences that Street and Smith decided to feature him in his own magazine and in April 1931 the first Shadow story appeared on the news-stands. It was written under the pseudonym of Maxwell Grant by Walter B. Gibson, a thirty-three-year-old magician and crimewriter who turned the disembodied voice with the chilling laugh into a mysterious crusader against evil, clad in black cape, slouch hat and concealing scarf, sporting twin Colt 45 revolvers and acting through a network of agents and multiple identities. The character was a potent mix of Zorro, the Scarlet Pimpernel, the cloaked and masked French master criminal Fantomas and Frank Packard's now forgotten New York clubman and crimefighter Jimmie Dale. *The Living Shadow* was a sensational success and the saga was launched. It ran in pulp magazine form from 1931 to 1949, eventually comprising 325 complete novels, 282 of them written by Gibson.[4]

The success of the novels led inevitably to the new version of *The Shadow* returning to radio in his own show. Gibson had nothing to do with the radio show and indeed it developed differently from the novels. In the books, the Shadow was in reality Kent Allard, internationally famous aviator, but when he was not being the Shadow, he posed as Lamont Cranston, big game hunter and explorer who was frequently away on expeditions. For the radio series, The Shadow really was Lamont Cranston, society playboy and dilettante. In place of a network of agents, he acquired a glamorous female companion Margo Lane, with whom he keeps in contact by shortwave radio. He also had a powerful weapon in his fight against crime. He had mastered in the Orient the technique of 'clouding men's minds' (a form of mesmerism taught him by an Indian yogi) so that they could not see him, only hear his voice and he used this ability to terrorize evildoers. It was a perfect radio device. The first actor to play the Shadow in his new incarnation was Robert Hardy Andrews, subsequently a prolific scriptwriter of radio soaps and later still of Hollywood films. But the most famous Shadow, even though he only played the role for the 1937–38 season was Orson Welles, who had earned an instant reputation as the *enfant terrible* of Broadway and who was to become an outstandingly versatile radio actor. Perhaps reflecting the Scarlet Pimpernel inspiration and the upper-class gentleman crimefighter tradition, Welles opted to give Cranston a clipped, quasi-English accent. His resonant, flexible voice was totally compelling and one of the programme's greatest assets.

The Shadow radio shows were strongly influenced by the contemporary Hollywood cinema. They were in effect half-hour aural movies, vivid, pacy and atmospheric, employing techniques such as montage to create atmosphere and advance the plot. Like the cliff-hanging cinema serials, the shows gloried in trapping the Shadow in impossible situations and seeing him extricate himself. In *The Society of the Living Dead*, for instance, he is trapped in a flooding mausoleum with a locked iron door.

The Shadow frequently pitted himself against what were seen as the major threats to American society in the 1930s; gangsters, sinister secret societies and rings of foreign spies and saboteurs. Even before the United States entered the war, they invariably had German names and German accents. Among his more exotic opponents were a Hindu temple dancer running a drug smuggling ring, a mad scientist experimenting on people with an ageing process and a deranged backwoods child-kidnapper. Each programme opened with the announcement: 'These half-hour dramatisations are designed to forcibly demonstrate to old and young alike that crime does not pay' and ended with the Shadow intoning 'The weed of crime bear bitter fruit. Crime does not pay. The Shadow knows'. Welles gave up the role of the Shadow in 1938 and it was taken on by a succession of radio actors (Bill Johnstone, Bret Morrison, John Archer, Steve Courtleigh, Bret Morrison again) until it finally came off the air in 1954, five years after *The Shadow* magazine had ceased publication. It had become an integral part of the imaginative lives of the successive generations of young Americans growing up in the 1930s, 1940s and 1950s. The radio success of The Shadow inevitably inspired movie spin-offs. There were a couple of low-budget Shadow features from the minor studio Grand National in 1937 and 1938 *The Shadow Strikes* and *International Crime* starring former idol of the silent screen Rod La Roque, a Columbia serial *The Shadow* made in 1940 with Victor Jory, a trio of Monogram B pictures *The Shadow Returns, Behind the Mask* and *The Missing Lady* starring Kane Richmond in 1946, and a 1958 Republic feature *Invisible Avenger* with Richard Derr. But none of them remotely realized visually the imaginative splendours and excitements associated with the radio version.

In the Grand National features the Shadow was played by ageing silent film star Rod La Rocque, approaching the end of his career. His Lamont Cranston is a stolid pipesmoking, trilby-hatted amateur criminologist, aided by his valet Henry. *The Shadow Strikes* (1937), directed by Lynn Shores and scripted by Al Martin and Rex Taylor, is a banal and pedestrian tale, flatly staged, devoid of music and poorly acted. It largely ignores the intrinsic appeal of the caped crimefighter and the requisite atmosphere of mystery, darkness and melodrama. Only briefly is Cranston seen in the Shadow's cape and slouch hat; otherwise he spends most of the film impersonating an amiable lawyer who is investigating the murder of eccentric millionaire Caleb Delthem and later his eldest nephew. Cranston discovers that the butler did it to ensure that his son, who was wooing one of the potential heirs to the Delthem fortune, would inherit.

International Crime (1938), directed by Charles Lamont and scripted by Jack Natteford, is a livelier and rather more entertaining film which transforms Cranston into a criminologist with a newspaper column in *The Daily Classic* and a regular radio spot on Station E-Mor, owned by the newspaper, where he is introduced as 'The Shadow'. He never appears in the Shadow's outfit though the caped and slouch-hatted figure appears as the logo on his column. There is no cackling laugh and no clouding of men's minds. He has an assistant, not Margo Lane but Phoebe Lane, an irritating and interfering junior reporter who is the niece of the paper's proprietor and is imposed on him by his editor. The film's main interest is that several scenes take place in the radio studios with Lamont broadcasting his column and delivering the recurrent message 'Crime Does Not Pay'. We see the broadcast being listened to by a married couple at home, a courting couple in their car, four small boys eagerly noting down the clues Cranston dispenses and by Police Commissioner Weston. Later a veteran safecracker named by Cranston on the air threatens him with a gun but is talked round while the broadcast is in progress. The plot has Cranston solving the murder of a millionaire banker by two foreign aristocrats, who want to prevent him making a major loan to the government of their unnamed home country.

By so doing, they hope to destabilize the government.

More faithful to the nature and ethos of the pulp novels is the fifteen-episode 1940 Columbia serial *The Shadow*, directed by James W. Horne and scripted by Joseph Poland, Ned Dandy and Joseph O'Donnell. In this version, the Shadow is pitted against the Black Tiger, a megalomaniac master criminal who is seeking to gain financial control of the city by a programme of dynamiting factories, sabotaging airlines, causing train crashes and assassinating or kidnapping leading industrialists. Although Margo Lane, described as Cranston's secretary, is included, the serial makes significant changes from the radio version. There is no use of the disembodied voice and the clouding of men's minds. Cranston instead uses a succession of disguises to fight the criminals. His principal guise, with the trademark black cape, slouch hat and black mask, is as The Shadow but he also impersonates Lin Chang, the bucktoothed Chinese proprietor of an Oriental bazaar. Cranston is not just the apparent playboy of the radio series but a brilliant research scientist who runs a laboratory that aids his criminological activities. Interestingly while the Shadow never becomes invisible, the Black Tiger does, causing himself to be bathed in a mysterious beam of light that reduces him to a disembodied voice speaking through the model of a tiger's head. The Tiger turns out to be one of the industrialists apparently fighting the crime wave. Everything in the film takes place at a frantic pace: fast and furious fights, spectacular crashes and explosions, car chases speeding round the permanently deserted streets of the Columbia backlot, and Cranston running everywhere. The saturnine Victor Jory is an effective Shadow, complete with striking cackle and knowing smile.

A character similar to Cranston emerged directly on the radio and made the transition to film. *Chandu the Magician* was a popular juvenile serial devised for radio in 1931 by Harry Earnshaw and Raymond R. Morgan. Chandu was the name given to an American magician Captain Frank Chandler, who is trained in India as a yogi and learns the practice of hypnotism and the ability to suggest the presence of people who are not in fact there. Scripted by Vera Oldham from the storylines devised by Earnshaw and Morgan *Chandu the Magician* ran from 1932 to 1936 in fifteen-minute episodes five nights a week. The first sixty-eight episodes had Chandu pitted against an Egyptian master criminal Roxor, who plans to take over the world by the use of a deathray invented by Chandler's brother-in-law Robert Regent, who is kidnapped and held prisoner in Roxor's Egyptian rock temple lair. Chandler's later adventures took him to equally exotic locations, including the lost continent of Lemuria. The original scripts updated and revised were broadcast anew on the Mutual network in 1948–49.

In 1932 the Fox Film Corporation adapted the original radio serial for the cinema. *Chandu the Magician* was co-directed by Marcel Varnel and William Cameron Menzies. The film starred Edmund Lowe as Chandu and Bela Lugosi as Roxor. The cinema allowed the story to be told with effects not possible on radio. The film opens with Chandu's initiation as a yogi. He performs the Indian rope trick, projects his astral self and walks barefoot across hot coals, all by virtue of special visual effects. Later he traces the captive Regent by use of a crystal ball. Captured and chained inside a mummy case which is thrown into the Nile, Chandu extricates himself, Houdini-style, and escapes.

Designed by Cameron Menzies, who had a well-developed taste for exotica, in stylized Oriental settings, the film consists of a series of captures, rescues and escapes, including Chandu's rescue of the woman he loves, Egyptian Princess Nadji, and his sister, brother-in-law and their family. It has a consistently delirious, dream-like feel, compromised only by Lowe's bland and inexpressive performance in a role he seems to have secured on the basis of the fact that he had played a magician in Cameron Menzies' previous directorial opus, *The Spider* (1931). The film is stolen by Lugosi's ripely melodramatic performance as Roxor, gleefully imagining the destruction of Paris and London by his deathray and devising ever more devilish tortures for his prisoners. Herbert Mundin provides some rather tiresome comic relief as Chandler's cockney batman, who keeps debating his drinking habits with a miniature version of himself, representing his conscience, scenes probably the responsibility of the French-born Varnel, whose subsequent career was spent entirely in the United Kingdom directing comedy films with Will Hay, George Formby, Arthur Askey and the Crazy Gang.

The film's relative lack of box-office success convinced Fox not to continue with a series of *Chandu* films. But independent producer Sol Lesser took up the character and produced for his company Principal Productions a twelve-episode serial *The Return of Chandu* (1934). The serial format brought it closer to its radio origins with a cliffhanger at the end of each episode. The film was based directly on the radio storyline that followed the initial narrative involving Chandu and Roxor. Barry Barringer adapted the radio scripts of Earnshaw, Morgan and Oldham for the screen. Another link with the radio was the presence of Cyril Armbrister, who had directed the radio serial, and was engaged as dialogue director for the film as well as playing a supporting role. The novelty was the casting of Bela Lugosi, promoted from his villain role in *Chandu the Magician* to the title role of the romantic hero, though no explanation is given as to why all-American Chandler had suddenly acquired a thick Hungarian accent.

In *The Return of Chandu* the magician's beloved princess Nadji, visiting

California, is subject to a succession of kidnap attempts by the cat-worshipping sect of Ubasti. The sect want to bring back to life their long-dead priestess Os-anna by sacrificing a genuine Egyptian princess. The sacrifice will also help to resurrect the lost continent of Lemuria, the remnants of which exist as a remote South Sea island. When Nadji is captured and taken to the island, Chandu and his family pursue the kidnappers. After surviving a succession of ordeals (poison dart, tiger pit, shipwreck, crushing rock, burning at the stake), Chandu succeeds in rescuing Nadji and destroying the cult and their temple. He deploys his powers of hypnotism, mind-reading, invisibility and the recitation of the deadly 'high incantation'. Lugosi is more convincingly mystical than Lowe as Chandu with most of the other actors delivering stagily overwrought melodramatic perform-ances. But the film is flatly and unimaginatively directed by Ray Taylor. The great gates of Lemuria turn out to be the gates on Skull Island from the set of *King Kong*, giving an epic flavour to the Lemurian scenes. The film was edited into two seventy-minute features in 1935, *The Return of Chandu* and *Chandu on the Magic Isle*. *The Green Hornet* was another superhero saga, running on American radio from 1936 to 1952. It was created by George W. Trendle, who had previously created the hugely successful *The Lone Ranger* series. Like *The Lone Ranger*, it was written by Fran Striker and originated on Detroit's Radio WXYZ, from where it was fed to the networks, successively Mutual, Blue and ABC. The Green Hornet was in reality Britt Reid, editor of *The Sentinel* newspaper. Wearing his hornet mask and leaving behind hornet seals to proclaim his involvement in fighting crime, his mission, as the programme's narrator put it, was 'He hunts the biggest of all game. Public enemies who try to destroy our America'. He is accompanied everywhere by his faithful Filipino valet Kato and speeds round in a supercharged car The Black Beauty. His commitment to humane values is em-phasized by his use of a specially devised gas gun which temporarily immobilizes his adversaries rather than killing them. Besides Kato, other regular characters in the series were Reid's blundering bodyguard, Michael Axford, who spoke in an outrageously cod Irish accent, and his bright and faithful secretary, Lenore Case. The show was introduced by Rimsky-Korsakoff's *The Flight of the Bumble Bee* and the car's journeys were accompanied by a hornet's buzz, specially created using a theremin. Each week the Hornet tackled racketeers and gangsters and then, during the war, spies and saboteurs. In 1939 Universal Pictures produced a thirteen-part serial based on the radio show. Directed by Ford Beebe and Ray Taylor, it was scripted by George Plympton, Basil Dickey, Morrison C. Wood and Lyonel Margolies. Fran Striker acted as adviser to the production and the result closely resembled the radio show, complete with *The Flight of the Bumble Bee* and the hornet's buzzing. Gordon Jones played Britt Reid but when he donned the Hornet's mask and got involved in a lot of physical action, the part was taken over by stuntman George de Normand with the voice dubbed by Al Hodge, who played the Hornet on radio from 1936 to 1943. Keye Luke, better known to cinemagoers as Charlie Chan's Number One son, played Kato, inexplicably transformed from a Filipino to a Korean, and Wade Boteler played Axford, his Irish accent as outrageously hammy and over-the-top as his radio counterparts, successively Jim Irwin and Gilly Shea. Like the radio series, each episode of the serial saw the Hornet tackling a particular racket. For the purposes of the serial, all the rackets were the work of a single crime syndicate whose mysterious leader is unmasked at the end. The crimes included an insurance swindle, protection rackets, illicit munitions smuggling, sabotage aimed at ruining and taking over bus and trucking companies, crooked building contracts using inferior materials and an attempt to fix the mayoral election to ensure the victory of an ally of the syndicate. Each racket was successfully exposed and defeated by the Hornet. Universal produced a sequel, *The Green Hornet Strikes Again* in 1944 with Warren Hull taking over the title role. *Nick Carter, Master Detective* (1943–55) had his origins in the Street and Smith dime novels beginning in 1886. He reached the screen in three stylish 'B' pictures, from MGM *Nick Carter, Master Detective* (1939), *Phantom Raiders* (1940) and *Sky Murder* (1940) starring Walter Pidgeon.

The 'private eye' was the hero of a new and distinctive type of American detective fiction – the 'hardboiled school'. The detective was a tough loner, a cynical professional but behind the hard exterior a bruised romantic who against the odds clings to a code of honour and decency. His beat was the city at night where society – both high and low – is sleazy and corrupt. The classic British detective of the golden age was the gentleman amateur, trained for nothing but ready for anything. He was well-spoken, impeccably mannered and moved with ease through all levels of society. The American hardboiled detective was his polar opposite. He was quintessentially embodied in two iconic American representations: Dashiell Hammett's Sam Spade and Raymond Chandler's Philip Marlowe. They were characters sufficiently similar to have been memorably incarnated on the cinema screen by the same legendary actor – Humphrey Bogart.

Their creators had certain similarities too. Both had served in the army in the First World War. Both were alcoholics and both learned their craft writing for the pulp detective magazines such as *Black Mask*. But there were significant differences. Hammett was a poor-born, self-educated Southerner, who had worked as a Pinkerton detective; Chandler, although born in Chicago, was raised in England and educated at Dulwich College before returning to the United States and embarking on a career as an oil executive, a job he came to hate and from which he was sacked in 1932, taking up writing as a means of earning a living. Chandler identified precisely the ways in which Hammett had changed detective fiction. Writing in *The Simple Art of Murder*, he said:

> Hammett took murder out of the Venetian vase and dropped it in the alley … Hammett wrote for people with a sharp, aggressive attitude to life. They were not afraid of the seamy side of things; they lived there. Violence did not dismay them; it was right down their street. Hammett gave murder back to the kind of people that commit it for reasons, not just to provide a corpse; and with the means at hand, not hand-wrought duelling pistols, curare and tropical fish. He put these people down on paper as they were, and he made them talk and think in the language they customarily used for these purposes. He had style, but his audience didn't know it, because it was in a language not supposed to be capable of such refinements … He was spare, frugal, hard-boiled, but he did over and over again what only the best writers can ever do at all. He wrote scenes that seemed never to have been written before.[5]

Chandler also defined the character of the private eye as hero:

> Down these mean streets a man must go who is not himself mean, who is neither tarnished nor afraid. The detective in this kind of story must be such a man. He is the hero; he is everything. He must be a complete man and a common man and yet an unusual man. He must be, to use a rather weathered phrase, a man of honor – by instinct, by inevitability, without thought of it, and certainly without saying it. He must be the best man in his world and a good enough man for any world. I do not care much about his private life … he is a relatively poor man, or he would not be a detective at all. He is a common man or he could not go among common people. He has a sense of character, or he would not know his job. He will take no man's money dishonestly and no man's insolence without a due and dispassionate revenge. He is a lonely man … he talks as the man of his age talks – that is, with rude wit, a lively sense of the grotesque, a disgust for sham, and a contempt for pettiness.[6]

Hammett's Sam Spade featured in only one novel, *The Maltese Falcon*, published in 1930, and a handful of short stories. But he became synonymous with the image of the 'private eye'. The name Sam Spade was an inspired one. Samuel Dashiell Hammett gave his detective his own unused first name – he was always known as Dash – and a surname indicating that this was a man who called a spade a spade and not a garden implement.

The book achieved perfect cinematization in a version written and directed in 1941 by John Huston, which remained faithful to the book and provided ideal visual matches to the characters created by Hammett; Humphrey Bogart as

Sam Spade, Mary Astor as Brigid O'Shaughnessy, Sydney Greenstreet as Caspar Gutman and Peter Lorre as Joel Cairo. It was not the first version of the book. Warner Brothers had produced two earlier versions. The 1931 *Maltese Falcon* (retitled *Dangerous Female* for television showings to avoid confusion) directed by Roy Del Ruth, was a tough, pacy thriller, raunchier and more sexually explicit than later versions as it predated the introduction of the Hays Code, the tightened-up censorship regulations under which Hollywood operated after 1934. Ricardo Cortez played Sam Spade as a suave womanizer and there were effective performances from Bebe Daniels as the femme fatale, here called Ruth Wonderly, and Dudley Digges as Gutman.

The 1936 remake, however, took unwarrantable liberties with the story while transforming it from a prototype *film noir* into a zippy, wisecracking sixty-six minute programmer renamed *Satan Met a Lady* and indistinguishable from the kind of film being regularly turned out on the Warner conveyor belt. Sam Spade was renamed Ted Shane and played by Warren William exactly as he had played two other celebrated sleuths, Philo Vance and Perry Mason, in earlier Warner Films. Gutman was recast as a woman, Madame Barabbas (played by Alison Skipworth) and Joel Cairo transformed from an effete Levantine into an ultra-correct Englishman, played by Arthur Treacher, Hollywood's perennial butler. But both these versions were to be eclipsed by Huston's definitive 1941 film.

Inevitably *The Maltese Falcon* featured in the various radio series devoted to the recreation of Hollywood films. A half-hour adaptation of the film was broadcast on 20 September 1943 in *The Lady Esther Screen Guild Theatre* with Bogart, Astor, Greenstreet and Lorre recreating their film roles. Another half-hour adaptation featured in *Academy Award Theatre*, broadcast on 3 July 1946, again with Bogart, Astor and Greenstreet, though not Lorre.

When *The Lux Radio Theatre* came to do an hour-long version of the film on 8 February 1943, none of the original stars were available and so in an alternative 'what might have been' version Edward G. Robinson, like Bogart a Warner Brothers star, played Sam Spade; Gail Patrick played Brigid O'Shaughnessy and Laird Cregar, Caspar Gutman. Robinson made his Spade more the snarling tough guy than the sardonic, world-weary adventurer that Bogart created. Cregar, another heavyweight actor, enjoyed himself as the fruitily orotund 'Fat Man' and Patrick was effective as the duplicitous anti-heroine.

Sam Spade became the star of his own radio series in 1946, *The Adventures of Sam Spade – Detective*, which ran successively on ABC, CBS and NBC until 1951. Howard Duff starred as Sam and the show was produced and directed by William Spier, a master of radio production who had created the spine-tingling

Suspense series. Hammett wrote none of the scripts. Indeed he had written almost nothing since 1934 and had been living on the royalties from his books and characters who included not just Sam Spade but also Nick and Nora Charles, the husband and wife detective team of MGM's popular *Thin Man* film series. But the radio writers captured the Hammett style very successfully. From 29 September 1946 to 16 March 1947 the scripts were written by Robert Tallman and Jo Eisinger and from 23 March 1947 until August 1949 by Robert Tallman and Gil Doud. Thereafter a variety of writers worked on the show. One of the hallmarks of the show was its humour, the wisecracks, the banter between Sam and his secretary Effie Perrine (Lurene Tuttle), the sendups. But Duff insisted it was not a spoof. 'We were fast-moving, pretty funny, and had some of the best writers in the business. But it wasn't all comedy. We did real heart-stoppers, too. We got down to the cases, as you have to when you're going to have life and death situations'.[7] All of the Hammett Sam Spade short stories were dramatized and there was a two-part sequel to *The Maltese Falcon* called *The Kandy Tooth* featuring the return of Caspar Gutman, played by Joseph Kearns. But the majority of the stories were originals devised by the series writers.

 But the show came to a sad end, a victim of the McCarthyite anti-Communist witch-hunt in 1940s and 1950s United States. The magazine *Hollywood Life* (13 July 1951) published one of many virulent anti-Hammett articles:

> Dashiell Hammett, noted author and creator of *The Thin Man* series and *Sam Spade*, deserves an American Tragedy title. Hammett is one of the most dangerous influential Communists in America. Communism has been his first love for many years, and he has aided the Moscow methods with thousands of dollars, and most of his spare time. Hammett is said to be responsible for selling the red banner to dozens of men and women including Howard Duff, alias Sam Spade. Duff is also a member of one or more red fronts and a definite red sympathizer. Truthfully Dashiell Hammett should be indicted for participating in subversive activities and aiding in matters which seek and conspire to overthrow the United States government.

Hammett was a Communist and active in the civil rights movement: Duff was not. Hammett's links with various Communist organizations had been regularly publicized since the House Un-American Activities Committee (HUAC) began its work in 1947. In 1949 Wildroot Hair Oil, the sponsor of the Sam Spade radio show, insisted that Hammett's name be removed from the show's credits. Then they decided to pull the plug on the show altogether. This decision prompted 250,000 letters from outraged fans urging its reprieve.[8] The show was continued but without Howard Duff. He bowed out with *The Femme Fatale Caper* on 17 September 1950. The show returned on 17 November 1950 with a new Spade, actor Stephen Dunne. An anti-Communist message was injected into the scripts as Sam rounded up Communist spies and fifth columnists and warned audiences against their plots and wiles. The series did not long survive Duff's departure and ended on 27 April 1951.

Howard Duff went on to become a successful film and television star in the kind of tough guy roles in which he had made his name on radio, beginning with the notable thrillers *Brute Force* (1947) where he was billed in the credits as 'radio's Sam Spade' and *The Naked City* (1948). In 1951 Dashiell Hammett went to prison for five months for contempt of court when he refused to disclose the whereabouts of four suspected Communists who had skipped bail. Released from prison in December 1951, he wrote nothing more before his death in January 1961. But on hearing of his death, columnist John Crosby wrote:

> Dashiell Hammett … was that rare thing – a shaker of the earth, an authentic. 'The Maltese Falcon' was one of the best books of its kind ever written. It struck the publishing world and the reading world like a thunderclap. Nothing has been the same since.[9]

Raymond Chandler's Philip Marlowe reached the screen at the height of Hollywood's golden age and inspired not one but two notable screen incarnations. Dick Powell, in a major career-changing role, moved from clean-cut song and dance man to worldweary private eye in Edward Dmytryk's superb *Murder, My Sweet* (UK title: *Farewell My Lovely*) (1944). Humphrey Bogart added Marlowe to his gallery of screen heroes in *The Big Sleep* (1946), memorably teamed with Lauren Bacall. Chandler's novels were famously complex and *The Big Sleep* more than most. It is said that when Howard Hawks was making the film, neither he nor any of the crew could figure out who killed the chauffeur. They cabled Chandler but he could not remember. For the record, the chauffeur committed suicide. But given Chandler's snappy dialogue, careful characterization and evocative settings, all beautifully reproduced in the film, no one much cared. There were two other Marlowes in the 1940s. Robert Montgomery directed and starred in *The Lady in the Lake* (1947) which used the ultimately tiresome gimmick of the subjective camera in which Montgomery was heard but not seen, as the camera acted as his eyes and gave his point of view. George Montgomery (no relation) starred in *The High Window* (1947), based on Chandler's 'The Brasher Doubloon'. It was a B picture, entertaining enough, but eclipsed by *Murder, My Sweet* and *The Big Sleep*.

Two of the Marlowe films were featured in the *Lux Radio Theatre*. On 11 June 1945 Dick Powell and Claire Trevor recreated their screen roles in an entertaining radio version of *Murder, My Sweet* and on 9 February 1948 Robert Montgomery and Audrey Totter recreated their screen roles in *The Lady in the Lake* which, without the first-person camera gimmick, actually worked better on radio.

But Marlowe acquired his own radio series, doubtless due to the box office success of *Murder, My Sweet* and *The Big Sleep*. *The Adventures of Philip Marlowe* made its debut on radio in 1947 with Oscar-winning actor Van Heflin as Marlowe. The eight-episode series was based directly on Chandler's short stories, opening with a memorable and evocative adaptation of 'The Red Wind'. Marlowe returned in 1948 in *The New Adventures of Philip Marlowe* with a new star, B-picture actor Gerald Mohr, of whose voice Chandler declared his approval. The scripts were not written by Chandler but by Mel Dinelli, Gene Leavitt and Robert Mitchell and were original stories. But Chandler's contract gave him script approval and he was regularly consulted by the writers to ensure Chandlerian authenticity. The result was a series that at its peak drew ten million listeners a week. Between 26 September 1948 and 15 September 1951, 114 episodes were broadcast.

During the 1940s Hollywood was dominated by film noir thrillers and detectives both tough and suave. Radio caught up in the late 1940s. By then most of the famous detectives had already established images and their regular appearances in film gave audiences a ready-made visual impression which the voices on radio were required to match and evoke. Interestingly most of the detectives were played on radio by radio actors rather than film stars. There was a well-established line of suave American gentleman sleuths.[10] S.S. Van Dine's Philo Vance had reached the cinema screen in fifteen films between 1929 and 1947, being played by William Powell, Basil Rathbone, Edmund Lowe, Warren William, Wilfrid Hyde White, Grant Richards, James Stephenson and William Wright. Three of the actors, significantly, were British (Rathbone, Stephenson, Hyde White), suggesting the transatlantic affinity of the gentleman sleuths. There were three Philo Vance series on American radio in 1945, 1946 and 1948–50, starring successively José Ferrer and Jackson Beck.

Nick and Nora Charles, the husband and wife detective team of Dashiell Hammett's *The Thin Man*, were brought to the screen by William Powell and Myrna Loy in six witty, sophisticated and immensely popular films by MGM between 1934 and 1947. They too reached the airwaves in a succession of series between 1941 and 1950. Nick was played variously by Les Damon, Les Tremayne, David Gothard and Joseph Curtin with Claudia Morgan as Nora throughout. Damon and Morgan learned to imitate the voices of Powell and Loy so effectively that some listeners believed they were Powell and Loy performing under pseudonyms.

Louis Joseph Vance's *The Lone Wolf* featured retired jewel thief Michael Lanyard who investigated crimes, accompanied by his butler Jamison. On screen in twenty-five films between 1917 and 1949 he was played by Bert Lytell, Melvyn Douglas, Francis Lederer, Warren William, Gerald Mohr and Ron Randell. On radio Gerald Mohr played him in a single series for Mutual which ran from 29 June 1948 to 1 January 1949.

Michael Arlen's *The Falcon*, man about town Gay Lawrence, featured in a well-liked RKO Radio series of thirteen films that ran from 1941 to 1946. The Falcon was initially played by George Sanders but when he wanted to leave the series, he was replaced by his real-life brother Tom Conway in *The Falcon's Brother* (1942). On radio, The Falcon, renamed Michael Waring, featured in a succession of series between 1943 and 1954, played by a succession of actors: Berry Kroeger, James Meighan, Les Tremayne, Les Damon and George Petrie. Two of them (Damon and Tremayne) also played Nick Charles, suggesting a certain similarity and interchangeability among the gentleman sleuths.

Rex Stout's fat, exercise-shunning detective Nero Wolfe, gourmet, orchid-grower and brilliant problem-solver was played in two 1930s films by appropriately bulky actors Edward Arnold (*Meet Nero Wolfe*) and Walter Connolly (*League of Frightened Men*). But he had a much longer radio career. *The Adventures of Nero Wolfe* (1943–44) featured Santos Ortega and Luis Van Rooten successively as Wolfe. *The Amazing Nero Wolfe* (1946) featured silent screen veteran Francis X. Bushman, who had played Messala in the 1926 *Ben-Hur*. *The New Adventures of Nero Wolfe* (1950–51) cast the screen's most famous fat man, Sydney Greenstreet, who with his distinctive throaty laugh and audience memories of his bulk on screen fitted the role perfectly.

Erle Stanley Gardner's lawyer sleuth Perry Mason, best remembered in his television incarnation by Raymond Burr (1957–66), had had an earlier screen life in six pacy Warner Brothers thrillers between 1934 and 1937, starring Warren William, Ricardo Cortez and Donald Woods successively as Mason. Gardner became increasingly dissatisfied with the Warner films as they changed the style, mood and character of the books in a deliberate bid to emulate the successful MGM *Thin Man* series. Perry Mason even marries his secretary Della Street to create the appropriate husband and wife team. *Perry Mason* ran on radio as a daily fifteen-minute serial from 1943 to 1955 with Bartlett Robinson, Santos Ortega, Donald Briggs and John Larkin successively taking the role. Gardner insisted on personal involvement to ensure fidelity to his characters. This was conceded and he wrote the original stories for the whole run of the series, though professional scriptwriters turned them into scripts which Gardner vetted before broadcasting.[11]

All these detectives were American but two British detectives joined them on the American airwaves. However, their adventures took place in the United States. *Bulldog Drummond*, the creation of 'Sapper', featured in twenty-one films between 1923 and 1951. In the early 'Sapper' novels Drummond with his ruthless black-clad extra-legal organization, The Black Gang, comes over as a violent Fascist thug. The cinema did him a distinct service by cleaning up his image, transforming him into a debonair gentleman adventurer and casting in the role such bona fide gentlemen as Ronald Colman, Jack Buchanan, Tom Conway, Ray Milland and Walter Pidgeon. On radio, from 1941 to 1949, Drummond, accompanied by his manservant Denny, was played by George Coulouris, Santos Ortega and Ned Weaver, with a short-lived revival in 1954 featuring Sir Cedric Hardwicke.

The Saint, created by Leslie Charteris (1907–93), was a twentieth-century swashbuckler, an amalgam of Robin Hood, A.J. Raffles and the Scarlet Pimpernel. His name, Simon Templar, was chosen to evoke the ethos of the medieval order of chivalry, the Knights of the Temple. He came to be seen as an embodiment of gentlemanly Englishness, combining a sense of heroic individualism, a sense of humour and a sense of duty. But over the years – and the character appeared continuously from 1928 to 1983 – Simon Templar's nature changed, partly in response to Charteris's move from England to the United States.

William Vivian Butler in *The Durable Desperadoes* saw the Saint evolving through five stages.[12] He was at first in 1928 romantic, piratical and energetic. From 1931 he evolved into an English gentleman adventurer, eccentric, versatile and given to versifying. After 1934, an Anglo-American Saint developed, smoother, older and less flamboyant. After 1942 the Saint became a Federal agent and detective pursuing Nazi spies and saboteurs. Finally, after the war he became a cosmopolitan, solitary, polished and endlessly globe-trotting. Charteris devised the distinctive stickman logo for the Saint and the whistled tune that is the Saint's musical signature.

When the Saint came to films in 1938 in a highly profitable series for RKO Radio Pictures, it was the Mark Three Anglo-American Saint. Louis Hayward starred in *The Saint in New York* and then George Sanders in five subsequent titles. One of them, *The Saint in London*, was filmed in the United Kingdom. Sanders became the face of the Saint for many people for many years. Charteris did not like Sanders' Saint – he wanted Cary Grant for the part – and when RKO switched Sanders to the almost identical role of the Falcon based on Michael Arlen's character, Charteris sued RKO for plagiarism and received an out of court settlement.

The Saint made his radio debut in 1939 on the commercial station Radio Eireann, played by Terence de Marney, who repeated the role on BBC Forces Radio in 1940 in a six-week series based on the original Charteris stories. But his principal radio incarnation was in the USA where between 1945 and 1951 the Saint's adventures were heard on various networks and voiced by five different actors, actors who were interestingly a mixture of American and British actors. This was the Mark Four Saint, the American Private Eye.

In 1945 the American radio and film actor Edgar Barrier played Simon Templar in a series of adaptations of Charteris stories with Charteris himself as script supervisor. The second series of twenty-six *Saint* programmes, for some of which Charteris wrote new *Saint* scripts later turned into short stories, starred Brian Aherne, Charteris's favourite among the radio Saints. But by far the longest run, 1947–50, was enjoyed by Vincent Price, whose velvet-voiced Saint was domiciled in New York. These were not Charteris originals but by other writers. This Simon Templar encountered those staples of late 1940s' cinema – fugitive Nazis, crooked fight promoters, corporate swindlers, seedy nightclub owners, jewel thieves and mobsters. The Saint retained his urbane bantering style but was now doing detective work.

When Price gave up the role, he was succeeded for the final 1950–51 series by first the American actor Barry Sullivan and later British actor Tom Conway. Conway, with his distinctive clipped voice and suave manner, was the brother of cinematic Saint George Sanders and became virtually an all-purpose detective, playing the Falcon, Bulldog Drummond and Norman Conquest on film and Sherlock Holmes and the Saint on radio. The Saint returned to the cinema in 1953 in a nondescript British B picture, *The Saint's Girl Friday*, for which Louis Hayward reprised the role he created in 1938. The radio Saint was to be eclipsed in the popular memory by Roger Moore's television incarnation which ran from 1962 to 1969.[13]

The Charlie Chan series was one of the longest-running detective series in films. It was based on a character created by Earl Derr Biggers, a Harvard-educated journalist turned thriller writer. Charlie Chan is a Chinese-born detective who works in the police department in Honolulu. He featured in six novels published between 1925 and 1933 when Biggers died. But the character carried on in films, eventually appearing in forty-six between 1926 and 1952. The classic incarnations were Warner Oland (sixteen films between 1931 and 1937), Sidney Toler (twenty-two films between 1938 and 1947) and Roland Winters (six films between 1948 and 1952).

The films were neatly constructed crime thrillers, rather stylishly made, particularly the ones produced by 20th Century Fox. One of the appeals of the series was the exotic locations to which Chan was sent, among them Rio, Panama, Egypt and Paris. *Charlie Chan in Shanghai* took him to the international settlement in Shanghai with its White Russian exiles and drug rings. *Charlie Chan at the Olympics* had him travelling on the airship *Hindenburg* to the 1936 Berlin Olympics where we get glimpses of Jesse Owens winning a medal.

But the principal appeal was the character of Charlie Chan himself. Charlie is the most positive role model of a Chinese man produced by Golden Age Hollywood, which makes it strange that in recent years Chinese-American groups have campaigned persistently to keep the films off television and video. They claim the characterization is demeaning. But Chan is clever, courteous, philosophical, wise, urbane and noble. He is a devoted husband and father, and he is far brighter than any of the white characters in the films. It is claimed that he speaks pidgin English. He does not. He speaks English as if it were a foreign language, very precisely. When a character in *Charlie Chan in Paris* addresses him in pidgin English, Chan sends him up. It is worth noting that the Chinese government in the 1930s and 1940s, who vociferously objected to and banned films which they decreed to be hostile depictions of China and the Chinese (*Shanghai Express*, *The Bitter Tea of General Yen*, *The Mask of Fu Manchu* among them) never objected to the Charlie Chan films. The Chinese actor Keye Luke who played Lee, Charlie's 'Number One Son', has defended the films as very positive and Warner Oland as a fine performer.[14]

Oland died in 1937 and Sidney Toler took over. He was a sharper-tongued, more incisive Chan but still basically goodnatured. In 1942 Fox abandoned the series and Monogram took over. Budgets were cut from $200,000 to $75,000 per film and the shooting schedule was a mere three weeks. But the characteristics of the series were maintained with Chan given a black assistant Birmingham Brown, played by top black nightclub comedian Mantan Moreland, his casting ensuring that the film played all the black cinemas in areas like Harlem.

Alongside the films, radio played its part in dramatizing the Chan stories. Between 2 December 1932 and 26 May 1933 on the Blue Network three of Biggers novels, *The Black Camel*, *The Chinese Parrot* and *Behind That Curtain* were dramatized in thirty-minute instalments. Genial, rotund character actor Walter Connolly played Charlie. There was a daily fifteen-minute episode *Charlie Chan* series on the Mutual Network between 17 September 1936 and 22 April 1938. Then between 5 October 1944 and 5 April 1945 Ed Begley starred as Charlie Chan in a new series of half-hour episodes, *The Adventures of Charlie Chan* on the Blue Network. Begley returned as Chan in a series of daily fifteen-minute episodes on ABC from 18 June to 30 November 1945 and on Mutual in a series of half-hour episodes from 11 August 1947 to 21 June 1948, being replaced by Santos Ortega before the end of the run (he also played Nero Wolfe, Bulldog Drummond and Perry Mason on radio).

The late 1940s in the cinema saw the advent of the location-shot, semi-documentary police drama epitomized by such films as *The Naked City* (1948) and *Call Northside 777* (1948). The actor Jack Webb played a small role in one of these docudramas, *He Walked By Night* (1948) and after discussions with the technical adviser, Sergeant Marty Wynn of the Los Angeles Police Department came up with a new concept, *Dragnet*. The idea behind *Dragnet* was to follow through one particular case with absolute realism. With the cooperation of the Los Angeles Police Department, Webb drew on authentic case files and the announcer would intone at the start of each show: 'The story you are about to hear is true, only the names have been changed to protect the innocent'. Jack Webb played the leading role of Sergeant Joe Friday and also directed the show, aiming to avoid all glamour and melodrama. The actors were encouraged to underplay, sequences were recorded on location and the demand for authenticity was such that Webb insisted that the programme include exactly the number of steps it took between floors of the LA Police Building. The series broke the taboo on broadcasting certain crimes and Friday investigated cases involving prostitution, pornography, drugs, child killing as well as robbery and murder. *Dragnet* ran on radio from 1949 to 1957 and created a trend which was followed by shows such as *The Lineup* (1950–53) and *Tales of the Texas Rangers* (1950–52). This meant that in its dying days, dramatic radio achieved a realism it had never before attained.[15] From 1952 to 1959 *Dragnet* ran simultaneously on television and there was a *Dragnet* feature film in 1954. The film and the television shows, like the radio shows, were directed by and starred Jack Webb, making *Dragnet* a supreme example of multi-media symbiosis.

In the United Kingdom, the detectives were either derived from established literary and cinematic sleuths (Sherlock Holmes, Sexton Blake, Father Brown) or were original radio creations who made their way eventually onto the cinema screen (Paul Temple, Dr Morelle, Dick Barton, PC 49, Inspector Hornleigh). Sherlock Holmes was as popular on British radio as he was on American radio and each country produced its definitive interpreter of the role (Basil Rathbone in the USA, Carleton Hobbs in the UK) (see Chapter 10).

In the December 1893 issues of the *Strand* magazine, Arthur Conan Doyle killed off Sherlock Holmes. The same month *The Halfpenny Marvel* published a story called 'The Missing Millionaire' written by a jobbing author Harry Blyth, using the pen-name Hal Meredeth. The stories introduced a character that came to be disparaged as 'the office boy's Sherlock Holmes' or 'The Poor Man's Sherlock Holmes'. But for several generations of the mass reading public Sexton Blake was *the* Baker Street detective, a more significant figure in the popular imagination even than Holmes.

The name was a masterstroke. Sexton Blake carried overtones of graveyards, mystery and death. Harry Blyth was paid nine guineas as a fee for the first story and the copyright in the character. But after writing seven stories, none of them actually very good, he died of typhoid fever in 1898. However, Blake's fictional career was to last more or less continuously from 1893 to 1978, running to over 4,000 stories by some 200 different authors.

As Blake took over the mantle of Holmes, he also took some of his attributes. Certainly they were similar in physical appearance. They both had rooms in Baker Street, devoted housekeepers and faithful assistants. But there were significant differences. Where Conan Doyle's stories were detective puzzles, celebrations of the fine art of deductive reasoning, the Blake stories were melodramatic thrillers, vivid, action-packed and fast-moving. Where Holmes never strays outside Western Europe in the published stories, Blake was constantly globetrotting and is almost certainly the most well-travelled of the fictional detectives. Holmes was a late Victorian, Blake a modern man of the streamlined inter-war years, his regular means of conveyance the bullet-proof Rolls-Royce as opposed to Sherlock's horse-drawn hansom cab. Holmes was a product of the middle-class world of *The Strand* magazine, which cost sixpence an issue. Blake was a product of the mass circulation story papers for working-class readers, epitomised by *The Half-Penny Marvel*, the paper launched by Alfred Harmsworth in 1893, which cost a halfpenny and in which Blake made his literary debut.

It was W.H. Back, an enterprising editor with the Amalgamated Press, who decided to build Blake into a replacement for Holmes, whose disappearance was still mourned by mystery-readers. This was when Blake was moved to Baker Street and equipped with dressing gown, pipe and violin. He was also given an assistant, Tinker, an orphan waif, who was a cross between Doyle's Billy the Page and Wiggins of the Baker Street Irregulars, and who was the perfect identification figure for juvenile readers.

There can be no doubting Blake's popularity. His adventures appeared in a wide variety of publications, but most notably in the weekly magazines *Union Jack* and its successor *Detective Weekly* more or less continuously from 1904 to 1940 and simultaneously in *The Sexton Blake Library*, monthly stories which appeared regularly from 1915 to 1963. Just as Sidney Paget created the visual image of Holmes, the visual image of Blake and his world was firmly and indelibly fixed by the artist Eric Parker (1898–1974) who for thirty years was responsible for most of the illustrations and cover pictures of the various Blake journals. His style was dynamic and atmospheric and he vividly depicted action scenes and imbued Blake with the hawk-like features and spare, athletic form that made him the ideal Holmes substitute.[16]

The appeal of the Blake stories in their heyday lay in the breathtaking action, the colourful locations and in particular the extraordinary gallery of villains who graced the pages of the Blake adventures. Each Blake writer had his own villain and the readers had their favourites too. There was the renegade police-man George Marsden Plummer, the renegade surgeon Dr Huxton Rymer, the elegant, opium-smoking adventurer Zenith the Albino, His Criminal Majesty King Karl of Serbovia, and then there were those leaders of conspiracies against the British Empire: sinister Chinese mastermind Prince Wu Ling, Head of the Brotherhood of the Yellow Beetle and the wealthiest man in China, sinister Egyptian mastermind Prince Menes, Head of the Ancient Order of Ra and leader of a white slave gang, and sinister Indian mastermind Gunga Dass. So vivid were these adventures that some readers believed firmly in the existence of Sexton Blake and Tinker.

Blake's popularity on the printed page inevitably meant translation to the other mass media. There were several Sexton Blake stage plays, the earliest produced in 1907. But the principal stage incarnation for Blake was the four-act play *Sexton Blake*, written by regular Blake author Donald Stuart and produced in London in 1930. The title role was taken by Arthur Wontner, who would become better known for playing Sherlock Holmes on stage and film. But he repeated the role of Blake in a gramophone record, *Murder on the Portsmouth Road*, also scripted by Donald Stuart.

The first Blake film appeared in 1909 and there were during the silent era thirteen half-hour Blake features. During the 1930s three quota films were produced in the United Kingdom starring George Curzon as Blake and Tony Sympson as Tinker: *Sexton Blake and the Bearded Doctor* (1935), *Sexton Blake and the Mademoiselle* (1935) and *Sexton Blake and the Hooded Terror* (1938), all based on *Sexton Blake Library* stories. Only the third of them, directed by George King, seems to have survived but it is an outrageously enjoyable slice of ripe melodrama, pitching Blake against 'The Snake', head of the Black Quorum organization and in reality stamp-collecting millionaire Michel Larron. Larron is played with lipsmacking relish by the master of old time melodrama, Tod

Slaughter. The narrative involving poisoned South American darts, a snake-filled death chamber and a gambling club full of trapdoors and secret television screens is packed with action and atmosphere and only George Curzon as Blake, determined but rather staid, lacks the appropriate dash, while Tony Sympson, too old for the role of Tinker, is irritatingly used as comic cockney relief.

The best screen Blake to date, dynamic, two-fisted and quick-witted was played by David Farrar in a brace of wartime films. *Meet Sexton Blake* (1944) and *The Echo Murders* (1945), directed and written by John Harlow, and based on works in the *Sexton Blake Library* were satisfyingly complicated dramas which pitted Blake against a new enemy – Nazi agents. The first of them included Tinker and housekeeper Mrs Bardell (the splendid Kathleen Harrison) with Blake on the track of the formula for a new metal alloy, but the second featured Blake alone, summoned to Cornwall to deal with murder and sabotage at a tin mine. David Farrar enjoyed himself as Blake as he recalled in his autobiography:

> A proposition was put to me to create Sexton Blake on the screen. Well, here … was something which was not likely to shatter the sophisticated circles of London's West End, and I reflected that Ronald Colman had, in his earliest days, made the Bulldog Drummond series and Basil Rathbone was churning out the Sherlock Holmes series regularly, so I thought it might be fun to create the oldest of all the famous sleuths of fiction. And fun it was, but very exhausting fun … Much of the fighting has, of course, to be fake, but on one occasion a heavyweight forgot to miss and my bruised mouth held up shooting on the film for three days. I knocked out countless villains, got into dreadful scrapes, smashed chandeliers, was thrown down flooded mineshafts – but always got my man … We broadcast an excerpt from one of the films in the *Music from the Movies* programme. I was interviewed over the air by Moore Raymond, who asked me: 'I suppose you've read dozens of Sexton Blakes, David?' to which I replied in the affirmative, but I confess I was lying – Sexton Blake never figured in my school curriculum.[17]

There would be one more cinematic Blake, Geoffrey Toone, in the sixty-seven-minute B picture, *Murder at Site Three* (1959), based on a novel by Blake author W. Howard Baker and directed by Francis Searle.

Blake's radio debut came in 1939 in a BBC serial *Enter Sexton Blake*, adapted from Berkeley Gray's *Three Frightened Men* by Ernest Dudley, soon to create his own radio detective Dr Morelle. George Curzon, evidently deemed to be identified with the role from his three film appearances, was recruited to play Blake with Brian Lawrence as Tinker. *The Detective Weekly* trumpeted its imminent appearance:

> ONLY TWO WEEKS – and then begins the great new wireless serial play bringing our famous Sexton Blake over the air to you for the first time. There have been

Sexton Blake films and today this grand character stands out as the most famous detective of fiction still in existence. When most of our fathers were young they read and were thrilled by the adventures of Sexton Blake of Baker Street, and today this great man and his assistant, Tinker, are more popular than ever – and with the fathers as well as the sons, and indeed, with mothers and daughters too. Sexton Blake is a personality everybody enjoys reading about – and now everybody will be able to hear him in one of his most thrilling cases broadcast by the BBC. *Enter Sexton Blake*, which is the title of the radio play, will have its first dramatic instalment on Thursday January 26 at 3.15 p.m. in the London Regional Programme, and also at 7.30 p.m. in the National Programme. From then on you will hear them at these times every following Thursday for twelve weeks.[18]

But Ernest Dudley deemed it a failure. He thought Brian Lawrence miscast as Tinker and felt that the story had not translated effectively from page to airwaves.[19]

Nevertheless audiences must have liked it well enough for it was followed in 1940 by *A Case for Sexton Blake*, adapted by Francis Durbridge, the creator of Paul Temple, from a story by Ted Holmes. It starred Arthur Young as Blake and Clive Baxter as Tinker. Sadly nothing remains from either serial in the archive and it is impossible to judge their effectiveness.

With the end of the Second World War, Blake's fictional life began to falter and drastic action was needed. In 1956 W. Howard Baker took over as Editor of *The Sexton Blake Library*. Blake and Tinker (more frequently referred to now by his given name Edward Carter and graduated from boy to young man) were moved to offices in Berkeley Square, given a glamorous secretary Paula Dane and the stories took on more of the hard-boiled style of the American pulps. *The Sexton Blake Library* was terminated in 1963 but Howard Baker brought the character back in a series of paperback novels published by Mayflower between 1965 and 1968. It ran to forty-three titles.

It was this revamped Blake who reached the radio for a definitive incarnation in seventeen half-hour programmes on the BBC Light Programme. It starred William Franklyn, suaver and smoother than previous interpreters as Blake, David Gregory as Tinker and Heather Chasen as Paula Dane. Although it was set in the 'Swinging Sixties', the scripts were by veteran Blake author Donald Stuart (1897–1980). He wrote thirty-eight stories for the *Sexton Blake Library* in the 1930s and for the radio series adroitly updated some of his vintage tales. For instance the episode *You Must be Joking* was a reworking of his Blake story 'The Green Jester', first published in *Union Jack* in 1930.

Producer Alastair Scott Johnston wrote in *Radio Times* (24 August 1967) that Sexton Blake was the 'grand-daddy of them all', adding:

These are all new stories specially written by Donald Stuart and we hope you will either enjoy being baffled, or, if you like to join in the game, trying to spot the criminal. We have done our best not to cheat and if we haven't made any ghastly mistakes, all the clues to help the amateur sleuths amongst you are there in the script, mixed up, of course, with innumerable red herrings. Sexton Blake has got to sort them out. Can you?

These half hours remain cleverly devised, exciting and consistently entertaining dramas, with an up-to-date spin, such as the unmasking of a Russian spy in MI5, the smashing of a drug ring using abandoned railway stations, victims of the Beeching cuts, as distribution centres, the capture of a serial killer nicknamed 'Bluebeard', and solving the Mafia killing of an informer. But there were also welcome echoes of the past such as the episode in which a sinister Chinese mastermind is developing poisonous fungi with which the entire population of the West could be destroyed.

At the same time as the radio series, there was an ITV television series of *Sexton Blake*, sixty half-hour episodes transmitted between 1967 and 1971. It starred Laurence Payne as Blake and Roger Foss as Tinker and unlike the Franklyn series, was set in the 1920s. But it had a tragic ending when Payne was injured in a sword duel and lost the sight in one eye as a result. Blake's final appearance both on screen and in print to date was in 1978 when Jeremy Clyde played him in a BBC serial by Simon Raven, *Sexton Blake and the Demon God*, an affectionate pastiche of the 1930s melodramas, which was novelised by John Garforth. In 2009 BBC Radio 2 broadcast *The Adventures of Sexton Blake*, a series of fifteen-minute episodes starring Simon Jones but it was a tiresome and silly parody of the inter-war stories.

Basil Radford and Naunton Wayne were first teamed in the Alfred Hitchcock thriller *The Lady Vanishes* (1938), a hugely entertaining film scripted by Frank Launder and Sidney Gilliat from the novel by Ethel Lina White. Most of the action takes place on a train crossing the mythical Central European country of Bandrika. Among the passengers are a couple of Englishmen, Charters and Caldicott, played by Radford and Wayne, who are hastening back to England for the Test Match. Cricket forms their sole topic of conversation. They had missed an earlier train when Charters had insisted on standing for twenty minutes for Liszt's *Hungarian Rhapsody* under the mistaken impression that it was the Hungarian National Anthem. When the train is stranded by an avalanche and they have to spend the night in a crowded hotel, they do not get anything to eat because they spend so long dressing for dinner that when they get down everything has been eaten. They complain constantly about the food and the accommodation.

But when the chips are down they come through with flying colours. The restaurant car of the train is uncoupled and besieged by the Bandrikan secret police who are seeking the British agent, Miss Froy, the eponymous vanishing lady. The only people in the car are all English because it is teatime. Musicologist Gilbert (Michael Redgrave) takes charge and organizes the defence and both Charters and Caldicott acquit themselves courageously. The English manage to escape and the master spy Egon Hartz (Paul Lukas) concedes defeat as they steam away: 'As they say in English, jolly good luck to them'. Charters and Caldicott arrive back to find that the Test Match has been washed out by rain.

The film established them as the archetypal Englishmen abroad, tweedy, pipe-smoking, cricket-loving, grumbling about everything that is unfamiliar or unEnglish but when it comes to a fight, fearless. It was an image audiences loved and Radford and Wayne became a cherished double act. Launder and Gilliat had invented the characters, who do not feature in the book, and so they were able to use them in other films. Charters and Caldicott featured in *Night Train to Munich* (1940), scripted by Launder and Gilliat for director Carol Reed. In this film, they assisted British secret agent Rex Harrison to help a Czech inventor and his daughter escape from Nazi Germany on the eve of the war. Launder and Gilliat featured Charters and Caldicott in their own first solo effort as directors, *Millions Like Us* (1943). Launder and Gilliat also scripted a comedy thriller serial for the BBC, *Crooks Tour*, in 1940, with Radford and Wayne as Charters and Caldicott. This was snapped up by British National and turned into a low-budget film, directed by John Baxter. Despite the cheap sets and stock footage of exotic locations, it remains an entertaining vehicle for the two hapless Englishmen abroad, this time on a coach tour of the Middle East. In a whirlwind journey which takes them from Bagdad to Istanbul, Budapest and a castle on the Hungarian frontier, Charters and Caldicott are mistaken for German agents and entrusted with a gramophone record which contains the Nazi plans to sabotage the oilfields. Charters and Caldicott encounter a desert sheikh who had been at public school with Charters and a glamorous nightclub singer who is a double agent working for the British as they narrowly escape a series of attempts by German agents to kill them and retrieve the record. Eventually they get the record safely back to London.

A second radio serial, *Secret Mission 609*, followed but this was not filmed. A falling-out between Launder and Gilliat and Radford and Wayne occurred in 1946 when Launder and Gilliat wrote Charters and Caldicott into their thriller *I See A Dark Stranger* but Radford and Wayne declined the parts because they were not big enough. Launder and Gilliat renamed the parts Goodhusband and

Spanswick and cast Tom Macaulay and Garry Marsh. Radford and Wayne continued to perform as a double act in such films as *Girl in a Million* (1946), *Quartet* (1948) and *It's Not Cricket* (1948). But because Launder and Gilliat owned the copyright in the characters of Charters and Caldicott, they refused to allow the BBC to produce new serials featuring the characters. Instead the BBC simply renamed the characters and Wayne and Radford played them exactly as before. They appeared in the comedy thriller serials *Double Bedlam* (1946), *Travellers Joy* (1947), *Crime, Gentlemen, Please* (1948), *Having a Wonderful Crime* (1949), *That's My Baby* (1950), *May I Have the Treasure* (1951) and *Rogues Gallery* (1952). The serials were scripted by a variety of different writers and Radford and Wayne appeared as Woolcott and Spencer, Berkeley and Bulstrode and Fanshawe and Fothergill while retaining the Charters and Caldicott characterisations. The partnership was only ended by Radford's death in 1952.

One of the most familiar theme tunes on British radio was Vivian Ellis's *Coronation Scot*, indelibly associated with the adventures of the best-loved husband and wife detective team on radio, Paul Temple and Steve. The Paul Temple series was to become the first and the longest-running detective series on British radio, first broadcast in 1938 and finally bowing out in 1968 after an incredible thirty-year run. The Paul Temple series was the brainchild of a young Bradford-born writer Francis Durbridge who while still a student at Birmingham University had been discovered as a writer by BBC producer Martyn C. Webster. Durbridge had written a play about a department store called *Promotion* but had always wanted to write thrillers. He approached Webster who invited him to submit an episode. He did and was commissioned. The first episode of the first ever Paul Temple serial *Send for Paul Temple* went on the air on 8 April 1938. But is was not yet the *Paul Temple* that was to become an integral part of regular radio listeners' imaginative landscape in the 1950s. There was no Peter Coke or Marjorie Westbury and no *Coronation Scot*. The title music was Rimsky Korsakov's *Scheherazade. Coronation Scot* was first used in 1947 on the serial *Paul Temple and Steve.* Paul Temple was played by Hugh Morton and Bernadette Hodgson played the girl reporter he subsequently married, whose real name was Louise Harvey but who was better known by her nom de plume Steve Trent. But all the labyrinthine complexity of plot and baffling details that endeared the stories to listeners were in place and the serial prompted a record 7,000 fan letters. The story had Paul Temple, novelist and criminologist, called in by Scotland Yard Commissioner Sir Graham Forbes, who was to remain a fixture in the series until the end, to help track down a mysterious jewel thief, known as The Knave of Diamonds. The identity of the villain, exposed in the final episode, was kept from the cast until the final read-through on the day of the broadcast and that remained the tradition throughout. A single episode from that first series, episode six, survives in the archive and still works as a suspenseful, atmospheric production.

Paul Temple was up and running and there were eventually to be a total of twenty Paul Temple serials and three one-off plays. Over the years there were to be six different Paul Temples – Hugh Morton, Carl Bernard, Barry Morse, Howard Marion-Crawford, Kim Peacock and Peter Coke. But with only a handful of exceptions, there was always and irresistibly Marjorie Westbury as Steve. Born in 1905, Marjorie Westbury had trained at the Royal College of Music and began her broadcasting career in 1933 as a singer. But she later turned to acting and in 1942 joined the BBC Drama Repertory Company and became one of the stalwarts of radio drama. She died in 1989 at the age of 84. Marjorie Westbury was only four foot ten inches tall and so her acting was largely confined to radio. As Steve she managed to sound both sexy and ladylike and conjured up a captivating image of poised, good-humoured and elegant femininity. Enyd Williams, then a young studio manager, remembered her: 'She was the absolute voice of radio in her day'. She was indeed voted Best Actress of the Year in the *National Radio Awards*, sponsored by the *Daily Mail*, in 1954 and 1955. As Steve, recalls Enyd Williams, 'You just knew she was the most glamorous, six foot blonde, the most marvellous woman'. In fact, she was so short she had to use an orange box to stand on to reach the microphone and her figure, as Peter Coke described it, was 'rather cottage loafy'. But 'she had this absolute magic with the microphone'.[20]

The longest-serving Paul Temples were Kim Peacock and Peter Coke. Peacock (1901–66) played the role between 1946 and 1953 in nine productions. Older and huskier voiced than Peter Coke, he was popular in the role but was replaced because according to Coke, 'he had become too slow'. Peter Coke took over in 1954 and played the role until the series ended in 1968. He was in eleven serials; seven originals and four remakes of earlier ones. It was Coke who thanks to regular repeats and the release of the series on audio cassette and CD, became the definitive Paul Temple, well bred, assured and incisive. Peter Coke, born in 1913, was educated at Stowe, trained at RADA and began acting in plays and films in the 1930s. But his career was interrupted by war service between 1940 and 1946. He resumed his stage career after the war and combined acting with writing, eventually having some ten plays to his credit. He was later to develop a second career as a shell-artist. He died in 2008 aged ninety-five. There is a gallery at Sheringham devoted to his work. He played Terry Palmer, one of the villains, in the 1950 production of *Paul Temple and the Vandyke Affair* and a police inspector in the 1953 film version of Durbridge's first television serial *The Broken Horseshoe* directed by Webster. But he was a regular actor in radio plays: 'I had a voice the microphone loved' he recalled. All the serials over thirty years were produced by Martyn C. Webster (1903–83). He became a master of the genre of radio thriller, producing in addition to Paul Temple, the *Appointment with Fear* series, the Philip Odell serials and some of the Sherlock Holmes plays with Carleton Hobbs and Norman Shelley. Enyd Williams recalled him as 'an enchanting human being. He was quite a small, dapper man and he had a most wonderful wicked sense of humour. He was a great practical joker'. On one occasion when Queen Mary was expected to attend a recording of *Saturday Night Theatre* and had to cry off because of a cold, he hired a complete Queen Mary outfit and turned up in it to the delight of the actors. She said 'He did the Paul Temples most beautifully and with tremendous care'. Peter Coke said he was 'a very, very clever producer – although you didn't realise it. He dealt with actors with such velvet gloves. He never raised his voice or got angry. He was such a nice man and he got his way with immense charm and great humour'. Webster was claustrophobic. He never used the lifts at Broadcasting House and he preferred to record his programmes in now long closed BBC outstations at Piccadilly and Tottenham Court Road.

One feature of the serials was their complex sound effects. Marjorie Westbury remembered with admiration studio manager Patience Sheffield's handling of them. In the days before advanced audio technology, the sound effects were all on gramophone records which had to be played in with split-second timing. 'In those days Patience was on grams. She would have eight timetables – eight'. She went on to describe a scene with Paul and Steve driving along, another car pursuing them, a crash and then police car and ambulance arriving: each of the different effects on a record. 'She never missed a trick – singlehanded'.[21] Peter Coke recalled an occasion when to get the right echo effect for a cave scene he and Marjorie recorded a scene in a gentleman's toilet. Another feature of the serials was Webster's use of a regular repertory company of actors. Time and again the names of James Thomason, Simon Lack, June Tobin, Ralph Truman, Olaf Olsen and Betty Hardy would turn up in the credits.

What was the appeal of the series? Peter Coke attributed it to the clever construction of the stories and the maintenance of suspense but also the relationship between Steve and Paul. 'The atmosphere between Marjorie and myself did contribute to the success because we were very close. A sort of warmth came over'. Marjorie agreed, pointing to 'All this nice comfy chat – a lot of badinage about how much I paid for my hats'. Many fans wrote in to ask if they were really married, which was a tribute to their acting skills, as neither of them ever married.

Fictional detectives have often been dedicated, wise, celibate figures, rooting out evil, hearing confessions, acting as substitute priests in a secular age. Paul Temple, despite the priestly overtones of his surname, did not. He was married and his partnership with Steve remains at the centre of the serials. It somewhat resembles the relationship of Dashiell Hammett's husband and wife detective team Nick and Nora Charles in the popular *Thin Man* film series starring William Powell and Myrna Loy. In the Temple serials, domestic detail counterpointed the detection, rendering the characters human and approachable.

In one respect, however, Paul Temple was in the classic tradition of English detectives – the gentleman amateur. He was thus the blood brother of the likes of Lord Peter Wimsey and Bulldog Drummond. In the novel version of *Send for Paul Temple*, Durbridge described him:

> Temple … was a modern embodiment of Sir Philip Sydney. Courtly in manners, a dominant character without ever giving the impression of domination. He was equally at home in the double-breasted dinner jacket he was now wearing, the perfect host entertaining his guests, or in a coarse, loose tweed suit striding along country lanes. Nobody was surprised to learn that he preferred rugby football to cricket, although he had played both. Now at the age of forty, he was past the violence of the game but still rarely missed an international match … The fact that he had never secured a blue was a constant source of regret. He had a habit of leisurely movement and retained traces of what, in his younger days, had been a very pronounced Oxford drawl. On the other hand, you felt that here was a man whose bulk would be no great hindrance to action, and that in a fight it was as well to have him on your side.[22]

Temple, educated at Rugby and Magdalen College, Oxford, the son of a general, earns his living as a crime novelist and a jolly good living it must have been for the first serial finds him living in a country house, Bramley Lodge, near Evesham. Later, he and Steve moved to a luxury flat in London, 127A Eaton Square, which was furnished with antiques, decorated with old masters and boasted a cellar full of vintage burgundy and claret from Justerini and Brooks. The ménage was completed by a rather tiresome cockney manservant, Charlie.

Throughout Paul showed a loving and chivalrous concern for Steve, wanting to protect her from violence and danger. But just as regularly, she insisted on staying at his side. Steve, who regularly faced kidnap and sometimes death, was quite resourceful when it came to dealing with opponents. Paul and Steve were constructed as complementary embodiments of masculinity and femininity, he gentlemanly, single-minded and an embodiment of deductive reasoning, she with a love of new hats and an infallible sense of intuition. If ever Steve said of someone, 'I don't like that man', he usually turned out to be the villain.

There was a comforting familiarity about the series, with standard ingredients regularly recurring. In each serial Paul would tackle a gang (of drug smugglers, diamond smugglers, jewel thieves, car thieves, counterfeiters or blackmailers) with a mysterious leader. You could be pretty sure that during the course of the serial, there would be a bomb in the car. Someone would be so badly beaten up that they would die. The car would be raked with bullets. Someone would impersonate Paul on the telephone. And many of the serials ended with that authentic 1950s event, the cocktail party, where Temple would dramatically expose the villain. In a nice nod to the home of the series, Durbridge began *Send for Paul Temple Again* with the murder of one of the participants in the popular discussion programme *The Brains Trust* at Broadcasting House.

Although earlier serials took place in Yorkshire, the Midlands and Scotland, by the 1950s the saga had settled down firmly in the Home Counties with the mayhem taking place around Farnham, Maidenhead, Guildford, Tenterden and St Albans. The series remains an infallible guide to the manners and mores of Middle England in that now almost impossibly remote era before the cultural revolution of the 1960s. In particular Paul Temple calls all the men by their surname and there is an almost mandarin politeness about introducing everyone. It reflects the hierarchy of politeness that once existed in which you called people you did not know 'Mr' or 'Miss', people you knew slightly by their surname and only very close friends by their Christian names. Nowadays under the influence of the United States, everyone is instantly on first name terms.

Radio success meant that Paul Temple rapidly became a multi-media personality. Many of the radio scripts were novelised. There was a Temple strip cartoon in the *Evening News* in the 1950s. Four of the serials were adapted as low-budget British B pictures, though none of them featured the radio casts. *Send for Paul Temple* (1946), directed by John Argyle, starred Anthony Hulme as Paul and Joy Shelton as Steve. It was based on the very first Temple serial. The remaining three all starred John Bentley, perennial star of British B pictures, as Paul Temple with first Patricia Dainton and then Dinah Sheridan as Steve. All three were directed for Butchers Films by Maclean Rogers. *Calling Paul Temple* (1948) was based on the 1945 radio serial *Send for Paul Temple Again*. *Paul Temple's Triumph* (1950) was based on the 1939 serial *News of Paul Temple*. *Paul Temple Returns* (1952) was based on the 1942 serial *Paul Temple Intervenes*. They suffered from the need to streamline and simplify in order to cram eight half-hour episodes into an average of eighty minutes. *Paul Temple's Triumph* took considerable liberties with the original, changing the setting (from Scotland to the New Forest) and the identity of the villain (from hotel owner Mrs Weston to amiable buffoon Oliver Ffollet, a character not in the radio serial). Entertaining enough within their limits, they were no substitute for the slow unfolding complexity of the radio versions. Between 1969 and 1971 a BBC television series of *Paul Temple*, not however scripted by Durbridge, was shown. It starred Francis Matthews who was a suave and stylish Paul and Ros Drinkwater, who made no impression at all as Steve. A sequence of self-contained adventures, often in foreign locations, the series lacked the vital cliff-hanging element of the radio serials.

It is a measure of the impact of the radio versions that when people of a certain age read Durbridge's Temple novels they hear the voices of Peter Coke and Marjorie Westbury. Marjorie Westbury was proof of the power of a voice. A woman in the West Country wrote to her, saying she loved her voice so much she was going to leave her all her money. Marjorie drove down to see the woman to show that she looked nothing like she sounded. This made no difference. The woman committed suicide, leaving all her money to Marjorie and making her independently wealthy. For despite their appearances in films, books, television and comic strip, Paul Temple and Steve remain ever and supremely the radio detectives.

The 1940s was the era when the psychiatrist became a popular hero in the cinema. Omniscient, compassionate and humane, the psychiatrist – Claude Rains in *Now Voyager*, Lew Ayres in *The Dark Mirror*, Leo Genn in *The Snake Pit* or Herbert Lom in *The Seventh Veil* – provided instant analyses of people's problems and pointed them towards the promise of a full recovery from whatever was troubling them psychologically or spiritually. It was but one small step from psychological problem-solving to detective work and in Dr Morelle, radio gained its most notable psychiatrist-detective.

Morelle was the creation of Ernest Dudley (1908–2006), actor turned prolific scriptwriter. He achieved nationwide celebrity in the 1940s as BBC Radio's *Armchair Detective* in a weekly series, beginning in 1942 in which he reviewed, with dramatised excerpts, the latest crime fiction. Dudley actually played himself in an unremarkable 1951 sixty-minute B-picture *The Armchair Detective* in which the radio detective proved a radio singer innocent of murder

Ernest Dudley put his immersion in detective fiction to good use. Dr Morelle was conceived in 1940 in a Bristol coal cellar where Dudley had taken refuge during the Second World War air raids. He had been commissioned by the Variety Department, which had been evacuated to Bristol, to provide a series of playlets for the popular variety show *Monday Night at Eight* which would set out a detective puzzle, the solution to which would be given at the end of the programme.

Dudley set out to create an entirely new kind of detective – the psychiatrist-detective. He based his character on an actor. He recalled: 'I always had a great admiration for an actor I had met once or twice in Paris – Erich von Stroheim. He had a most unpleasant personality but he was attractive to women'.[23] Stroheim, billed as 'The Man You Love to Hate', had cornered the market in arrogant Prussian army officers and would go on during the Second World War to play Rommel in the Hollywood film *Five Graves to Cairo*.

Dudley's first choice of name for the character Corelli was vetoed by the producer, who thought it might offend the family of the romantic novelist Marie Corelli and so he settled on Dr Morelle (he never had a Christian name), and devised for him a spoof *Who's Who* entry which appeared in the published version of the first series of Morelle stories:

> Educated Sorbonne, Rome, Vienna. M.D. Berne, 1923; Lecturer and Research Fellow, Sorbonne, 1928; Research Fellow, Salzburg Hospital, 1931; Lecturer in Medico-psychological aspects of criminology to New York Police Bureau, 1934; Lecturer and medico-psychiatrist to police bureaux of Geneva, Rome, Milan and Paris, 1935–1937. Published: miscellaneous papers on medical and scientific subjects. Writings for journal include 'Auguste Dupin versus Sherlock Holmes – a study in Ratiocination', *London Archive and Atlantic Weekly*, 1931. Address: 221 B Harley Street, London W.1. Recreations: Criminology and fencing (European Fencing Champion (epee) Switzerland, 1927–28–29.) Clubs: None.

A nice nod there to the master Conan Doyle in Morelle's London address. Like all great detectives, Morelle had a set of distinctive characteristics and idiosyncrasies. He smoked Egyptian Le Sphinx cigarettes through a cigarette holder, carried a swordstick and had no romantic or sexual interest in women.

Morelle's regular foil and sidekick was his fluttery and feather-brained secretary Miss Frayle whom he constantly bullied and belittled, a role Ernest Dudley created for Jane Grahame, a popular radio actress who happened to be his wife. Dudley recalled: 'One of the odd things about Dr Morelle was his relations with Miss Frayle. When the series first went out … what caused a minor sensation was the way Dr Morelle was so rude. Secretaries from all over the country wrote to say how horrible he was to poor Miss Frayle'.

Meet Dr Morelle, featured as a segment of *Monday Night at Eight*, initially ran from 20 July 1942 to 25 March 1943. It returned for another run from 15 April to 29 July 1946. The role of Dr Morelle was created by Dennis Arundell. He had played Lord Peter Wimsey on stage in 1936. But this was a very different kind of role. Ernest Dudley attributed much of the programme's success to Arundell's performance. Dudley recalled:

> Dennis Arundell was a very intelligent actor – he was an intellectual as an actor and as a person – and he brought to Dr Morelle a terrific air of knowledge and intellect … He had made a special hit as the murderer in *Gaslight*. He was a terrific actor in those sinister parts. He got it in his voice. At the same time he was sexually attractive to women.

Sadly no recordings of the series survive in the BBC Archives. The final run of *Meet Dr Morelle* (13 October 1947 to 26 March 1948) featured a new actor, Heron Carvic. Arundell had tired of playing the role but Carvic was selected for the similarity of his voice to Arundell's.

In 1957 Dudley revived Dr Morelle for a series of thirteen half-hour episodes on the BBC Light Programme called *A Case for Dr Morelle*. It ran from 23 April to 16 July 1957. The series was produced by Leslie Bridgmont and starred the well-known character actor Cecil Parker as Dr Morelle and Sheila Sim as Miss Frayle. It is the only series for which recordings survive in the archive. Dudley was happy with the longer running time as it gave him the chance to develop Dr Morelle and his methods and his relationship with Miss Frayle in greater detail than the original ten-minute format.

The milieu for the stories was – like so many detective series of the 1940s and 1950s – very largely middle-class. The stories frequently centred on murder, literally a matter of life and death in those years when murder was still a capital crime. Often Dr Morelle would be led into a case of detection by the problems of one of his patients, as in *A Confession of Guilt*. He used a classic combination of observation and deduction in tackling his cases, as in *The Black Ruby*. Dr Morelle frequently used his authority and his psychological knowledge to trick suspects into confessing as in *The Will*, *Act of Violence* and *The Wedding Dress*. He proved apparently supernatural events to be due to human agency in *The Black Ruby* and *The Wedding Dress*. He remained throughout cool and imperturbable, even when faced with the possibility of his own murder as he was when he investigated the mysterious death of the Baroness de Beauville at the Wigmore Hotel in *Alarm Call*.

The radio success of Dr Morelle inevitably led to his translation into other media. In 1949 Hammer, as part of their programme of filming radio successes, produced *Dr Morelle and The Case of the Missing Heiress*. Directed by Godfrey Grayson, it was scripted not by Ernest Dudley but by Ambrose Grayson and Roy Plomley and based in part on a play which did not involve Morelle. Although another radio favourite, Valentine Dyall, 'The Man in Black' played Morelle, he did not appear until halfway through the story which was for the most part a drab and dreary country house murder mystery. Dudley however did collaborate on a stage play *Dr Morelle* with Arthur Watkyn. It was produced at the Q Theatre in 1950 with Dennis Arundell returning to the role of Morelle and also directing. In addition Ernest Dudley wrote fourteen books chronicling the exploits of the doctor. Morelle was one of the most memorable of the British radio detectives and thrilled millions week after week with his unique combination of arrogance and omniscience.

Inspector Hornleigh Investigates achieved remarkable popularity during the 1930s. It began as a series of dramatic sketches which featured in *Monday Night at Seven*, being first heard on 31 May 1937. It consisted of Hornleigh and his assistant Sergeant Bingham questioning the witnesses to a crime. Hornleigh would deduce the identity of the criminal from a fatal slip made by a suspect and the audience would be invited to guess the solution which would be revealed at the end of the programme. The series was created by Hans Wolfgang Priwin, a refugee from Nazi Germany. Subsequently changing his name to John P. Wynn, he became a BBC stalwart, devising long-running quizzes such as *Brain of Britain* and thriller series like *Inspector Scott Investigates*. Hornleigh was played by S.J. Warmington, who was killed in the London Blitz in 1941, and Bingham by Ewart Scott. The popularity of the character led to a series of stories in the *London* magazine, a stage play starring John Longden in 1938 and three films.

Inspector Hornleigh (1938), scripted by Bryan Edgar Wallace, son of the more famous Edgar, and directed by experienced American B-picture director Eugene Forde was a thoroughly entertaining detective mystery which conformed to the familiar format – the committing of the crime, the questioning of the witnesses and the fatal slip by which Hornleigh identified the culprit. It all hinged on the intriguing plot premise of the theft of the budget box of the Chancellor of the Exchequer just before he is due to deliver the budget. Subsequently three of the members of the gang responsible are murdered. Hornleigh successfully solves all the crimes. The main difference in the films was the characterization. Where on the radio both inspector and sergeant were played straight and spoke conventional English, on film Hornleigh was portrayed as a lugubrious but canny cockney by Gordon Harker and Bingham as a dimwitted, wild-eyed, accident-prone Scotsman by Alistair Sim. One of the principal themes of all three films was the comic byplay between the two of them.

The remaining two films were both directed by Walter Forde (no relation to Eugene), a master of the comedy thriller genre. *Inspector Hornleigh on Holiday* (1939) was scripted by Frank Launder and Sidney Gilliat and began with Hornleigh and Bingham staying at the amusingly observed Balmoral Guest House in storm-lashed Brighthaven. They become involved in the investigations into the murder of a fellow guest. This results in the uncovering of an insurance swindle in which dead bodies from the Queen Anne hospital are substituted for those of the insured members of the Chelsea Bridge and Social Club in faked accidents. The brains behind the operation turns out to be the matron, who is a man in drag.

By the time of *Inspector Hornleigh Goes To It* (US: *Mail Train*) (1940), the war was on and Hornleigh and Bingham are assigned to investigate pilfering from army stores and stumble on a ring of fifth columnists, which includes a chatty barmaid, a dentist and a public school headmaster. It culminates in an exciting finale on the night mail from Carlisle – with footage from the celebrated GPO documentary *Night Mail* – as the gang are rounded up. Val Guest and J.O.C. Orton scripted from a story by Frank Launder.

Dick Barton was a radio phenomenon. It was Norman Collins, the newly appointed Controller of the Light Programme, a man with a populist understanding of audience tastes, who in 1946 conceived of the idea of a daily fifteen-minute serial of the 'cloak and dagger' kind. John MacMillan, an Australian who had before the war worked for Radio Luxembourg and Radio Normandy, was appointed project director and he called in Martyn C. Webster, celebrated as the producer of the *Paul Temple* serials, to assemble the team. Webster selected Neil Tuson as producer and Edward J. Mason and Geoffrey Webb to write the scripts. It was to be produced, like the first *Paul Temple* serials in Birmingham, perhaps to distance Broadcasting House in London from such low-brow fare.

Detailed biographies were constructed for the leading characters, Dick Barton, and his sidekicks, 'Snowy' White and 'Jock' Anderson. Dick Barton was born in 1912 in High Wycombe and educated at King Edward Grammar School, High Wycombe, and Glasgow University. Before the war he had been an engineer on large-scale construction projects. During the war, he served with the commandos, winning the Military Cross and being demobbed as a captain on 5 November 1945. As a former officer at a loose end after demobilisation and seeking excitement, Barton exactly resembled Bulldog Drummond at the end of the First World War. Like Drummond, Barton gathered sidekicks around him. But there was a difference. Drummond and his chums were public school educated, upper-class gentlemen. Barton, an undoubted officer and a gentleman, was a grammar school boy and his sidekicks were working-class NCOs.; cockney 'Snowy' White (who had been his platoon sergeant in the commandos) and Scotsman 'Jock' Anderson, a sergeant in the 51st Highland Division, their accents easily differentiated from the cultured received pronunciation tones of Barton. The facetious bantering style Barton adopted towards arch-villain Wilhelm Kramer exactly echoed Bulldog Drummond's approach to his arch-enemy

Carl Peterson. The final element, the theme tune, was the inspired choice of Neil Tuson, selected from the gramophone library of pre-recorded music, Charles Williams' 'The Devil's Gallop'.

The series *Dick Barton – Special Agent* made its debut on the Light Programme at 6.45 p.m. on 7 October 1946 and ran for six months each year until it bowed out on 30 March 1951 after 711 episodes. During the run there were three Dick Bartons. The first was Noel Johnson, who left after a pay dispute and soon turned up on Radio Luxembourg as Dan Dare. The second from 7 February 1949 was Duncan Carse, in real life an Arctic explorer and oceanographer. He was succeeded on 14 April 1950 by Gordon Davies, a controversial choice as he had been a conscientious objector during the war. He played the role for the rest of the run. John Mann and Alex McCrindle played 'Snowy' and 'Jock' respectively throughout the series.

Scriptwriter Geoffrey Webb recalled the constraints under which they worked:

> There must be a story – the stronger the better – which can be got across to the listener in dialogue form. The dialogue must say all that the author intends it to say, and at the same time to be pronounceable … Sound effects and speech are the only media available to the radio writer to get his story across. He must remember those limits when he is writing, bearing in mind that his material impinges on only one sense, the ear … one of the primary requirements of the thriller serial is that the story must move along at a cracking pace … Barton is said to be the fastest thing in radio – American radio included – and this is undoubtedly one of the secrets of his universal appeal … An effort is made to design each programme in such a way that there are at least three dramatic peaks in the fifteen minutes, so that a dramatic intensity/time graph would look roughly like a letter 'W'.[24]

By January 1947 *Dick Barton* had become a massive hit, with 15 million listeners. It became clear that it appealed particularly to children and juveniles, much as the Sexton Blake stories had when published weekly before the war in *Union Jack* and later *Detective Weekly*. But this was a signal for the beginning of criticism of the series for keeping children from doing their prep, feeding them with sensationalism and love of violence and inculcating hatred of foreigners, many of the same criticisms that were attracted by popular Victorian melodramas, 'penny dreadfuls' and Hollywood films.

An array of teachers, probation officers, magistrates and chief constables began bombarding the press with denunciations of the series. Other voices were raised in its support, among them other magistrates, directors of education, medical officers, psychiatrists, the writers of newspaper editorials, and Herbert Morrison, Lord President of the Council in the Labour government.[25] The BBC took fright and prepared a code of conduct for writers of the serial, known informally as 'The Thirteen Commandments'. First issued on 27 August 1947, it insisted that Barton be intelligent as well as hardhitting, should only use force as a last resort, never commit a criminal offence, should never lie, should not indulge in sex, drink or swearing. Barton's violence was to be limited to 'clean socks on the jaw'. He should not involve innocent members of the public. The villains should avoid sadistic behaviour. Horrific and supernatural effects should be avoided. Political themes were 'unpopular as well as being occasionally embarrassing' and should be avoided. A ban on the use of cut-throat razors was added later.[26] The new guidelines meant the elimination of Barton's girlfriend, Jean Hunter.

Barton had his enemies even within the BBC. There were those who thought it too downmarket for such an august organization. Director-General Sir William Haley was advocating its termination as early as March 1947 and Val Gielgud, Head of Drama, described it as 'a purely mechanical piece of puerility' in December 1949.[27] Eventually however, Barton was killed off. *Dick Barton* was doomed by rising production costs, the continued misgivings of senior BBC executives, the prevailing cultural climate of concern with the moral panic about juvenile delinquency and the appointment of the Beveridge Committee in 1949 to consider the future of broadcasting, which had the BBC fearful of accusations of 'dumbing down'.

The Barton production team moved on to create a very different daily serial, that 'everyday story of country folk', *The Archers*, which following its debut in 1951 is still running and still popular today. But Dick Barton left some cultural echoes. There was a Dick Barton annual in 1949 and a book by Geoffrey Webb about the making of the serial. Barton appeared in the comic *The Comet* in 1953. In 1977 Elwyn Jones, the respected scriptwriter of *Z-Cars, Softly, Softly,* and *Barlow at Large*, novelised three of the earliest *Barton* scripts in the volume, *Dick Barton – Special Agent.* In 1979 Southern Television produced a twenty-six part series of fifteen-minute episodes of a *Dick Barton* series, set in the late 1940s. It avoided parody and captured something of the tone and flavour of the radio series. A series of *Dick Barton* send-ups were produced on the stage between 1999 and 2003.

It is a measure of the contempt in which the BBC's flagship serial was held within the corporation that only a handful of episodes were preserved for the archives. When in 1972 it was decided to revive the first *Barton* serial as part of the celebrations of the BBC's Silver Jubilee, it was discovered that nothing survived from 1946. So a new production was made with the original cast reassembled and Raymond Raikes, who had worked on the original series, directing. When in 1989 BBC audio wanted to release a version on audiotape commercially, they discovered that yet again the BBC had failed to keep the remake. Fortunately Miss Pat Hetherington of Carlisle, a lifelong Barton devotee, had taped it and her recording was able to be released commercially and has been preserved for posterity. It is a superb example of the serial form, gripping, fastmoving, atmospheric and absolutely entrancing.

Bulldog Drummond, who first appeared in print in 1920, had been a regular figure on the screen in the United Kingdom and the United States throughout the 1930s, incarnated by a variety of actors, including Ronald Colman, Ralph Richardson, Ray Milland, John Lodge and John Howard. The radio success of Dick Barton meant that the cinema inevitably beckoned for this latter-day Drummond and Hammer acquired the film rights to the series. There were to be three low-budget Barton films which all achieved box-office success. Hammer retained 'The Devil's Gallop' theme music but dispensed with the radio cast entirely. The first of the trilogy, *Dick Barton – Special Agent* (1948), shot at Marylebone Studios, one of the smallest studios in the United Kingdom, and on location at Chichester Harbour, is ludicrously inept, deficient in almost every department. A thriller needs pace, action and thrills. This has none. It was shot on a handful of cheap sets with a startlingly talentless cast, most of whom either overact or fail to act at all. The score is shaky and tinny; the action scenes dismally staged. Jock and Snowy are used as comic relief and involved in deeply unfunny slapstick sequences. This almost total failure can be laid at the door of the director and co-writer Alfred Goulding, who was an extraordinary choice to make a thriller. Goulding, an Australian and former vaudevillian, had had a career in Hollywood and the United Kingdom almost entirely confined to comedy. In silent days he had worked with Harold Lloyd, Hal Roach and Mack Sennett. In the United Kingdom in the 1930s he had directed a succession of leading comics: Sydney Howard (*Splinters in the Air*, 1937), Claude Hulbert (*Olympic Honeymoon*, 1936), Leslie Fuller (*One Good Turn*, 1936), Stanley Holloway (*Sam Small Leaves Town*, 1937). His most notable achievement had been the Laurel and Hardy comedy, *A Chump at Oxford* (1940). The script, co-written by Alan Stranks, best known for the light-hearted *PC 49* radio series, featured a group of former Nazis, posing as Swedish scientists, who plan to introduce cholera bacilli into the British water supply and wipe out the population. In acknowledgement of his dedicated schoolboy following, the script included an intrepid schoolboy Snub, who reads about Dick in his comics and helps him out on his mission. During the course of the film Dick suffers attacks by sniper, poison dart and acid, and being tied up – for no apparent reason – inside a suit of armour. He survives all this but not the dismal writing and direction. It only has to be compared to the splendid Republic serials of the 1940s or the Paramount Bulldog Drummond series of B pictures in the 1930s to see how defective *Dick Barton* is. Its Hollywood counterparts had speed, pace, style, vigorously staged action scenes and competent acting. *Dick Barton* had none of these attributes.

There was a change of director for the next two films. Godfrey Grayson, a wartime documentarist who had directed the location scenes on the Gainsborough thriller *Snowbound*, was just embarking on a long and undistinguished career directing B-picture detective stories and thrillers first for Hammer and later the Danzigers. He brought with him his brothers Ambrose, who provided the stories, and Rupert, who wrote the scores. The next film, *Dick Barton at Bay* (1950), made second but released third, at least dispensed with the comedy but it also dispensed with Jock Anderson and Jean Hunter, who had both featured in the first film. It was shot like the first film at Marylebone Studios. Like *Dick Barton – Special Agent* it included an enterprising schoolboy Tommy to help Dick. This film centred on the kidnapping of inventor Professor Mitchell and his new death ray by monocled, shaven-headed, piano-playing masterspy Sergei Volkoff. Taking over the lighthouse at Beachy Head, Volkoff plans to use the ray to shoot down the British defence mission heading for a vital meeting in a fleet of planes and thus ensure world domination for his country which is not named but is self-evidently Russia. Dick foils his plans and Volkoff falls to his death from the lighthouse. Slow, stagey and badly acted, it did at least include an atmospheric chase through the streets of Limehouse as a secret agent (played by a youthful Patrick McNee) is tracked and killed, a murderous attack on Dick by a Chinaman and the inventive use of the lighthouse setting for the denouement.

By far the best of the trilogy was *Dick Barton Strikes Back* (1949), shot third but released second. Interiors were taken at Viking Studios, Kensington, but there was extensive location-shooting: at London Airport, London Zoo and in Blackpool. This had Dick, once again accompanied only by Snowy, on the trail of a weapon more deadly than the atomic bomb. It turns out to be a gigantic tuning fork emitting sonic rays which shrivel the brain and kill people while leaving the buildings standing. Two villages are wiped out before Dick and Snowy track the villains to Blackpool where they set up their weapon on top of the Tower, planning to wipe out the town's population as part of the plan for world domination by an unnamed country. It is once again evidently Russia as the plot is masterminded by a renegade peer Lord Armadale (James Raglan), who describes himself as 'a fellow traveller', and who is assisted by a suave and sinister foreigner Fouracada (Sebastian Cabot) and a band of circus gypsies. For once the fights are convincing, the villains are competently acted and there is a genuinely exciting finale with Dick clambering over Blackpool Tower before knocking Lord Armadale down a lift-shaft. Evidently Grayson's documentary background came into its own when filming the vivid and realistic scenes around the Tower, Winter Gardens and Golden Mile in Blackpool. Unlike the radio series, in which politics was taboo, the last two Barton films can be seen as part of the United Kingdom's contribution to Cold War propaganda.

The greatest asset of the series is Don Stannard, clean-cut, square-jawed and with an appropriately straightfaced, urgent delivery: 'Whatever devilry you are up to, you won't get away with it this time', etc. He was about to begin shooting a fourth film, *Dick Barton in Africa*, when he was killed in a car crash in 1949 at the age of 44. It was decided that the series could not continue without him and it was terminated. Interestingly three of the four titles in the series, *Dick Barton at Bay*, *Dick Barton Strikes Back* and the unmade *Dick Barton in Africa* had titles echoing the 1930s Bulldog Drummond film series, suggesting that this is the model the film-makers were seeking to emulate.

Where Paul Temple began on radio and then appeared in published novelisations of the serials, Philip Odell began in a novel, moved to radio but returned to print in novelisations of the serials, which Collins the publisher promoted as 'famous from radio thrillers'. Philip Odell was a very different detective from Paul Temple, more in the American hardboiled model than the gentlemanly English sleuth. There were strong echoes of Chandler's Philip Marlowe. But he proved very popular with BBC listeners. He was originally created by Lester Powell in a 1946 novel *A Count of Six*, a powerful and exciting thriller in which ex-Office of Strategic Services (OSS) agent Odell goes undercover in post-war Germany to track down a new and deadly bacteria gas developed by the Nazis which has gone missing. Transformed into a private detective based in London, he then featured in seven serial plays. The first was *Lady in a Fog*, an eight-part serial, which began on 6 October 1947. He returned in *The Odd Story of Simon Ode* (1948), *Spot the Lady* (1949), *Love from Leighton Buzzard* (1950), *The Lady on the Screen* (1952), *Test Room Eight* (1958) and *Tea on the Island* (1961). The original *Lady in a Fog* was remade in 1958. Martyn C. Webster produced both versions. Lester Powell introduced the character to listeners in a *Radio Times* article (5 October 1947):

> The character I dislike most in all fiction is the 'mastermind detective'. I find him unreal, frequently a prig and always a bore. Consequently Philip Odell … is not a mastermind. He makes mistakes in a human way and puzzles out the solution of a

problem much as you or I would. He is, I hope, a person you can believe in … He is no mastermind but he has a good mind in a literal sense. Odell is humanitarian, interested and concerned in people. He has an instinctive understanding of their foibles and motives and neither condemns nor approves. In *Lady in a Fog* you can see him at his best … You can hear – and *see* (for Odell will narrate the story in the manner of a movie camera) all that he hears and sees.

Odell is Irish, son of a Dublin schoolmaster, educated at Trinity College Dublin, with a view to a medical career. But with the outbreak of the Spanish Civil War, he joined the International Brigade and fought for the republican cause. After the victory of France, he emigrated to the United States, became a government agent and joined the OSS, serving in North Africa and France. His plan was to return to Ireland after the war but it was at this point that he was diverted by the *Lady in the Fog*, which led to a career in England as a private detective.

Robert Beatty, the rugged Canadian actor, was cast as Philip Odell and played him with a mixed Irish-American accent and an appropriately convincing tough guy attitude. *Lady in a Fog* saw him enlisted by the beautiful Heather McMara to solve the suspicious death of her brother and this leads him into a satisfyingly complex tale of murder, blackmail and revenge, involving Odell being incarcerated in and then escaping from a private lunatic asylum where he has been taken and drugged, like Marlowe in *Farewell My Lovely* (similarly the hothouse opening of *Simon Ode* recalled the opening of Chandler's *The Big Sleep*). Beatty played Odell in all the radio serials and Lester Powell dedicated *Shadow Play*, the 1949 novelisation of *The Odd Story of Simon Ode*, to Beatty.

The series inspired only one film, the inevitable Hammer B picture, rechristened *Lady in the Fog* (US title: *Scotland Yard Inspector*) (1952), directed by Sam Newfield and scripted by Orville H. Hampton. Reducing the four hours of the serial to a mere eighty-two minutes, it was done in typical low-budget style with an underpopulated nightclub, a single slow-moving police car and an imported American star Cesar Romero playing Odell as a trench-coated reporter rather than private eye trading wisecracks with the plodding Scotland Yard men. Although it included the murders, the blackmail and the insane asylum, there were many changes in the characters, their motives and their relationships. The radio version remained infinitely more satisfactory.

The most unlikely of the original radio detectives was the humble bobby on the beat, PC 49. He was unlikely because the dominant cultural tradition in the United Kingdom was until the 1950s the stereotype of the lovable, accident-prone, comically incompetent bobby. This stretched back to Gilbert and Sullivan's chorus of policemen in *The Pirates of Penzance* lugubriously singing 'A policeman's lot is not a 'appy one' and it included the popular music hall comedians Sandy Powell and Robb Wilton bungling their police duties and the succession of British comedy stars who have donned the blue uniform to play comic constables – Jack Hulbert, Stanley Holloway, Will Hay, George Formby, Gracie Fields, Norman Wisdom and the 'Carry On' team. It is a tradition summed up by Charles Penrose's perennially popular record 'The Laughing Policeman'.

This consistent, lovably comic image was an important means of defusing discontent. For there was a longstanding suspicion and hatred of the police – the 'plague of blue locusts' as they were known – in some sections of the working class. But another reason why the police were so often comic was that they were themselves working-class and before the 1940s in popular culture the working classes were almost invariably comic. The amateur sleuths were serious because they were – by and large – gentlemen and it was they who dominated the crime-fighting scene on film, stage and radio. This was changed by the advent of PC 49. PC 49 was Archibald Berkeley-Willoughby, educated at public school and trained at Hendon Police College, and thus a far cry from the old, slow-witted, slow-talking, 'Allo, allo, allo, what's going on here then' cockney copper.

The Adventures of PC 49 ran on radio from 1947 to 1953, 112 episodes in all, and it is still fondly remembered today even though only three episodes are known to survive in the archives. The creator of the series was Alan Stranks. Born in Melbourne, Australia, he had begun his career as a cub reporter before turning to writing for Australian radio. Migrating with his family to England, he wrote several radio plays for the BBC before coming up with the idea for PC 49. He explained in an article in 1952 how he came up with the idea:

> One morning I went to New Scotland Yard to make inquiries about a point of police routine. When I arrived at the yard, I was greeted by a sergeant on duty at the door … 'So, you're one of the blokes who writes all this nonsense about special agents, private investigators and such-whats, are you?' I admitted that I was. 'Well, you just listen to me!' he barked. 'Don't you think it's about time some of you writers gave credit where credit is really due?' Slightly puzzled, I asked him to explain what he meant. 'It's about time you realised', he announced sternly, 'that almost ninety-nine percent of the crimes committed in this country are solved by the keen observation and the devotion to duty of the ordinary bloke on the beat … Give the 'bobby' a break – there's no-one deserves it better' … As I walked along the Thames Embankment twenty minutes later, … I was excitedly turning over in my mind an entirely new character … a plain, everyday policeman … I realised that in spite of the dull routine of 'pounding the pavement' and 'bashing the beat' there were many moments in a policeman's life which could be extremely exciting. I learned that in the history of the Force, both in peace and war, many had been killed or gravely injured in their service to the public … Before twenty-four hours had passed the first P.C. 49 adventure was written.[28]

The title probably derives from the popular Edwardian music hall song *P.C. 49*, recorded by Harry Fay in 1910, and recalling the misadventures of a comic cockney copper.

The series was produced by Vernon Harris of the Variety department. He selected Brian Reece for the title role after he had played a role in Harris's production for radio of the musical *Bless the Bride*, displaying the appropriate light touch for the part, and Joy Shelton for his fiancée Joan Carr after his wife heard her step at the last minute into a role in a live production without rehearsal and deliver a faultless performance.[29] The regular cast was completed by Leslie Perrins as Detective Inspector Wilson and Eric Phillips as Detective Sergeant Wright.

It was a very happy show to work on, as Joy Shelton recalled.[30] She thought Brian Reece perfect as Archie: 'Brian had a lovely quality – he was not an actory-actor. He was a real person … He was a tall, gangly person, so full of energy and life'. The regulars became like a family. The broadcaster Susan Stranks, Alan's daughter, confirms that 'the cast was a very happy mob'. Joy Shelton also loved working with Vernon Harris, who as a director was 'marvellous. He was warm … he was funny … he knew exactly what he wanted … ace on timing … but wonderful with discipline. If the need arose, he could suddenly come down on you'. This was particularly true in the case of 'corpsing', when actors got fits of the giggles. Each episode took a day and a half to make: one day to rehearse with recording the next morning.

Archie's principal ambition was to prove himself a detective. But whenever he got the chance, his eager-beaver enthusiasm and tendency to blunder into dangerous situations exasperated his superior officers. Despite the comic banter, Archie had a shrewd brain and regularly applied the classic detection techniques of observation and deduction, as in the surviving episode *The Case of the Black Diamonds*. P.C.49 also had a social conscience, regularly coming to the aid of ex-convicts and prisoners' families, as in *The Case of the Perfect Fiddle*. The mixture of comedy and thrills that Alan Stranks achieved in his scripts was one of the keys to the success of the series as Susan Stranks recalled: 'The humour was generated not only by the plots but through the relationship of Brian Reece and Joy Shelton and the relations with the Chief Inspector and Detective Sergeant were also quite humorous. It made for a very good light comedy presentation of sometimes quite serious stuff'.[31] Alan Stranks was a stickler for research, making friends of senior officers at Scotland Yard as well as underworld figures, in his pursuit of authentic stories.

The popularity of the series is evidenced by the way its catchphrases entered the language: 'Out you go, 49' and 'Oh, my Sunday helmet' in particular. Like

Dick Barton the series became particularly popular with children. So although it was originally broadcast in the late evening, the BBC repeated it in the early evening for the younger listeners. This popularity with children led to the newly launched *Eagle* comic hiring Alan Stranks to script a comic strip of PC 49, which ran from 1950 to 1957. But being a boys' comic, it was deemed wise to drop the romance with Joan and substitute PC 49's involvement with a Boys Club, to provide identification figures for the young readers.[32]

There were also two films from Hammer, *The Adventures of P.C. 49* (1949) and *A Case for P.C. 49* (1951). Both films were scripted by Vernon Harris and Alan Stranks, the first directed by Godfrey Grayson and the second by Francis Searle. Both were crisply shot but had the usual hallmarks of the low-budget B-picture, small casts and limited sets. Both were also much more violent than the radio series. In *The Adventures of P.C. 49*, PC 49 goes undercover to expose a ruthless gang hijacking lorry loads of bonded whisky and cigarettes, killing a night watchman and driver in the process. In *A Case for P.C. 49*, PC 49 investigates the murders of a millionaire and a gang boss and the framing of an ex-convict for the crimes. But neither was entirely satisfactory. In *The Adventures of P.C. 49* only Eric Phillips from the regular cast was on hand. Brian Reece was unavailable because of stage commitments and Hugh Latimer played Archie with Patricia Cutts as Joan. But it signally lacked the humour of the radio version. For *A Case for P.C. 49* Brian Reece and Joy Shelton were back in their familiar roles and there was humour but the story was uninteresting.

Alan Stranks undertook a punishing work schedule. For alongside *P.C.49*, he was also scripting during 1951–52 another radio police series, *Flint of the Flying Squad*, starring Bruce Seton, as well as his *Eagle* comic strips and four PC 49 annuals. In addition, he was a busy and successful song lyricist, one of whose songs 'All' won the British heat of the Eurovision song contest. Susan Stranks recalled his work routine: 'He was a great night bird. He always worked to deadlines. He would doodle a lot putting off the time when he had to commit to a plot. He always used to leave it to the last minute'. She recalled him pacing the back garden of their house chainsmoking as he thought out his plots. Alan Stranks died while on holiday in Spain, still only in his fifties. PC 49 is his lasting legacy. PC 49 looked back to the musical comedy policemen of the interwar years but also forward to the next great development in the dramatic representation of the police – social realism. In January 1950, three years after PC 49 made his radio debut, a film was released which permanently changed the popular image of the police. It was *The Blue Lamp*, whose central figure PC George Dixon was gunned down by hoodlum Dirk Bogarde halfway through the film. In 1955 Dixon was revived by his creator Ted Willis on television and Jack Warner returned to his film role and was to play it continuously until 1976; in all some 434 episodes. The series confirmed the transformation of the cultural image of the police. But we should not forget that it was PC 49 on radio who paved the way for the revaluation of the 'ordinary copper patrolling his beat'.

Notes

1   J. Fred MacDonald, *Don't Touch That Dial!: Radio Programming in American Life, from 1920–1960*, Chicago: Nelson Hall, 1996, p. 155.
2   Howard Haycraft (ed.), *The Art of the Mystery Story*, New York: Grosset and Dunlap, 1946, p. 304.
3   John Dunning, *The Encyclopedia of Old-Time Radio*, New York: Oxford University Press, 1998, p. 277.
4   For the history of 'The Shadow' see Walter B. Gibson, *The Shadow Scrapbook*, New York: Harcourt Brace Jovanovich, 1979, and Thomas J. Shimeld, *Walter B. Gibson and The Shadow*, Jefferson, NC: McFarland, 2003.
5   Raymond Chandler, *The Simple Art of Murder*, New York: Vintage Books, 1988, pp. 14–15.
6   Chandler, *The Simple Art of Murder*, p. 18.
7   Martin Grams Jr., *The Radio Adventures of Sam Spade*, Arlington, VA: OTR Publishing, 2007, p. 34. See this book for a full history of Sam Spade on radio.
8   Dunning, *Encyclopedia of Old-Time Radio*, p. 14.
9   Quoted in Diane Johnson, *Dashiell Hammett: A Life*, New York: Random House, 1983, p. 199.
10 For an excellent account of detectives in the cinema, see William K. Everson, *The Detective in Film*, Secaucus, NJ: Citadel, 1972.
11 For a full account of the media career of Perry Mason see J. Dennis Bounds, *Perry Mason: The Authorship and Reproduction of a Popular Hero*, Westport, CT: Greenwood Press, 1996.
12 William Vivian Butler, *The Durable Desperadoes*, London: Macmillan, 1973, pp. 115–32, 206–14, 227–37.
13 For a full account of The Saint's media career see Burl Barer, *The Saint: A Complete History*, Jefferson, NC: McFarland, 1993.
14 For a full account of Charlie Chan in films see Ken Hanke, *Charlie Chan at the Movies*, Jefferson, NC: McFarland, 2004.
15 On the career of Jack Webb and *Dragnet* see Daniel Moyer and Eugene Alvarez, *Just the Facts, Ma'am: The Authorized Biography of Jack Webb*, Santa Ana, CA: Seven Locks Press, 2001.
16 For a complete history of Sexton Blake see Norman Wright and David Ashford, *Sexton Blake: A Celebration of the Great Detective*, Maidstone: Museum Press, 1994.
17 David Farrar, *No Royal Road*, Eastbourne: Mortimer Publications, 1947, pp. 127–8.

18   Wright and Ashford, *Sexton Blake*, pp. 150–2.

19   Author's interview with Ernest Dudley, broadcast on BBC Radio 4, *The Radio Detectives*, 3 June 1998.

20   Author's interviews with Enyd Williams and Peter Coke, broadcast on 20 May 1998 on BBC Radio 4, *The Radio Detectives*. All quotes from Enyd Williams and Peter Coke are taken from these interviews. Only ten of the original twenty-four serials survive but Patrick Rayner has billiantly recreated three of the lost serials with Crawford Logan and Gerda Stevenson.

21   Marjorie Westbury interview in *Dick Barton and All That*, BBC Radio 4, 31 October 1982.

22   Francis Durbridge, *Send for Paul Temple*, London: Chivers Press, 1992, pp. 27–8.

23   Author's interview with Ernest Dudley, broadcast on 8 June 1999, BBC Radio 4, *The Radio Detectives*. All quotes from Ernest Dudley about Dr Morelle come from this interview.

24   Geoffrey Webb, *The Inside Story of Dick Barton*, London: Convoy Publications, 1950, pp. 50, 52, 54.

25   Webb, *The Inside Story of Dick Barton*, pp. 110–45; James Chapman, '"Honest British Violence": Critical Responses to *Dick Barton – Special Agent* (1946–1951', *Historical Journal of Film, Radio and Television*, 26 (October 2006), pp. 537–59.

26   Chapman, 'Honest British Violence', pp. 558–9; Webb, *The Inside Story of Dick Barton*, pp. 43–9.

27   Chapman, 'Honest British Violence', p. 540.

28   Alan Stranks, *On Duty with P.C. 49*, London: Juvenile Productions Ltd., 1952, p. 94–6.

29   Vernon Harris interview in *Dick Barton and All That*, BBC Radio 4, 31 October 1982.

30   Author's interview with Joy Shelton, 12 August 1999.

31   Author's interview with Susan Stranks broadcast on BBC Radio 4, *The Radio Detectives*, 15 June 1999.

32   Author's interview with Norman Wright broadcast on BBC Radio 4, *The Radio Detectives*, 15 June 1999.

5

Broadcasting films

By common consent, the most popular and the best produced dramatic show on American radio was *The Lux Radio Theatre*. It ran from 1934 to 1955, regularly won awards as the best dramatic show on the air and at its height reached an estimated forty million listeners weekly. The show was the brainchild of the J. Walter Thompson advertising agency, who were promoting Lever Brothers products (notably Lux Flakes and Lux Soap) and had regularly been using stars' endorsements of the products in advertising. Thompsons suggested that Lever Bros sponsor an hour-long dramatic show which would adapt leading Broadway plays and feature popular stars of the day. Lever Brothers agreed and the *Lux Radio Theatre* was born.[1]

The first programme was broadcast on the NBC network on 14 October 1934. It was a dramatization of Austin Strong's play *Seventh Heaven* and featured film stars Miriam Hopkins and John Boles in the leading roles. The show was produced in New York, hosted by a fictitious Broadway producer, Douglass Garrick (played by John Anthony). The first season of the show featured a good selection of Broadway plays and a good range of leading stage stars (Leslie Howard, Helen Hayes, Paul Muni, Pauline Lord and Ina Claire, among them). The first series won the Radio Editors of America Award for best dramatic programme.

But the show went out at 2.30 p.m. on Sunday, which was not considered a prime slot, and so for the second season which began on 28 July 1935, the show moved to the CBS network and was assigned the prime slot of 9.00 p.m. on Monday evening, which it was to hold for the next eighteen years. The second season began to place greater emphasis on the performance of Hollywood film stars rather than Broadway stage stars and the plays starred such performers as Joan Crawford, Bette Davis, Clark Gable, Edward G. Robinson and Douglas Fairbanks Jr. But it was a major problem getting Hollywood stars to travel to New York for a one-off radio show and in 1935 the ratings began to slip. Danny Danker, a Thompson executive, suggested a drastic solution – moving the entire show to Hollywood and adapting current movie successes with top stars. So in 1936 production of the show moved to Hollywood and it was recorded live in the Music Box Theatre on Hollywood Boulevard before an audience of a thousand; it moved in 1940 to the Vine St Playhouse but remained a live show. One of the reasons it was so good was a generous budget which allowed five days of rehearsal, twice as long as any other show, an orchestra of twenty-five musicians conducted by 20th Century Fox's musical director Louis Silvers, and fees of $5,000 a show for the top stars. The studios cooperated fully, letting the programme have their scripts cheaply, releasing their stars to appear and regarding it basically as a comparatively cheap way of advertising their films to a mass audience. The announcement with which the show now began, 'Lux presents Hollywood', emphasized the movie angle and although a sprinkling of plays was still done, the majority of the shows were now adaptations of films, if possible with their original stars but if not possible, with different stars who give us in effect an alternative history of Hollywood. The move from New York to Hollywood was epoch-making. Within a year it was reported that 90% of the top radio shows had also relocated from New York to Hollywood. The transformation of the *Lux Radio Theatre* resulted in an immediate doubling of its audience.

The *Lux Radio Theatre* differed in two important ways from the films it dramatized. Although Hollywood had superseded Broadway as a popular attraction, the show retained a theatrical structure. It was performed in three acts, the host referred to 'our play', to the curtain rising, to actors coming to the footlights to take a curtain call and so forth. It indicates both that the theatrical structure retained prestige and that a three-act format allowed for commercials without compromising the flow of the dramatic action. Second, the show had a host who narrated the story, covering the inevitable gaps that occurred when a visual drama was transposed into an aural medium. But he also introduced and chatted to the stars, promoted the product and created an intimate feel without ever losing a sense of authority. The programme allowed the listeners vicarious participation in the romance and glamour of Hollywood as stars endorsed their household goods like Lux flakes, there were interval interviews with backroom staff of the movies – screen test directors, historical advisers, wardrobe directors, composers, dance directors – and there was friendly banter and the use of nicknames between the host and the stars. It all created the 'illusion of intimacy' that fuelled celebrity culture.

One of the programme's major assets was its host, this time a real-life presenter and not a fictional producer. It was Cecil B. De Mille, who was billed, presented and promoted as the producer of the show. It was a masterly choice for De Mille was one of the very few film directors who was known to audiences as a personality. Most of them were merely names among the screen credits. De Mille, who had been directing films since 1914, was a showman and a self-publicist, an ex-actor and playwright, who self-consciously acted out the role of the 'great director'. He was associated with spectacle, grandeur and the epic and his name lent some prestige to the show. De Mille took to the role of producer of the *Lux Radio Theatre* with great aplomb. For much of the show's run, the fiction was maintained that De Mille actually produced the show. He did not. He was only its host and presenter. But reviewers sometimes wrote about the 'De Mille touch' in the production and it is clear that the fiction was widely believed. The effective producer was Danny Danker who assembled an expert radio production team. De Mille adored his role on the show and wrote about it in his autobiography in a way which gives us an insight into the power and importance of American radio in its heyday:

> If we had been foolish enough to retire in 1935, I wonder if I might have missed the experience which brought me closer to the American people than anything else I have ever done. It began in 1936, when I was approached by representatives of Lever Brothers, the powerful international firm of soap makers, with an idea. Their idea was a new radio programme. Lever Brothers thought, very accurately as it turned out, that the programme would sell soap. I saw in it an opportunity to bring the living theatre, good drama, possibly great drama, into the living-rooms of American homes; and I hasten to add that I was not repelled by the salary offered me if I would take part in this enterprise – $2,000 a week. In the 1930s, radio was almost, if not quite, as bad a word among motion picture people as television was to become later; but I thought, also accurately I believe, that the proposed radio programme would help, not hurt, motion pictures, for its basis was to be the dramatization of stories that had been filmed, played by actors and actresses from motion pictures. The first broadcast of the Lux Radio Theatre went on air on June 1, 1936, when I first spoke the words 'Greetings from Hollywood, ladies and gentlemen' … Week after week, we had a live audience of about 1,000 people, to give the players and the director the lift that only a living audience can provide. But the great audience of the Lux Radio Theatre was America. For nearly nine years after that June evening in 1936, I spoke 'Greetings from Hollywood' on Monday nights to an ever-growing audience, in homes across the whole broad country, in hospitals, later in camps and installations of the armed forces, wherever there was a radio within range of the Columbia Broadcasting System; and every Monday night after an hour of good entertainment, I signed the programme off the air with 'this is Cecil B. De Mille saying goodnight to you from Hollywood'. On peak Mondays there were something like forty million listening to the Lux Hour. I like big numbers; but what the Lux programme meant to me cannot be measured in any numbers. It meant families in Maine and Kansas and Idaho finishing the dishes or the school work or the evening chores in time to gather round their radios. It meant the shut-ins, the invalid, the

blind, the very young, and the very old who had no other taste of the theatre. It meant people, not in the mass but individuals, who did me the honour of inviting me into their homes; people to whom I was no longer a name filtered through the wordage of imaginative press agents, but a person whom they knew. And I would be less human than even my critics would allow, if I were not touched when people, recognizing me on trains or in stores or on the street, in almost any city I visited, told me they liked those Monday evenings and my 'greetings' and 'goodnights'. It cost me very much more than $100,000 a year when a letter came to me in 1944, telling me that I could no longer conduct the Lux Radio Theatre.[2]

What happened was that in 1944 the American Federation of Radio Artists (AFRA) decided to fight Proposition 12 which was due to appear on the Californian Election Ballot. Proposition 12 allowed every Californian as of right to obtain a job without first joining a union. AFRA levied a one dollar fee from its members to campaign against the proposition. De Mille, who supported the proposition, refused to pay the levy. AFRA expelled him and he was no longer able to appear on radio. His last show *Tender Comrade* was broadcast on 22 January 1945. Ironically, in view of De Mille's prominence among Hollywood's anti-Communist campaigners after the war, *Tender Comrade* was later denounced as Communist propaganda. There were bitter exchanges between De Mille and AFRA, during the course of which AFRA exploded the myth of De Mille the Lux producer by revealing that he was just the host and narrator and only ever turned up for the dress rehearsal and the actual performance. The departure of De Mille was a serious blow to the series and they tried out a succession of actors, producers and directors as guest hosts, among them Lionel Barrymore, Walter Huston, Thomas Mitchell, Brian Aherne, Mitchell Leisen, Preston Sturges, Hal Wallis, Mark Hellinger, Irving Pichel and John Cromwell, before settling on a new permanent host, who made his debut introducing *Destry Rides Again* with James Stewart and Joan Blondell on 5 November 1945. The new host was long-time Warner Brothers contract director William Keighley. He had been an actor and had a good speaking voice. But he can hardly be said to have been a household name.

William Keighley was to host the show for seven seasons before he retired from directing and went to live in Paris. He was replaced as host by Irving Cummings, another former actor turned director. He had been for many years a director at 20th Century Fox and had already retired when he began hosting the *Lux Radio Theatre* with their version of *Two Weeks With Love* on 8 September 1952. He hosted the show for the rest of its run. For its twentieth season, 1954–55, the *Lux Radio Theatre* returned to NBC and moved to Tuesdays at 9.00 p.m. It introduced the gimmick of broadcasting Lux's twenty greatest movies to celebrate the show's twentieth anniversary. *Lux* chose the following films, some of them receiving a third airing:

My Man Godfrey (1936) with Jeff Chandler and Julie Adams
The Awful Truth (1937) with Cary Grant and Irene Dunne
Wuthering Heights (1939) with Merle Oberon and Cameron Mitchell
Alexander Graham Bell (1939) with Robert Cummings
How Green Was My Valley (1941) with Alexis Smith, Michael Rennie and Donald Crisp
The Song of Bernadette (1943) with Ann Blyth and Charles Bickford
Now, Voyager (1944) with Dorothy McGuire
Together Again (1944) with Maureen O'Hara
Great Expectations (1946) with Rock Hudson and Barbara Rush
Stairway to Heaven (1946) with David Niven and Barbara Rush
Gentleman's Agreement (1947) with Ray Milland and Dorothy McGuire
The Bishop's Wife (1947) with Cary Grant and Phyllis Thaxter
Miracle on 34th Street (1947) with Edmund Gwenn
Mother Wore Tights (1947) with Dan Dailey and Mitzi Gaynor
Treasure of the Sierra Madre (1948) with Edmond O'Brien and Walter Brennan
Edward, My Son (1949) with Walter Pidgeon
Battleground (1949) with Van Johnson and George Murphy
All About Eve (1950) with Ann Blyth and Claire Trevor
Five Fingers (1952) with James Mason and Pamela Kellino
Trouble Along the Way (1953) with Van Johnson and Joanne Dru

Two of the titles (*Great Expectations* and *Stairway to Heaven*) were British. *Lux's* top year for films was evidently 1947, though by general critical consent 1939 has been deemed Hollywood's greatest year. Apart from the completely forgotten romantic comedy, *Together Again*, which had originally starred Irene Dunne and Charles Boyer, these were all notable or popular titles. In several cases, the original stars recreated their screen roles: Cary Grant (*The Awful Truth*, *The Bishop's Wife*), Irene Dunne, Merle Oberon, Donald Crisp, Charles Bickford, David Niven, Edmund Gwenn, Dan Dailey, James Mason and Van Johnson (*Battleground*). But Lever Brothers had begun sponsoring the *Lux Television Theatre* in 1950. By 1954 they were cutting costs on the radio show by featuring only one star per programme. The show was finally cancelled at the end of the 1954–55 season, clear confirmation that television had superseded radio as the domestic mass medium of choice. But during its twenty-year run, the *Lux Radio Theatre* gives us a powerful insight into the relationship between Hollywood and its public.

It enables us to assess the popularity of particular stars and particular films at the time and not retrospectively, which is often how their popularity is decided today. The fact that the shows were done live enables us to chart the reaction of the audience to a favourite film in a way that was not possible in cinemas. In the productions, which were recorded at the time on disc, we hear the audience 'oohing' and 'aahing' and laughing at the jokes. In particular we hear their reaction to the stars and the announcements. When, for instance, it is announced at the end of *This Love of Ours* on 4 February 1946 that next week's show will be *Now, Voyager* with Bette Davis and Gregory Peck there is an almost orgasmic gasp of delight from the audience. However, when at the end of *In Which We Serve* on 21 June 1943 it is announced that next week's show will be *The Great Man's Lady* with Barbara Stanwyck and Joseph Cotten, there is total silence, suggesting indifference to the choice.

We also have some guidance on audience preference in films. For the host regularly invited the audience to write in recommending films for adaptation. Cecil B. De Mille, for instance, says when introducing the production of *Wuthering Heights* that this has been specifically requested by listeners. One index of popularity is the number of times a particular film was dramatized on the *Lux Radio Theatre*. The record is held by *Seventh Heaven*, which was done four times – in 1934, 1938, 1944 and 1951 – but this is slightly misleading as it was the first ever Lux broadcast and tended to be revived as an anniversary programme. More significant perhaps are those titles that were done three times. They constitute a kind of canon of Lux classic movies. There were fourteen and they are, in alphabetical order: *The Awful Truth, Berkeley Square, The Bishop's Wife, Burlesque, Edward, My Son, How Green Was My Valley, The Letter, Miracle on 34th Street, Mother Wore Tights, Now, Voyager, One Sunday Afternoon, Smilin' Through, A Tale of Two Cities* and *Wuthering Heights*. It is a combination of sentimental Christmas stories, backstage dramas, family sagas, love stories and melodramas.

Ninety-three titles were done twice and they are principally love stories, films such as *Intermezzo, Jane Eyre, Love Affair, Love Letters, Magnificent Obsession, One Way Passage, Random Harvest, Rebecca* and *A Star is Born*. Conversely, certain genres are conspicuously under-represented. There were altogether 926 *Lux Radio Theatre* productions. Only one was a horror film (*The Phantom of the Opera*) and that version was always more opera than phantom; only sixteen were gangster films and only twenty-two Westerns. Of the twenty-two Westerns, fifteen of them date from the post-war years, though they included some of the all-time great productions, among them *My Darling Clementine, Red River, She Wore a Yellow Ribbon, Destry Rides Again, Winchester 73* and *Shane*. This was probably because the Western was a specifically masculine genre. But there was also the fact that the Western was strongly dependent on its visuals. The Westerns which worked best on radio were those which in addition to scenery and action featured strong character studies. This explains why *Red River*, *She Wore a Yellow Ribbon* and *Broken Arrow* transferred successfully to radio and *Virginia City* did not. *Red River*, broadcast on 7 March 1949, was based on Howard Hawks's epic 1948 cattle drive saga and featured John Wayne recreating his screen role of the tough cattle baron whose stubborn determination leads to him being ousted from leading the drive by his adopted son. Wayne also starred in *She Wore a Yellow Ribbon*, broadcast on 12 March 1951, recreating his screen role as Captain Nathan Brittles, the cavalry veteran on his final mission before retirement in John Ford's 1949 film. *Broken Arrow*, broadcast on 22 January 1951, was a powerful and moving version of the 1950 20th Century Fox production which was one of the earliest pro-Indian films. It was due to feature the original stars of the film, James Stewart, Jeff Chandler and Debra Paget. But when Stewart fell ill, Burt Lancaster stepped very capably into the role at short notice. *Virginia City*, on the other hand, broadcast on 26 May 1941, was a comparatively unexciting version of the 1940 Warner Brothers American Civil War film with Errol Flynn recreating his original screen role of undercover Union Army officer. The Michael Curtiz-directed film depended heavily on its large-scale action scenes, escapes, chases, stagecoach hold-up, wagon train trek and guerrilla attack and these were simply not reproducible on radio on the same scale. The low representation of the violent, the unrespectable and the masculine among film subjects coupled with the preponderance of comedy, musicals and love stories strongly suggests that the programme is aiming at a family audience with a high proportion of women, who are after all the advertisers' target audience. This also dictates the set of values being promoted weekly. These are overwhelmingly marriage and the family, romantic love and mother love, duty, service and sacrifice.

The *Lux Radio Theatre* played its part in Second World War propaganda. The eighth season of the programme opened on 14 September 1942 with its first war-related show, *This Above All* starring Tyrone Power and Barbara Stanwyck. War-related programmes thereafter figured regularly until the end of 1944 after which there were no combat films dramatized and only two war-related programmes before the end of the war itself, evidence of the war weariness which was widely reported to have set in.

There were dramas based on the exposure and denunciation of Nazi ideology (*Hitler's Children*, *This Land is Mine*, *The Master Race*). There were programmes about the contribution of women on the home front (*The War Against Mrs Hadley*,

Tender Comrade) and as nurses at the front (*So Proudly We Hail*). There were a succession of powerful and moving combat films, celebrating the heroism of the Marines (*Wake Island, Guadalcanal Diary*), the navy (*The Navy Comes Through, Destroyer*), the army air force (*Air Force*) and the merchant marine (*Action in the North Atlantic*). The big action set pieces in these films, which were predominantly visual, could not be reproduced on radio and were replaced by narration and sound effects and their prominence consequently reduced. This had the effect of concentrating on the interplay of characters stressing the camaraderie, stoicism, dedication and self-sacrifice of the servicemen. Unlike the films, the radio versions were generally narrated by one of the characters, describing his experiences, feelings and reactions and thus establishing an intimacy with the audience. The characters usually included one who was disgruntled and complaining and needed to have 'why we fight' explained to him and at the same time to the audience. The complainer invariably ended up participating fully and enthusiastically in the war effort. The characters included both officers and enlisted men to underline the democratic and fully integrated nature of the war effort. The propaganda was not limited to the programme. The full participation of the Hollywood community in the war effort was stressed. At the end of *This Above All* and *Wake Island* it was announced that within days the stars of these films, Tyrone Power and Robert Preston, would be joining up. In the chats with the stars at the end of the programme, their involvement in overseas United Service Organizations (USO) tours entertaining the troops and in domestic war bond rallies to raise money for the war effort was regularly discussed. At the end of *The War Against Mrs Hadley* it emerged that De Mille's son and the son of Edward Arnold, one of the stars of the programme, were both in the army and the husband of co-star Fay Bainter, a distinguished naval officer in the First World War, was heading up civil defence in Santa Monica. There were also regular exhortations for listeners to assist the war effort by joining, for example, the merchant marine and the nursing service. The United Kingdom and her people received their tributes in dramatisations of *This Above All, In Which We Serve* and *Mrs Miniver*, though interestingly none of the films celebrating the heroism of 'our gallant Russian allies' made it to the *Lux Radio Theatre. In Which We Serve* was the only British-made film to be featured in the *Lux Radio Theatre* during the war. Noel Coward's film, which intercut the experiences of the crew of *HMS Torrin* with the trials and tribulations of their family at home, had achieved remarkable critical and box-office success in the United Kingdom. Dilys Powell in *The Sunday Times* (29 September 1942) called it 'the best film about the war yet made in this country or America'. But it struck powerful chords elsewhere. The film was chosen by the United States Board of Review as the outstanding film of 1942 and Coward was awarded in 1943 a special Oscar for his outstanding production achievement. The Russian director V.I. Pudovkin wrote of it 'It's a splendid job, overwhelming in its complete and well-thought out frankness … You can see the real face of England in it'.[3] The *Lux Radio Theatre* production was a highly effective and very moving adaptation with Ronald Colman and Edna Best taking the roles of Captain Kinross and his wife, played in the film by Noel Coward and Celia Johnson. They were supported by a talented cast of British-born radio actors to ensure vocal authenticity.

Mrs Miniver was one of the most profitable and influential films of the war. Directed by William Wyler, the MGM film was released in 1942. It earned MGM's highest ever domestic gross for a film and a foreign gross second only to the silent epic *Ben-Hur*. It was estimated that thirty-three million Americans had seen it by March 1943. It was awarded six Oscars and was credited with cementing the Anglo-American alliance for the war effort. The popularity of the film was such that it inspired a weekly thirty-minute serial on CBS, *Mrs Miniver* (1943–44), which saw the family evacuated to the United States and charted their experiences there.[4]

The *Lux Radio Theatre* broadcast of *Mrs Miniver* on 6 December 1943 featured three of the stars of the film (Greer Garson, Walter Pidgeon and Henry Wilcoxon) and contrived to reduce a 134-minute film to a sixty-minute radio play. The programme celebrates family life, with its focus on the Miniver family (father, mother, three children) and their life during 1939 and 1940. It endorses marriage (Clem and Kay Miniver are a happily married and devoted couple) and heterosexual romance (Vin and Carol fall in love and marry). It highlights in particular the role of the mother – as home-maker, as support for her husband and children but also as active participant in the war effort (she captures a downed German airman). It focuses on a cohesive local community, featuring village, church, flower show.

The programme personalizes the British war effort by focusing on a family with which the American audiences can identify. The radio programme (unlike the film) is narrated by Mrs Miniver, emphasizing the role of the wife and mother in the story. It shows the effects of the war on an average family – husband to Dunkirk, son to the RAF, mother capturing German pilot, daughter-in-law killed. It establishes a class-structured society (personalized as Lady Beldon) but defuses it by gently mocking Vin's armchair socialism and having him marry Lady Beldon's granddaughter, and by Lady Beldon being humanized. The idea of the 'People's War' emerges through the narrative and is explicitly underlined in the vicar's final sermon. The Christian aspect of the struggle is emphasized by the role of the church and the vicar and the singing of 'Onward Christian Soldiers'. After the war, *Lux* did its bit for the Cold War by broadcasting radio versions of four anti-communist dramas, *The Red Danube* (broadcast on 19 March 1951), *My Son John* (27 October 1952), *Man on a Tightrope* (7 December 1952) and *Pick-up on South Street* (21 June 1954).

And what of the stars? Although *Lux* aimed to secure the actual stars of the film for the radio broadcast, sometimes they were not available (out of the country, away on location or simply ill). On one famous occasion Gary Cooper and Jean Arthur were scheduled to appear in the radio version of *The Plainsman* but both went down with flu. Arthur played Calamity Jane with a raging temperature and a doctor in attendance, and Fredric March was drafted in at twenty-four-hours' notice and with only one read-through to play Wild Bill Hickok. On other occasions stars got to play roles for which they might well have been considered or perhaps not. Ronald Colman was David O. Selznick's first choice for Maxim De Winter in the film of *Rebecca* and turned it down. But he did it on *Lux*. Alan Ladd and Hedy Lamarr played the Bogart and Bergman roles in *Casablanca*. Greer Garson played Katharine Hepburn's role in *The African Queen* opposite Humphrey Bogart. Errol Flynn took on Leslie Howard's role in *British Agent* and Gary Cooper's in *Lives of a Bengal Lancer*. Edward G. Robinson played Sam Spade in *The Maltese Falcon*. Basil Rathbone took on Claude Rains' role in *The Phantom of the Opera*. Humphrey Bogart took on Jean Gabin's role in the radio version of *Moontide*. Rock Hudson played Pip in *Great Expectations*. Clifton Webb played the title role in *The Man Who Came to Dinner*.

Do the most popular stars to appear on the *Lux Radio Theatre* tell us anything about the values it was promoting? Twelve male stars and six female stars made more than fifteen appearances in the *Lux Radio Theatre*. Fred MacMurray held the record for male star appearances with twenty-eight. After him the most popular stars were Cary Grant, Don Ameche, Ray Milland, George Brent, Brian Aherne, Joseph Cotten, Walter Pidgeon, Herbert Marshall, Ronald Colman, William Powell and Robert Young. The top female performer with twenty-six appearances was Loretta Young, followed by Claudette Colbert, Barbara Stanwyck, Irene Dunne, Olivia de Havilland and Anne Baxter. These lists overwhelmingly reflect two sets of images: honest, decent, down-to-earth, all-round Americans, and ladies and gentlemen with a strong leavening of British performers. *Lux*'s fondness for promoting family values extended to a penchant for featuring husband and wife teams in their plays: Hedy Lamarr and John Loder, Joan Crawford and Franchot Tone, Tyrone Power and Annabella, Orson Welles and Rita Hayworth,

Ronald Colman and Benita Hume, Joan Fontaine and Brian Aherne, Al Jolson and Ruby Keeler, Fredric March and Florence Eldridge and Barbara Stanwyck and Robert Taylor. Almost all the stars of Hollywood's golden age appeared at least once on the *Lux Radio Theatre*, with only a handful of exceptions: Greta Garbo, Luise Rainer, Fred Astaire and Boris Karloff among them. But significantly in the 1950s the new generation of stars was conspicuous by its absence, even if their films were being done on the show. Marlon Brando, Richard Burton, Tony Curtis, Doris Day, Grace Kelly and Jose Ferrer never appeared on the *Lux Radio Theatre*, an indication perhaps of its declining importance in promoting the stars' careers.

The importance in the culture of radio stars is attested by the fact that several times on *Lux*, existing film properties were specially tailored to fit their established radio characters. Jack Benny and Mary Livingstone appeared in two venerable and much filmed stage farces, *Brewster's Millions* (filmed in 1914, 1926 and 1935) and *Seven Keys to Baldpate* (filmed in 1917, 1925, 1929 and 1935). In the very funny production of *Seven Keys to Baldpate*, broadcast on 26 September 1938, Benny and Livingstone played themselves with Cecil B. De Mille also appearing as himself in his only dramatic performance on the show. The comedy centred on De Mille, having been pestered by Benny for a film role, sending him off to an allegedly haunted house to fulfil his boast that he could write a film script in twenty-four hours. Jim and Marion Jordan, the much-loved Fibber McGee and Molly of radio, were given two *Lux* vehicles, again specially re-written to fit their radio characters. *Mama Loves Papa*, broadcast on 8 April 1940, was based on the 1933 Paramount domestic comedy starring Charles Ruggles and Mary Boland. *The Whole Town's Talking*, broadcast on 24 February 1941, was based on John Ford's 1935 gangster comedy which had starred Edward G. Robinson and Jean Arthur.

It is interesting to note which directors were best represented in the *Lux Radio Theatre*. If we test the series against the pantheon of greatest Hollywood directors established by Andrew Sarris,[5] the pantheon comes off badly. Although Orson Welles appeared three times on *Lux* as an actor (in *Jane Eyre*, *Break of Hearts* and *A Tale of Two Cities*), none of his films was adapted for the radio series. There were similarly no Max Ophuls films broadcast. There was only one Jean Renoir (*This Land is Mine*) and only one Josef von Sternberg (*Morocco*); only two Fritz Lang films (*Cloak and Dagger* and *The Woman in the Window*) and only four Ernst Lubitsch films (*Desire*, *The Shop Around the Corner*, *Heaven Can Wait* and *Cluny Brown*). The three pantheon directors who came off best were Alfred Hitchcock, John Ford and Howard Hawks. Nine of Hitchcock's nineteen American films were broadcast, three of them twice (*Suspicion, Rebecca, Strangers on a Train*). The others were *Mr and Mrs Smith, Shadow of a Doubt, Notorious, Spellbound, The Paradine Case* and *I Confess* plus his British film *The 39 Steps*. Of the thirteen films Hawks made during the lifetime of the *Lux Radio Theatre* nine were broadcast: *The Criminal Code, Come and Get It, Ceiling Zero, Only Angels Have Wings, His Girl Friday, Ball of Fire, Air Force, To Have and Have Not* and *Red River*. Nine of Ford's thirty-four films were broadcast. But only two of them were Westerns (*My Darling Clementine* and *She Wore a Yellow Ribbon*) and apart from *How Green Was My Valley* (broadcast three times), it is a very unrepresentative selection: *The Brat, Mary of Scotland, Arrowsmith, Prisoner of Shark Island, The Whole Town's Talking*, and *When Willie Comes Marching Home*. Conspicuously missing were many of what are generally regarded as Ford's masterpieces: *The Informer, The Hurricane, Stagecoach, Young Mr Lincoln, Drums Along the Mohawk, The Grapes of Wrath, The Long Voyage Home, They Were Expendable, Fort Apache, Wagonmaster, Rio Grande, The Quiet Man*, and *The Sun Shines Bright*.

On the other hand, perhaps not surprisingly, Cecil B. De Mille, the programme's host, was well represented. Six of the ten films he made during the programme's run made it onto the air: *The Plainsman, The Buccaneer, Northwest Mounted Police, Reap the Wild Wind, The Story of Dr Wassell* and *Samson and Delilah*. But perhaps the director whose work was most in tune with the kind of family values *Lux* wanted to promote was Frank Capra. Between 1934 and 1951 when he temporarily ceased directing, every one of his films was adapted for the radio except for his black comedy *Arsenic and Old Lace* and his three political films (*Mr Smith Goes to Washington, Meet John Doe* and *State of the Union*).[6] Like Hollywood itself, *Lux* tended to avoid political subjects and such notable political films as *The Great McGinty, Keeper of the Flame, Citizen Kane, Wilson, Tennessee Johnson, All the Kings Men*, and *A Lion is in the Streets* did not make it into the *Lux Radio Theatre*.

Something else we can learn from *Lux* is the comparative popularity of British films in the United States. For *Lux*, the period 1945–49 was evidently the golden age of British films: for while it did six British films from the 1930s (*The Scarlet Pimpernel, The Thirty Nine Steps, Pygmalion, Sorrell and Son, The Sidewalks of London* (UK title: *St. Martin's Lane*) and *Goodbye, Mr. Chips*) and four from the 1950s (*The Browning Version, The Winslow Boy, Breaking the Sound Barrier* and *The Mudlark*), it did eight from the 1940s and five of them were done twice – *Brief Encounter, The Seventh Veil, Great Expectations, The Third Man* and *A Matter of Life and Death* (under its US title *Stairway to Heaven*). The others were *Adam and Evalyn, In Which We Serve* and *Vacation from Marriage* (UK title: *Perfect Strangers*).

Although there is a comparatively small number of British films represented in the *Lux* output, considerably more are based on Hollywood films set in the United Kingdom or the British Empire or featuring British stars. A number of reasons have been advanced for the utilization of the United Kingdom, British themes and British actors in Hollywood films of the 1930s and 1940s. One is economic. Margaret Farrand Thorp in 1939 noted that the United Kingdom was the largest market for American films outside Hollywood and that deference to British ideals and values made good sense.[7] Another is the tightening of the Hays code and the purging from the screen of sex, violence and contemporaneity which led to Hollywood studios turning to Victorian novels and in particular classic British novels for respectable properties. A third is the technological advance of the introduction of sound which led to a rush to acquire and film stage plays, many of them British. But there was another dimension: the cultural dimension.

A shared Anglo-American transatlantic culture underpinned the so-called 'special relationship' which saw regular traffic in fiction, drama and entertainment between the two countries. The Americans took to such quintessentially British figures as Shakespeare, Dickens, Scott, Kipling, Conan Doyle and Gilbert and Sullivan with as much enthusiasm as the British took to such quintessentially American writers as Fenimore Cooper, Longfellow, Washington Irving and Bret Harte.

What linked many of these writers and spanned the Atlantic during the nineteenth and twentieth centuries was a commitment to chivalry. It was in the nineteenth century that the image of the gentleman had been reformulated as a latter-day version of the medieval knight, the embodiment of the virtues of bravery, loyalty, courtesy, modesty, purity, honour and *noblesse oblige*. Exactly the same proliferation of chivalry took place in the United States, where in the nineteenth century gallantry, honour and *noblesse oblige* became deeply embedded in the national psyche. As John Fraser has written in his masterly study of this phenomenon, *America and the Patterns of Chivalry*:

> The family of chivalric heroes has been by far the largest and most popular one in the twentieth-century American culture, and its members, in whole or in part, have entered into virtually everyone's consciousness. They include, naturally, the legion of knightly Westerners in print and celluloid sired by Owen Wister's *The Virginian* and their Indian counterparts. They include Robin Hood, Errol Flynn's especially, and Zorro, and the Scarlet Pimpernel, and gentlemen buccaneers like Rafael Sabatini's Captain Peter Blood … They include the officers and gentlemen of *Lives of a Bengal Lancer*, and the gentlemen rankers of *Beau Geste,* and the First World War aviators of *Dawn Patrol* … They include honest cops like Dick Tracy, and fearless investigative reporters, and incorruptible district attorneys, and understand-

ing young doctors like Doctor Kildare. They include battered but romantic private
eyes like Raymond Chandler's Philip Marlowe … They include gentlemen knights
like Prince Valiant and nature's gentlemen like Tarzan … They include Superman
and Buck Rogers. They include men about town like Philo Vance, the Saint, and
Dashiell Hammett's Nick Charles, and the figures played by Fred Astaire … They
include gentlemanly English actors like Ronald Colman and George Sanders, and
gentlemanly American ones like Douglas Fairbanks Jr and William Powell, and all
those immortals, Gary Cooper, Spencer Tracy and the rest who have epitomized
American gallantry and grace.[8]

Many of these characters and actors appeared on American radio. To this company of heroes, there should certainly be added Sherlock Holmes and Dr John
H. Watson, for whom chivalry was as real and meaningful a code of life as it was
to their creator Sir Arthur Conan Doyle.

It is an extraordinary fact but every year from 1930 to 1950 with the sole
exceptions of the years 1937 and 1938, Sherlock Holmes appeared for thirty-nine
weeks a year on American radio. From 1939 to 1946 the well-loved team of Basil
Rathbone and Nigel Bruce played Holmes and Watson, making these very British
characters an integral part of the imaginative inner lives of successive generations
of Americans. But the Holmes series was only part of a substantial British presence on American radio. American radio dramatized the American adventures of
Bulldog Drummond and the Saint. There were at least four series dealing with
Scotland Yard (*Whitehall 1212*, *Scotland Yard*, *Pursuit* and *Hearthstone of the
Death Squad*). Mr and Mrs Miniver emigrated to the United States for a 1944
radio series *Mrs Miniver*. When Orson Welles launched his celebrated Mercury
Theatre on the Air in 1938 there were initially twenty-two broadcasts, including
of course the famous *War of the Worlds* by H.G. Wells, with the action relocated
to the United States, but of the remaining twenty-one no fewer than ten were
either based on British books involving British characters or were about British
characters: *Dracula*, *Treasure Island*, *A Tale of Two Cities*, *The Thirty Nine Steps*,
The Man Who was Thursday, *Jane Eyre*, *Sherlock Holmes*, *Oliver Twist*, *Around the
World in 80 Days*, and *The Pickwick Papers*. There was also a Shakespeare play
(*Julius Caesar*) for good measure. The presence of three Dickens adaptations is
significant. It confirms what guest host Frank Craven said when introducing
the *Lux* adaptation of *A Tale of Two Cities* in 1945, which starred Orson Welles
as Sydney Carton: 'Between the people of the English-speaking world are many
strong and common bonds such as a sense of fair play and a love of tolerance
and to these bonds may be added a common love of Dickens'.

The value of radio as evidence of this common culture is that unlike films,
these radio shows were made for the USA and Canada alone with no UK export

intentions and must therefore be seen as evidence of America's cultural assumptions, though during the war *Lux* was broadcast on short-wave on American Forces Network and could in theory have been picked up in England.

The *Lux Radio Theatre* above all demonstrates that extraordinary symbiosis that existed between Hollywood and network radio in the heyday of both media. They cross-fertilized, enriched and reinforced each other regularly in their shared mission to reassure the mass audience about the essential soundness of American society and America's social values.

There was nothing like the *Lux Radio Theatre* in the United Kingdom. For the BBC dramatizations of films came a very long way after stage plays and classic novels. Sometimes a story would be dramatized on radio to capitalize on the publicity generated by a film version. Such as the 1939 serialization of A.E.W. Mason's recently filmed *The Four Feathers*. The war saw some increase in radio versions of films. On 25 February 1940 BBC Wales produced a radio version of the Ealing Studios film *The Proud Valley*, adapted by Jack Jones, and featuring several of the film cast. Paul Robeson who played the black stoker David Goliath who sacrifices his life to save his Welsh mining colleagues in a pit disaster did not appear but his songs and other music from the film soundtrack were used.[9] The most popular plays of 1942 were radio versions of the hit Fox film *How Green Was My Valley*, the prestige British production *Young Mr Pitt* starring Robert Donat and Thorold Dickinson's 'careless talk costs lives' drama documentary *The Next of Kin*, again featuring several of the film cast (Stephen Murray, Nova Pilbeam, Reginald Tate and Phyllis Stanley). *How Green Was My Valley* was broadcast with a cast of Welsh actors in a sixty-minute version on 11 May 1942 and again on 2 August 1942; *The Young Mr Pitt* in a sixty-minute version on 30 August 1942. *The Next of Kin* was broadcast on 6 July 1942. The production of *Young Mr Pitt* was reviewed by *The Manchester Guardian* (2 September 1942):

> The broadcast of 'The Young Mr Pitt' on Sunday, with Robert Donat as Pitt, was good, though somewhat sketchy. It was adapted from the film of that name, and produced by Dallas Bower. It depended entirely on Robert Donat, and as he is an exceptionally good radio actor, with a vibrant, energetic voice, his success was the measure of the broadcast's success. One cannot but feel that a very much better radio story could have been made without using the film as a basis. In many cases the film foundation is a source of weakness rather than of strength. In this broadcast Fox, though ably played by Robert Morley, was a very dim and foolish figure; whatever Charles James Fox may have been, he was not this.
>
> One would like to hear some time a broadcast feature about Pitt, combining the work of an historian and a practised radio writer. Indeed many great Parliamentary figures of our past could be recreated in broadcasting. The history of the House of Commons has been done once, in a good broadcast early this year; and a series of

broadcasts earlier than that reproduced famous 'occasions' in the House. But there is still room for historical broadcasts, which could be lively and dramatic as well as soundly historical, about great political leaders, Whigs and Tories, and Prime Ministers of the past. Such programmes could and should be written for radio, without waiting for the stimulus of films to give a ready-made subject.

In 1941 there was an unusual prestige film adaptation. It was a radio version of Sergei Eisenstein's 1938 film *Alexander Nevsky* produced as a tribute to 'our gallant Soviet allies'. The film which dramatically depicted the victory of the Russians over the cruel Teutonic Knights was turned into a poetic radio drama by Louis MacNeice. It was produced by Dallas Bower and done live at Bedford Corn Exchange with a cast headed by Robert Donat and Peggy Ashcroft. It was broadcast on 8 December 1941, the day after Pearl Harbor.[10] It is a powerful example of poetry as propaganda with its mixture of patriotic exhortation, epic evocation of the battle on the ice, graphic denunciations of German atrocities, and ringing paeans of praise for peace, freedom and solidarity. MacNeice's words were underscored by Sergei Prokofiev's majestic music for the film, performed by the BBC Symphony Orchestra and chorus conducted by Sir Adrian Boult.

After the war, BBC radio began to take more notice of the cinema. There were film magazine programmes, containing reviews, previews, interviews, film music features and round table discussions. *Picture Parade* featured on the Light Programme from 17 April 1946 and *Film Time* on the Home Service from 27 May 1948. They were succeeded eventually by *Moviegoround* which ran from 1956 to 1969. There was also a very strange concept, *From a Seat in the Circle*, in which David Southwood would describe an excerpt from a current film release while sitting in the cinema.

Another development which had no parallel in the United States was the broadcasting of adapted film soundtracks. Radio producer Peter Eton wrote in *Radio Times* (2 April 1948) that he was 'against broadcasting soundtracks because the quality is rarely up to the standard required by BBC engineers' and 'because a film tends to lose most of its appeal when stripped of vision and translated into sound'. But there were a few exceptions to this and Eton broadcast several adapted soundtracks in special editions of his *Picture Parade* programme. In 1948 there were sixty-minute adaptations of *The Unfaithful*, the Warner Brothers melodrama with Ann Sheridan, Zachary Scott and Lew Ayres, the British films *My Brother Jonathan* and *Broken Journey*, the 20th Century Fox comedy *Sitting Pretty* with Maureen O'Hara, Robert Young and Clifton Webb and the crime thriller *Call Northside 777* with James Stewart. The success of these programmes was such that the prejudice against soundtracks was overcome and in 1949 a regular Sunday afternoon programme was introduced, *Sunday Cinema*, featuring sixty- or later forty-five-minute adaptations of recent screen successes. They included in that year the Hollywood films *Letter to Three Wives*, *The Treasure of the Sierra Madre*, *The Best Years of Our Lives*, *House of Strangers*, *Top of the Morning*, *Goodbye, Mr Chips*, *Mr Blandings Builds His Dream House* and *Lost Horizon* and the British films *Blithe Spirit*, *Kind Hearts and Coronets*, *The Interrupted Journey*, *Trottie True*, *The Chiltern Hundreds*, *Brief Encounter* and *The Seventh Veil*. Two of the titles, *Lost Horizon* and *Goodbye, Mr. Chips*, were pre-war successes but both were based on novels by the British writer James Hilton. At a time when several radio versions of films appeared every week on American radio, only between two and four radio versions of films a year were produced on the BBC. They tended to be prestige British film productions.

In 1947 there were four film adaptations, all British films. On 7 May 1947 there was a sixty-minute version of the current Herbert Wilcox production *The Courtneys of Curzon Street* with the screen stars Anna Neagle and Michael Wilding recreating their screen roles for the radio. Then on 27 June 1947 there was a ninety-minute radio version of the Carol Reed film *Odd Man Out* with an entirely different cast from the film, headed by James McKechnie, Joyce Redman and Max Adrian.

Beginning on 25 August 1947, Alastair Sim, Rosamund John, Judy Campbell and Megs Jenkins starred in their original screen roles in *Green for Danger*, adapted as a serial in six half-hour episodes by Lester Powell from the film by Frank Launder and Sidney Gilliat and the novel by Christianna Brand. On 29 September there was a sixty-minute radio version of the David Lean film *Brief Encounter* with Thea Holme and Bryan Coleman in the roles played on screen by Celia Johnson and Trevor Howard. On 4 May 1955 Wendy Hiller and James McKechnie would star in a new radio version of this perennial favourite.

In 1948 there were three radio versions of films, two of them British. *Spring in Park Lane*, broadcast on Easter Monday, 29 March 1948, featured Anna Neagle, Michael Wilding, Nigel Patrick and Nicholas Phipps in their original screen roles from Herbert Wilcox's hit romantic comedy. On 9 August 1948 *A Matter of Life and Death* was produced in a radio adaptation by Lester Powell of the celebrated Michael Powell and Emeric Pressburger film fantasy. Marius Goring and Abraham Sofaer recreated their original film roles as the Heavenly Messenger and the Judge. David Farrar and Kathleen Byron took the roles played in the film by David Niven and Kim Hunter. For Christmas, there was a radio version of the seasonal Hollywood comedy, *Miracle on 34th Street*, about an old man playing Father Christmas in a big department store. It starred Robert Beatty, Milton Rosmer, Finlay Currie and Joyce Heron.

In 1949, there were further radio versions of films. *Man on the Run* was based on the film written and directed by Lawrence Huntington and adapted for radio by Robert Stannage in collaboration with the author. This crime thriller about a shopgirl who helps a deserter involved in a jewel robbery starred Derek Farr and Joan Hopkins in the cinema. On radio it starred Sebastian Shaw and Joan Hopkins. On Whit Monday, 6 June 1949 there was a radio version of the latest Wilcox–Neagle–Wilding film *Maytime in Mayfair* with Anna Neagle and Michael Wilding recreating their screen roles. *The Saturday Night Theatre* production on 18 June was *The Lady Vanishes* based on the Frank Launder and Sidney Gilliat script for the 1938 Hitchcock thriller. Michael Hordern and Belle Crystall starred with the roles of Charters and Caldicott taken by Alastair Duncan and Norman Shelley. *The Last Days of Dolwyn* (10 August 1949) was a radio version of Emlyn Williams' 1948 film about the drowning of a Welsh village to form a reservoir. Edith Evans, Emlyn Williams and Richard Burton recreated their film roles and the production utilised John Greenwood's score for the film.

On 17 May 1950 Googie Withers made her dramatic radio debut in a version of the powerful 1947 Ealing drama, *It Always Rains on Sunday* in which she had starred on the screen. On 9 February 1951 the Home Service broadcast a radio version of the 1950 production *Chance of a Lifetime*, the controversial film written by Walter Greenwood and Bernard Miles about a group of workers taking over a business and manning it as a co-operative. Both major cinema circuits had refused to show it until the intervention of the Labour government to compel its screening. The radio version, narrated by Howard Marion-Crawford, featured Bernard Miles in his original screen role and Norman Shelley in the part originally played by Basil Radford. On 11 April 1951 Nigel Balchin's screenplay for the 1947 British film *Mine Own Executioner* was adapted for radio with Anthony Jacobs, Grizelda Hervey and Malcolm Hayes in the leading roles taken on screen by Burgess Meredith, Dulcie Gray and Kieron Moore.

The post-war practice of Hollywood studios shooting big-budget films abroad to take advantage of so-called 'frozen funds', company profits which could not be removed from individual countries in order to stimulate local production, led to the previously unexpected presence of major stars in the United Kingdom. The BBC was able to take advantage of this on several notable occasions. On 31 May 1950 Gregory Peck, who was in the United Kingdom to film *Captain Horatio Hornblower R.N.*, could be heard in a radio version of his 1949 Second World War combat drama *Twelve O'Clock High*. The radio production co-starred

Robert Beatty, who was also appearing in *Hornblower*, and Ben Lyon, star of the First World War flying epic *Hell's Angels* twenty years earlier. On 30 May 1951 the BBC achieved another coup in their adaptation of Robert E. Sherwood's play *The Petrified Forest*, directed by Martyn C. Webster. Bette Davis, who was in the United Kingdom to star in the film *Another Man's Poison* with her husband Gary Merrill and Emlyn Williams, recreated for radio her role in the 1936 Warner Brothers film version. Gary Merrill and Emlyn Williams co-starred.

If anything, the number of film adaptations diminished during the 1950s as the emphasis remained squarely on the theatre as the primary source of radio drama. But the 1950s did see one extraordinary hybrid. Beginning on 16 June 1955 there was a four-part radio serial based on the soundtrack of the Walt Disney hit film *20,000 Leagues Under the Sea* but the film soundtrack was supplemented by additional dialogue and incidents from the book, performed by radio actors, who presumably impersonated the voices of the film's stars, Kirk Douglas, James Mason, Paul Lukas and Peter Lorre. This weird venture seems not to have been repeated.

Notes

1 For a full history of the *Lux Radio Theatre* see Connie Billips and Arthur Pierce, *Lux Presents Hollywood*, Jefferson, NC, and London: McFarland, 1995.

2 Cecil B. De Mille, *Autobiography*, London: W.H. Allen, 1960, pp. 316–18.

3 Anthony Aldgate and Jeffrey Richards, *Britain Can Take It: British Cinema in the Second World War*, London: I.B. Tauris, 2007, p. 210.

4 H. Mark Glancy, *When Hollywood Loved Britain*, Manchester: Manchester University Press, 1999, p. 134.

5 Andrew Sarris, *The American Cinema: Directors and Directions, 1929–1968*, New York: Dutton, 1968, pp. 40–81.

6 The Capra titles adapted for *Lux* were *It Happened One Night, Broadway Bill, Lady for a Day, Mr Deeds Goes to Town, Lost Horizon, You Can't Take It With You, It's a Wonderful Life, Riding High*, and *Here Comes the Groom*.

7 Margaret Farrand Thorp, *America at the Movies*, New Haven, CT: Yale University Press, 1939, p. 294.

8 John Fraser, *America and the Patterns of Chivalry*, Cambridge: Cambridge University Press, 1982, p. 12.

9 *Radio Times*, 23 February 1940.

10 Barbara Coulson, *Louis MacNeice at the BBC*, London: Faber, 1980, pp. 56–7.

6

The radio studio as performance space

There are few more prosaic settings than a radio studio, usually an anony-mous-looking room with table, chairs, curtains and control panel. But it was imbued with glamour by the nature of what was created within that space. In one of the earliest theoretical studies of the medium, Rudolf Arnheim conveyed something of that romance:

> I hope that there will be found in this theoretical book some of the many extraor-dinary sensations associated with the broadcasting house and the wireless receiver. The carpeted rooms where no footstep sounds and whose walls deaden the voice, the countless doors and corridors with their bright little light-signals, the mystify-ing ceremonial of the actors in their shirt-sleeves who, as if attracted and repelled by the microphone, alternately approach and withdraw from the surgical charms of the metal stands; whose performance can be watched through a pane of glass far away as in an aquarium, while their voices come strange and near from the control-loudspeaker in the listening room; the serious young man at the control-board who with his black knobs turns voices and sounds off and on like a stream of water; the loneliness of the studio where you sit alone with your voice and a scrap of paper and yet before the largest audience that a speaker has ever addressed; the tenderness that affects one for the little dead box suspended by garter-elastic from a ring … the joy of the writer who may create unhindered fantastic spirit-plays in the realm of thought … and finally of the long exciting evenings at the loudspeaker where, a god or a Gulliver, you make countries tumble over each other by a twist of your hand, and listen to events that sound as earthly as if you had them in your own room, and yet as impossible and far-away as if they had never been.[1]

The best cinematic depiction of radio studios in action can be found in the documentary film *BBC – The Voice of Britain* (1935), commissioned by the BBC from the GPO Film Unit and directed by Stuart Legg with significant input from others in the unit, notably John Grierson, Cavalcanti, Evelyn Spice and Harry Watt. It encapsulates in a succinct fifty-six minutes a day in the life of Broadcasting House, newly built and opened in 1932, monumental, solid and reassuring. With credits unfolding to the strains of Eric Coates 'Knightsbridge March', the theme tune of the popular programme *In Town Tonight*, the film opens with a pan down from the clouds via an aerial to the face of Broadcasting House. There is a close-up of the corporation's Latin Motto and the religious service opens the day's broadcasting, with a hymn ('Glorious Things of Thee are Spoken') and a bible reading. The voices of the radio are heard over shots of people going about their daily lives, a recurrent visual trope which stresses the relationship between the wireless and its listeners. The narrator explains that the BBC belongs to the people who pay their ten shillings a year licence fee. 700 people work in the 350 offices. The post is delivered, 2,000 letters a day, and we hear a montage of voices praising, blaming, complaining, enquiring; and a series of extracts from replies. At an executive planning meeting, the Director of Talks and his assistant Lionel Fielden plan the talks schedule. Val Gielgud, the head of Drama, discusses the allocation of studio space for drama rehearsals and Eric Maschwitz, the head of Variety, and producer John Watt discuss the unacceptability of a proposed joke. Derek McCulloch, 'Uncle Mac', the head of *Children's Hour* also bids for studio allocation, quipping mischievously that *Children's Hour* is far more important than *Macbeth*. The legal department discusses potential law suits about names. A maintenance man checks on mice infestations. Smartly dressed page boys in the art deco corridors swap cigarette cards of radio personalities, including Stuart Hibberd, the chief announcer, who we then see in the canteen selecting a cake. Henry Hall and the BBC Dance Orchestra are seen in morning rehearsal. Disc jockey Christopher Stone tries out records for his programme, deliberately smashing one by a crooner. Potential performers are auditioned. Sound effects (rain, wind, thunder, horses, bubbling cauldrons) are tried out for *Macbeth*. Producer John Sharman listens to comedy duo Clapham and Dwyer doing their cross-talk act and warns them not to include suggestive material and that they must not exceed seven minutes. Producer Howard Rose rehearses the three witches from *Macbeth*, one of whom is the celebrated documentarist Humphrey Jennings. Bryan Michie rehearses tap dancers. *Radio Times* rolls off the presses, with a voice ritually reciting programme details. The voices from the Empire Service are heard, with Sir John Reith extolling the role of that Service. The engineering work of the BBC is explained and we see an outside broadcast of the Oxford and Cambridge Boat Race. On *Children's Hour* a woman reads about the quest for the golden fleece from Charles Kingsley's *The Heroes* over shots of children listening intently. The song *The Teddy Bear's Picnic* is played over shots of a teddy bear's picnic in a suburban garden. A lesson in practical mapmaking and creating a local exploring notebook is given in Schools Broadcasting with children at their schoolroom desks listening. An outside broadcast from Aberdeen is given permission to overrun and we see the message being passed to BBC Birmingham, Manchester, Leeds, Newcastle and Edinburgh. The BBC Symphony Orchestra under Dr Adrian Boult perform Beethoven's Fifth Symphony with people at home listening. An SOS message is broadcast to a fishing boat on the Viking Bank about the illness of one of the crewmen's mother. The microphone, we are told, has produced new means of distributing opinion and we see Ramsay Macdonald, Stanley Baldwin, George Lansbury, Sir John Simon, Sir Josiah Stamp, Maurice Dobb, Gerald Heard, David Low, J.B. Priestley, H.G. Wells, Commander Stephen King-Hall, G.K. Chesterton and George Bernard Shaw in action. The BBC link up with Montreal for an account by Captain Bisset of the *Ascania* of his rescue during the recent Atlantic gales, and broadcast the funeral of King Alexander of Yugoslavia via Radio Paris, heard over newsreel footage of the event in Belgrade. The liner *Queen Mary* is launched by King George V and Queen Mary, with the voices of the King and Queen heard over newsreel footage of the launch. Singer Nina Mae McKinney performs 'Dinah' in the studio. A cross section of homes is seen as the variety show proceeds with singing of 'I Cover the Waterfront'. A police message is broadcast appealing for information about a robbery and urging anyone with such information to telephone Whitehall 1212. Gracie Fields is heard singing 'So tired of waiting' over shots of London at night, workers going home and people in a pub. A music hall artist sings 'Knocked 'em in the Old Kent Road'. Henry Hall and his band perform 'Piccadilly Ride' and 'Sweetmeat Joe, the Candy Man' over scenes of lovers saying goodnight. Henry Hall signs off with the theme tune 'Here's To the Next Time'. Then the duty announcer declares: 'This is the end of the National Programme for tonight. Goodnight everyone, goodnight'. The camera pans up the façade of Broadcasting House and into the ether as Big Ben strikes midnight.

Graham Greene, writing in *The Spectator* (2 April 1935), mischievously suggested that the film was intended to be a satire on the BBC. In fact it is an invaluable historical record of the life of the BBC in the 1930s, stressing its social, cultural and political inclusiveness and doing so in a wholly engrossing manner. As Rachael Low put it, 'it has an outstandingly elaborate soundtrack in the group's new counterpoint style … the camera, cutting and soundtrack keep the mass of material moving with great facility'.[2]

The ubiquity of radio was such that established literary classics could be reworked to accommodate the radio age. Mark Twain's *A Connecticut Yankee at the Court of King Arthur*, which satirized the conventions of medieval romance and challenged the idea that the Middle Ages were superior to the present, was published in 1889. In 1931 it was adapted as a vehicle for Will Rogers. Rogers was one of America's best-loved humorists, a cowboy philosopher whose nationally syndicated newspaper columns and radio broadcasts had him dispensing homely folk wisdom in a down-to-earth and humorous style. He made regular radio appearances from 1922 but in 1930 was given his own weekly show. He returned with a weekly show in 1933–35, always donating his fees to charity. When he was killed in a plane crash in 1935, the nation mourned.

In *A Connecticut Yankee* (UK title: *A Yankee at King Arthur's Court*), directed by David Butler and written by William Conselman, Twain's story was updated to 1931. Rogers' Hank Martin, a blacksmith in the novel, now runs a radio shop and local radio station WRCO in Harkdale, Connecticut. The film opens with him introducing the quartet 'The Four Farmhands' in the makeshift studio and then signing off for the night. Called upon to deliver a battery to a sinister country house, he encounters a mad inventor who believes that he can pick up sounds and voices from the past with his apparatus. As trumpets are heard and the court of King Arthur is announced on the apparatus, Hank is knocked out by a falling suit of armour and wakes up in Camelot. Arrested and sentenced to be burned at the stake as a monster, he demonstrates his 'magic' powers by using a lighter and predicting an eclipse of the sun. He is knighted as Sir Boss and made prime minister. Thereafter he sets out to modernize Camelot, introducing a telephone system, a factory for making armour, advertising which he describes as a process for getting you 'to spend money you haven't got on things you don't want'. He wins a joust by lassoing his opponent from his horse. The tournament is described by a radio sports commentator, sponsored by the armour factory. When Arthur's daughter Alisande is kidnapped by his sister Morgan Le Fay, Hank and Arthur set out to rescue her but are captured and imprisoned. Page boy Clarence organizes a rescue mission, which involves a fleet of Baby Austins, an autogyro dropping bombs and knights armed with sub-machine guns. The prisoners are rescued but Hank is knocked out by falling masonry and wakes up back at the inventor's house. It is then revealed that what they had thought was sounds from the past is in fact a radio broadcast of *King Arthur and His Knights*. Hank happily returns home. Rogers' relaxed, naturalistic, head-scratching, 'Aw Shucks' performance contrasts nicely with the self-consciously melodramatic acting and archaic dialogue of the Arthurian characters. The contrast was enhanced by Rogers' practice of rewriting his lines and adlibbing, a practice director David Butler happily encouraged: 'by doing that, we got a lot of funny lines'.[3]

Kate Douglas Wiggin's *Rebecca of Sunnybrook Farm*, published in 1903, was a much-loved slice of sentimental Americana about a fatherless child sent to live on a farm with a stern aunt, spreading sweetness and light and changing for the better the lives of those she encounters. It was filmed in 1917 with Mary Pickford and in 1932 with Marian Nixon. 20th Century Fox saw it as an ideal vehicle for their child star Shirley Temple and assigned director Allan Dwan to the project in 1938. Dwan recalled:

> They owned the book, which was … sort of a *Pollyanna* – pretty sticky. I said, 'this *could* be made into something interesting'. And I had Raymond Griffith again (as producer) so I was able to say, 'Let's go after it with an update attitude – put some music in it – give Shirley something to sing – let's get radio in', Radio was very popular then. And we injected all that. The book, *Rebecca of Sunnybrook Farm*, is nothing like that. In fact when we were through, all we had left was the title and the names of the characters.[4]

Not surprisingly the credits read that the screenplay by Karl Tunberg and Don Ettlinger was 'suggested by the story by Kate Douglas Wiggin'.

The film opens and closes in the smart art deco studios of the Federal Broadcasting Company and largely concerns product promotions. Radio producer Anthony Kent (Randolph Scott) is searching for a little girl who can sing and will be 'Little Miss America', the voice of Crunchy Grain Flakes on the Crunchy Grain Flakes Hour. He finds little Rebecca Winstead (Shirley Temple), loses her, finds her again living on Sunnybrook Farm with her aunt Matilda, overcomes the aunt's objections to broadcasting and in an outside broadcast from the farm makes her a star. Her greedy stepfather turns up to claim her, sells her contract to the rival Baby Bath Soap Hour but she fakes laryngitis, is dropped by them and reunited with Kent and Crunchy Grain Flakes and makes a triumphant studio debut in 'The Toy Trumpet', singing and dancing with Bill Robinson, both of them dressed as toy soldiers. She also contrives to unite three pairs of lovers by the end of the film.

A cheerful, tuneful vehicle for Fox's most profitable star, then at the height of her popularity, it also contains a mild satire of radio with its rival producers, demanding sponsors and the potential hazards of live performance. There is a nice little cameo from Franklin Pangborn as the organist Hamilton Montmarcy, who is kept on standby to play the organ in the event of on-air problems. He has waited for ten years for his chance to do this and when summoned after Rebecca's voice fails he sits down at the organ and faints.

The film *Pot O'Gold* (UK title: *The Golden Hour*) was directly inspired by the first big money giveaway show in the United States. Radio historian John

Dunning wrote of it:

> The rise of *Pot O'Gold* was a radio phenomenon. But its fall came almost as fast, and when it bowed out its credibility was shaken and its audience reduced to a fraction of what it once commanded. The lure of *Pot O'Gold* was rooted in simple human greed. Each week a sponsor gave away $1,000 to people who answered their telephones when the *Pot O'Gold* host called. There were no questions to answer; people … didn't even have to be listening. All they had to be was home to answer the phone: they would then be told that *Pot O'Gold* was calling from New York and that $1,000 was being sent to them at once by telegraph.[5]

The telephone number was chosen by successive spinnings of a wheel of fortune and the spinnings were interspersed by musical numbers performed by Horace Heidt and his Musical Knights. The show ran from 1939 to 1941 but its popularity declined when bad telephone connections thwarted potential winners. A revival in 1946–47 failed to re-establish the show's popularity.

A fictional backstory for the show was provided by the amiable comedy *Pot O'Gold* (1941), directed by George Marshall, scripted by Walter de Leon and produced by James Roosevelt, the son of the President. The film combined a Capraesque populist comedy with seven musical numbers. James Stewart, the beloved American Everyman, starred as the decent smalltown music-shop proprietor Jimmy Haskell who plays the harmonica, has no money but is happy. His music-hating uncle, C.J. Haskell (Charles Winninger), is a miserable and despotic capitalist tycoon, the proprietor of Haskell's Health Foods. He is trying to purchase and demolish the boarding house next door, run by cheerful motherly Ma McCorkle and her daughter Molly (Paulette Goddard) who allow the unemployed musicians of Horace Heidt's orchestra to practice on their terrace, driving C.J. mad. When Jimmy loses his shop, he comes to the city and throws in his lot with the McCorkles and the orchestra. C.J. is decoyed out of town and Jimmy takes over running Haskell's Happiness Hour, a radio programme sponsored by C.J. on the Globe Broadcasting Company. Jimmy arranges for the Horace Heidt orchestra to appear on the show with Molly as their singer. But when Molly discovers that Jimmy is C.J.'s nephew, she retaliates by announcing on the air that the show will give away a thousand dollars a week. Jimmy then devises the Pot O'Gold show to do it, the show is recreated in an art deco radio studio, C.J. is reconciled by the success of the show and Jimmy and Molly announce their imminent marriage. No one seems to have noticed the irony of hitching a populist morality tale about the joys of the simple life and the need to humanize rich capitalists to a show appealing, as John Dunning put it, to audience greed.

The Jackpot (1950), directed by Walter Lang and scripted by Phoebe and Henry Ephron, is a both funny and charming account of how a radio quiz show could seriously disrupt ordinary life. James Stewart and Barbara Hale play Bill and Amy Lawrence, a typical mid-Western middle-class couple. They live in Glenville, Indiana, and have two children (Phyllis and Tommy). She is a housewife; he works for Woodruff's department store. Then one day the Federal Broadcasting Company telephone to say that he has been selected to receive a call from the quiz show *Name the Mystery Husband* and he stands to win $24,000-worth of goods. He successfully names Harry James and wins. Then his troubles begin. Hosts of prizes arrive including a pony, a swimming pool, tins of soup, plants, watches, furniture, washing machines plus an interior decorator to remodel their house and a glamorous painter to paint Bill's portrait. As confusion mounts, Bill loses his job, his marriage is threatened by Amy's suspicions of an affair between him and the painter Hilda Jones, he is arrested when he tries to sell off jewellery to a racketeer in Chicago and finally he learns he has to pay $7,000 tax on his prizes. But it all ends happily with Bill reinstated at work, getting a promotion and saving his marriage. It is wonderfully acted by Stewart as the goodhearted, increasingly harassed paterfamilias and a sterling cast; Barbara Hale as his devoted wife, Alan Mowbray as the posturing interior decorator, Fred Clark as Bill's longsuffering boss, Patricia Medina as the glamorous portrait painter and James Gleason as a hardbitten local newspaper man.

The fictional quiz programme was very obviously based on *Stop the Music*, a sensationally successful giveaway show of 1948 in which a variety of different items were won by whoever identified a mystery tune when called on the telephone by the programme. Its success on ABC killed off the long-running radio show of Fred Allen which was its competition on NBC and effectively terminated his radio career. He made a few films and sporadic television appearances, despite detesting the medium ('they call it a medium because nothing on it is ever well done') before his death in 1956.

Another quiz show satire which was both sparkling and sophisticated, was provided by *Champagne for Caesar* (1950), directed by Richard Whorf and written by Hans Jacoby and Fred Brady. It centres on Beauregard Bottomley (Ronald Colman), an unemployed genius, who knows everything but cannot get a job. When he is turned down for a research job by Milady Soap, he determines to bankrupt the company going on *Masquerade for Money*, the quiz show sponsored by Milady Soap. In a sign of the times, the show is broadcast simultaneously on radio and television. Having glimpsed the show on television in a shop window, Bottomley declares the show and its host Happy Hogan 'the forerunner of intellectual destruction in America'. Going on the show, Bottomley wins week after week. Sales of the soap and the ratings for the show go up and up. In despair, the devious and dottily autocratic company boss, Burnbridge Waters (Vincent Price), takes the show off the air. When sales plummet, he has to restore it to the airwaves. Bottomley continues to win, doubling his money every week. Waters hires the beautiful Flame O'Neill (Celeste Holm) to romance Bottomley and discover his weakness so that he can be sabotaged. He claims not to understand Einstein's law of thermodynamics. When he is then asked about it on the show, his definition is pronounced incorrect until Dr Einstein rings up from Princeton to confirm Bottomley's definition. He is finally beaten when asked to name his social security number and gets it wrong. He is reunited with Flame with whom he has fallen in love. He reveals that he had done a deal with Waters to lose in return for stock in the company and his own radio show but he genuinely did not know his own social security number. There are fine performances from Ronald Colman, his charm and wit humanizing the intellectuality, and Vincent Price as the egotistical autocrat surrounded by yes-men and going into trances to gain inspiration. Added piquancy was given by the fact that the charmless quiz master Happy Hogan was played by Art Linkletter, host of the longrunning daily audience participation show *House Party* which ran from 1945 to 1967.

One of the more unlikely broadcasting crazes in both the United Kingdom and the United States was the spelling bee. Spelling contests with instant prizes, they were all the rage in the United States in 1937 and came to the United Kingdom in 1938 where they were staged, according to the BBC, strictly for educational purposes.[6] They featured in Ealing Studios' episodic comedy musical *Let's Be Famous* (1939), directed by Walter Forde and written by Alan MacKinnon and Roger MacDougall. The film was intended to showcase Betty Driver as the successor to Gracie Fields, who had left Ealing for 20th Century Fox. Driver strikingly resembled Fields in style, tone, looks and breezy Lancashire manner. She was teamed with Irish comedian Jimmy O'Dea in a story featuring the adventures and misadventures of an Irish postmaster Jimmy Houlihan (O'Dea) and Liverpool lass Betty Pinbright (Driver) as they both seek to break into broadcasting. The background to the film is the rivalry between the BBC and commercial radio, here represented by the fictional Radio France. Jimmy, summoned by the BBC to appear in a spelling bee, wrongly believes he is being invited to participate in a celebrity concert. Arriving at Broadcasting House, he wrecks the spelling bee by singing 'The Minstrel Boy' and causing a riot. Meanwhile Betty wins a crooning competition in Liverpool and is signed by agent Johnnie Blake (Patrick Barr) to star in Radio France's *Golden Glow Hour*, advertising bath soap. Betty has a hit singing a Fields-type optimistic anthem 'I've Got a Hunch – Happy Days Are Here Again'. Ironically the film was released in June 1939 and three months later the country was at war. Jimmy, famous because of the BBC riot, is signed to appear in the rival *Silverene Hour*. But he and his agent 'Finchie' Finch (Sonnie Hale) get drunk and in a deeply unfunny sequence wreck the Radio France broadcast by improvising a running commentary on the programme using the available sound effects. Although the authorities try desperately to stop them, their broadcast proves to be a comedy hit and the two soap companies compete to sign them as a new comedy duo.

Professional Sweetheart (UK title: *Imaginary Sweetheart*) (1933), directed by William Seiter and written by Maurine Watkins, was an amusing satire on commercial radio. Ginger Rogers starred as Glory Eden, who, billed as the 'Purity Girl of the Air', is the singing star of a radio show, the *Ippsie-Wippsie Hour*, sponsored by Ippsie-Wippsie, 'the washcloth of dreams' and broadcast from New York. Glory is so disgruntled over the restrictions placed on her to preserve her image – no cigarettes, no liquor, no make-up, no boyfriends, no nightclubbing – that she refuses to sign a new contract. Her sponsors decide to manufacture a romance for her and recruit a fan, a cleancut country boy from Kentucky, Jim Davey (Norman Foster). She falls genuinely in love with him and they are married on the air. But when he discovers it has all been a publicity stunt, he carries her off to his cabin in Kentucky and she settles down to a life of bucolic domesticity. However, when she hears a new Ippsie-Wippsie girl – her black maid – singing in her place, and swinging up her sentimental song, she furiously signs with a rival company, Kelsey dishrags. But all ends happily when the two companies merge and she returns to the show with Jim on hand to recite uplifting poems. Curiously, for her one song, 'My Imaginary Sweetheart', Ginger Rogers was dubbed by another singer, Etta Moten.

The film opens in the New York studio with the show being broadcast and glutinously insincere speeches from the announcer and the singer. But behind the scenes, Glory is threatening to swear on the air if she does not get her own way over some new clothes and as her voice is heard singing, we see the sponsor and his staff arguing furiously in dumbshow behind the soundproof window of the control room. The broadcast wedding has the announcer rehearsing the audience in their applause and the minister hamming up the service for the microphone. Later we witness all the behind the scenes shenanigans of the rival sponsors and their scheming staffs as they try to upstage each other.

William Haines became one of MGM's brightest stars during the 1920s with his bright and breezy, wisecracking, all-American boy persona. But he became one of the leading casualties of the arrival of sound. The same personality in the talkies with its remorseless wisecracking and mugging soon became tiresome. In a bid to resurrect his career MGM put him into two films with the novelty of a radio background and with much of the action taking place in a radio studio.

Remote Control (1930) is a brisk and lively comedy which runs little more than an hour. Unusually it credits no scenarist and no director, suggesting behind the scenes problems with rewriting and re-shooting. At least three directors, all with established comedy backgrounds, are known to have worked on the film (Edward Sedgwick, Nick Grinde and Mal St Clair). However, there are no signs of strain on the screen and the film works perfectly well on its own terms. Haines plays William Judd Brennan, who, losing his job at a music store, joins the radio station WPN, threatened with closure because of falling listening figures and declining advertising revenues. The film extracts humour from Brennan's auditioning of a string of hopeless performers, his go-getting attitude to securing new contracts and his own performances as station announcer and as Uncle Elmer, reading bedtime stories to children, frightening them with his animal noises and accidentally setting his false beard on fire. Drama is provided when Dr Leonard Kruger, leader of a criminal gang, joins the station as resident clairvoyant and uses his broadcasting slot to send coded messages to his gang. The gang kidnap Brennan after robbing the participants in an outside broadcast from a hotel roof of the Junior League Follies. But Brennan manages to get a message to the police who round up the gang. Entertaining enough and retrospectively interesting for its radio studio setting, the film did little to halt the slide in Haines's fortunes.

Are You Listening? (1932), directed by Harry Beaumont, sought to provide a change of pace for Haines. For it is a straightforward melodrama with Haines as a radio gag writer who is falsely accused of the murder of his wife, tricked into making a confession on a radio phone-in and then subjected to a manhunt coordinated by radio broadcasters. He is eventually exonerated. The change of image did nothing to restore Haines's popularity and in 1934 he abandoned his film career to become an interior decorator, earning considerable success in particular for remodelling the homes of the stars, many of them his friends and former colleagues.[7]

Paramount cashed in on the desire of radio audiences to see their favourites in the flesh with a series of what were in effect musical revues, the *Big Broadcast* series, tuneful and entertaining reminders of the musical content of 1930s broadcasts. *The Big Broadcast* (1932), directed by Frank Tuttle and written by George Marion Jr., had a wafer-thin plot. George Burns, playing himself, runs station WADX in New York. He goes broke and sells the station to wealthy Texas oilman Leslie McWhinney (Stuart Erwin), who to promote the station mounts *The Big Broadcast*. There is a double romantic subplot. McWhinney falls for Anita Rogers (Leila Hyams) who in turn falls for singer Bing Crosby, playing himself, and first seen being mobbed by his fans outside the radio studios. Crosby, on the rebound from being jilted by his fiancée Mona Low (Sharon Lynn), responds to Anita's obvious attraction. But when Mona returns, he is reunited with her and Anita realizes she actually loves the shy and devoted McWhinney.

But the *raison d'être* of the film is the succession of popular musical acts who appear. They include Kate Smith, 'the greatest name in radio – the songbird of the South' who had a hit fifteen-minute show *Kate Smith and her Swanee Music*, which was heard several times a week; Cab Calloway and his band playing his signature tune 'Minnie the Moocher'; the Mills Brothers performing their signature tune 'Tiger Rag'; Vincent Lopez and his orchestra; Arthur Tracy, 'The Street Singer', singing 'Here Lies Love'; the Bosworth Sisters singing 'Crazy People' and tenor Donald Novis, who had won the title 'America's most promising youthful vocalist' in 1928, singing 'Trees'. Several popular announcers, Don Ball, James Wallington, Norman Brokenshire and William Brenton, also appeared with name plates in front of them in case people failed to recognize them.

The stars did what they were famous for on the air. George Burns and Gracie Allen did several cross-talk acts. Bing Crosby sang 'Please, Lend A Little Ear to my Pleas' and his signature tune 'Where the Blue of the Night Meets the Gold of the Day'. *The Big Broadcast* itself is intercut with the comic attempts of Stuart Erwin to acquire a record of Bing singing, believing him too drunk to appear. He eventually finds one and gets it to the studio but it is accidentally destroyed and Erwin is reduced to attempting an impersonation of Bing until Bing actually turns up and takes over the song.

The Big Broadcast of 1936 (1935), directed by Norman Taurog from a script by Walter de Leon, Francis Martin and Ralph Spence, also featured a radio station, WHY, facing bankruptcy and closure. The station owner Spud Miller (Jack Oakie) poses on the air as 'Lochinvar, the Great Lover' wooing female audiences with sentimental poems and love songs, actually performed by his partner Smiley (Henry Wadsworth). Countess Ysabel de Narglia (Lyda Roberti) falls in love with his voice and discovering the imposture kidnaps them both, and takes them to the island of Clemente where her overseer, jealous of them, seeks to kill them. Miller has entered station WHY in the international broadcasting competition and they delay their deaths by broadcasting from the island through the Radio Eye (effectively a television) invented by George Burns. They win the competition and are rescued from the murderous attentions of the overseer by United States marines.

The Radio Eye device allows the incorporation of a variety of acts. These include Bing Crosby singing 'I Wished on the Moon', Ethel Merman singing 'It's the Animal in Me', Ray Noble and his orchestra, Ina Ray Hutton and her all-female Melodiers, Amos 'n'Andy, performed by Gosden and Correll in blackface, a domestic sitcom sketch with Charlie Ruggles and Mary Boland, a dramatic sketch with Sir Guy Standing, Gail Patrick, David Holt and Virginia Weidler about a small boy giving a blood transfusion to save his sister, the spectacular tapdancing of the Nicholas Brothers and Bill 'Bojangles' Robinson, the Vienna Boys Choir and vaudeville act Willie West and McGinty doing a slapstick stage routine about the building and demolishing of a new house.

The Big Broadcast of 1937 (1936), directed by Mitchell Leisen and scripted by Walter de Leon and Francis Martin, opened with a male trio singing 'Hi, ho, the radio' which detailed the ubiquity of the medium and then proceeded to a comic musical take on the relations of the radio station and its sponsors. Jack Benny stars as Jack Carson, manager of the National Network Radio Company (NNRC). He needs to keep his new sponsors George and Gracie Platt (Burns and Allen) of Platts' Golf Balls, happy. When they first arrive at the studio Carson is producing a dramatic sketch with a comic display of sound effects, a vast middle-aged woman playing a teenager and Carson himself acting with an outrageous Australian accent. But the lucrative sponsorship is threatened when singer Frank Rossman (Frank Forest), star of the top-rated NNRC show, threatens to pull out unless something is done about Gwen Holmes (Shirley Ross), disc jockey at a local station who is continually sending up his records. Manager Bob Miller (Ray Milland) persuades Carson to sign her up for the network and he romances her to keep her quiet. She falls in love with him but when she discovers their schem-ing, she sets her cap at Rossman, makes a successful singing debut on the *Platts' Golf Ball Hour*, and their romance leads Carson to plan an on-the-air wedding for the radio sweethearts. Unable to go through with it, Gwen flees but when Miller declares his love for her over the air, they are reunited and married on the air. The Platt Golf Ball Hour features both the Benny Goodman Orchestra and Leopold Stokowski and his symphony orchestra performing 'Impregnable Fortress'. There are songs from Frank Forest, Shirley Ross and Martha Raye, energetically performing 'Vote for Dr Rhythm'. Burns and Allen do their cross-talk acts. Director Mitchell Leisen recalled: 'I loved working with Jack Benny and George Burns and Gracie Allen. Burns and Allen supplied a lot of their own gags and I just let them go'.[8] Bob Burns, a folksy regional comedian in the Will Rogers mould, wanders round the studio trying to find Stokowski and successively interrupting a lonely hearts programme, a science programme and a health and beauty show. From 1936 he had been a regular with his Arkansas anecdotes on Bing Crosby's *Kraft Music Hall* radio show and from 1942 to 1947 he had his own show *The Arkansas Traveller*.

The last of the series, *The Big Broadcast of 1938* (1937), again directed by Leisen and scripted by de Leon and Martin with Ken Englund, coupled together two inter-war phenomena – radio and the luxury liner. The background is a race between two super-liners, *S.S. Colossal* and *S.S. Gigantic* across the Atlantic from New York to Cherbourg. The *Gigantic* is powered by radio waves and much of the action revolves around an on-board concert being broadcast from the ship. The star of the film was W.C. Fields as the shipping line owner's eccentric brother who causes all kinds of comic havoc on the voyage. Fields insisted on including his venerable golfing and billiards routines in the film. But there were also speciality acts from Mexican singer Tito Guizar, Shep Fields and his Rippling Rhythm Orchestra, Kirsten Flagstad of the Metropolitan Opera singing Brunhilde's aria 'To-Jo-To-Ho' from *Die Walkure*, Martha Raye, singer and comedienne, doing a song and comic dance with half a dozen sailors and Dorothy Lamour singing 'You Took the Words Right Out of my Heart'. There was a lavish, elegantly staged sequence, 'The Waltz Lives On', choreographed by Leroy Prinz, surveying the different dance styles from 1850 to 1938.

The film was principally notable for the screen debut of Bob Hope, playing radio announcer Buzz Fielding. He only got the job because Jack Benny turned the role down. But Hope delivered gags, sang and danced and made such an impression that his career was effectively launched. He would become a fixture on American radio with a weekly thirty-minute variety show that ran on CBS and NBC from 1938 to 1958. The film's slender narrative was eked out by three exiguous romances (between Leif Erickson and Dorothy Lamour, Bob Hope and Shirley Ross and Martha Raye and Lynne Overman).

The film was directed by Mitchell Leisen who found W.C. Fields undirectable ('He was the most impossible ornery son of a bitch I ever tried to work with'). In despair Leisen assigned Ted Reed to shoot Fields' golfing and billiard sketches and had a heart attack the night after he had completed the film. Leisen recalled with some justice 'The only part that was any good was "Thanks for the Memory"'. This sequence had Bob Hope and Shirley Ross as an estranged couple recalling their past together. It was done with just the right amount of pathos and stands out from the rest of the film which is frankly something of a hodge-podge. It won an Oscar for best song of the year and became Hope's signature tune.[9]

Radio Stars on Parade (1945), directed by Leslie Goodwins, was another of

RKO's low-budget round-ups of current radio favourites. The plot premise had two talent scouts, played by comic actors Wally Brown and Alan Carney, seeking to launch their new singer Frances Langford. This was simply an excuse to take her on a round of visits to radio studios and catch glimpses of popular shows, culminating in Ralph Edwards's *Truth or Consequences*.

During the war, 20th Century Fox produced a series of tuneful and nostalgic musicals celebrating the evolution of key institutions of American popular culture: the music business (*Tin Pan Alley*), amusement parks (*Coney Island*), the musical stage (*The Dolly Sisters, Lillian Russell*) and Hollywood (*Hollywood Cavalcade*). Radio received its tribute in *The Great American Broadcast* (1941), directed by Archie Mayo and scripted by Don Ettlinger, Edwin Blum, Robert Ellis and Helen Logan. This entertaining light musical which combined romance, songs and enthusiastic enterprise featured two radio pioneers, Rix Martin (John Payne) and Chuck Hadley (Jack Oakie) who in 1919 teamed up to make a commercial success of the newly invented wireless. Their revolutionary idea is to provide entertainment over the air. Their first attempt, broadcasting a musical show from the roof of a warehouse in New Jersey, is amusingly depicted as a violent storm and torrential rain disrupt proceedings, the equipment overheats and Hadley has to join the operatic troupe when a key member fails to turn up. In the end, the tent roof collapses, drenching them all. They have greater success with a pioneering outside broadcast covering the historic Jess Willard–Jack Dempsey fight in Toledo. But the two friends part when Rix falls in love with Chuck's girlfriend, singer Vicki Adams (Alice Faye). Hadley teams up with wealthy Bruce Chadwick (Cesar Romero) and launches the successful New York radio station WAB. Rix marries Vicki and they struggle to find finance for their station WNX. When Vicki gets Chadwick to invest in WNX, she and Rix quarrel and he walks out. Vicki goes to work for WAB as a singer. But Chuck contrives to reunite them when he implements Rix's idea of a nationwide hook-up of radio stations and stages the Great American Broadcast. The smart art deco radio studio serves as the stage for a variety show with the Inkspots and the Wiere Brothers performing alongside Vicki and Rix.

The British film *Radio Parade of 1935* (1935) (US title: *Radio Follies*), directed by Arthur Woods, is a remarkable film, nothing less than a thoroughgoing satire of the BBC, embodying all the contemporary criticisms of the institution and its programmes and actually parodying real-life individuals. It is largely set in the fabulous art deco setting of the headquarters of the NBG, which ostensibly means the National Broadcasting Group but which the public would have understood to mean 'No Bloody Good'. Both exterior and interiors approximate to the new

Broadcasting House in Portland Place. The Director-General, William Garlon (Will Hay) is stuffy, autocratic and reclusive. The character was originally to have been called William Garland; Garland equals Wreath; Wreath recalls Sir John Reith, BBC Director-General. In the film, he never listens to the programmes, is never seen by the staff, sits in an office surrounded by pictures of himself and in the washroom experiments at parting his hair like Hitler. He has a series of ex-officer assistants who are basically 'yes men'. His deputy, the Blimpish Major-General Sir Frederick Ffotheringhay (Davy Burnaby) is evidently intended as a portrait of Reith's deputy, Admiral Sir Charles Carpendale, who, according to Val Gielgud had 'a formidable reputation of a quarterdeck manner and brusque questioning about one's public school and one's athletic achievements'.[10] Garlon accidentally encounters Jimmy Clare (Clifford Mollison), the complaints manager – he receives 6,000 complaints a day. Clare insists on escorting him round the studios and showing him the programmes. They include a screeching soprano and a string trio, a huge fat man with his feet up dictating 'Keep Fit' instructions, and a completely incomprehensible talk. There is a dance band, but they are only allowed to play chamber music. Jimmy, who declares the existing programmes 'rotten', suggests a giant variety show to liven up the schedules. Garlon is reluctant ('We don't want to be bothered with new ideas') but agrees, encouraged by his daughter Joan (Helen Chandler) who goes to work as Jimmy's secretary.

Jimmy recruits many of the leading variety artists for his show but on the eve of broadcasting, leading impresario Carl Graham of the Theatres Trust holds all the artists to their contracts with him, forbidding them to appear and ef-fectively sabotaging the show. This is exactly what George Black of the General Theatres Corporation did in the early 1930s as he feared the emptying of his theatres by the rival attraction of the wireless. Jimmy rises to the challenge by recruiting talent he finds among the staff at the NBG Headquarters and in an extraordinarily prophetic sequence, puts the concert out on the newly invented medium of television via large screens set up in public places and in colour. The screen bursts from black and white into the pastel shadings of Dufaycolour for two final big musical numbers, Alberta Hunter and a black chorus singing a powerful anti-racist song 'Black Shadows', and dancer Fred Conyngham taking the lead in 'Miss Susan Brown' which involves dancers, singers, orchestra and expressionist sets. The broadcast is a hit and Jimmy proposes to Joan.

The film contrasts the elitist and unappealing fare provided by the NBG with two entertainment forms known to be popular with the people. One is the Hol-lywood musical with big dance numbers staged by the American choreographer Buddy Bradley in the kind of kaleidoscopic patterns, shot from overhead, that characterised the Warner Brothers musicals of Busby Berkeley. The opening is superb: the staff arrive at the NBG Headquarters singing 'Good Morning', secretaries, telephonists, page boys, announcers etc. The announcers sing 'We're the men who thrill the nation/with an Oxford intonation' before using a throat spray, the Western Brothers deliver a mournful musical weather forecast and the senior executives deposit their top hats before taking the salute from the massed ranks of the employees. Later the executives, who proclaim Jimmy's plans to be 'Bolshevism', fall into line when Garlon gives his consent and perform the musical number 'Doing the Newer than New', along with the entire NBG staff. The final Dufaycolour numbers are also in the grand Hollywood manner.

The other populist form is the music hall and the film is chock full of music hall favourites, many of them playing NBG staff. Lily Morris and Nellie Wallace memorably perform two songs as a pair of charladies. Gerry Fitzgerald and Arthur Young perform a romantic ballad as window-cleaners. Haver and Lee do a comic routine with sound effects. The Carlyle Cousins perform as singing telephonists. The Three Sailors do a knockabout act as the Complaints Department. Claude Dampier does a comic piano-tuner act. Clapham and Dwyer appear as a couple of reporters. Billy Bennett appears as the Commissionaire. In addition singer Eve Becke, comedian Ted Ray, cabaret artist Ronald Frankau and impressionist Beryl Orde do their acts, Beryl Orde impersonating Maurice Chevalier, Jimmy Durante, Mae West and Mabel Constanduros. A final instructive fact worth noting is that John Watt, who co-wrote the original screen story for *Radio Parade of 1935*, was to become head of BBC Variety in 1937, and began to implement the policy he had advocated in comedic terms in this hugely entertaining film.[11] It became one of the few British musicals to get a release in the United States. A previous film, *Radio Parade* (1933) with a similar line-up of music hall and broadcasting favourites had not enjoyed an American release and no known copy of the film now survives.

In the United Kingdom as in the United States, the simplest and the laziest way of displaying radio personalities to the cinema-going public was in the form of filmed revues. Thus *On the Air* (1934), directed by Herbert Smith, was a musical in which radio stars on holiday helped a local vicar stage a concert. The film featured comedy double acts Clapham and Dwyer and Scott and Whaley, singers Derek Oldham and Eve Becke, speciality act Wilson, Keppel and Betty, xylophonist Teddy Brown, music hall veteran Harry Champion, Roy Fox and his Band and Buddy Bradley's Dancing Girls. *Variety Hour* (1937), directed by Redd Davis, had a storyline in which comedians try to make good on radio. It contrived to include performances by Clapham and Dwyer, Brian Lawrence and his Lansdowne Band, the Norwich Trio, tap dancer Jack Donahue, baritone Raymond Newell, singer Helen Howard and the Music Hall Boys, and cowboy band Carson Robinson and his Pioneers. *Radio Pirates* (1935), directed by Ivar Campbell, had a café proprietress, radio salesman and composer set up a pirate radio station to solve their financial problems and the resulting show featured Hughie Green, Teddy Brown and Roy Fox and his band. These films were the rather amateurish British equivalent of Hollywood's *The Big Broadcast* series.

Bernard Vorhaus was an American director who came to the United Kingdom in the 1930s and turned out a succession of pacy, stylish B pictures on minimal budgets, usually for Julius Hagen's film factory, Twickenham Studios. Several of them (*The Ghost Camera, The Last Journey, Cotton Queen*) have retrospectively earned critical admiration. Speaking in 1986, Vorhaus nominated *Street Song* (1934) as 'the worst thing I've done'. A film was needed on the floor at Twickenham to meet the demands of the quota and Vorhaus had a week to provide a script. Vera Allinson wrote the script from a story by Vorhaus and fellow American Paul Gangelin. Vorhaus recalled: 'I couldn't rewrite and direct at the same time. It was awful'.[12] Viewed today, the film is actually a lively and charming musical if overly sentimental, particularly the scenes involving an appealing younger brother with a cute performing dog. The boy is knocked over by a van in the street and his recovery is ensured by the goodhearted villain voluntarily exculpating the hero, on the run from the police for a crime he did not commit.

The film's title song is actually Franz Liszt's *Liebestraum* set to new English lyrics and sung four times by John Garrick. Garrick plays a fugitive street-singer Tom Tucker who is given shelter by impoverished pet-shop owner Lucy Gray (Rene Ray) and her brother Billy (John Singer). Tom seeks to break into broadcasting and in one characteristically inventive Vorhaus sequence he pursues bandleader Roy Hall (an obvious combination of the names of popular bandleaders Roy Fox and Henry Hall) through the London streets to Broadcasting House. However, when he tries to sing to him with his accordion he is drowned out by the sound of drills from nearby road-menders. Eventually getting into the studio, he sings 'Painting Pictures' with the band before he is evicted. He is wrongly arrested by the police but eventually cleared and following demands from the listening audience, makes his radio debut with the band and is set for stardom. The film ends with a shot of Broadcasting House, testimony to the importance of the medium to the popular culture of the day.

Something rather more substantial was attempted in Associated British Pictures' *Music Hath Charms* (1935). The supervising director was Thomas Bentley with individual segments directed by Alexander Esway, Walter Summers and

Arthur Woods. This is an immensely engaging, tuneful and pacy surrealistic musical covering a day in the life of Henry Hall and the BBC Dance Orchestra, featuring singers Hildegard and Dan Donovan. It begins with Henry Hall shaving and being serenaded on his birthday by the band with 'Many Happy Returns of the Day'. He bids goodbye to his children and drives to work as 'I'm Feeling Happy' is played on the soundtrack. At Broadcasting House, the band rehearse 'There's No Time Like the Present', 'A Honey-Coloured Moon' and 'In My Heart of Hearts' and we later see their lunchtime and teatime broadcasts. One of the band remarks that their music touches the lives of people all round the world but a cynical secretary doubts whether it makes much difference. The film then demonstrates the effect of the band's music on a variety of situations. Marjorie and Jack, a young couple engaged in a breach of promise case, are reconciled in court by the music. George and Joan, a mountaineering couple, stranded by mist in the Scottish mountains are led to safety in a cottage by the sound of the band's music. A potentially disastrous shipboard romance between a married woman and a caddish Lothario is scotched by the music. In Africa, two white men besieged by natives are saved when they are soothed by the sound of the music. Henry Hall and the band take a group of deprived children to the countryside to celebrate Henry Hall's birthday and are stranded there, getting back to Broadcasting House only in the nick of time for the 5.15 performance. This gave rise to what Henry Hall recalled as 'the most important and original part of the film', a musical sequence devised by arranger Benjamin Frankel in which Hall arrives alone in an empty studio for the broadcast, starts playing the piano and one after another the musicians come in from all corners of the studio and join in the music. 'The scene and the music moved step by step from a trio to a quartette, to a quintette, to an octette, until the full orchestra raised melody and counter-melody to a rousing and effective finale. The brilliant musical arrangement was matched by first-class camera work, and was an example of how to blend parts into a successful whole'.[13] The film ended with a montage of people of all walks of life listening to the band's broadcast. The whole film was predicated on the principle of the ubiquity and the unifying and integrating nature of the wireless, linking city and country, rich and poor, jungle and ocean, the United Kingdom and the Empire. It is at once a vindication of radio and of popular music and its transformative effect. Hall recalled 'the film enjoyed considerable success – it made money', and the *Daily Herald* proclaimed Henry Hall an unexpected star.[14]

Not just bandleaders but also BBC announcers, reporters and newsreaders rapidly became celebrities in their own right, giving rise to the phenomenon described in the comic song 'Little Betty Bouncer loved an announcer down at the BBC' where the radio voice inspires romantic devotion. The same idea lay behind Jessie Matthews' film debut, *Out of the Blue* (1931), a painfully laborious and heavy-handed screen version of the popular musical comedy *Little Tommy Tucker*. A hackneyed narrative of romantic misunderstandings in a series of typical 1930s settings (English country house, Biarritz hotel, West End night-club), it nevertheless enabled Jessie to demonstrate her undoubted star quality. Its only novelty lay in the idea of 'Tommy' Tucker (Jessie Matthews) daughter of an impoverished baronet, falling in love with the voice of BBC announcer Bill Coverdale (Gene Gerrard, who also directed the film), known as 'Uncle Bartholomew'. The film opens with a glimpse of a studio where a group of pal-pably bored radio actors are performing a thriller, full of shots and shouts, while playing patience and reading the newspaper. This is followed by Bill Coverdale reading the script of a programme about stately homes. Later, growing steadily more drunk, he commentates on the Radio Ball, anticipating by some six years the famous occurrence when an audibly drunk Commander Tommy Woodrooffe commentated on the 1937 Spithead Naval Review ('The fleet's lit up'). After various complications, Bill and 'Tommy' are united.

The Happy Family (1952) (US title: *Mr Lord Says No*), directed by Muriel Box and scripted by Muriel and her husband Sydney Box, is an engaging Ealin-gesque comedy about a family – the Lords – whose corner shop is scheduled to be demolished to make way for the Festival of Britain site. They barricade themselves in and are besieged but eventually defeat the Whitehall bureaucrats and save their home. The progress of the siege is regularly reported from the BBC by an effete newsreader (Michael Ward). But more significantly a BBC roving reporter Maurice Hennessey, amusingly played by Tom Gill as an eager-beaver silly ass, climbs into the shop to report the siege from the inside. He confides that it is his ambition to escape from his exile on *Woman's Hour* and to take over *Down Your Way*. He reports on the siege in the approved manner of a BBC cricket commentary.

The Dick Barton phenomenon inspired an affectionate send-up in a comedy film, *Helter Skelter* (1949), directed by Ralph Thomas and scripted by Patrick Campbell. This extraordinary film seems to be aiming to be a British *Hellzapoppin* (1942), the fastmoving surrealistic farce starring the vaudeville team of Olsen and Johnson. *Helter Skelter* throws in everything it can think of in a hit-and-miss *mélange* of impersonations, parodies and sketches, some of them funny and some of them not. There is an unfunny parody of the saucy Hollywood costume drama *Forever Amber* with the characters speaking a mixture of modern slang and Wardour Street 'Merrie England' dialect. There are cabaret acts (singer Shirl Conway and ventriloquist Robert Lamouret and his Duck). There are glimpses of stars in current Gainsborough films (Glynis Johns as the mermaid in *Miranda* and Dennis Price as Byron in *The Bad Lord Byron*). Richard 'Mr Pastry' Hearne pops up in a variety of guises and as a *deus ex machina*.

But radio is the principal subject. The film opens, imitating *In Town Tonight* as the 'mighty roar of London's traffic' is halted to find out who is 'On the Prowl Tonight'. Various new radio personalities appear. Jimmy Edwards (*Take It From Here*) and Harry Secombe (*Listen My Children*) play a psychiatrist and his assistant trying to cure the heroine of hiccups by showing her an extract from the 1929 slapstick comedy *Will You Believe It?* which is actually very amusing. Jon Pertwee (*Waterlogged Spa*) plays a manic headwaiter doing a variety of voices.

However, *Dick Barton* is the principal theme. Heiress Susan Graham (Carol Marsh) falls in love with the actor (David Tomlinson) playing the lead in the hit BBC serial *Nick Martin – Special Investigator*, which appears nightly on the Light Programme at 6.45 p.m., like *Dick Barton*. The joke is that Nick Martin is portrayed as terrified of his fans and dominated by his battleaxe mother, who writes the scripts for the show.

We see the broadcasting of the *Nick Martin* show in the studio with Nick and his sidekicks Chalky and Taffy (Snowy and Jock) battling the arch-villain Gennaro amid a variety of sound effects. When his mother tries to break up the romance, Susan goes to Broadcasting House in search of Nick. There we get glimpses of the panel game *Twenty Questions*, Valentine Dyall (celebrated as 'The Man in Black') narrating the spoof *Scrapbook for 1066* and Terry-Thomas doing his famous sketch as a BBC announcer on a record programme who in the absence of records has to impersonate the singers, notably Paul Robeson doing 'Green Pastures'. Susan ends up locked in a cupboard in the studio and Nick refuses to broadcast until she is found. This precipitates a national crisis. The Director-General (Ronald Adam) insists that the show must go on – in contrast to his real-life counterpart who wanted to scrap it. The nation is mobilized to find her. Finally Field Marshal Montgomery appeals to Nick's patriotism to go ahead with the broadcast. As the show begins, Susan is found in the cupboard. She and Nick fall into each other's arms and Terry-Thomas is drafted in to do all the voices for the show.

Head Over Heels (1937), directed by Sonnie Hale, was an untypically disappointing entry in the series of lavish Gaumont British musicals showcasing the singing and dancing talents of Britain's premier musical comedy star Jessie Matthews. It had a fine score by Hollywood tunesmiths Mack Gordon and Harry

Revel. But this hardly compensated for the trite storyline of a romantic triangle in a redundant Parisian setting that was short on both the elegant style and comic embellishment that had characterized earlier Matthews vehicles.

Jessie plays an aspiring singer-dancer, Jeanne Corbet, torn between a flashy actor Marcel Larrimore (Louis Borell) and a shy radio engineer Pierre Brissard (Robert Flemyng). Marcel leaves her for a Hollywood star but Pierre ensures that she achieves stardom as 'The Lady in Blue' singing jingles for soap and toothpaste on the fictional commercial station Radio Seine. The actor comes back into her life but she settles for the faithful Pierre, who has invented an automatic programme selector for radio which will make his fortune. The film includes two lengthy sequences set in the art deco studios of Radio Seine, the first a concert with Jeanne singing to an appreciative studio audience, and the second, a bust-up on the air when Jeanne confronts the star for whom Marcel deserted her in a verbal spat, eagerly listened to by the wider radio audience.

Edith Meiser, prolific radio writer and producer, penned a detective mystery, *Death Catches Up with Mr Kluck* under the pen-name Xantippe (the acid-tongued wife of Socrates). It was published in 1935 in Doubleday's *Crime Club* series. Doubleday proudly proclaimed that not only was it a classic murder mystery but also 'a devastating and ruthless satire of radio' in which 'Many prominent radio figures, thinly disguised, move through the pages of the book'. It also argued that the reader would learn from the book 'a good deal about the mad, ludicrous and significant business of radio'.[15]

Much of the action takes place in Radio Forum, the New York headquarters of the Consolidated Broadcasting Company (CBC). Caesar Kluck of Kluck's Korjul, 'America's favourite soft drink', powerful programme sponsor and detested womanizer, is murdered. Subsequently Joe the Italian porter is also murdered. Radio engineer Benjamin Franklin Butts investigates, aided by Christina 'Steenie' McCorkle, sharp-tongued continuity writer for the advertising agency which holds the Kluck's Korjul account. The whole plot hinges on a knowledge of the layout of the radio headquarters, the techniques of broadcasting, programme timings and schedules and executive decision making. The engaging aspect of insiderdom is reinforced by the sardonic footnotes with which the book is peppered, such as note 1 on page 131 which refers to a performance by the Bachelor Bakers' male quartette: 'All quartettes wrangle … Next to adagio dancers, quartettes (male or female) hold the long distance record for continuous wrangling' or note 4 on p. 133: 'To the sponsor, the commercials are the really fascinating part of his program. The average sponsor will raise more hell if the company's name or product is mispronounced by a seventy-five dollar a week announcer than he will if his Four

Thousand Dollar a performance star drops dead in front of the microphone'.

Eventually Butts proves that the murderer is announcer Dave Butler, who confesses. He killed Kluck because Kluck had hooked him and his wife on cocaine and then seduced the wife. Joe was killed because Marie Butler was his niece and he knew about the motive Butler had. Butler then jumps out of the window to his death. Meanwhile romance has blossomed between Butts and 'Steenie'. The novel was filmed by Universal as a B picture in 1938 under the title *Danger on the Air*, directed by Otis Garrett with Donald Woods as Butts and Nan Grey as the heroine, rechristened Reenie McCorkle. It retained the humour alongside the murder mystery. But Dave Butler's motivation was changed. In the film, he was avenging the death of his father who had committed suicide after being ruined by the financial machinations of Caesar Kluck. Cocaine and seduction was too hot for 1930s cinema.

One of Sidney Toler's Monogram Charlie Chan mysteries, *The Scarlet Clue* (1945), directed by Phil Rosen from a George Callahan script, was largely set at the Cosmo Radio Center, where Charlie has tracked subversives trying to steal government radar secrets. During his investigations, Charlie encounters a grandiloquent Shakespearean actor reduced to earning a living as 'The Mad Monster', a soap opera with a man playing the elderly grandmother and a dictatorial sponsor constantly berating the cast of her sponsored programme for incompetence. There is a series of murders: the radio station manager, who is one of the subversives, a soap actress blackmailing him and a soap actor about to provide Chan with vital information. After several attempts on his life, Chan exposes the murderer and secret leader of the spy ring, Mrs Marsh, the sponsor, who plummets to her death down a liftshaft.

During his earlier incarnation as Charlie Chan at 20th Century Fox where he enjoyed bigger budgets and more accomplished production values, Sidney Toler encountered radio in *Charlie Chan at the Wax Museum* (1940), directed by Lynn Shores. This gripping and atmospheric thriller was set almost entirely in a wax museum, Dr Cream's Museum of Crime, during a thunderstorm, and came complete with chamber of horrors, a prowling criminal with a bandaged face, a chess-playing automaton, secret rooms and sliding panels. The Museum of Crime was the setting for a weekly outside broadcast called 'The Crime League'. Charlie Chan and rival criminologist Dr Von Brom are guests on the show, discussing an old case on which they had disagreed. Von Brom is murdered and so too is the bandaged criminal. Chan exposes the host and director of the programme, Tom Agnew, played by radio actor Ted Osborn, as the culprit. He is another criminal, believed dead, who had had his face changed by plastic surgery.

The Unsuspected (1947) is an engrossing thriller, directed in grand Gothic style by Michael Curtiz, full of shadows, billowing curtains and drenching rain. The central figure is velvet-voiced Victor Grandison, 'writer, art collector and teller of strange tales'. He is a radio personality whose weekly show from New York has him vocally caressing the lurid details of famous murder cases and expounding his theory that the most successful murderer is the unsuspected. Grandison is played in a tour de force performance by Claude Rains, himself an accomplished radio performer as well as screen actor. He had achieved stardom initially entirely through his voice as he played the title role in *The Invisible Man* (1933). The film opens and closes in a radio studio. In between Grandison murders his secretary, his niece and her husband and tries to murder his ward, on whose millions he has been living. The live broadcasts of his show were intended to provide him with alibis for the murder of the secretary and the death of the ward. But the alibis fail when it is demonstrated that he left early after the first broadcast in time to commit the murder and his ward is revived before she succumbs to drugged champagne. The police close in as he is broadcasting and he abandons his script to deliver something unprecedented in broadcasting history – a full confession for three murders and the admission that he is himself the unsuspected. It makes a riveting finale. Interestingly, his radio producer is a woman, Jane Moynihan (Constance Bennett), who works with him on his scripts.

Val Gielgud (1900–81), head of Drama at the BBC, and Eric Maschwitz (1901–69), head of Variety (writing as Holt Marvel), collaborated on a series of thrillers in the 1930s. The first and most successful of them was *Death at Broadcasting House*. Gielgud recalled that he and Maschwitz went on holiday to the South of France, took a BBC secretary with them and dictated 70,000 words in sixteen days. The book was published in the United Kingdom in 1934 by Rich and Cowan, serialized and published also in the the United States. A copy was sent to Sir John Reith who 'wrote a charming letter of commendation, finding fault only with our invention in that we had described him as calling a special meeting of the Governors to consider the result of murder on the sacred premises! This, he wrote, he would never have dreamed of doing'.[16] The sequence was omitted from the film version. The authors thought it had cinematic possibilities. Gielgud wrote: 'Broadcasting House, if only as a new building and rather a box of tricks, was still 'news'. Most people seemed curious to know what went on behind its concrete battlements; seemed eager to enjoy any opportunity of 'seeing the wheels go round'. They tried all the well-known companies without success but sold the idea to a new concern, Phoenix Films, set up by three young men, Hugh Perceval, formerly a publicity man with Gainsborough, director Reginald Denham, and screenwriter Basil Mason. Their intention was to produce low-budget, quality films with particular emphasis on first-class photography. On *Death at Broadcasting House*, Perceval produced, Mason scripted and Denham directed. They shot the film in twenty-nine days, budgeting it at around £16,000, and spending £18,000, but released in 1934, it eventually grossed £90,000. The contemporary critics loved it for its ingenious story, unique setting and the excellent photography of ace German cinematographer Gunther Krampf.[17]

Phoenix assembled a fascinating cast for their film version. The youthful Jack Hawkins and Donald Wolfit, both destined for greater things, played small supporting roles, a programme researcher and the murder victim respectively. The detective, Inspector Gregory, was played by the ever-reliable Ian Hunter, making one of his last British film appearances before departing for a long and honourable career in Hollywood. His performance is crisp and authoritative in contrast to the shrill and often inept playing of the director's wife as the heroine, actress Joan Dryden. As Lillian Oldland, the lady had been a star of British silents but after changing her name to Mary Newland with the coming of sound she had only moderate success and was nearing the end of her career. Also on hand were Henry Kendall playing fashionable West End playwright Rodney Fleming in languid sub-Coward manner and Val Gielgud himself as radio producer Julian Caird, complete with swirling cape and slouch hat and echoing in voice and profile his brother, Sir John Gielgud. The scriptwriter had added what Gielgud called 'some indifferent low comedy relief' in the form of silly ass Guy Bannister with his catchphrase 'H-h-h-how did you arrive at that?' who spent the film wandering around Broadcasting House trying to provide himself with an alibi for the time of the murder.[18] He would play Lord Peter Wimsey in a subsequent Phoenix production, *The Silent Passenger*.

Retrospectively the film has considerable interest both in its setting (Broadcasting House) and its background (the production of a radio play). The authenticity of the sets and technical detail is guaranteed by the experience of the two authors and their use of the blueprints of the Broadcasting House studios to ensure absolute accuracy. The general public believed the film had been shot at Broadcasting House but in fact apart from the handful of exterior shots, the interiors were all re-created at Wembley Park Studio where the film was actually shot. There is something inescapably glamorous about the gleaming art deco interiors, the studios, offices, listening rooms, and concert hall and undeniably fascinating about the mechanics of radio play production. It demonstrates the multi-studio approach with actors, musicians and sound effects in three different studios. It was favoured by the pre-war BBC, unknown in the the United States but abandoned in the United Kingdom during the war due to lack of studio space and never revived. Its aim was to create what Gielgud calls 'aural perspective'. We encounter the control panel, the signal lights, the sound effects creation and the actors grouped around the old-fashioned microphone with scripts. A key role is also played by the Blattnerphone, a system of recording on steel tape for rebroadcast on the Empire service. It allows the police to play back the murder committed on air.

The film provides a cross-section of the activities in Broadcasting House with chorines tap-dancing in front of the microphones, jaunty dance bands, dinner-jacketed announcers and a benignly paternalist Sir John Reith figure, here called Sir Herbert Farquarson (Robert Rendel). In the book he is General Farquarson and evidently based on Admiral Carpendale. Added flavour is provided by the 'look, it's none other than' glimpses of announcer Eric Dunstan, critic Hannen Swaffer, humorist Gillie Potter, political commentator Vernon Bartlett and singers Eve Becke and Elizabeth Welch. The 'behind the scenes of a famous institution' story was a clever crowd-puller at the time and is in retrospect a valuable historical document: other examples are *Death on the Set* (1935) behind the scenes in a film studio and *The Arsenal Stadium Mystery* (1939) with its recreation of Highbury.

An effective radio production of the story, adapted by Sue Rodwell and recorded on location in Broadcasting House, was directed by Enyd Williams and broadcast on 2 March 1996. It starred Peter Sallis as Detective Inspector Spears, John Moffat as Julian Caird and Jeremy Clyde as Rodney Fleming, with Bill Nighy as Leopold Dryden, Diana Quick as Isabel Dryden, Julian Glover as Stuart Evans and Graham Crowden as General Farquarson, given a Scottish accent to suggest Reith.

The film has the classic 'golden age' detective story format. Small part player Sydney Parsons (Donald Wolfit), the victim in the specially written radio play *Murder Immaculate* by Rodney Fleming, is strangled on the air, heard by twenty-five million listeners. Inspector Gregory investigates, questioning cast and production staff and finally by the use of a Blattnerphone recording of the play tricking the culprit into confessing. The murderer is Rodney Fleming, who was being blackmailed by Parsons. Fleeing arrest, he is accidentally electrocuted and the film ends with a BBC announcer solemnly apologizing for a technical hitch.

The Twenty Questions Murder Mystery (1949) was directed by Paul Stein from a script by Patrick Kirwan and Victor Katona. The central idea of the film is that reporter Robert Beatty unmasks a killer who has been sending in clues as questions to the popular BBC quiz programme, which ran from 16 March 1947 to 28 July 1976. The film featured the questionmaster Stewart MacPherson, panellists Jack Train, Richard Dimbleby, Jeanne de Casalis and Daphne Padel, and 'mystery voice' Norman Hackforth who announced to the audience the object the panellists had to guess.

The ingenious murder mystery *The Voice of Merrill* (1952), directed and written by John Gilling, hinges on that brief period in popular culture when it was possible for a storyteller on radio such as A.J. Alan to achieve national celebrity. Appropriately the film opens and closes with a shot of Broadcasting House. Alycia Roach (Valerie Hobson), unhappily married to bombastic playwright Jonathan Roach (James Robertson Justice), arranges for the BBC to broadcast some of her husband's early stories submitted under a pseudonym. She then persuades Roach to allow her lover, struggling writer Hugh Allen (Edward Underdown), to read them on the air. The series called *The Voice of Merrill*, in which we see Allen reading from a script in a BBC studio introduced by the celebrated BBC announcer Alvar Lidell, becomes an instant hit and press and public clamour for the true identity of the mysterious Merrill. Roach, suspecting that his wife intends to kill him, produces a final Merrill story *Confession* in which Allen will confess on the air to the recent unsolved murder of a female blackmailer. Roach dies and Alycia is suspected but an autopsy reveals he died of natural causes. Allen reads the story, which contains details only the real murderer could know. When the police arrive to arrest him, he admits that he did not write the stories and Roach is identified as the murderer. The only flaw in the story is that the BBC would not have permitted a story to be read without there being a rehearsal and in the film the audience is expected to believe that Allen is reading it for the first time actually on air.

Two of the most notable radio commentators became immortalized on film. Walter Winchell (1897–1972) was a phenomenon of the radio age. An estimated fifty million Americans either listened to his weekly radio show or read his daily newspaper column, syndicated to more than two thousand newspapers. His biographer Neal Gabler recorded:

> It was said that when he switched papers in New York, two hundred thousand readers followed him, and one report attributed nearly half the readership of the Hearst newspaper chain to Winchell's column. Presidents courted him, and government officials of America's foreign enemies castigated him by name. Hit songs were written about him, and Hollywood coaxed him to star in two movies, both of which were box office successes. For a time you could walk down any street on a warm Sunday night at nine o'clock, when his broadcast aired, and hear his disembodied voice

wafting from open windows, giving ghostly validation to his own slogan: 'Winchell … HE SEES ALL … HE KNOWS ALL'.[19]

He wrote in smart, slangy prose, inventing new words to describe birth, marriage, divorce and romance. To marry was to 'merge' or to be 'Lohengrinned', to divorce to be 'Reno-vated' or 'Phffft', a birth was a 'blessed event', romance was 'making whoopee'. He helped to transform American journalism by creating the modern gossip column which fostered a culture of celebrity based on the doings of the big names in New York, Washington and Hollywood. Dubbed 'the Boswell of Broadway', he evoked for ordinary people an exciting world of socialites, showfolk, gangsters, musicians and nightclubbers.

Winchell began as a vaudeville performer before he started publishing backstage gossip in *Vaudeville News*. In 1924 he was taken up by the tabloid *New York Evening Graphic* with a column 'Your Broadway and Mine'. In 1929 he joined William Randolph Hearst's *New York Mirror* and he remained a fixture in the Hearst newspapers until he finally lost his column in 1967. In 1931 he began broadcasting a gossip column as part of NBC's *Lucky Strike Dance Hour*. In shirt sleeves, hat on the back of his head, with his traditional greeting 'Good Evening, Mr and Mrs America and all the ships at sea' and his staccato delivery he rapidly became a radio star. He developed celebrated feuds (with drama critic St John Ervine and the powerful Broadway producers the Shubert Brothers who banned him from their thirty theatres). A mock feud was invented with bandleader Ben Bernie which had them trading inventive insults over the air to the delight of listeners. It became part of American radio and there were similar mock feuds between Jack Benny and Fred Allen, W.C. Fields and Charlie McCarthy and Bob Hope and Bing Crosby. In December 1932 he got his own fifteen-minute gossip slot on the *Jergens Lotion Programme* in which he dispensed the latest celebrity gossip using a telegraph ticker to signal each item and to impart an air of urgency. By 1935 his was one of the top-rated shows on the air. The programme ran from 1932 to 1948 and then for a variety of sponsors he continued on the air until 1959. He simultaneously had a television show from 1952 to 1958. But by the late 1950s he was looking and sounding increasingly old-fashioned.

During the 1930s he came to idolize Franklin Roosevelt and became a journalistic populist, an early opponent of Hitler and Fascism, campaigned for US intervention in Europe and supported the war effort. After the war he became a fervent opponent of the Soviet Union and a supporter of Senator McCarthy's anti-Communist crusade. From 1959 to 1963 he narrated the hit television series *The Untouchables* featuring Eliot Ness and his campaign against 1920s gangsters. His delivery was perfect for period evocation but confirmed that he had himself become part of history. By the 1960s he had lost his radio and television shows and eventually his slot and the world moved on.

But Winchell also made an impact on the cinema. He provided the original story, a potent mixture of nightclub life and organized crime, for the entertaining film *Broadway Through a Keyhole* (1933), directed by Lowell Sherman. The film opens with Winchell broadcasting a typical column with his trademark sideswipes at bandleader Ben Bernie. Thereafter his newspaper columns and broadcasts punctuate the film at regular intervals. The story has racketeer Frank Rocci (Paul Kelly) falling in love with chorus girl Joan Whelen (Constance Cummings). He buys a club and makes her a star. But when a rival gangster makes an attempt on his life, Frank sends Joan to Florida for safety. There she falls in love with bandleader and crooner Clark Brian, played by bandleader and crooner Russ Columbo. When Frank orders her back to New York, Clark Brian confronts him and declares his love for Joan. Frank nobly steps aside. But after Joan is kidnapped by a rival gang, Frank is mortally wounded helping to rescue her. Dying in hospital, he gives Joan and Clark his blessing and listening to the sounds of Broadway, he hears Winchell on the radio proclaiming him a hero. The film was given added authenticity by the presence in the cast of legendary nightclub entertainers Texas Guinan as a clubowner and Blossom Seeley as an ageing gangster's moll and of vaudevillian Eddie Foy Jr. playing himself. What those in the know recognized was that the script was based on the true story of the love of gangster Johnny 'Irish' Costello for singer Ruby Keeler and his eventual standing aside when she fell in love with singer Al Jolson.

Winchell himself became a model for the dramatic portrayal of the American journalist: fast-talking, quick-witted, cynical and unscrupulous. Damon Runyon caricatured him as Waldo Winchester. Winchell was the obvious model for Alvin Roberts, the New York gossip columnist who is the central figure in the play *Blessed Event* (itself a Winchellism) by Manuel Seff and Forrest Wilson. Filmed in 1932 by Warner Brothers and directed by Roy Del Ruth, it starred Winchell lookalike Lee Tracy as Roberts. With dialogue delivered at a machine-gun rattle, this gleeful black comedy has Alvin Roberts achieve success as gossip columnist on *The Daily Express* with a scurrilous column entitled 'Spilling the Dirt', which gets him his own radio show. He conducts a running feud with crooner Bunny Harmon (Dick Powell), blackmails his editor, uses the paper to conduct personal vendettas, ruins innocent people's lives by exposing their secrets and is regularly threatened with murder by his victims. But he escapes the various attempts and rises ever upwards.

Winchell was also the model for radio reporter Larry Wayne, played by a

miscast Lew Ayes, in *Okay America* (UK title: *Penalty of Fame*) (1932), directed
by Tay Garnett and scripted by William Anthony McGuire and Scott Pembroke.
In this film the reporter gets caught up in the kidnapping of a politician's daughter
by an Al Capone-type gangster (Edward Arnold). Wayne arranges for the payment
of the ransom but is subsequently murdered by the gangster while he is on the
air broadcasting his radio column. The original intention had been for Winchell
to play Larry Wayne but negotiations with Universal broke down.

MGM's lavish and tuneful *Broadway Melody of 1936* (1935), directed by Roy
Del Ruth, showcased the dazzling dance talents of Eleanor Powell. Top-billed
Jack Benny plays the scheming columnist Bert Keeler of *The World-Tribune*,
known as the 'Voice of Broadway'. There is no doubt who Keeler is supposed to
be. He has Winchell's trademark hat and telegraph ticker, his staccato delivery
and uses Winchellisms such as 'blessed event'. Keeler is conducting a feud with
Broadway producer Bob Gordon (Robert Taylor), who regularly turns up at his
office to punch Keeler on the nose. Keeler's latest wheeze to embarrass Gordon
occurs when he discovers that Gordon lacks a star for his new show. He invents
a fictitious French star, La Belle Arlette and reports Gordon's frantic pursuit
of her. However when Gordon's former hometown sweetheart Irene Foster
(Eleanor Powell) turns up seeking an audition and is turned down by Gordon,
she audaciously poses as Arlette, secures the star part, triumphs and reignites
her romance with Gordon.

Winchell himself made it to the screen in two films for 20th Century Fox, both
directed by Sidney Lanfield, which featured his 'feud' with Ben Bernie. The very
funny *Wake Up and Live* (1937) was scripted by Harry Tugend and Jack Yellen.
Much of the action takes place in the fabulous art deco setting of the Federal
Broadcasting Company's Radio Center. The life of the Center is effectively evoked
in background vignettes: Barnett Parker as a snooty chorusmaster disdainfully
leading the community singing of 'Camptown Races'; a massive opera star fainting from microphone fright; the tour guides being drilled and disciplined like a
regiment with failure leading to dishonourable discharge. The film opens with
Ben Bernie and his band performing at the Hi-Hat Club and Winchell doing his
regular radio broadcast, his trademark hat on the back of his head, and rattling
off the latest gossip about film stars, socialites and gangsters (for the purposes of
the film all fictional). The film is thereafter punctuated by band performances
and Winchell broadcasts all peppered with his invented Winchellisms. The film
highlights their exchange of insults on the air. Their rivalry is crystallized when
they both engage in the search for a mysterious tenor who accidentally broadcasts
during Bernie's radio show and is dubbed 'The Phantom Troubadour' (echoing

the real radio performer known as 'The Masked Tenor'). The singer is actually Eddie Kane (Jack Haley), a vaudeville performer who suffers from 'mike fright' (the microphone turns into a grinning devil before his eyes), and has had to take a job as a tour guide at Radio Center. His identity is discovered by radio singer Alice Huntley (Alice Faye), whose uplifting show *Wake Up and Live* has been cancelled by the sponsors as too dull and lacking in jokes. She sets out to cure him of his 'mike fright', during the course of it enabling him to broadcast unwittingly from her apartment by setting up a microphone that he believes to be a dummy. Both Winchell and Bernie claim to have found the 'Phantom Troubadour' but Bernie produces a masked impersonator and Winchell uses a record. An unscrupulous agent kidnaps Eddie but he escapes and encouraged by Alice, conquers his 'mike fright' and makes his debut in a broadcast from the Manila Club with Ben Bernie. Bernie and Winchell declare a truce. Bernie and Winchell convincingly play themselves and deliver their insults with relish. Winchell is also given two very funny assistants, wisecracking Patsy Kelly and cigar-chewing, acid-tongued Ned Sparks. Ironically Haley's singing voice was dubbed by Buddy Clark – making him the real 'Phantom Troubadour'. A follow-up film, *Love and Hisses* (1937) had Winchell and Bernie tussle over the promotion of a new discovery, French singer Simone Simon who after various shenanigans is successfully launched. But it was disappointingly routine and lacked the comic sparkle of *Wake Up and Live*.

In the meantime Winchell had been perfect casting as the fast-talking, unscrupulous reporter Hildy Johnson with James Gleason as his manipulative editor Walter Burns in the *Lux Radio Theatre* presentation on 28 June 1937 of *The Front Page*, the classic Ben Hecht–Charles MacArthur play about journalism. The play had opened on 14 August 1928 in New York and was an immediate hit with Winchellesque Lee Tracy as Hildy and Osgood Perkins as Walter. The role of Hildy fitted Winchell like a glove and might have been modelled on him but for the fact that the play was based on Hecht and MacArthur's experiences as journalists in Chicago in the 1920s and Hecht and MacArthur's Hildy Johnson was based on a real-life Hildy Johnson who worked his way up from copy boy to top reporter and died in 1931 aged 45. Walter Burns was based on a real-life editor Walter Crawford Howey.

Winchell was introduced by presenter Cecil B. De Mille as 'the most original, most highly paid, most copied and most widely known amongst reporters'. The story, which had been notably filmed in 1931 with Pat O'Brien and Adolphe Menjou, has Hildy trying to leave journalism, get married and go into book publishing while the lure of a front page story and the machinations of his editor combine to prevent him. The radio version is fast-talking, fast-moving, establishing a pace which never lets up. The banter between the newsmen crackles and Winchell is excellent. But Winchell's enduring reputation was determined by none of these films. Instead it was a film far removed from the musicals and comedies of the 1930s that fixed his image for posterity – Alexander Mackendrick's caustic masterpiece, *The Sweet Smell of Success* (1957). It originated in a 1950 *Cosmopolitan* story by Ernest Lehman, who had once fed gossip titbits to Winchell. Lehman turned it into a script for the independent company Hecht-Hill-Lancaster. The script was then extensively reworked by the brilliant left-wing playwright Clifford Odets. The result was an unsparing exposé of the corrosive power of the Broadway columnist, J.J. Hunsecker. Known as 'The Eyes of Broadway', Hunsecker's column is published in the *New York Globe* and he also has his own television show. He rules the roost, like Winchell did at the Stork Club, from his regular table at the nightclub 21 where he is courted by people seeking his favour. His column is described as a mixture of 'slimy scandal' and 'phoney patriotics', the very charges levelled against Winchell by his critics. He revels openly in the power he exercises over politicians, showbusiness people and policemen. Hunsecker is portrayed as cruel, vindictive, egocentric and paranoid. Readers of the original story and viewers of the film identified this at once as a portrait of Winchell. The film contains two outstanding performances from Burt Lancaster as the icily aloof and venomous Hunsecker and Tony Curtis as the frantically hustling press agent Sidney Falco who, to get items into Hunsecker's column, resorts to ever more desperate stratagems – blackmail, pimping, anti-Communist smears and police violence. The plot of the film hinges on Hunsecker using Sidney to break up a romance between his sister Susan, to whom he is obsessively devoted, and a young jazz musician, and details the increasingly dishonest and illegal means Sidney goes to, in order to retain the favour of the columnist, who himself smears the boy in his column. In the end, Sidney fails, Susan leaves her brother and Hunsecker has Sidney beaten up by his police henchmen. The episode recalls Winchell's use of his column to smear an admirer of his daughter Walda. The urgent jazz score, evocative black and white photography of New York at night, the pungent dialogue, the nervous intensity and relentless pace of life combine to convey exactly the right atmosphere of corruption and the abuse of power.[20]

Just as colourful as Winchell but more upmarket was the critic and broadcaster Alexander Woollcott (1887–1943). One of the most influential theatre critics in New York, he became equally significant in the world of books. In his twice-weekly fifteen-minute radio programme *The Town Crier* (1933–38) on CBS he told stories, related gossip and delivered reviews of books and plays, speaking directly to middle-class, middle-brow America. 'Within a few months', *Literary Digest* reported, 'his voice was familiar to everyone in America who owned a radio, and he had only to mention that he had gone "quietly mad" over a book to have the country go mad too'. Two typical beneficiaries of Woollcott's enthusiasm were James Hilton's *Goodbye, Mr Chips* and Pearl Buck's *The Good Earth*, propelled to the top of the best-seller lists following his endorsements.[21] So distinctive a character was he with his unique combination of erudition, sentimentality and venom that he inspired, it is said, the screen characters Waldo P. Lydecker in *Laura* and Addison DeWitt in *All About Eve*.[22] He also seems to lie behind the character of broadcaster Victor Grandison in *The Unsuspected*. Like Grandison, Woollcott was a 'gleeful connoisseur of murder and macabre' and Grandison's introduction to his programme 'This is Grandison speaking' directly echoes Woollcott's 'This is Woollcott speaking'. But Woollcott's most celebrated incarnation was as Sheridan Whiteside in *The Man Who Came To Dinner* by two of Woollcott's New York friends, playwrights Moss Hart and George S. Kaufman. There was never any doubt about who the play was based on as the authors dedicated it to 'Alexander Woollcott. For reasons that are nobody's business' and gave him a percentage of the take in view of the use they were making of his character and idiosyncrasies.

The play related how Sheridan Whiteside, author, lecturer and broadcaster, known as 'the idol of the airwaves' descended on the mid-Western town of Mesalia, Ohio. Slipping on the ice and breaking his hip, he moves in with the Stanley family and causes havoc by virtually taking over the house and receiving a stream of visitors, phone calls and gifts. The play and film captured the essence of 1940s celebrity culture with Whiteside receiving telephone calls from Eleanor Roosevelt, Winston Churchill and Ethel Barrymore and referring in passing to his friendship with Somerset Maugham, the Duke and Duchess of Windsor, Jascha Heifetz, Gypsy Rose Lee, Deanna Durbin, and Haile Selassie. One of the highlights of the film is the Christmas outside broadcast from the Stanleys' living room in which Whiteside delivers a glutinously sentimental address, accompanied by a boys' choir. Whiteside is sponsored by Cream of Mush; Woollcott was sponsored by Cream of Wheat.

The film is dominated by Monty Woolley's definitive performance as Whiteside, a self-centred, vituperative, endlessly scheming egotist. But there is added humour in the fact that many of the other characters are also based on real-life figures in Woollcott's social circle. There are notable performances from Reginald

Gardiner as the English playwright Beverly Carlton, a thinly disguised Noel Coward; Jimmy Durante as the girl-chasing Hollywood comedian Banjo, based on Harpo Marx, and Ann Sheridan as the social-climbing stage star Lorraine Sheldon, based on Gertrude Lawrence.

The play had actually been inspired by a visit paid in 1938 by Woollcott to Moss Hart's home in Pennsylvania where he had insulted the host, his guests and his taste in architecture, furniture and friends, denounced the servants for dishonesty and demanded that all the heating in the house be switched off. Hart and Kaufman cast a disgruntled drama professor from Yale, Monty Woolley, as Whiteside. The play opened in New York on 16 October 1939 and received fourteen curtain calls. It was an instant hit and made Woolley an immediate star. While Woolley played the part in New York, Clifton Webb took it on in a second company performing in Chicago and finally Woollcott himself played the part in a third company, first on the West Coast and later the East Coast. The Warner Brothers film version, directed by William Keighley and released in 1941, was described by Bosley Crowther in *The New York Times* as 'Unquestionably the most vicious but hilarious cat-clawing exhibition ever put on the screen, a deliciously wicked character portrait and a helter-skelter satire'.[23] Woollcott himself suffered a heart attack during a live broadcast of a round table discussion on Hitlerism in 1943 and died several hours later.[24]

The Great Man (1956), based on a novel by Al Morgan, directed and co-written by and starring José Ferrer, took a far more disenchanted view of the radio industry than the comedies and musicals of the 1930s and 1940s. The film, sharply observed, well acted and capably directed, exposed the industry as cynical, hypocritical and manipulative. Adopting the same structure as *Citizen Kane* and with first-person narration by the star, the film has investigative reporter Joe Harris (Ferrer), assigned to research and present a radio tribute to a major radio personality, 'comedian, philosopher and friend of the people' Herb Fuller, recently killed in a car crash. The film consists of a series of interviews with people who knew Herb and a completely different picture of the deceased emerges – unscrupulous, callous, manipulative and egotistical. The interviewees include the local radio station proprietor (Ed Wynn, himself an early star of radio) who gave Herb his first break and was badly let down by him; the drunken singer (Julie London) who had been his mistress and whom he had physically abused and his former manager (Keenan Wynn), who reveals that Herb's greatest broadcast, one appealing for blood for wounded soldiers and apparently done from the Rhine front line, was actually done from the safety of a studio in Paris where he was on a bender. Having compiled a wholly false and insincere tribute,

Joe goes on the air, abandons his script and tells the true story of Herb. He expects the sack but the company president is delighted, dubs him 'Mr Integrity' and gives him his own show. The cynicism of the media is perfectly displayed in two beautifully written and played scenes. In one, two company executives discuss arrangements for Herb's lying-in-state and decide to turn a cinema into a special chapel and since Herb had no religion, to bring in choirs from all the major religious denominations. In the other, interviews are held with a selection of the mourners at the lying-in-state and later in the studio, cut and edited to change the emphasis of what was being said. Interestingly in 1957 Elia Kazan directed *A Face in the Crowd* which similarly exposed a beloved folksy philosopher and television personality as a cruel and egotistical sham. Together with *The Sweet Smell of Success* and *The Great Man*, *A Face in the Crowd* represents a new stage in the representation of the media, born perhaps of the experience of the McCarthyite period, which stresses the ability of radio and television to falsify, manipulate and deceive audiences. It is a far cry from the uncritical celebration of radio that Hollywood undertook in previous decades.

Notes

1   Rudolf Arnheim, *Radio*, London: Faber and Faber, 1936, pp. 19–20.
2   Rachael Low, *Documentary and Educational Films of the 1930s*, London: Allen and Unwin, 1979, p. 83.
3   David Butler with Irene Kahn Atkins, *David Butler: A Director's Guild of America Oral History*, Metuchen, NJ: Scarecrow Press, 1993, p. 108.
4   Peter Bogdanovich, *Allan Dwan: The Last Pioneer*, London: Studio Vista, 1971, pp. 109–10.
5   John Dunning, *The Encyclopedia of Old-Time Radio*, New York: Oxford University Press, 1998, pp. 551–2.
6   Valeria Camporesi, *Mass Culture and National Traditions: The BBC and American Broadcasting 1922–1954*, Fucecchio, Italy: European Press Academic Publishing, 2000, p. 121.
7   William J. Mann, *Wisecracker: The Life and Times of William Haines*, New York: Viking, 1998.
8   David Chierichetti, *Hollywood Director*, New York: Curtis Books, 1973, p. 103.
9   Chierichetti, *Hollywood Director*, pp. 119–22.
10 Val Gielgud, *Years in a Mirror*, London: The Bodley Head, 1965, p. 48.
11 On *Radio Parade of 1935* see John Ellis, 'British cinema as performance art: *Brief Encounter, Radio Parade of 1935* and the circumstances of film exhibition', in Justine Ashby and Andrew Higson (eds), *British Cinema Past and Present*, London: Routledge, 2000, pp. 95–109.
12 Bernard Vorhaus quoted in Geoff Brown, 'Money for speed', in Jeffrey Richards (ed.), *The Unknown 1930s*, London: I.B. Tauris, 1998, p. 190.

13 Henry Hall, *Here's To the Next Time*, London: Odhams, 1955, p. 141.

14 Hall, *Here's To the Next Time*, p. 141.

15 Xantippe, *Death Catches Up With Mr Kluck*, Garden City, New York: Doubleday, Doran and Co., 1935, p. i.

16 Gielgud, *Years in a Mirror*, p. 138.

17 Val Gielgud, *Years of the Locust*, London; Nicholson and Watson, 1947, pp. 130–1 and Gielgud, *Years in a Mirror*, p. 139.

18 Gielgud, *Years of the Locust*, p. 131.

19 Neal Gabler, *Walter Winchell: Gossip, Power and the Culture of Celebrity*, London: Picador, 1995, p. xii.

20 Philip Kemp, *Lethal Innocence: The Cinema of Alexander Mackendrick*, London: Methuen, 1991, pp. 137–62.

21 Joan Shelley Rubin, *The Making of Middlebrow Culture*, Chapel Hill: University of North Carolina Press, 1992, p. 292.

22 Steven Bach, *Dazzler: The Life and Times of Moss Hart*, New York: Alfred A. Knopf, 2001, p. 188.

23 Quoted in Gene Ringgold, *The Films of Bette Davis*, New York: Citadel Press, 1970, p. 114.

24 Howard Teichmann, *Smart Aleck*, New York: William Morrow, 1976, p. 253.

7

War and politics

The Second World War was a radio war. Radio in wartime was informational and inspirational. It provided news, entertainment, propaganda. Speeches on the radio by the national leaders, Roosevelt in the United States and Churchill in the United Kingdom, lifted morale. The links between cinema and radio became ever closer. Three notable British films derived their titles from recurrent phrases in the news bulletins: *One Of Our Aircraft Is Missing*, *The Next of Kin* and *Fires Were Started*. Two of the memorable radio voices of the war were the novelist and playwright J.B. Priestley, whose broadcast *Postscripts* after the news made him the most listened-to broadcaster in the United Kingdom after Churchill and the journalist and war correspondent Quentin Reynolds who broadcast to the United States from London in strongly supportive terms. Both of them were recruited by the documentary movement, which came into its own during the war. Both provided what were in effect radio essays with pictures. Reynolds introduced and narrated *London Can Take It* (1940) and *Christmas Under Fire* (1940) which were aimed at the American audience and paid tribute to the courage, determination and morale of the British people in the face of German bombing. Priestley wrote and narrated *Britain at Bay* (1940), a clarion call to the British people to join in the war effort in defence of freedom.

King George VI's main contribution to inspirational broadcasting was his annual Christmas message to the United Kingdom and the Empire. One of these led directly to a film. He ended his 1939 Christmas message by quoting from a poem by Minnie Louise Haskins, *The Gate of the Year*:

> I said to the man who stood at the Gate of the Year, 'Give me a light that I may tread safely into the unknown' and he replied, 'Go out into the darkness, and put your hand into the hand of God. That shall be to you better than light, and safer than a known way'.

He concluded 'May that Almighty Hand guide and uphold us all'. Film tycoon J. Arthur Rank, a devout Methodist, was so moved by this that he commissioned an inspirational film to be built around it. He turned for it to Norman Walker, who had directed Rank's award-winning first feature film venture, *Turn of the Tide* in 1935. Walker took his cue from an earlier passage in the King's speech:

> We look with pride and thankfulness on the never-failing courage and devotion of the Royal Navy … and when I speak of our navy today, I mean all the men of our Empire who go down to the sea in ships, the mercantile marine, the mine-sweepers, the trawlers and drifters, from the senior officers to the last boy who has joined up.

In doing so, he turned back to the world of fisherfolk featured in *Turn of the Tide*. In *The Man at the Gate* (1941), he tells the story of a fisherman's wife who has lost two sons to the sea and when her remaining son, a wireless operator on a steamer, is reported lost after the ship is sunk by German bombs, she loses her faith in God. She comes to believe that 'there's no love left in the world and only fear, hatred and cruelty'. But listening to the King's Christmas broadcast and the Haskins poem, she regains her faith and repeats his words 'better than light and safer than a known way'. Immediately after the broadcast comes news on the radio that her son has been rescued and landed safely in Scotland. The King's words have restored faith and hope.

From the beginning, radio featured in films about the war. *The Lion Has Wings* (1939), the first feature film of the conflict, was made by Alexander Korda in six weeks flat, following the outbreak of the war. An out-and-out propaganda piece, it blended documentary and newsreel footage with staged dramatic scenes and feature film extracts to show why the United Kingdom was fighting Germany. In one of the staged sequences, two middle-class women, played by stars Merle Oberon and June Duprez, listen to the declaration of war on the radio, standing up as the national anthem is played at the end. In Noel Coward's box-office hit *In Which We Serve* (1942), recounting the story of a ship *H.M.S. Torrin* from its launch in 1939 to its sinking in the battle of Crete in 1941, the crew also hear the declaration of war broadcast throughout the ship from the radio. When Chamberlain declares 'You can imagine what a bitter blow this is to me', John Mills, as seaman Shorty Blake, responds 'It isn't exactly a bank holiday for us', a direct echo of Coward's opposition to Chamberlain's pre-war policy of appeasement. Catching up with the progress of the war on the six o'clock news became a nightly ritual, as seen for instance in Frank Launder and Sidney Gilliat's *Millions Like Us* (1943). Keeping in touch with home through the radio was a feature of overseas service as when an army unit out east in *The Way Ahead* (1944) gather round a wireless set to listen to an evocative talk on the English countryside.

The radio was ever-present in recreations of actual wartime episodes. In 1946 director Brian Desmond Hurst took survivors of Arnhem back to Holland to restage that fatal campaign, mingling original combat footage and documentary recreations. For the film Canadian war correspondent Stanley Maxted repeated his historic despatches for the BBC and throughout soldiers followed the progress of the action on the wireless. In *For Freedom* (1940), a semi-documentary recreation of the battle of the River Plate, Robert Beatty played an American correspondent reporting on the sinking of the *Graf Spee*, a sequence repeated in Michael Powell and Emeric Pressburger's large-scale Technicolor restaging of the story in *Battle of the River Plate* (1955) with Lionel Murton playing the correspondent. In Powell and Pressburger's wartime tribute to the Dutch resistance, *One of Our Aircraft is Missing* (1942), the members of the resistance tuned in surreptitiously to the BBC.

Dangerous Moonlight (US title: *Suicide Squadron*) (1941), directed by Brian Desmond Hurst and scripted by Terence Young, was a classic romantic melodrama in which a Polish concert pianist (Anton Walbrook) falls in love with and marries an American millionaire's daughter (Sally Gray). Their romance is, however, threatened when despite her opposition, he joins the Polish air force in England. The film opens with scenes in Poland in which the outnumbered Polish air force prepares for a final mission and the radio continuously plays Chopin's *Polonaise* in A Major as a sign that Warsaw is still holding out against the Germans, recreating the historical fact that Polish radio played the national anthem continuously until Warsaw surrendered. RKO Radio Pictures, who produced the film in the United Kingdom, had so little faith in the film that they licensed it to a minor studio, Republic, for release in the United States, only to reacquire it when Richard Addinsell's *Warsaw Concerto*, specially composed for the film, became a worldwide hit. In *Night Train to Munich* (1940), the Czech interior minister used the radio to alert the population to the German invasion.

Anthony Asquith's charming and funny *The Demi-Paradise* (1943), written and produced by White Russian émigré Anatole de Grunwald, was the British cinema's principal contribution to Anglo-Russian friendship and tribute to 'our gallant Russian allies'. Laurence Olivier gave a brilliant performance as a bemused Russian engineer who comes to England in 1939 and whose preconceptions about the United Kingdom are gradually disproved as he comes to appreciate the secret of the United Kingdom's survival and success. The radio plays a part at two key moments. The BBC record Beatrice Harrison playing *Chanson Hindoue* on the cello to the nightingales in the garden of a country house, evidence to the Russian of the true spiritual nature of the British, and a recreation of an actual event, and later the engineer hears Churchill on the radio pledging the United Kingdom's support for Russia after the German invasion of the Soviet Union.

No film-maker testified to the ever-present wartime role of radio better than Humphrey Jennings. He was one of three directors – with Harry Watt and Pat Jackson – who for the GPO Film Unit shot *The First Days* (1939). It began with people all over the country switching on their radios to hear the historic broadcast by Prime Minister Neville Chamberlain announcing the declaration of war on Sunday 3 September 1939, a broadcast that would become very familiar from its regular use in feature films and documentaries about the war: 'I am speaking to you from the cabinet room of 10 Downing Street ...'

Listen to Britain (1942), the film many regard as Jennings' masterpiece, is a sound picture of twenty-four hours in the United Kingdom at war. It meshes music, sound and image perfectly to create a picture of the organic wholeness of a people and their culture. It wordlessly integrates and accords equal respect to all elements of the population in what was being projected as a 'People's War': men and women, adults and children, soldiers and civilians, factory workers and teachers, Britons and Canadians. Along with the trill of birdsong, the roar of Spitfires, the rumble of tanks, the clip-clop of horses' hooves, the hiss of steam engines, the clang of Big Ben and music of all kinds, highbrow and lowbrow, the radio provides a thread of continuity. The BBC time signal – the pips – introduces Joseph McLeod: 'This is the BBC Home and Forces Programme. Here is the news'. Thereafter there is a montage of overseas broadcasts: 'London Calling' and the strains of 'The British Grenadiers'. There is a snatch of a 'Keep Fit' programme and 'Music While You Work', with girls on the production line joining in 'Yes, My Darling Daughter'. In his only feature-length documentary *Fires Were Started* (1943), a tribute to the courage of the firefighters, the wife of one of them, Jacko, listens to the radio news report of the raid on London: 'it does not appear that casualties are likely to be heavy', unaware that her husband has perished doing his duty.

The Silent Village (1943) was Jennings' imaginative transposition to South Wales of the massacre of the Czech mining village of Lidice after the assassination of *Reichsprotektor* Reinhard Heydrich. The film depicts the occupation of the village by the Nazis and the resistance by strikes, sabotage and the production of an underground newspaper. But after Heydrich is assassinated, the village of Cwmgiedd is singled out for retribution. The men are shot, the women removed to a concentration camp and the village burned to the ground. After the shooting of Heydrich, the film is punctuated by close-ups of the radio as a succession of announcements are made: the shooting, the arrests and executions, the death of Heydrich and finally the destruction of the village and the obliteration of its name. But the film ends on an upbeat note as we are told the name of Lidice has been immortalized, lives in the hearts of miners the world over and will further inspire the struggle for freedom.

Jennings' haunting *A Diary for Timothy* (1945) follows the first few months of the life of Timothy Jenkins, born near Oxford on 3 September 1944, the fifth anniversary of the outbreak of the war. It seeks to explain the war effort to him and expresses hopes for the future which will not involve a return to the bad old pre-war days of unemployment, division and deprivation. It is a film which despite its upbeat ending with news reports of American, British and Russian advances in 1945, is extraordinarily melancholy in tone. It embraces the news of the Arnhem disaster, the flying bombs, extensive bomb damage, queues, rain and as narrator Michael Redgrave says of December 1944: 'death and darkness, death and fog … death came by telegram to many of us on Christmas Eve'. It conveys through its imagery, its E.M. Forster-scripted commentary and Richard Addinsell's plaintive musical score an aching sense of war weariness, a longing for it all to be over but underlying it a determination to see it through. Just as in *The First Days*, so radio is an integral part of the last days of the war. The film opens in a BBC studio with Frederick Allen reading the first news of the day on Sunday 3 September 1944 and thereafter a succession of different BBC announcers, some in their shirtsleeves, can be seen and heard announcing the assault on Arnhem, the German counterattack in the Ardennes, the Russian advance into Germany, the allied air attacks on Berlin and the allied crossing of the Rhine. We also hear some of the historic firsthand account of Arnhem by the Canadian war correspondent Stanley Maxted.

The Crown Film Unit also produced *The True Story of Lilli Marlene* (1944), directed and written by Humphrey Jennings, a dramatic reconstruction of the way in which a song broadcast by the enemy was appropriated and transformed by the British. It highlights the role of radio request programmes in maintaining troops' morale. It is narrated by Marius Goring who, describing the record of 'Lilli Marlene' as an Eighth Army trophy of war, recounts the history of the song which tells of the yearning of a girl for her soldier sweetheart. The words were written in 1923, the music in 1938 and it was recorded by the Swedish singer Lale Andersen. It went unnoticed until 1941 when the Germans entered Belgrade, took over the radio station and initiated a programme *Message from Home*, a series of messages and record requests played for the Afrika Korps. 'Lilli Marlene' becomes an instant hit with the troops. Denis Johnston, the BBC war correspondent, relates how he found soldiers in the British Eighth Army listening to it. The Germans continue to play it and the BBC analyse it for propaganda content. It is played every day until the surrender of Stalingrad and then Radio Belgrade cease to play it. In the United Kingdom new words are put to the music and Lucie Mannheim performs it, delivering with evident relish the line 'Hang Hitler from the lantern of Lilli Marlene'. News arrives that Lale Andersen has been imprisoned in a concentration camp for sending messages home saying 'All I want is to get out of this terrible country'. The song now marches with the Eighth Army and the allied forces liberating Europe and is finally seen and heard in a scene projecting forward to a peaceful post-war London.

A shoddy and cheaply made fictionalization of the story of the song appeared in 1950, *Lilli Marlene*, directed by Arthur Crabtree and written by Leslie Wood. For all its stock characters and clichéd situations, its retrospective value lies in the fact that it is a compendium of many of the wartime aspects of broadcasting. The film is narrated by American war correspondent Steve Moray (Hugh McDermott), whose broadcasts on the progress of the war in the Western Desert punctuate the film. He tells the story of Lilli Marlene (Lisa Daniely), daughter of a French father and German mother, who before the war had inspired the German composer to write the song after a brief holiday romance. The song later became a favourite of the Afrika Korps. In 1942 Lilli Marlene is discovered working as a waitress in her uncle's café in a small town in North Africa. The Germans plan to use her for propaganda purposes. But she is captured by the British and demonstrates her real loyalties by singing 'Lilli Marlene' in French and English to the men of the Eighth Army. In an impromptu concert she not only sings her own song but also the Vera Lynn wartime favourite 'We'll Meet Again'. The Germans are desperate to get her back and attempt to kidnap her during the concert but fail. She is flown to Cairo to broadcast to the Allies but a second successful German bid to kidnap her sees her returned to Germany where she is brainwashed and ends up making propaganda broadcasts in which she reads out messages from English POWS to their families, while continuing to sing 'Lilli Marlene', now in German. In 1946 she turns up at the first Alamein reunion at the Albert Hall and is reunited with Steve, with whom she is in love, and it is revealed that the messages she was broadcasting from Berlin contained coded information for British Intelligence. She ends up leading the assembled veterans in the title song. Not only does the film include two of the most popular broadcast songs of the war and first-hand accounts of the campaigns by a war correspondent, it features Richard Murdoch as an entertainments officer, recreating his role from the popular radio comedy *Much Binding in the Marsh*, first broadcast in 1944 and to which reference is made in the dialogue. It also features Estelle Brody, the silent film star who is now also broadcasting to the troops and sings 'Mademoiselle from Armentieres', the First World War hit which had become the title of her most successful film in 1926. Neil Tuson, the producer of *Dick Barton – Special Agent*, turns up briefly as a BBC producer. Michael Ward, in an extraordinary piece of miscasting, appears as probably the most outrageously camp Nazi agent ever seen on film.

The role in the nation's affections occupied in the 1930s by Gracie Fields was taken during the war by Vera Lynn, who became known as 'The Forces Sweetheart'. She became the British equivalent of Lale Andersen, German radio's 'Lilli Marlene'. Vera's radio request programme, 'Sincerely Yours', in which she sang sentimental songs and delivered personal messages to the servicemen overseas from their loved ones at home, was from its initiation in 1941 a hit with listeners. Her image, as she writes in her autobiography, was 'a believable girl-next-door, big-sister, universal fiancée'. Her repertoire was 'for the most part … sentimental, wistful songs. They may have been the ones I was best at, but they were also the ones the troops asked for'.[1] The Board of Governors, the BBC Music Department and a gaggle of MPs and retired military men became concerned that a diet of such songs would undermine the morale of the troops and that they should be given regular doses of virile, martial music. In 1942 the *Brains Trust* even debated a question 'Is Vera Lynn's programme harmful to morale?'. The BBC launched an 'Anti-Slush War', initially welcomed by the press.[2] But within weeks the public were protesting, the popular press swung in behind them and Vera Lynn was vindicated. As she wrote herself: 'As I saw it, I was reminding the boys of what they were *really* fighting for, the precious personal things rather than the ideologies and theories'.[3]

Her radio success led directly to films. Vera Lynn starred in three made respectively in 1942, 1943 and 1944, the most successful being the first, which inevitably bore the title of her signature tune, *We'll Meet Again* (1942). Directed by Phil Brandon, it had a storyline loosely based on Vera's own career. In the film, she plays Peggy Brown who is appearing in a West End musical during the Blitz and is accidentally discovered by the BBC. She spends much of the film doing good. She comforts a boy whose mother has been killed in the Blitz and a professor whose life's work has been destroyed. She unites an estranged couple – she, superintendent of an orphanage, he a Scottish soldier – and supervises their wedding, singing 'Ave Maria' at it. She tells the girl: 'It's up to us now more than ever to stand by these men of ours. We must make our loyalty, our sacrifice equal to theirs'.

The BBC is central to the story. Peggy starts out as a dancer but is discovered to have a voice when the audience for the show in which she is appearing, *Piccadilly*

Belles, stay behind in the theatre during an air raid. After a rousing rendition of 'God Save the King', Peggy leads them in a spirit-lifting 'cheer-up' song 'Be Like the Kettle and Sing', until the all-clear sounds. Struggling composer Frank Foster gets her to record privately his latest song 'After the Rain'. Bandleader Geraldo, playing himself, gets Peggy an introduction to BBC executive Hastropp and she delivers a copy of the record to his office. It is forgotten until accidentally played when a programme is under-running. Peggy becomes an instant star and Geraldo plays the song with his orchestra at his nightclub, with Peggy singing.

The BBC is embodied by kindly, wise and paternalistic executive Hastropp (Frederick Leister) and his comically anxious and officious secretary Miss Bohne (Betty Jardine). They now manage her broadcasting career. Peggy's stardom is cemented by an appearance on the hit show *Variety Hour* and she gets her own show *Sincerely Yours*. She uses a St Andrew's Day broadcast to inform the soldier whose marriage she facilitated that his baby has been born. She visits mother and baby in hospital and sings a lullaby to the children 'Goodnight, my baby, goodnight'. The film ends with an outside broadcast of a concert for the RAF with Peggy singing 'Sincerely Yours' and 'We'll Meet Again', the audience joining in. The film represents a defiant cinematic rejection of the 'Anti-Slush War' but also contains interesting glimpses of the BBC at war with guest appearances by John Watt and John Sharman of the Variety Department and announcer Alvar Liddell, and with the fictional Hastropp juggling schedules, improvising and dealing with wartime hazards to keep the BBC broadcasting.

The idea that secret information was being transmitted to the enemy via coded messages on the radio was one of the rumours being circulated during wartime. It featured in three other films. *Who Done It?* (1942), directed by Erle C. Kenton, was one of a popular series of comedy films starring that deeply unappealing duo, Bud Abbott and Lou Costello, the former a hectoring bully, the latter a loud, accident-prone idiot child. Most of the action takes place in the ultra-modern studios of the GBS, General Broadcasting System, whose executive director, Colonel Andrews (Thomas Gomez) is electrocuted in a steel chair in front of the live audience for the show *Murder at Midnight* as he prepares to make an important announcement. His Czech doctor is subsequently also murdered. Abbott and Costello, two soda jerks who are aspiring radio writers, are mistaken for detectives and start investigating the murders, assisted by the producer of *Murder at Midnight*, Jane Little (Louise Allbritton) and her boyfriend, the show's scriptwriter Jim Turner (Patric Knowles). The investigation takes place amid Abbott and Costello's traditional slapstick knockabout and quickfire gag routines. Eventually it is decided to restage the broadcast to expose the murderer and he is revealed as one of the company's employees who is transmitting to an enemy power vital information about naval shipping movements through coded messages slipped into radio broadcasts. Colonel Andrews and Dr Marek had broken the code and therefore had to be eliminated. The film ends with Abbott and Costello chasing the spy onto the roof of the radio building and Costello dangling from the radio aerial and receiving electric shocks before the spy is captured. The studio setting allows glimpses of a variety show and a lottery show *Wheel of Fortune* as well as the mystery show *Murder at Midnight*. There is also the inevitable comedy routine involving radio sound effects. The idea of a woman producer of mystery shows was not at all far-fetched as former actresses Helen Mack and Edna Best both produced radio mystery shows during the 1940s.

In *Let George Do It* (1940), directed for Ealing Studios by comedy maestro Marcel Varnel, borrowed from Gainsborough for the purpose, the United Kingdom's top male box-office star George Formby leant his talents to the war effort in his familiar persona of the gormless but goodhearted Lancashire lad who successfully muddles through whatever predicament he has to face. In *Let George Do It*, band-leader Mark Mendez (Garry Marsh) is communicating information about British shipping to Nazi U-Boats via a code contained in the musical arrangements played by his band in their concerts broadcast on the radio from the Hotel Majestic, Bergen. George, acting as a British secret agent, joins the band as a ukulele player, obtains the musical code and after various comic misadventures ensures the capture of Mendez. In the lively and atmospheric Hollywood thriller *International Lady* (1941), directed by Tim Whelan, an FBI agent (George Brent) and an MI5 operative (Basil Rathbone) join forces to put paid to the activities of a Norwegian opera singer (Ilona Massey) who via musical codes in songs in her broadcast concerts is transmitting instructions for the sabotage of American planes intended for the United Kingdom.

There is something of a Hitchcockian flavour to the narrative of *International Lady* and Hitchcock himself featured radio in the climax of one of his best thrillers, *Foreign Correspondent* (1940). In this film, American foreign correspondent Johnny Jones (Joel McCrea) helps rescue a Dutch statesman kidnapped by the Nazis and exposes the Universal Peace Party as a Nazi front. Along with the exciting action set-pieces punctuating the film, the narrative charts the education of an initially ignorant and detached American who becomes fully apprised of the issues at stake and committed to the war against the Nazis.

The film was shot between 18 March and 29 May 1940 at a cost of $1,484,167. The action covered the period 20 August to 3 September 1939, ending with the outbreak of war and the shooting down by a German battleship of the clipper in which the leading characters are flying back to the United States. The final scene had Joel McCrea, Laraine Day and George Sanders discussing their experiences and reporting back to the *New York Globe* from the rescue ship. But shortly after completing the filming, Hitchcock paid a visit to England to see his mother and experienced the atmosphere in the country where Germany had begun bombing industrial and military targets in the North and the Midlands. In Hollywood, producer Walter Wanger was anxious to include the latest war news (the fall of Poland, Holland, Denmark and France) and so Ben Hecht was drafted in to write a new final scene. It was scripted and shot in a single day, 5 July 1940, in time for the film to open on 27 August. In a radio studio in London, Johnny Jones broadcasts to the United States as the German bombs fall on London in a manner uncannily prefiguring the broadcasts from Edward R. Murrow and Quentin Reynolds to the United States from London.

> JONES: Hello America. I've been watching a part of the world being blown to pieces. A part of the world as nice as Vermont, Ohio, Virginia, California and Illinois lies ripped up and bleeding like a steer in a slaughterhouse. And I've seen things that make the history of the savages read like Pollyanna legend.
> ANNOUNCER: We're going to have to postpone the broadcast.
>
> (*At this point sirens begin to wail and lights flash as bombs begin to burst outside the studio.*)
>
> JONES: Don't postpone nothing, let's go on as long as we can.
> ANNOUNCER (*to Carol*): Ma'am, we've got a shelter downstairs.
> JONES: How about it, Carol?
> CAROL: They're listening in America, Johnny.
> JONES: O.K. We'll tell them. I can't read the rest of this speech I have because the lights have gone out. So I'll just have to talk off the cuff. All that noise you hear isn't static, it's death coming to London. Yes, they're coming here now. You can hear the bombs falling on the streets and homes. Don't tune me out – hang on – this is a big story – and you're part of it. It's too late now to do anything except stand in the dark and let them come as if the lights are all out everywhere except in America.
>
> (*Music – 'America' – begins to play softly in background of speech and continues through end credits.*)
>
> JONES: Keep those lights burning, cover them with steel, ring them in with guns, build a canopy of battleships and bombing planes around them and, hello, America, hang on to your lights, they're the only lights in the world.

Five days after Hitchcock shot his epilogue, the London Blitz began. *Foreign Correspondent* was to become one of the films complained of by American isolationists who maintained that Hollywood was seeking to drag the United States into a European war. A Congressional Committee was even set up to examine the truth of these charges but its hearings were overtaken by the Japanese attack on Pearl Harbor and America's entry into the war.[4]

Leo McCarey will probably be remembered as a director of great moments rather than great movies. He himself admitted in an interview that he liked moments in all his films and if these could be put together he might have had something. McCarey's special brilliance lay in his talent for improvisation and it is from this talent that his great moments sprang. But it is a talent which is also a limitation. For while improvisation can create great moments, it can rarely create great movies. The key to understanding McCarey's films is something he once said in an interview about what films should be. He said that every film should be something of a fairy tale: 'I'll let someone else photograph the ugliness of the world. It's larceny to remind people of how lousy things are and call it entertainment'.[5] His best films (*Ruggles of Red Gap*, *The Awful Truth*, *Going My Way*, *Good Sam*) are examples of the genre known as 'the fantasy of good will'.

McCarey's contribution to the war effort, *Once Upon a Honeymoon* (1942) demonstrates perfectly McCarey's strengths and weaknesses as a director. For he chooses to tell a fairy-tale romantic comedy, as the title suggests, but sets it against the background of war-torn Europe to enable him to comment on Fascism. The result is two films in one. On one level we get delicious comedy with Ginger Rogers as Kate O'Hara, an American showgirl married to an Austrian baron, and Cary Grant as Pat O'Toole, a newspaperman who pursues her from capital to capital. There are some memorable McCarey moments: notably Cary posing as an Austrian fitter measuring Ginger for a new dress and a scene where Cary tries to get Ginger drunk in Warsaw and ends up roaring drunk himself.

But on the other, ostensibly more serious, level we have the anti-Fascist message intertwined with some populist comment on being yourself – 'yourself' being preferably a solid, down-to-earth, red-blooded American. The film opens in Vienna in 1938 with Katie O'Hara, burlesque dancer from Brooklyn posing as Philadelphian socialite Katherine Butt-Smith (pronounced Bute-Smith) complete with snobbish la-de-dah accent and airs and graces, telephoning her mother to tell her that she has netted a baron and is going to marry him. The film charts her gradual awakening to what is going on in Europe and her steady abandonment of the airs and graces and affected highbrow culture under the guidance of Pat, who represents the red-blooded American tradition. At the beginning of the film she switches off the radio in the middle of Seyss-Inquart's broadcast announcing that Austria is to be absorbed into the Reich. She is not interested. But she becomes interested when she sees at first hand the persecution of the Jews, the German sterilization policy and the concentration camps, in which she and Pat are confined for a short time after helping a Jewish chambermaid to escape from Poland. She also learns about the fifth-column activities of her husband, Baron von Luber (Walter Slezak), 'Hitler's personal finger man' who sprints round Europe softening up Czechoslovakia, Poland, Norway and finally France for the German invasion. The r*eductio ad absurdum* of this activity is the short scene which opens with von Luber having dinner with a man in Norway who assures him that he will find conditions favourable in Norway and to whom he replies, 'I'm sure I will, Mr Quisling' and ends with a shot of von Luber strolling into the villa Laval in Paris. Even Hitler is reduced to a bit part, glimpsed walking down a hotel corridor.

The film ends with Katie demonstrating her commitment to the democratic cause by pushing her erstwhile husband, the Baron, overboard from a liner bearing him to the United States to continue his devilish work, after he has lectured her about the masses not wanting to think and great men being needed to do it for them. Scrappy, ramshackle and ultimately ludicrous, the film demonstrates McCarey's inability to handle a 'serious message picture'. He goes so far out that he enters the realm of the absurd. But at least one can salvage the comedy and the felicitous teaming of Cary and Ginger.

O'Toole, who starts out as a newspaperman, becomes during the course of the film a radio news analyst. We see him broadcasting from Warsaw amid the Nazi bombing and warning against the danger from fifth columnists. But the big broadcasting scenes come in a Paris radio studio where Pat has agreed to broadcast to the United States to explain Germany's peaceful intentions. He contrives to sabotage it by using colloquial American expressions suggesting the opposite of what he is saying. He also builds up Baron von Luber as a greater figure than Hitler, causing the baron to be sent for by the Führer.

The Lady Has Plans (1941), directed by Sidney Lanfield and written by Harry Tugend, was a comedy thriller set in wartime Lisbon. Ray Milland starred as Ken Harper, the United Broadcasting Company's foreign correspondent, stationed in Lisbon and reporting on the air on developments in Europe. Sidney Royce (Paulette Goddard) is sent to work for him and mistaken for an espionage agent who has the plans for a new torpedo tattooed on her back and aims to sell them to the highest bidder, the Germans or the British. When the truth is discovered, Sidney, Ken and Ronnie Dean (Roland Young) of the British Embassy join forces to lure the agents and the Nazis into a trap. A special hook-up is arranged from a hotel lobby which allows Ken to broadcast to the United States the Nazis' plans and the arrest of the spies. The situation gives rise to a number of well-worn comedy routines (switching around drugged drinks, mixing up rooms, mistaken identity), all smoothly and unobjectionably packaged into a glossy and entertaining conveyor-belt studio product with lavish sets, sprightly direction and accomplished performances, notably from Roland Young as a bumbling British agent.

In both the United Kingdom and the United States films were made drama-tizing the deployment of clandestine radio as part of anti-Nazi resistance in Germany. *Freedom Radio* (1940) (US title: *Voice in the Night*), was directed by Anthony Asquith and scripted by a large team of writers, Anatole de Grunwald, Basil Woon, Jeffrey Dell, Roland Pertwee, Bridget Boland, Louis Golding, Gor-don Wellesley, Wolfgang Wilhelm and George Campbell, suggesting a succession of rewrites. It seems to be dramatizing the activities discussed in *Freedom Call-ing!*, an anonymous account of resistance radio by 'The representative in Great Britain of the Freedom Station' published in 1939.[6]

It is set in Berlin in 1939 and is a hard-hitting drama which explores the use of radio by both the regime and its opponents. The wife of Hitler's Viennese throat doctor, Karl Roder (Clive Brook), actress Irena Roder (Diana Wynyard), is appointed director of Popular Pageantry for the Reich. They become estranged by her pro-Nazi sympathies and his progressive alienation from the regime. This is caused by the murder of his friend Father Landbach for asking his congrega-tion to pray for a list of arrested people; by the rape by a Gestapo officer and subsequent imprisonment in a concentration camp of the fiancée of a young radio engineer; by the arrest of a succession of friends, including the Jew Heini; by the arrest of Granny Schmidt for listening to music on a foreign radio sta-tion; and by the dehumanization of his brother-in-law Otto after he joins the Gestapo. Sickened by the use of radio by the Nazis for propaganda, Dr Roder, his friends Emil and Rudolf and the young radio engineer Hans set up a transmitter to broadcast Freedom Radio, telling the truth about the regime. They achieve a coup by cutting into a speech of Hitler's at one of the rallies staged by Irena. The footage of the rally comes from Leni Riefenstahl's *Triumph of the Will*.

The Nazis institute a nationwide search for the transmitter and the Freedom Radio moves from place to place to avoid detection. Emil is killed fleeing from the Nazis. Irena recognizes Karl's voice in the broadcasts. When Karl warns of the imminent invasion of Poland, Irena comes to believe Karl is right in his belief that Hitler wants war and not peace. She joins him in a broadcasting van where they are detected and both shot. But Freedom Radio remains on the air, with Hans broadcasting.

Hollywood produced its own equivalent of *Freedom Radio* in *Underground* (1941). Warner Brothers had produced the first thorough-going anti-Nazi film, *Confessions of a Nazi Spy* in 1939 but according to Vincent Sherman, who was assigned to direct *Underground*, it had not made money and so *Underground* was downgraded to B picture status. But Sherman was keen to make it. He was handed a screenplay by Edwin Justus Mayer and Oliver H.P. Garrett but he rewrote it with Charles Grayson. Sherman recalled: 'I have never worked longer hours or more intensely on any film, but I relished every minute of it because I felt that I was helping to alert the world to the menace of Hitler and the Nazis. It was also a time when the United States was still in the throes of isolationism. The America Firsters were still dominating the thinking of the country, supported by Father Coughlin and Charles Lindbergh, who were favourably disposed towards the Nazis. The picture was branded by certain politicians as "war mongering"'.[7]

Sherman asked for and got as stars the Dutchman Philip Dorn and the German Kaaren Verne and insisted on peopling the supporting cast with refugee German actors and actresses for authenticity. But the studio insisted on him using contract star Jeffrey Lynn who was American and had never played anything like the convinced Nazi he was called upon to play in *Underground*. Sherman worked intensively with him to extend his emotional range and he gave arguably his best screen performance.

The film centres on the operation by the anti-Nazi underground in Berlin of an illicit radio station, 'The Voice of Freedom', which talks of the true conditions in Germany and urges resistance to the tyranny of Hitler. References to the bombing of Rotterdam, the flight of Hess to the United Kingdom and the sinking of the *Bismarck* give the story an extra edge of topicality. Chemist Eric Franken (Philip Dorn) leads the radio group which operates from a mobile van and a boat, just like the radio in *Freedom Radio*. Colonel Heller (Martin Kosleck) and his soldiers seek to track down the radio. Eric's brother Kurt (Jeffrey Lynn), an army officer who has lost an arm at the front, returns home and defends the war as a struggle to restore Germany's place in the world. He helps Heller track down the underground radio and the operators are seized, among them Eric. But when Kurt witnesses the torture of his father and brother, he joins the underground. As Eric and the others are led out to execution by guillotine, the underground radio broadcasts its message of defiance.

Moving and powerful, the film struck a chord with audiences. Sherman recalled that it received good reviews and did 'smashing business'. Costing $300,000 to make, he claims that it netted two million and led to Sherman's promotion to A features. Warners' records show that it cost $309,000 and brought in $1,307,000 in domestic and foreign rentals to Warners. *Confessions of a Nazi Spy* cost $681,000 to make and brought in $1,531,000 in rentals but this included the proceeds of reissues of the film during the war when it had become more topical. Sherman may be right in suggesting that *Confessions of a Nazi Spy* made little profit on its first release.[8]

Two of the Axis propaganda broadcasters became famous. One was William Joyce, known as 'Lord Haw-Haw', who in supercilious upper-class tones broadcast war news in English from Germany with his much imitated introduction 'Germany calling, Germany calling'. The other was Tokyo Rose, whose seductive voice over the airwaves sought to demoralize the American troops in the Pacific. Both of them inspired lively B pictures. Columbia's *Appointment in Berlin* (1943), directed by Alfred E. Green and written by Horace McCoy and Michael Hogan, centred on an ex-RAF officer Keith Wilson (George Sanders) who flees to Berlin, claiming to have become disillusioned with life in the United Kingdom. He becomes a broadcaster in the 'Haw-Haw' mode, delivering Nazi-slanted war news to the United Kingdom. In reality he is a British agent sending back vital information by a word code in his broadcasts. When he is unmasked by the Germans, he is killed while trying to escape back to the United Kingdom. Tokyo Rose was made the subject of a lively Paramount B picture in 1945, *Tokyo Rose*, directed by Lew Landers. American POW Pete Sherman (Byron Barr) is chosen to be interviewed on the air by Tokyo Rose (Lotus Long). But he wrecks the broadcasting studio and escapes. He then concocts and carries out a plan to kidnap Tokyo Rose and thus terminate her broadcasts.

Radio and politics became inextricably mixed in the United States in the 1930s. Franklin Delano Roosevelt became par excellence the 'radio president' making over 300 radio addresses between 1933 and 1945. His addresses became popularly known as 'fireside chats' and created that vital 'illusion of intimacy'; they were the only occasions when all the networks and stations cleared the airwaves for the same broadcast. An estimated 72% of the American population tuned in.[9] Roosevelt believed that 'nothing since the creation of the newspaper has had so profound an effect on our civilization as radio'.[10] He was a natural broadcaster with an easy style, simple language, mastery of timing and delivery, and no regional accent. From 1932 the Democrats had a 'director of radio'. The Republicans only caught up in 1936. Roosevelt became the first presidential candidate in history to deliver his acceptance speech over the radio. Roosevelt was a better and more accomplished broadcaster than his Republican opponents in 1940 and 1944, Wendell Willkie and Thomas E. Dewey. But Roosevelt was not the only politician to master broadcasting. He was challenged by Huey Long, the populist Governor of and later senator from Louisiana, and Father Charles Coughlin, the 'radio priest', a Catholic cleric who had a broadcasting tower built next to his church and was a forerunner of the later televangelists. Both were violently anti-Roosevelt and both expert broadcasters with wide appeal. Long felt the 'New Deal' did not go far enough and campaigned against concentrated wealth in his 'Share the Wealth Association' and Coughlin denounced 'Communists, Jews, socialists, capitalists and international bankers' as responsible for the country's ills.[11] They both represented serious challenges to Roosevelt but were eliminated from the political scene, Long by assassination in 1935 and Coughlin by being forced off the air by 1941 as his broadcasts became so fascistic they earned the approval of the Nazi newspaper *Der Sturmer*.[12]

The Federal Radio Act of 1927 had encouraged the development of news broadcasting but two events in 1932 ensured the success of radio news, the reporting of the kidnapping of the Lindbergh baby and the election returns in the Hoover–Roosevelt election in which radio beat the newspapers with the news. By 1940, 81% of American families said the news was an integral part of their listening, via regular bulletins, or commentaries by the new phenomenon of the news analyst like Lowell Thomas or H.V. Kaltenborn or by the dramatized news stories that featured in the docudrama series *The March of Time*.[13]

These developments were directly reflected in American political films, for example the political trilogy of Frank Capra, *Mr Smith Goes to Washington*, *Meet John Doe* and *State of the Union*. *Mr Smith Goes to Washington* (1939) is a full-throated, big-hearted paean to American democracy. Jefferson Smith (James Stewart), idealistic head of the Boy Rangers in an unnamed mid-Western state, is appointed to succeed a senator who has died suddenly because the party bosses under Jim Taylor (Edward Arnold) believe him too naïve to detect the graft and corruption in which they are engaged. When Smith discovers the truth, he decides to fight the party machine and takes up a lost cause. Capra reveals the full extent of the machine's power. Control of newspapers and radio stations enables them to manipulate public opinion and they are well on the way to putting their front man, the popular and respected but corrupt Senator Joseph Harrison Paine (Claude Rains) in the White House. Smith is framed and faced with imprisonment but makes a twenty-three-and-a-half-hour speech to the Senate which eventually prompts Paine to confess his guilt and expose the corruption. The climactic Senate scenes are reported on the radio with the respected political commentator H.V. Kaltenborn, playing himself, as he explains the nature of a 'filibuster' – 'democracy in action' – and charts the progress of the debate.

Meet John Doe (1941) seeks to warn the United States of the danger of domestic fascism. Financier and oil magnate D.B. Norton (Edward Arnold) takes over an old-established newspaper and fires many of the staff. One of them, Ann Mitchell (Barbara Stanwyck), writes a powerful final article purporting to be from one 'John Doe' threatening to jump off the tower of City Hall on Christmas Eve as a protest against social injustice. The article causes a sensation. Everyone wants to know who Doe is and Ann, to save face, produces a down-and-out baseball player, Long John Willoughby (Gary Cooper) who becomes John Doe. She writes a successful series of articles in his name and he broadcasts on NBC, eulogizing 'the little man' and talking of the virtues of freedom and goodwill. John Doe clubs spring up all over the United States and the John Doe philosophy of good neighbourliness sweeps the country. When the movement is at its height, Norton reveals his plan to use it to further his own fascist ambitions. John determines to expose him at a big John Doe convention being covered by all the radio networks and with real-life announcers Mike Frankovich, John B. Hughes and Knox Manning appearing as themselves. But Norton silences John by having the microphones cut off and having his private police force beat up John's supporters. John is exposed as a fake and feels he can only redeem himself by throwing himself off the tower but Ann Mitchell and a group of his earliest supporters rally round and dissuade him from jumping and he agrees to continue the fight against Norton and his fascist ambitions and the film closes to the triumphant strains of Beethoven's 'Ode to Joy'.

In *State of the Union* (1948), based on a hit Broadway play by Howard Lindsay and Russell Crouse, millionaire aircraft manufacturer Grant Matthews (Spencer Tracy), a classic Capra 'Good Man', is being propelled towards the Republican nomination for the presidency by hard-bitten Kay Thorndike (Angela Lansbury), head of the Thorndike Press who aims to be the power behind the throne. Deluded by visions of the White House, Matthews tones down his views (such as support for world government), compromises his ideals and goes along with the machinations of the party machine and corrupt self-serving interest groups. But at the end, helped by his wife Mary (Katharine Hepburn), he regains his idealism. He uses a radio programme designed to boost his image to denounce the interest groups supporting him and the idleness of the voters who allow themselves to be deceived and manipulated by crooked politicians. Then he embarks on a campaign to eradicate corruption from public life. Taken together the three films graphically illustrated the way in which radio had transformed American politics and highlighted the ways in which it could be used to assist the democratic process or if it fell into the wrong hands, to undermine it.

The way in which politics would be transformed by radio is hinted at in Stanley Kramer's superb film version of the Scopes Trial, *Inherit the Wind* (1960). In 1925 in Tennessee schoolteacher John Scopes was prosecuted for teaching the Darwinian theory of evolution. The court case pitted the fundamentalist former Presidential candidate William Jennings Bryan against the atheistic liberal lawyer Clarence Darrow. The protagonists, thinly disguised as Matthew Harrison Brady and Henry Drummond, were played by Fredric March and Spencer Tracy, both on top form, and the film is a full-throated defence of free speech and free thought and an assault on bigotry and prejudice. At the end of the trial, an engineer sets up a microphone to broadcast the trial verdict to Chicago. Drummond immediately appreciates that this new invention will transform the world and the cynical journalist E.K. Hornbeck (Gene Kelly) pronounces the doom of the old style oratory of Brady, which will prove totally unsuited to the intimacy of the new media.

There was no British equivalent to the American political film. Such films as there were (*Young Mr Pitt, The Prime Minister, Fame is the Spur*) mainly dealt with the pre-radio era, though radio figured briefly with the Prime Minister mobilizing the population for evacuation in the Boulting Brothers' *Seven Days to Noon* (1950) in which a renegade scientist is threatening to explode an atomic bomb in London.

Two pre-war Hollywood films focused on the use of radio to attempt to undermine the British Empire. *Storm Over Bengal* (1938), directed by Sidney Salkow and written by Dudley Waters, was a fast-moving, rip-roaring imperial thriller, in which a native ruler, Rahman Khan, planning a full-scale uprising, uses a shortwave radio station in the hills to broadcast inflammatory speeches to all of India. The uprising is foiled by the gallantry of Captain Jeffrey Allison (Patric Knowles) who blows up an ammunition dump destroying the radio station and kills the native leader.

The Sun Never Sets (1940), directed by Rowland V. Lee from a script by W.P. Lipscomb, charted the threat from radio in Africa. Hugo Zurof, a multi-millionaire armaments manufacturer (Lionel Atwill) is ostensibly leading a scientific expedition to the Gold Coast to study insect life. Under cover of the expedition, he sets up a clandestine radio station broadcasting subversive messages with the intention of stirring up war and furthering his ambition to become world dictator. His plans are thwarted by two brothers, British District Officers Clive (Basil Rathbone) and John Randolph (Douglas Fairbanks Jr.). John infiltrates the radio station and broadcasts a warning which allows Clive to lead a bombing squadron to destroy the radio station and the millionaire.

Radio had a role to play too during the Cold War, in particular in two films in which God intervenes in the modern world directly. *The Next Voice You Hear* (1950), directed by William Wellman and scripted by Charles Schnee, was liberal MGM producer Dore Shary's cinematic reaction to the anti-Communist hysteria sweeping the United States. The voice of God is heard on the radio preaching the need for love, faith, peace and freedom. The voice is greeted first by scepticism, then fear and finally it inspires a religious revival as people flock to churches, synagogues and mosques and vow to change their lives for the better. It focuses in particular on the impact of the broadcasts on a typical American family, the Smiths: Joe and Mary Smith (played by James Whitmore and Nancy Davis, the future Mrs Ronald Reagan), their son Johnny and Aunt Matilda. Everyone becomes nicer, more loving and more neighbourly after hearing the broadcast.

God chooses to speak through radio again in *Red Planet Mars* (1952), directed by Harry Horner and written by John L. Balderston and Anthony Veiller. Taking the opposite viewpoint to *The Next Voice You Hear*, it is an absurd piece of anti-Communist propaganda from the height of Cold War paranoia. Chris Cronyn (Peter Graves), a scientist with a Carnegie Foundation grant, contacts Mars by radio. He receives back a series of messages about life on Mars which causes economic and social panic in the West. Then comes a series of religious messages which sparks off a Christian revival in Russia. The Soviet regime is toppled and a provisional government established under the Patriarch of Moscow. Then the messages stop and a renegade Nazi turns up to reveal that he sent the messages and aims, as a self-proclaimed disciple of Satan, to destroy the regimes of both East and West. But then a real message comes in from Mars, the voice of God proclaiming peace and goodwill to all men. The Nazi shoots at the transmitter, blowing up himself and the scientist. But the Christian revival now sweeps the world and the President of the United States bestows his blessing on it. During the course of the 1950s the rise of television would eclipse the role of radio in politics, so that by 1958 the candidates in the election for the mayor of Boston in John Ford's *The Last Hurrah* are broadcasting their electoral appeals on the new medium.

Notes

1   Vera Lynn, *Vocal Refrain*, London: W.H. Allen, 1975, pp. 97–8.
2   Siân Nicholas, *The Echo of War: Home Front Propaganda and the Wartime BBC 1939–45*, Manchester: Manchester University Press, 1996, pp. 238–9.
3   Lynn, *Vocal Refrain*, p. 99.
4   Matthew Bernstein, *Walter Wanger, Hollywood Independent*, Minneapolis: University of Minnesota Press, 1994, pp. 158–63.
5   Jeffrey Richards, *Visions of Yesterday*, London: Routledge, 1973, p. 254.
6   Jo Fox, '"The Mediator": Images of radio in wartime feature film in the United Kingdom and Germany' in Mark Connelly and David Welch (eds), *War and the Media:*

Reportage and Propaganda 1900–2003, London: Tauris, 2005, pp. 92–111.

7   Vincent Sherman, *Studio Affairs*, Lexington, KY: University of Kentucky Press, 1996, pp. 94–5.

8   Sherman, *Studio Affairs*, pp. 91–6. On the box-office grosses see H. Mark Glancy 'Warner Bros film grosses, 1924–1951, the William Schafer Ledger', *Historical Journal of Film, Radio and Television* 15 (1995), pp. 55–74.

9   Robert J. Brown, *Manipulating the Ether: The Power of Broadcast Radio in Thirties America*, Jefferson, NC and London: McFarland, 1998, p. 21.

10   Brown, *Manipulating the Ether*, p. 9.

11   Brown, *Manipulating the Ether*, p. 87.

12   On Roosevelt, Coughlin and Long, see also Bruce Lenthall, *Radio's America: The Great Depression and the Rise of Modern Mass Culture*, Chicago and London: University of Chicago Press, 2007, pp. 83–141.

13   Susan Douglas, *Listening In: Radio and the American Imagination*, Minneapolis: University of Minnesota Press, 2004, p. 162.

8

The multi-media Pimpernel

The Scarlet Pimpernel, in reality Sir Percy Blakeney, Baronet, is a character who decisively fixed the image of the French Revolution in the minds of successive generations of British readers. The books, the play and later the films charting his adventures established beyond doubt that the French revolutionaries were a bloodthirsty, beastly, ungentlemanly mob and that a well-brought-up aristocrat could run rings round them, particularly if he were an English aristocrat. In the Pimpernel saga, liberty, equality and fraternity came off a definite second best to chivalry, duty and *noblesse oblige*. Paradoxically, this most English of English heroes was the creation of a Hungarian emigré aristocrat, Baroness Emmuska Orczy (1865–1947), who had settled in England at the age of fifteen.

Fascinated by history, she had tried her hand at writing and had had several short stories accepted for periodical publication. While staying in Paris in 1901 she conceived of a French Revolutionary story set against the background and scenes she explored during her visit. But she lacked a central character. He came to her one day as a vision, as she explained in her autobiography:

> I first saw him standing before me – don't gasp, please – on the platform of an underground station, the Temple. I had been to see someone on the *Daily Express*, *à propos* of some minor work, and was waiting for my Inner Circle train for Kensington. Now, of all the dull, prosy places in the world, can you beat an Underground Railway Station? It was foggy too, and smelly and cold. But I give you my word that as I was sitting there, I saw – yes, I saw – Sir Percy Blakeney just as you know him now. I saw him in his exquisite clothes, his slender hands holding up his spyglass: I heard his lazy drawling speech, his quaint laugh … it was a mental vision, of course, and lasted but a few seconds – but it was the whole life-story of the Scarlet Pimpernel that was there and then revealed to me.[1]

Recounting the story in a radio talk in 1934, she spoke in that once fashionable upper-class English accent which pronounced its *a*'s as *e*'s (romentic, fect, stending), indicating the extent to which she had become incorporated into the English class system.

With the central character established, she sat down and wrote the novel *The Scarlet Pimpernel* in five weeks flat ('I … look on those five weeks as some of the happiest in my life'). But no publisher would touch it. Undaunted, Baroness Orczy and her husband, artist and illustrator Montagu Barstow, turned it into a play and it was taken up by actor-manager Fred Terry (1863–1933) and premiered at the Theatre Royal, Nottingham, in autumn 1903. The Baroness recalled that it was 'lavishly produced and cast to perfection with Fred Terry as Sir Percy Blakeney, a role which fitted him like the proverbial glove, and Julia Neilson, beautiful and emotional as Marguerite' and that audience approval was 'not only ungrudging but enthusiastic' and the local press was 'enthusiastic in its praise'. But when Terry sought a partnership with manager Frank Curzon to bring it into London, Curzon declared: 'This is all right for the provinces, but it won't do for London. The Press for one will never stand it'.[2] But Terry believed in the play, persisted with it and opened it in London at the New Theatre on 5 January 1905. The press poured scorn on the production, with the *Daily Mail* leading the charge: 'the Scarlet Pimpernel is a little flower that blossoms and dies in one day, which is the obvious fate of this play'.[3] Audiences fell but Terry persisted, 'papered' the house with friends and then gradually word of mouth spread, audiences picked up and the public took the play to their hearts. Fred Terry and Julia Neilson kept it in their repertoire until Terry retired in 1929, eventually chalking up 3,000 performances.

Sir John Gielgud, who was Fred Terry's great-nephew, saw several of his productions, including *The Scarlet Pimpernel* and recorded his impressions of Terry, Neilson and their plays:

> Fred Terry, who was always known as 'Golden Fred', was a great, jolly man … But he had a most violent temper. He was an enormous eater, gourmand, gambler, as well as a splendid actor and a great personality. He married the beautiful Julia Neilson, who was a very affected, mannered actress, but she had moments of charm. He used to make her life hell at rehearsals and his company was terrified of him … his productions … seemed to have an extraordinary sweep about them, and an immense care for detail. He used to kill his company with hard work, making them rehearse all day. A new play might take as much as a year to prepare because Fred could not learn his lines and insisted on directing himself, getting into fearful rages and losing his hat by sitting on it in the stalls. All the noises behind the scenes – royal processions approaching or the Massacre of St Bartholomew – were rehearsed and executed to perfection. Make-up, clothes, scenery and lighting – everything was meticulously harmonized … Fred would be violent about anything in a play that he did not think was manly and noble. The heroines were white, and the villains black, and that was that. But he had an enchanting quality. He was funny, engaging and a real card in many ways.[4]

Baroness Orczy witnessed both the rage – ten minutes of violent abuse of a minor actor late in responding to a call from Terry – and the painstaking attention to detail: 'I watched him one day for twenty minutes teaching the Prince of Wales in Act II how to manage his sword, and how to sit down gracefully without getting his legs entangled in it. Twenty minutes – and never once losing patience'.[5]

Despite the admiration and gratitude Baroness Orczy felt to Fred Terry, there was eventually a court case between them in 1924 about *The Scarlet Pimpernel*. The Baroness was regularly approached for the film rights to the story. But Fred was adamantly opposed to the cinema: 'Fred Terry was an avowed and bitter enemy of the films, which he looked upon as successful rivals of theatrical enterprise … When the word cinematograph cropped up Fred Terry saw red'.[6] The Baroness took the case to court and lost. It was confirmed that she had copyright in the book but that performing rights in the play belonged to Terry and Neilson and that the film rights could not be sold except by agreement of the two sides.

This decision also confirms the fact that the original play by Orczy and Barstow was partially rewritten by Terry to make it more suitable for the stage. Julia Neilson recalled: 'Our chief criticism of the original version was that all the exciting events happened "off stage". The audience never saw any of the Pimpernel's wonderful exploits which were spoken of so freely by the other characters'.[7] So Terry and Louis Calvert rewrote the opening scene of the rescue of the Countess de Tournai and her daughter, making it 'a most effective opening scene, because as they both argued, the audience had seen the Pimpernel *do* something and so were more ready to accept the heroic feats performed between the acts'. The fourth act was also rewritten by Calvert and Terry in association with Orczy and her husband because, Orczy says, Terry did not want to end the play disguised as a scruffy and disreputable old Jew and so it climaxed with 'no sea, no rocks, no soldiers, and Terry bowing his last as handsome as ever before'.[8] The original finale preserved in the novel has a grim seacoast setting, Percy disguised as an old Jew and saving Marguerite while in disguise. The play ends in a well-lighted, comfortable inn with Percy in his gentlemanly finery to the end. Baroness Orczy recorded with some bitterness that she and her husband attended only a few rehearsals; 'we felt that we were not wanted … One felt that the remarks or criticisms of the merest scene-shifter were of more importance … than those of the author of the play'.[9]

The essential playability and sheer exuberant theatricality of Fred Terry's stage version was confirmed by the triumphant revival of the play in 1985. Adapted by Beverley Cross and directed by Nicholas Hytner, it was a glorious mixture of action, comedy and song, staged with elegance, vigour and invention. Sir Donald Sinden was superb as Sir Percy, handling comedy and action with equal aplomb and there were excellent performances from Joanna McCallum, the image of her celebrated mother Googie Withers, as Marguerite, Charles Kay as a saturnine Chauvelin, Alex Jennings as the glacial Robespierre and Rowland Davies as the bluff and hearty Prince of Wales.

The success of the play ensured the success of the novel, eventually published by the small firm of Greening and Company on 12 January 1905. It is 'affection-ately' dedicated to 'Julia Neilson and Fred Terry, whose genius created the roles of Sir Percy and Lady Blakeney on the stage'. Unlike the initial reaction to the play, 'Praise from every section of the Press was wholehearted'.[10] It had run through twenty-seven impressions by the start of 1907, eventually selling three million copies, being translated into sixteen languages and inspiring eleven sequels.

Several important factors explain the durability of the Pimpernel in the popular imagination. He is one of the most notable examples of the 'masked avenger', a staple figure in swashbuckling literature and film. He is in a sense the ultimate wish fulfilment figure. For his double life (by day a respectable law-abiding gentleman, by night a daredevil adventurer, a master of disguise and stratagem, righting wrongs, fighting tyrants, wooing lovely ladies) provides the perfect metaphor for the audience of the swashbuckling genre who live out vicariously fantasies of romance and adventure of a kind generally absent from everyday life. The ingredients (double life, chases, escapes, disguises) were com-mon to all 'masked avenger' dramas. It is the adventure factor which perhaps best explains the durability of such figures as the Scarlet Pimpernel, Zorro and Scaramouche. All are variations on the same theme and all have taken off from their literary origins to acquire an independent folklore existence. The masked avenger also has a political role to play in that the existence of aristocratic in-dividuals able to right wrongs by their own efforts precludes the need for the masses to take matters into their own hands by way of revolution. It was precisely mass popular revolution in France that caused the evils the Scarlet Pimpernel was called upon to oppose.

The second appeal was to national identity. Sir Percy Blakeney to the fash-ionable world of eighteenth-century London is merely a brainless fop but to the persecuted aristocracy of revolutionary France he is a fearless champion and saviour. But in both facets of his character he combines two qualities – he is a gentleman and he is English. Baroness Orczy recorded that she set out to give 'a perfect presentation of an English gentleman' and the Home Secretary Sir William Joynson-Hicks told her: 'I love your character so because he is so very English. You have put your finger on what is best and truest in English character' and another politician told her 'I like your Blakeney so much; he is such a gentleman'.[11]

A third appeal is the romance. Sir Percy is deeply in love with his beautiful French wife, the actress Marguerite St Just, but comes to believe her guilty of betraying an aristocratic family to the revolutionaries and the guillotine. The couple represent an attraction of opposites; he English, she French, he monarchist, she republican, he aristocrat, she bourgeois. The central dilemma haunts the first novel. Thereafter in sequels Marguerite is often in danger and Sir Percy has to rescue her, reaffirming their enduring love.

The Scarlet Pimpernel was, however, very much a figure of the Old World. The United States, which had a lingering regard for the French Revolution, never liked him enough to produce films based on his exploits. Apart from a 1917 Hollywood version of *The Scarlet Pimpernel* starring Dustin Farnum, the films were produced exclusively in England. But the idea was too good to waste and was transferred to the more congenial setting of Spanish California by Johnston McCulley, whose serial story *The Curse of Capistrano*, published in *All-Story* magazine in 1919, gave the world the 'American Pimpernel', by day Spanish dandy Don Diego Vega, and by night the black-masked righter-of-wrongs known as 'Zorro' – the Fox.

The principle behind the characters remains the same. Zorro, though he fights gubernatorial despotism, does not seek to alter the system or to take California out of the Spanish Empire. He is only concerned to remove a corrupt functionary and is otherwise every bit as staunch an upholder of aristocratic Establishmentarianism as Sir Percy. But Zorro is more of a true swashbuckler than Sir Percy. He uses a sword where Sir Percy relies on his wits and his blueblooded ingenuity to get him through. In fact the contrast between the all-action, all American Zorro and the languid, sardonic Sir Percy in many ways reflects the difference between the American and British character.

The earliest British Pimpernel film, *The Elusive Pimpernel*, dates from 1919. Produced by Stoll Pictures and directed by Maurice Elvey, it stars Cecil Humphreys as Sir Percy, Marie Blanche as Lady Marguerite and Norman Page as the arch-enemy Chauvelin. Based on Baroness Orczy's first sequel to her original success, the film opens in 1792 with the Revolutionary tribunal, presided over by a leering Robespierre, howling for aristocratic blood and discovering that they have been foiled again by Sir Percy Blakeney – 'a typical aristocrat of the time' as the titles call him. Chauvelin is ordered to destroy him and seeks to do so by kidnapping his wife, while Sir Percy busies himself rescuing the De Marny family from the deadly embrace of Madame Guillotine. When called upon to choose between his wife and his duty, Sir Percy's choice is unhesitating ('Much as I love you, my dear, I have a greater love – my honour'). But he is not called upon to push the choice to its logical conclusion, for with a merry laugh and an insolent parting note he escapes with his wife and the captive aristocrats 'to England, home and safety'. The film, viewed today, is inexpressibly tedious, slow-moving and heavy-handed. In short, it is typical of British costume films of the period: quaint naturalistic exteriors and cheap, unconvincing interiors (even the cells have painted cobwebs), inept direction and a cast of enthusiastic but untalented amateurs who look as if they have been recruited from the local Village Institute Dramatic Circle.

Henry Kolker's *I Will Repay* (1923) (US title: *Swords and the Woman*) was based on another of the Orczy sequels and starred Holmes Herbert as Sir Percy and Hollywood star Pedro de Cordoba as Paul Deroulède. Deroulède is a lawyer and gentleman who, having got mixed up with the Revolution, falls in love with aristocrat Juliette de Marnay. Love opens his eyes to the evils of the Revolution and he and his lady love are rescued from the vengeance of the *sans-culottes* by Sir Percy. *The Bioscope* called it 'a most capable presentation of a deservedly popular story'.

Lastly, in 1928 Matheson Lang starred in *The Triumph of the Scarlet Pimpernel* (US title: *The Scarlet Daredevil*), for director T. Hayes Hunter and producer Herbert Wilcox. Set in 1794, it had Sir Percy save his wife from the guillotine by framing the woman who had helped to kidnap her. It included a large-scale sword-fighting scene on a huge staircase with Sir Percy successfully disposing of ten gendarmes. Matheson Lang was praised for his 'grace, agility and personal charm' and for his great skill in make-up disguise.

It was only after Fred Terry died that a film of *The Scarlet Pimpernel* could be made. Alexander Korda made a bid for the rights and Julia Neilson sold him the rights to certain scenes and business created for the play while Baroness Orczy sold the rights to the book and they divided the proceeds. It is clear, however, that the film is essentially based on the play, though credited only to the novel.[12]

Korda originally envisaged Charles Laughton in the leading role but when this was announced in the press, there was such a hostile reaction from fans complaining about his physical unsuitability that Korda switched the part to Leslie Howard, who was to achieve a personal triumph in the part. Baroness Orczy recorded: 'Leslie Howard was certainly very attractive, very charming, he knew how to make love, but he was not Fred Terry. Fred Terry was the ideal Sir Percy and there cannot be two ideals in one's mind of the one character … he had the charm of manner, the beautifully modulated voice, the humour, and the dominating personality'.[13]

The 1935 film *The Scarlet Pimpernel* became the definitive screen version and one of the most fondly remembered British films of the 1930s. What was seen by many as a characteristically British film was in fact largely the work of Hungarians. Like Baroness Orczy, producer Alexander Korda, co-scenarist Lajos Biro and art director Zoltan Korda were Hungarians. So too was that most perfect English-man Leslie Howard née Steiner, Hungarian by birth but educated at an English public school. Like Baroness Orczy, Alexander Korda had come to identify totally with his adopted country, producing a series of high quality films celebrating the English upper classes, British history and the British Empire and eventually earning himself a knighthood. It was from this unlikely Magyar medley of talent that the perfect screen version of *The Scarlet Pimpernel* derived.

But it only reached the screen after intense production difficulties. Rowland Brown, the talented American director of gangster classics *Blood Money* and *Quick Millions*, was signed to direct but within weeks of commencing was taken off the picture. Korda apparently felt that he was making the story too grim and gory, shooting it in fact like a gangster film. When Brown refused to alter his approach, Korda took over the direction himself. The film was eventually handed over to the American editor, Harold Young, who completed it and received the sole directorial credit. However, according to Raymond Massey who played Chauvelin, Korda supervised Young and the direction 'throughout the months of shooting remained an unofficial but smooth collaboration'.[14] This is entirely convincing as *The Scarlet Pimpernel* stands out as the most notable achievement in Young's otherwise entirely routine directorial career.

Despite the difficulties, Raymond Massey would recall in his autobiography: 'I never had such fun working in a movie as I did in *The Scarlet Pimpernel*. Of all the heavies I have played on the screen, the most wicked and the most fun to do was Chauvelin … there was a spirit in that company, a feeling of confidence, a sort of *élan* which I had often found in the theatre but never sensed in any other movie'.[15]

In spite of its celebrity, the film does have its weaknesses. The production values are, as always in Korda's films, excellent and memorably evoke the el-egance and grace of upper-class eighteenth-century England. But the film could have done with more of the blood and thunder Brown was accused of trying to introduce. There is perhaps too little of the Pimpernel and too much of Sir Percy for successful balance between the two identities to be maintained. Deeds are reported rather than seen and this leads sometimes to a sense of anticlimax.

The film is also seriously underscored. The music, credited to Arthur Benjamin, consists almost solely of *La Marseillaise* played over the credits and *Eine Kleine Nachtmusik* played at the ball.

However, the film provides perfect visual match-ups of Percy, Marguerite and Chauvelin in the stars Leslie Howard, Merle Oberon and Raymond Massey. Howard, with his soft voice, lazy manner, blond, dreamy-eyed, donnish good looks was equally at home in rescuing aristocrats (at one point, gleefully disguised as an old hag) and in fooling the world as a fop. The foppish pose is beautifully conceived and played and involves several memorable encounters, among them a bantering exchange with a crusty old colonel, a lively controversy with the exasperated royal tailor about the length of the Prince of Wales's sleeve and his cheeky send-up of the dour Chauvelin.

Merle Oberon, with her rosebud mouth, lustrous dark hair and porcelain beauty, makes a convincing image of perfection for which a man would gladly sacrifice his life. Raymond Massey adds another memorable portrait to his brilliant 1930s gallery of historical villains. The raised eyebrow and slicked-down black hair, the bright penetrating eyes and uniquely twisted mouth combine to create an appropriately saturnine and intense contrast to the fair-complexioned and relaxed Sir Percy.

The message of the film is conveyed in the early scenes which establish a striking counterpoint between the settled, natural order of things in the civilized, monarchical United Kingdom, whose champion is the Pimpernel, and the disturbed, unnatural state of revolutionary France, personified by Chauvelin. The film opens with the Guards regiments parading in front of the Palace of St James in London. The Prince of Wales (Nigel Bruce) watches from an open window, and when the spectators see him, they doff their hats and bow. The loyalty, honour, order and quiet national pride which this scene conveys is immediately contrasted with France at the same time. The guillotine is at its grisly work of mass execution, the blood-crazed mob roar their approval and degraded old hags sit knitting at the foot of the scaffold. The film cuts ironically to the legend 'Liberté, Egalité, Fraternité' engraved on a mirror. So much for the new order of things.

Throughout the film we are never allowed to forget that the Pimpernel is English and what is more represents the best of England. 'I confess I feel a little proud when I think that the Pimpernel is an Englishman', observes the Prince of Wales. Sir Percy himself strolls into an ambush whistling 'God Save the King' and when condemned to death by Chauvelin, memorably recites John of Gaunt's 'This England' deathbed speech from *Richard II*. The whole ethos is perfectly summed up in the unforgettable final scene on the ship carrying the Blakeneys safely home to England. Arm in arm, they gaze through the mist, straining for a first glimpse of the white cliffs. Suddenly there is a cry from the rigging 'Land Ahead'. Percy says 'Look Marguerite … England' and the final music swells on the soundtrack. It was Korda who devised the last line, saying 'After that, they'll have to cheer'.

But just as important as being English is being a gentleman, and Percy is the living embodiment of the innate superiority of the English gentleman. He airily mocks his enemy Chauvelin ('Devilish clever, the French, how they speak that unspeakable language of theirs, I will never know'). He also teaches him how to tie a cravat. Chauvelin is not a gentleman and therefore does not know how to do it. Percy regards the activities of the Pimpernel as sport and this also distinguishes him from Chauvelin, for whom everything is in deadly earnest. Under these circumstances, the intended jokey statement of the old colonel about the French Revolution, 'If we didn't have our foxhunting and pheasant shooting, we'd be cruel too', emerges as an entirely valid justification of the existing British system of values and government, as embodied by the Scarlet Pimpernel. Costing £143,521 to produce, it had netted £204,300 in box office receipts by 1937, making it the most profitable Korda production apart from the *Private Life of Henry VIII*.[16] It was reissued in 1942 and 1947.

The success of *The Scarlet Pimpernel* inevitably prompted a sequel, *The Return of the Scarlet Pimpernel* (1938). Based on the novel *The Elusive Pimpernel*, it was directed by Hans Schwartz and scripted by Lajos Biro, Arthur Wimperis and Adrian Brunel. Curiously enough, it is more cinematic but less charismatic than the original. In spite of the flaws, the previous film had in Leslie Howard, Merle Oberon and Raymond Massey actors with genuine star quality, an incandescence which somehow obscured the static and sometimes anti-climactic nature of the production. The new version had Barry K. Barnes as Sir Percy, Sophie Stewart as Marguerite and Francis Lister as Chauvelin, all good actors but without that extra dimension which would have put them in the star firmament. Barnes gives as stylish, witty and elegant a performance as one could possibly wish, however, without effacing memories of Leslie Howard. He is particularly good in a succession of disguises: deaf, elderly colonel, snaggle-toothed simpleton, French guards officer, window-cleaner. Sophie Stewart is meltingly lovely and there is an eye-catching performance from the smoulderingly handsome young James Mason, on loan from Fox British where he was making 'quota quickies'. He plays the French deputy who leads the attack on Robespierre in the Assembly. Francis Lister's Chauvelin is a lesser figure than Massey's, more the subtle schemer and less the elemental Satanic villain. At the end he has to be saved by Percy from the righteous indignation of the mob. Directed (Hans Schwartz), produced (Arnold Pressburger) and photographed (Mutz Greenbaum) by refugees from Nazi Germany, the film was conceived by the writers to 'remind audiences of Hitler and the Nazis'.[17]

Structurally it is a better film than *The Scarlet Pimpernel*. It has pace, lightness and just the right note of insouciance, and Lazare Meerson's stylized eighteenth-century sets are every bit as good as Vincent Korda's were in the original film. A strong narrative, filled with well-staged chases, rescues, ambushes and escapes, centres on Sir Percy's attempts to rescue Marguerite, kidnapped and taken to France in a bid to trap him. Percy accomplishes this aim by stirring up the Assembly to overthrow Robespierre and bringing an end to the Reign of Terror. Only an Englishman would think of causing the downfall of a regime in order to save his wife.

There is a much more satisfying balance between the activities of Sir Percy and those of the Pimpernel than in the previous film. But the inspiration of his actions remains the same and is stressed in a similar intercut opening. France is ruled now by Robespierre, seen in long-shot in his office, a distant, cold, all-powerful figure. The Revolution runs according to his dictates. But the summary arrests, summary executions and howls of the mob are intercut with the elegance, poise and sportsmanship of a period cricket match on a country house lawn, with Percy in a ruffled shirt wielding a straight bat. The contrast between France (dictatorship and the mob) and England (the aristocracy at play) is thus established from the outset. Once again the Prince Regent appears to lend sanction to the actions of the Pimpernel and he and his friends toast 'England and Freedom' (the two being synonymous) and sing 'Here's a health unto his majesty', reminding us of the system for which they are fighting.

The original *Scarlet Pimpernel* was remade by Korda in 1949–50. Although it was titled *The Elusive Pimpernel*, it was directly based on the 1935 film and not the eponymous novel. Korda did a deal with Hollywood producer Samuel Goldwyn, who had loved the original version, to finance a new version in colour. Korda wanted the producing team of Michael Powell and Emeric Pressburger to do the new version. But they were extremely reluctant. They both hated remakes, preferring to work on original projects. But they had just signed a five-picture contract with Korda and after holding out for a year, succumbed to his blandishments. Powell suggested remaking it as a musical. But this was vetoed by Korda, who wanted a straight remake of the 1935 version. They were, however, allowed to go to France, shooting on location at Mont St Michel and the chateaux of Chaumont, Loches, Usse, Chambord, Villandry and Blois, as well as later in Bath, London and Marlborough. Powell and Pressburger were able to use their customary collaborators, cameraman Christopher Challis and camera operator Freddie Francis, production designer Hein Heckroth, art director Arthur Lawson and composer Brian Easdale. Powell then proceeded to shoot it as 'the lightest of soufflés, treating it with affection but refusing to take it seriously, and contrasting scenes of the English aristocracy dancing and gambling with others of the bureaucracy that was taking over France in the name of the people … Hein's and Arthur's costumes and sets, Brian Easdale's musical score, and the colour photography of Chris Challis and Freddie Francis, were delightful and new. Such colours, such make-ups, such contrasts, had never before been seen in three-strip Technicolor'.[18]

There is no doubt that the film is consistently sumptuous to look at, each shot framed like a canvas. Canary yellow, burgundy red and Regency striped carriages race hell for leather across the rolling downs; revolutionaries storm a chateau by trampling on the multi-coloured flower beds and formal patterned garden; Sir Percy, in candy-striped dressing gown, turban and with a cockatoo on his shoulder, poses inside a picture frame to baffle the mob before leading them on a merry dance round the chateau.

Powell and Pressburger sought to freshen the old story by setting key scenes from the original in new locations. The sequence in which Sir Percy recites his new rhyme 'They seek him here, they seek him there, those Frenchies seek him everywhere' and enfuriates Colonel Winterbottom, set in 1935 in Black's Club, now takes place in a Turkish bath with Percy dodging about between clouds of steam. The prize fight between Dan Mendoza and Gentleman Jackson attended by the Prince of Wales and Percy in the 1935 version is replaced by a carriage race to Brighton. The finale, originally taking place in an inn in Boulogne, now takes place in the abbey on Mont St Michel with the incoming tide trapping the French soldiers and allowing the Pimpernel and party to escape on his yacht.

Powell imbues the proceedings with the air of a magic performance, using camera trickery to enhance the effect. In one single tracking shot, a cart full of escaping aristocrats drives into a barn at one end and emerges from the other end as an elegant carriage. Percy in the picture frame suddenly comes to life. When Chauvelin sneezes, having taken pepper in mistake for snuff, the screen is filled with exploding fireworks. The final escape from Mont St Michel is done as a series of sleight of hand stratagems.

In retrospect Powell concluded that in shooting the film, 'I had fallen into the oldest trap in the world; the trap of the picturesque … It's a particular curse of the British cinema … actors plus costumes plus twentieth century landscapes equals coloured picture postcards'.[19]

But this was not his only problem, there was the casting. He had wanted Rex Harrison for the role of Sir Percy. But he was compelled to cast David Niven, who was under contract to Goldwyn and was part of the deal. Niven did not want to do it. He hated costume parts and had just spent eight months on loan to Korda playing the title role in the disastrous historical epic *Bonnie Prince Charlie* ('one of those huge florid extravaganzas that reek of disaster from the start').[20] He was not comfortable doing the disguises ('it's just not my sort of stuff', he told Powell).[21] But he could not afford to go on suspension and so did everything he could to make things difficult for Goldwyn, insisting on taking his six weeks' holiday entitlement before starting the film and then travelling to England by boat and train instead of plane. Niven certainly does his best with the part ('he was a most conscientious worker' recalled Powell) but as an essentially twentieth-century actor was fundamentally miscast as a swashbuckler.[22]

Powell was even more unhappy with his leading lady. He had wanted the French roles played by French actors and sought a French actress such as Michele Morgan for Marguerite Blakeney, who was of course a French actress. Korda insisted on Margaret Leighton because she was under contract and had only recently been Niven's co-star in *Bonnie Prince Charlie*. Powell dismisses her brutally in his autobiography: 'She looked like a horse and had cross-eyes … She wasn't a film actress. She had a breathy Manchester voice with overtones of Brighton'.[23] Basically she was too serious and too English an actress for the role of Marguerite.

His first choice for Chauvelin had been Marius Goring but Powell and Goring agreed that it was too soon after he played the Heavenly Messenger in *A Matter of Life and Death* as an eighteenth-century French aristocrat to tackle another eighteenth-century French role. So he cast Cyril Cusack, 'an actor of subtlety and power'.[24] Cusack's black-clad Chauvelin was a malign spider scuttling out from behind columns and statuary to work his mischief rather than the Satanic elemental figure projected by Raymond Massey.

However, when Goldwyn saw a roughcut of the film, he hated it, and refused to put up his agreed investment. 'He wanted a colour copy of the old film, and no incidentals', said Powell.[25] He cabled a list of changes to Korda that he wanted made. Disheartened, Powell and Pressburger complied. There was extensive reshooting before the film could be released. It cost £450,000 to film originally with retakes adding £27,000. In the film as it now stands much of the dialogue is taken directly from the 1935 screenplay. Goldwyn was still unhappy with it and in fact did not release it in the United States until 1955 in black and white, retitled *The Fighting Pimpernel* and shorn of twenty minutes.[26] When *the Elusive Pimpernel* was released in the United Kingdom, the press, while praising the colour, settings and costumes, were united in damning the film as long-winded, arty-crafty, confusing, diffuse and fatally lacking in pace. Powell concluded: 'The French have a word for it. When a film is a failure, they call it a *navet*, a turnip … *The Elusive Pimpernel* was a super-super-turnip'.[27] Although Powell paints Goldwyn as the villain of the piece, Charles Drazin robustly defends his attitude and actions, on the basis of correspondence he has studied.[28]

Korda's original *Scarlet Pimpernel* film reached American radio in an effective adaptation for *The Lux Radio Theatre*, broadcast on 12 December 1938. Leslie Howard recreated his original role and Olivia de Havilland assumed the role of Marguerite, playing it, unlike Merle Oberon, with a French accent. Denis Green played Chauvelin and a supporting cast of British actors (Walter Kingsford, Vernon Steele, Ramsay Hill, Eric Snowden and Reginald Sheffield) was assembled to provide vocal authenticity. De Mille, in introducing the show, declared Sir Percy Blakeney to be Howard's greatest role and he performed it with all the elegance, lightness and style of his film portrayal. He neatly contrasted the drawling, foppish Blakeney vocal characterisation with the urgent, authoritative Pimpernel tone, as well as assuming the voices of an elderly priest and an old hag during his disguises. In making the radio adaptation, scriptwriter George Wells had had to devise new scenes to cover verbally pivotal scenes in the film with little or no dialogue. So opening with a montage of voices establishing the myth of the Pimpernel, the script included a scene in a barber's shop where Sir Percy, disguised as a priest, learns about the current state of affairs in Paris and the imminent execution of the de Tournais whom he later rescues, and a bantering confrontation in Lord Grenville's library between Percy and Chauvelin. In the film, Percy is apparently asleep on a chaise longue throughout the scene, something not reproducible on radio.

Baroness Orczy's original novel *The Scarlet Pimpernel* was serialized in six half-hour episodes on the BBC Light Programme, starting on 5 July 1949. Marius Goring played the Pimpernel, Catherine Salkeld, Marguerite and Geoffrey Wincott, Chauvelin. Producer Archie Campbell, describing the Pimpernel as 'the most admirable' of his schoolboy heroes, acknowledged the popularity of the character in an article in the *Radio Times* (1 July 1949):

> Surely almost everyone who has reached his or her years of discretion can claim at least a bowing acquaintanceship with the Scarlet Pimpernel. Those who have not read the Baroness Orczy's famous novel at least once in their lives have probably seen

one or more of the films based on it, while earlier and more fortunate generations will have memories of the play.

He concedes that the adaptation by thriller writer Lester Powell, creator of Chandleresque private eye Philip Odell, is a 'free' one and 'listeners will hear much in this version which certainly had no place in the original'. But it followed the general outline of the original narrative.

The Scarlet Pimpernel returned to the airwaves in 1952, thanks to the initiative of the innovative and enterprising radio producer Harry Alan Towers. Towers, who before the war had worked for Radio Luxembourg and during the war had produced programmes for forces radio, set up a company called Towers of London in 1945 to produce and sell pre-recorded programmes worldwide. One of his ideas was to use recently released films as the basis for radio series. This had the advantage of capitalizing on the existing publicity for the story and the public's appetite for the characters. He broke into the all-important American market in 1951 with *The Lives of Harry Lime* starring Orson Welles, a radio series inspired by the hit film *The Third Man* in which Welles had played the notorious black marketeer in post-war Vienna. Filmed in 1949, it had been released in the United States in 1950 and had been adapted for radio in *The Lux Radio Theatre*, broadcast on 9 April 1951. Although Alexander Korda held the film rights to *The Third Man* itself, Towers discovered that Graham Greene retained the rights to the actual character of Lime and did a deal with him for the radio rights. Towers followed a similar procedure when he followed up the Warner Brothers film success *Captain Horatio Hornblower R.N.* (1950) with a radio series *Horatio Hornblower* starring Sir Michael Redgrave which dramatized the entire sequence of C.S. Forester novels in half-hour episodes, first broadcast in the United Kingdom and the United States in 1952. It was Welles who inadvertently gave Towers the idea for a *Scarlet Pimpernel* series when he remarked that one episode of *The Lives of Harry Lime* was turning Lime into the Scarlet Pimpernel. Once again Towers discovered that Sir Alexander Korda and London Films held the film rights to the original novel, which had just been remade as *The Elusive Pimpernel* (1950). But Towers simply acquired from Baroness Orczy's son John Montagu Barstow the radio rights to one of the original novel's many sequels, *The Adventures of the Scarlet Pimpernel* and used that as the basis for a fifty-two episode radio series. Towers recalled that Korda was 'livid' at being outwitted again by Towers but Towers managed to soothe his injured feelings and 'we became great friends'.[29] The radio series was scripted by the American radio writer Joel Murcott, whose previous assignment had been *Tales of the Texas Rangers*, but he evidently steeped himself in Baroness Orczy's writings to achieve the right tone for the stories. The programmes were directed by Tig Roe, later head of light entertainment at Associated Rediffusion Television. They were recorded on disc at the independent IBC Studio, Portland Place, opposite the BBC but much used by Radio Luxembourg and Radio Normandy to make their programmes.

Marius Goring, coincidentally Michael Powell's first choice to play Chauvelin in *The Elusive Pimpernel*, and previously the BBC's Pimpernel, took the title role of Sir Percy Blakeney. There was only one other actor in a continuing role, David Jacobs, playing the Pimpernel's principal henchman, Lord Tony Dewhurst. The veteran broadcaster David Jacobs, then a young actor not long out of the forces, recalled the period as a most exciting time in his life. He had encountered Towers during the war when, both in uniform, they were working in Ceylon for Overseas Recorded Broadcasting making programmes for the forces. Out of uniform after the war, Towers would use Jacobs regularly in his programmes but always left it until the last minute to book his actors to ensure that they were 'hungry' to perform. Apart from Goring and Jacobs in their continuing roles, there was an unofficial repertory company of actors, playing a variety of roles week by week but not credited as was then the custom. Jacobs found Goring 'absolutely brilliant and marvellous to work with. Such a friendly fellow. He couldn't have been funnier'. Goring regularly cracked jokes to maintain a relaxed and friendly attitude in the studio. This was necessary as it was extremely hard work. They regularly recorded four programmes a day. But Jacobs recalled: 'They were not slipshod. They were very well done, well edited and the effects department worked overtime to get everything right.'[30]

The series went out in the United Kingdom over Radio Luxembourg, starting on 1 December 1952 and in the United States on NBC from 21 September 1952. The series dispensed with Marguerite and concentrated squarely on adventure. Each episode was narrated by Marius Goring as Sir Percy and with the aid of the evocative narration and excellent sound effects resulted in fastmoving, atmospheric half-hour adventures, regularly featuring chases, sword duels and gunfights. Many of the stories involved disguises – as pedlar, beggar, coachman, sailor, smuggler, soldier, chimney sweeper, public letter writer, crone, even Chauvelin himself – achieved aurally by change of voice.

The rescue of threatened aristocrats, often by ingenious stratagems, was the subject of many of the episodes. But alongside such figures as the Duc de Montreux and his daughter, the Duc de Farigny and his family, Duchess Marguerite St Anne, Vicomte de Villiers and Count de Fresne, the Pimpernel and his friends also rescued a poor provincial schoolmaster Jean-Pierre Lamont, a merchant Fernand Michel, a flower girl Emilie Rombeau and her father, English children held hostage in the abbey at Rheims, and the servants of the royal family, all condemned to death, indicating that the mission of the Pimpernel was wholly democratic and not elitist.

In addition to the regular rescues, Sir Percy foiled Chauvelin's plans to murder the French Ambassador in London and frame the Pimpernel for the crime; to assassinate the Prince of Wales and his closest confidants; and to poison the entire British military and political establishment at a banquet given by an emigré aristocrat, the Marquise de Vannes, who was in Chauvelin's pay. Actual figures from the period made guest appearances in the stories: the Prince of Wales, Captain Horatio Nelson, Lieutenant Napoleon Bonaparte, William Pitt and the Duke of Wellington.

Indicative of the time in which the series was made, there was a definite Cold War slant to some of the stories. The French called each other 'comrade' as often as they did 'citizen'. There was reference to 'the People's Police' arresting suspects. In one episode, Lord Tony Dewhurst, captured by Chauvelin, was subjected to brainwashing – bright light, sleep deprivation and confinement in a white-painted cell. *The Flight of Madeleine Delon* featured a group of poor, starving French people who continue to worship secretly in the abandoned cathedral despite the official ban on religion. The Pimpernel and his band rescue them, earning the joyous cry from their leader: 'To England, to eat, to work, to worship in freedom'. In many of the costume drama series of the 1950s – *The Adventures of Robin Hood* and *William Tell* for example – there is a story echoing the contemporary fears of the H-bomb – about the invention and timely destruction of a fearsome super-weapon. In *The Scarlet Pimpernel* the episode *The Disappearance of Sykes* featured a mad English inventor John Sykes who had developed a powerful new explosive, capable of wreaking massive destruction. He sells it to the French and the Pimpernel succeeds in destroying the formula and killing him before it can be used against England.

Goring was so attached to the role of Sir Percy Blakeney that he was soon involved in the transfer of the character and the series to television. *The Adventures of the Scarlet Pimpernel* was a series of eighteen black and white half-hour episodes produced by Towers of London for television and shot at the National Studios, Elstree. It was co-produced by Goring with Dennis Vance and David Macdonald, who were the principal directors on the series. Apart from Goring as Sir Percy, the series had regular cast members appearing in almost every episode; Stanley Van Beers as Chauvelin, Alexander Gauge, who had played the part in an episode of the radio series, as the Prince of Wales and an entirely new figure, the Countess de la Valliere, Chauvelin's agent in London, played by Goring's wife, the German actress Lucie Mannheim. But there was a change of henchmen. In the pilot episode for the series *The Hostage*, directed by Michael McCarthy, the henchman as on the radio was Lord Tony Dewhurst, played by Robert Shaw. But he was missing from the rest of the series, replaced by two new henchmen, Sir Andrew Foulkes (Patrick Troughton) and Lord Richard Hastings (Anthony Newlands). As the series was filmed in 1954 the likelihood is that Shaw was unavailable as he was making his big-screen debut in *The Dambusters*, which was being filmed at the same time. Interestingly many of the television episodes were direct reworkings of the radio scripts. The very first episode *The Hostage* in which the Pimpernel and Dewhurst rescue Suzanne de Fleury and then her son, being held hostage by Chauvelin, was based on the first episode of the radio series. Thereafter *Sir Percy's Wager*, *The Sword of Justice*, *The Elusive Chauvelin*, *The Winged Madonna*, *The Ambassador's Lady* and *Sir Andrew's Fate* were all based on radio originals. Each episode began like the radio series with Goring reciting the famous Pimpernel rhyme:

> They seek him here, they seek him there,
> Those Frenchies seek him everywhere,
> Is he in heaven, is he in hell,
> That damned elusive Pimpernel.

But, presumably for censorship reasons, on the radio series, 'damned' was replaced by 'durned' and on television by 'cursed'. The series was shown in the United States, syndicated to local television stations, in 1955 and on ITV in the United Kingdom between 24 February and 24 June 1956. Despite the grace and good humour of Marius Goring, evidently enjoying himself in the role, the series on television lacked the flair of its radio counterpart. Cramped, drab sets, functional direction, limited action scenes and economical visuals all combined to give the series a threadbare, cutprice look, markedly inferior to the vivid vistas of the imagination summoned up by the radio stories: the teeming Paris streets, the howling mob, the clashing armies, the surging seas and the glittering court at Carlton House.[31]

London Films returned to *The Scarlet Pimpernel* in 1982 with a two-and-a-half-hour telefilm, directed by Clive Donner. It was scripted by William Bast and based on two Orczy novels *The Scarlet Pimpernel* and *Eldorado* but incorporated scenes and dialogue directly from the 1935 film version, and a climax lifted from *The Elusive Pimpernel*. The now familiar story of Percy, Marguerite and Chauvelin was expanded by the inclusion of the romantic affairs of Marguerite's brother, Armand St Just and the rescue by the Pimpernel of the Dauphin Louis, the heir to the French throne, from the Temple prison. Lavishly shot at Blenheim Palace,

Ragley Hall, Broughton Castle and Milton Manor and boasting elegant costumes and sets, it also had a splendid Sir Percy in Anthony Andrews, a statuesque Marguerite in Jane Seymour, and in Ian McKellen a Chauvelin more human and more humorous than before, if no less fanatical about the Revolution, with added emotional depth in the revelation of his frustrated love for Marguerite and embitterment at her choice of Sir Percy as a husband. It came to a very satisfying conclusion with a lively sword duel between Percy and Chauvelin and the escape of the Pimpernel and his party from the island fortress of Mont St Pierre which is cut off by the tide from the mainland and allows Percy's yacht to reach them.

London Films were involved once again in 1998 in collaboration with the BBC and A and E network in the United States in a series of three ninety-minute films, handsomely produced and consistently exciting, shot on location in the Czech Republic. The new *Scarlet Pimpernel* series was scripted by Richard Carpenter and directed by Patrick Lau. Richard E. Grant was perfectly cast as the Pimpernel, precisely combining the aristocratic poise with the derring-do. Elizabeth McGovern, miscast as Marguerite, was never convincing as the beautiful French actress Marguerite St Just. But there were two highly effective villains, Martin Shaw as Paul Chauvelin, cunning and fanatical, and Ronan Vibert as the icily menacing, softly-spoken Robespierre. Although *The Scarlet Pimpernel*, the first of the three episodes, retold the basic story familiar from the 1935, 1950 and 1982 versions, there were changes. Chauvelin was now much more cruel and the action far more violent than in previous versions. Chauvelin tortures League member James Danby to death, shoots the injured Tony Dewhurst in the head and has his informer Minette Roland's throat cut when she tries to double-cross him. The second episode, *Valentin Gautier*, depicts the savagery on both sides in the royalist resistance to the Revolution in the Vendée. It also develops the relationship of Percy and Marguerite as one of equals as they verbally spar, take part together in rescues and enjoy a mutually fulfilling sexual relationship. The third episode, *A King's Ransom* features a plot by Chauvelin and a murderous transvestite actress to kidnap the imprisoned Dauphin and hold him to ransom. It is foiled when the Pimpernel rescues the boy and kills the 'Chevalier d'Orly' in a climactic duel. Chauvelin avoids disgrace by substituting another boy for the Dauphin in the state orphanage where he was held.

A second series of three ninety-minute episodes was produced in 2000. Elizabeth McGovern was written out of the series by the providential death of Marguerite in childbirth. Martin Shaw had moved on but Ronan Vibert continued as Robespierre, providing an effective foil to Sir Percy. The style, dash and brio of the previous series were maintained. In *Ennui*, scripted by Matthew

Hall and directed by Graham Theakston, Percy assuages his grief at the death of Marguerite by helping a determined French aristocrat rescue her captive parents from France. In *Friends and Enemies*, scripted by Alan Whiting and directed by Simon Langton, Percy rescues a brilliant scientist and his sister who have invented a deadly new explosive. He also exposes a traitor in the League and takes time out to commission a picture of Blakeney Hall from J.M.W. Turner. Finally in *A Good Name*, scripted by Rob Heyland and also directed by Simon Langton, Percy has to rescue an aristocratic English poet, wrongly identified as the Pimpernel, and his French sweetheart who turns out to be Robespierre's lovechild. Now single again, flirting with the ladies, delivering acid one-liners and employing a range of ingenious gadgetry in his rescues and escapes, Percy comes across even more strongly as something of an eighteenth-century James Bond. There for the moment the record stops. But we can be certain that the enduring appeal of the characters and the theme – the timeless struggle for freedom against tyranny and oppression – will ensure the return of the Pimpernel in some guise or other in the course of time.

Notes

1 Baroness Orczy, *Links in the Chain of Life*, London: Hutchinson, 1947, p. 97.
2 Orczy, *Links in the Chain of Life*, p. 101.
3 Orczy, *Links in the Chain of Life*, p. 106.
4 John Gielgud, *An Actor and His Time*, Harmondsworth: Penguin, 1981, pp. 25–6.
5 Orczy, *Links in the Chain of Life*, p. 103. There is a detailed account of Fred's performance by one of his company in Julia Neilson, *This for Remembrance*, London: Hurst and Blackett, 1940, pp. 205–13.
6 Orczy, *Links in the Chain of Life*, p. 164.
7 Neilson, *This for Remembrance*, p. 189.
8 Neilson, *This for Remembrance*, p. 190; Orczy, *Links in the Chain of Life*, p. 102.
9 Orczy, *Links in the Chain of Life*, p. 102.
10 Orczy, *Links in the Chain of Life*, p. 107.
11 Orczy, *Links in the Chain of Life*, pp. 7, 98.
12 Neilson, *This for Remembrance*, p. 193; Orczy, *Links in the Chain of Life*, p. 165.
13 Orczy, *Links in the Chain of Life*, pp. 164–6. The choice of Laughton may have been dictated by the fact that by the end of his career as the Pimpernel Fred Terry was actually very fat and had to sit out the minuet. See Gielgud, *An Actor and His Time*, p. 26.
14 Raymond Massey, *A Hundred Different Lives*, London: Robson Books, 1979, p. 188.
15 Massey, *A Hundred Different Lives*, pp. 187–90.
16 Margaret Dickinson and Sarah Street, *Cinema and State*, London: BFI, 1985,

p. 86.

17 Adrian Brunel, *Nice Work*, London: Forbes Robertson, 1949, p. 180.

18 Michael Powell, *Million-Dollar Movie*, London: Heinemann, 1992, p. 55.

19 Powell, *Million-Dollar Movie*, p. 52.

20 David Niven, *The Moon's a Balloon*, London: Hamish Hamilton, 1971, pp. 253–4.

21 Powell, *Million-Dollar Movie*, p. 54.

22 Powell, *Million-Dollar Movie*, p. 21.

23 Powell, *Million-Dollar Movie*, p. 19.

24 Powell, *Million-Dollar Movie*, p. 26.

25 Powell, *Million-Dollar Movie*, p. 60.

26 Kevin Macdonald, *Emeric Pressburger: The Life and Death of a Screenwriter*, London: Faber and Faber, 1994, p. 316.

27 Powell, *Million-Dollar Movie*, p. 18.

28 The story of the filming is told in Powell, *Million-Dollar Movie*, pp. 17–28, 46–60; Macdonald, *Emeric Pressburger*, pp. 303–7, 315–18; Christopher Challis, *Are They Really So Awful?*, London: Janus, 1995, pp. 78–9. Charles Drazin defends Goldwyn's attitude and reactions as justified, citing correspondence with Powell and Korda in support of his view, in *Korda: Britain's Only Movie Mogul*, London: Sidgwick and Jackson, 2002, pp. 309–16.

29 Harry Alan Towers interview, *The Radio Adventurers*, BBC Radio 4, 30 September 2003.

30 Author's interview with David Jacobs, *The Radio Adventurers*, BBC Radio 4, 30 September 2003.

31 The fledgling BBC television service broadcast a production of the original Orczy-Terry play *The Scarlet Pimpernel* with Margaretta Scott and James Carney on 5 February 1950.

9

Tarzan of the airwaves

Everyone has heard of Tarzan, the white man raised by apes in the African jungle who became a legendary warrior and fought for good against evil. He was the most famous creation of a prolific and popular writer of romantic adventure novels, Edgar Rice Burroughs (1875–1950). The books have been translated into thirty-one languages. Like many of the most enduring characters in popular culture, Sherlock Holmes, Raffles, Dr Fu Manchu, Bulldog Drummond, for example, Tarzan has acquired an existence independent of his creator. The Tarzan that many remember is the product of the MGM film series inaugurated in 1932 and starring the former Olympic swimming champion Johnny Weissmuller. However the Tarzan of the MGM films differed in many respects from the character created by Edgar Rice Burroughs in his 1912 novel *Tarzan of the Apes* and developed in twenty-five subsequent books. MGM's Tarzan was a monosyllabic noble savage of indeterminate origin, living in a tree house with a pet chimpanzee and eventually mating with Jane Parker, the daughter of an English trader. Burroughs' Tarzan was an articulate and well-educated Englishman, John Clayton, Lord Greystoke, who, although raised by apes after the murder of his parents, eventually travelled to Europe, became fluent in English, French, German and Swahili and acquired a vast plantation in East Africa, where he ruled a tribe of faithful natives, the Waziri. He married Jane Porter, the daughter of an American professor Archimedes Q. Porter.

Burroughs claimed that the first novel emerged from his reflections on the relative importance of nature and nurture in the shaping of a human being. In Tarzan, the aristocratic blood and breeding ensures an essential nobility which survives his years of struggle and violence in the primitive ape world. This instinct, for instance, dictated his rejection of cannibalism, which the local blacks enthusiastically practiced.

Burroughs believed in the Darwinian theory of evolution, defending it in an article he published in 1925 at the time of the Scopes Trial in Tennessee.[1] But this did not mean that he saw modern white civilization as 'the ultimate achievement of evolution'. As Erling B. Holtsmark puts it: 'The reductive view would have us believe, for example, that in Burroughs all animals are, on the evolutionary scale, inferior to all men, all blacks are inferior to all whites, all forms of religion are expressions of primitive superstition, and so forth'. On the contrary, the books yield abundant evidence that Burroughs considered some animals superior to some humans, some blacks superior to some whites and some religious views based on reasoned speculation.[2] Burroughs himself wrote:

> It pleased me … to draw comparisons between the manners of men and the manners of beasts and seldom to the advantage of men. Perhaps I hoped to shame men into being more like beasts in those respects in which beasts excel men, and these are not a few … I wanted my readers to realize that man alone of all the creatures that inhabit the earth or the waters below or the air above takes life wantonly; he is the only creature that derives pleasure from inflicting pain on other creatures, even his own kind. Jealousy, greed, hate, spitefulness are more fully developed in man than in the lower orders. These are axiomatic truths that require no demonstration.[3]

Burroughs' Africa was a place of the imagination for he had never been there. Detail seems to have been derived from H.M. Stanley's classic work of exploration, *In Darkest Africa* (1890) and Burroughs made elementary errors, for example including a tiger in the magazine version of *Tarzan of the Apes* before changing it to a lioness for the book version when it was pointed out that there were no tigers in Africa.[4] But Burroughs admitted: 'I can write better about places I have never seen than those I have seen'.[5]

He was a natural storyteller, capable of fast-moving narratives, vivid description and the imaginative creation of social and religious systems. But the continuing popularity of Tarzan testifies to the enduring power of the underlying themes of the novels, which have been summed up by his biographer Irwin Porges as: 'the conflict of heredity and environment; the lone man pitted against the forces of nature; the search for individual freedom; escapism – flight from the boring routines of daily life; a destructive civilization with man, its representative, displaying all its vices, as opposed to the simple virtues of nature's creatures'.[6]

Erling B. Holtsmark has persuasively argued that in style, technique, characters and contents, the Tarzan novels are the latest manifestation of a well-established literary tradition. He writes:

> Burroughs declares himself a member in good standing in the long tradition of heroic literature that, for us, begins with the Homeric epics. Burroughs' masterly adaptations of various techniques from the epics of Greece and Rome underscore and sustain this powerful sense of the heroicness of the world and the action he in turn has created.[7]

By close analysis and comparison, he sees that Burroughs shares the key characteristics of the ancient Greek and Roman style as seen in the *Iliad*, the *Odyssey* and the *Aeneid*, in particular polarity, chiasmus and parallelism. He argues that Burroughs, like his classical predecessors, uses landscape – in this case the jungle – as commentary on the psychology of his characters. He sees Tarzan, regularly described by Burroughs as godlike and with his physique compared to that of the Greek gods and the Roman gladiators, as the archetypal epic hero, blood brother of Heracles, Achilles, Perseus, Orestes and countless others. In particular he sees him as an analogue of Odysseus and sees distinct parallels between the *Odyssey* and Burroughs' *Son of Tarzan*. Tarzan's own story has many of the elements of the classic paradigm of the hero narrative as distilled by Lord Raglan in his *The Hero*.[8] The themes of the Tarzan narratives are those of classical myth: beauty and the beast, burials, clothing, disguises, disease and wounds, food and eating, hunting, abduction, capture and imprisonment, escape, shipwreck, rebirth, ransom, treasure, love triangles, marriage and identity and heritage.[9]

It is interesting to note that Burroughs, although American, chose to make his hero British, but then ensured his marriage to an American, suggesting a commitment to the idea of a transatlantic alliance to ensure the supremacy of the Anglo-Saxon race, an idea that also inspired Arthur Conan Doyle.[10] Tarzan also becomes something of a hero of the British Empire when he is not off discovering lost civilizations. He helps the British in East Africa against the Germans (*Tarzan the Untamed*, 1919), foils Communist agents seeking the gold of Opar to finance worldwide revolution (*Tarzan the Invincible*, 1931; *Tarzan Triumphant*, 1932) and in *Tarzan and the Foreign Legion* (1944), he is to be found in Sumatra fighting the Japanese while serving as a colonel in the RAF.

Burroughs' immediate literary inspiration may also have been British. For it is hard to believe that Tarzan (whose name means 'white skin' in the language of the apes) was not a direct echo of Rudyard Kipling's Mowgli (whose name means 'frog' in the language of the wolves), the Indian boy raised by wolves, who features in *The Jungle Book* and *The Second Jungle Book*, published respectively in 1894 and 1895. Burroughs claimed Romulus and Remus as the direct inspiration for Tarzan. But Robert W. Fenton has pointed out the close parallels between passages of Kipling and passages of Burroughs.[11] Just as Mowgli communicated directly with a range of anthropomorphic animals, Baloo the bear, Akela the wolf, Bagheera the panther, Shere Khan the tiger, Kaa the python, Tabaqui the jackal, and Hathi the elephant, so too did Tarzan with Numa the lion, Tantor the elephant, Sheeta the panther/leopard, Histah the snake, Horta the boar, Bolgani the gorilla, Sabor the lioness, Wappi the antelope and Manu the monkey.

So popular was the character of Tarzan with young readers that an organization was set up to cater for them in 1916. The Tribes of Tarzan (later the Tarzan Clans) was rather similar to the Boy Scouts, whose junior branch, the Wolf Cubs, was directly modelled on *The Jungle Book*. The members of the Tribes of Tarzan took an oath promising to abide by the Tarzan code which clearly indicates what kind of role model Tarzan was intended to provide:

> A Tarzan tribesman will always be truthful, honest, manly and courageous. He will obey the laws of health and cleanliness. He will smile in defeat and will be modest in victory. He will do unto others what he would have others do unto him.[12]

Ultimately, however, the Tribes of Tarzan could not compete with the Boy Scouts of America, established in 1910.

It was inevitable that Tarzan would be portrayed in the cinema and he duly made his screen debut in *Tarzan of the Apes* (1918), produced by the newly formed National Film Corporation of America. Tarzan was portrayed by burly, barrel-chested Elmo Lincoln, who had played 'the mighty man of valour', bodyguard to Prince Belshazzar, in D.W. Griffith's *Intolerance* (1916). Enid Markey played Jane. But almost at once Burroughs encountered the problem he was continually to face with film producers. The script by Fred Miller and Lois Weber was a reasonably faithful adaptation of the first Tarzan novel. But producer Bill Parsons was continually making changes during filming to accommodate changes in the shooting schedule. The film was shot in Louisiana, incorporating background footage taken in Brazil. There were repeated rows with Parsons but the completed film was a great success and reportedly made over $1 million.[13] Parsons promptly produced a sequel, *The Romance of Tarzan* (1918) in which Tarzan followed Jane to the United States and there saved her from bandits. Burroughs protested about this fabrication but found his hands were tied by the contract he had signed with Parsons. He hoped for better luck when he sold the rights to *The Return of Tarzan* to the Great Western Producing Company which cast New York fireman Gene Pollar as Tarzan in a version of the novel, retitled *The Revenge of Tarzan* (1920) for the screen but the film had poor production values and a contrived script. Burroughs' objections to the change of title were ignored. So it was back to the National Film Corporation of America who wanted to produce a serial version of *Son of Tarzan* (1921) in fifteen episodes. Bill Parsons was by now dead and Burroughs approved the script of the new venture. Lithe Hawaiian actor Kamuela Searle was cast as Korak, son of Tarzan, and ex-opera singer P. Dempsey Tabler played the by now middle-aged Tarzan. It has regularly been reported that Searle died of injuries sustained during the film and that shooting had to be completed using a double. But John Taliaferro has queried this, pointing out that he subsequently appeared in another film, *Fool's Paradise* in 1921 and according to his brother died of cancer in 1924.[14]

Elmo Lincoln returned to the role of Tarzan, billed as 'The Tarzan of Tarzans', for another fifteen-episode serial, *The Adventures of Tarzan* (1921), based partly on *The Return of Tarzan* and partly on *Tarzan and the Jewels of Opar*. It was written and directed by Robert F. Hill and was successful at the box office. But it only served to increase Burroughs' discontent. He did not like Elmo Lincoln as Tarzan and repeatedly told producers and Lincoln himself that he did not conform to Burroughs' conception of Tarzan.

> In the first place Tarzan must be young and handsome with an extremely masculine face and manner. Then he must be the epitome of grace … My conception of him is a man a little over six feet and built more like a panther than an elephant.[15]

He poured all his bitterness about the film-makers into a letter to his brother Harry in 1922:

> The producers never read the stories, and it is only occasionally, I imagine, that the director reads them … As far as I know, no one connected with the making of a single Tarzan picture has had the remotest conception of either the story or the character, as I conceived it. Whatever beauty there was in the character of Tarzan or in the stories themselves, was not brought out, but the pictures paid well in box-office receipts, and really that is all that counts.[16]

He was to channel his discontents with the film industry into one of the later Tarzan novels, *Tarzan and the Lion Man* (1933) in which he mercilessly satirized a Hollywood film company (BO Films) which goes on safari to Africa to make a Tarzan-type film, *The Lion Man*. There is an alcoholic racist film director; a crass production executive who wants a tiger sequence, though there are no tigers in Africa; a snooty leading lady who keeps fainting and the Lion Man himself, Stanley Obroski, a world champion marathon runner ('He don't have to act but he looks great stripped'), who turns out to be a coward and eventually dies of fever. The story ends with Lord Greystoke in Hollywood auditioning for the role of Tarzan in a film to be produced by Prominent Pictures. He is turned down: 'Not the type. Not the type at all'. An adagio dancer Cyril Wayne is signed for the role. It may not be mere coincidence that in the same year Paramount released a blatant Tarzan imitation, *King of the Jungle*, featuring Kaspa the Lion Man, played by Buster Crabbe.

In 1926 Burroughs sold the rights to his 1923 novel *Tarzan and the Golden Lion* to FBO who produced a film version in 1927. James Pierce, an All-American footballer, was cast as Tarzan and Burroughs considered him perfect for the role. But critics denounced the film as far-fetched, Pierce dismissed it as a 'stinkeroo', and Burroughs called it 'a silly mess'.[17] But Pierce met and married Burroughs' daughter Joan. The final silent film incarnations were two more fifteen-part serials, *Tarzan the Mighty* (1928) and *Tarzan the Tiger* (1929), based on Burroughs' *Jungle Tales of Tarzan* and *Tarzan and the Jewels of Opar* respectively. They starred Frank Merrill, a former champion gymnast and stuntman, particularly successful in the vine-swinging sequences. Burroughs complained that *Tarzan the Mighty* bore almost no resemblance to its alleged source, *Tarzan the Tiger* bore a closer resemblance to its source but repeated an error originally made by Burroughs and later corrected by introducing tigers into Africa. Universal were considering a third Tarzan serial with Merrill when, following the introduction of sound, his voice proved unsuitable for the talkies and he retired from film acting.

The arrival of sound would see the emergence of the most famous screen Tarzan of them all – Johnny Weissmuller. MGM decided on a talkie version of *Tarzan of the Apes* following its success with the African adventure *Trader Horn*. A photographic expedition to Africa had resulted in far more location footage than could be used in *Trader Horn* and this was utilized to provide background imagery for the new film, which was principally shot at Toluca Lake, north of Hollywood. The film was directed by W.S. Van Dyke, who had also directed *Trader Horn*. The adaptation was made by Cyril Hume with dialogue provided by – of all people – Ivor Novello, who was spending a short and largely unproductive period in Hollywood as a scriptwriter. It is Novello who has been erroneously credited with the line 'Me Tarzan – You Jane'. In fact no one spoke it. The line was simply 'Tarzan – Jane'. Obliged to provide an original story because the screen rights to the novels were tied up by the silent versions, Hume abandoned Burroughs' narrative and constructed a screenplay centred on the jungle trek by two fortune hunters to find the legendary elephants' graveyard with its priceless hoard of ivory, and the romance between Tarzan, the mysterious, inarticulate white man in the jungle and Jane, the sophisticated daughter of an English trader (played by MGM contract star Maureen O'Sullivan). Even Tarzan's pet chimp was removed: Burroughs' Nkima became MGM's Cheeta. The transformation of Tarzan from an articulate British aristocrat into an inarticulate 'noble savage' succeeded in downplaying the obviously colonialist element of the novels though it can never be wholly eliminated with a white lord of the jungle. MGM did not select an actor to play Tarzan but in view of the large amount of swimming, fighting and vine-swinging, they chose an athlete – Johnny Weissmuller, who had won five swimming gold medals in the 1924 and 1928 Olympics. The graceful vine-swinging sequences actually had the celebrated aerialist Alfredo Codona doubling for Weissmuller. MGM signalled its distancing from Burroughs by titling the film *Tarzan the Apeman* rather than *Tarzan of the Apes*. The resulting film was a major box office success. Costing $660,000 to make, it netted $2,540,000 at the box-office worldwide. MGM immediately ordered a sequel.[18] In effect, it was a remake of *Tarzan the Apeman* focusing on another trek to the Mutia Escarpment in search of the elephants' graveyard and developing the romantic relationship of Tarzan and Jane.

Tarzan and His Mate (1933), scripted by James Kevin McGuinness and Howard Emmett Rogers, is actually a more exciting and sexier film than its predecessor despite a fraught production process. The film was begun under the direction of MGM's ace art director Cedric Gibbons who wanted to break into film direction and although the film is credited to him, he was removed from the film and replaced by Jack Conway, who recast, reshot and completed the film, without credit. It remains the best of the MGM Tarzans. The film included attacks by cannibals and gorillas and fights between Tarzan and a lion, a rhinoceros and a crocodile. The underwater crocodile fight sequence was to be reused in two future Tarzan films. The rip-roaring finale had Jane and her companions attacked by cannibals and lions and rescued by Tarzan with contingents of gorillas and elephants. The physical charms of Weissmuller and O'Sullivan were emphasized by the skimpiness of their outfits. Jane's costumes had to be lengthened in later films as the censorship code was tightened up in 1934. But in 1933 it was possible to include a balletic underwater swimming sequence with 1932 Olympic gold medallist Josephine McKim, who won as a member of the 4x100 metre freestyle relay, doubling for Jane completely naked. The Breen Office, the film censors, banned the sequence but MGM circulated three different versions of the film, one of them containing the nude footage, until the censors caught up with them and they had to eliminate the sequence entirely.[19] It made $2,239,000 worldwide but the inflated production costs of $1,286,000 seriously reduced the profit margin.

One of the much-imitated elements of the film was the distinctive Tarzan yell. Gabe Essoe explained its genesis:

> Tarzan's famous yell as we know it today was a product of MGM's sound department and was not perfected until 1934. They laid four different sound tracks (the bleat of a camel, howl of a hyena, growl of a dog, pick of a violin's G string) over Johnny Weissmuller's yodel, which was played at a lower speed and an octave higher. They timed it so that each of the sounds played a fraction of a second after the preceding one.[20]

Subsequently Weissmuller learned to imitate the sound and his voice replaced the recording. The sound engineers also devised higher and lighter calls for Jane and Boy.

Burroughs, however, remained deeply unhappy with the screen Tarzans. His daughter Joan recalled:

> Dad found it hard to reconcile himself to the movie versions of the Tarzan stories, and never did understand the movie Tarzan. He wanted Tarzan to speak like an educated Englishman instead of grunting. One time we saw a movie together and after it was all over, although the audience seemed enthusiastic, my father remained in his seat and kept shaking his head.[21]

MGM did not have exclusive rights to Tarzan. For independent producer Sol Lesser had acquired an option to make Tarzan films from another producer who had done a deal with Burroughs in 1928. He exercised it in 1933 to produce *Tarzan the Fearless* which was made both as a feature film and a twelve-episode serial. If Burroughs had hoped for a more faithful version of his books, he was to be disappointed. Lesser took the MGM film as his model, casting Buster Crabbe, the 1932 Olympic swimming gold medallist in the 400 metres freestyle, as Tarzan. A much cheaper and more rough and ready production than MGM's, Lesser's film, shot in the San Fernando Valley, directed by silent screen veteran Robert F. Hill (who had directed Elmo Lincoln as Tarzan) and scripted by prolific serial writers Basil Dickey and George Plympton, *Tarzan the Fearless* had Tarzan helping an expedition to find a missing scientist who had been searching for the lost cave-city of Zar only to fall into the hands of its idol-worshipping, Egyptian-style inhabitants. The lively serial-style adventures had Crabbe's vigorous and likeable Tarzan rescuing assorted characters from lion, crocodile and Arab slave-traders. Buster Crabbe repeated Weissmuller's monosyllabic noble savage creation, though the film acknowledged that he was the rightful Lord Greystoke, and in his romance with Mary Brooks, the scientist's daughter, emulated Weissmuller's courtship of Jane.

Reviewers inevitably compared the film to MGM's, to the detriment of Lesser's film, and Buster Crabbe moved on to star in eighty feature films and to play Flash Gordon in three memorable serials for Universal. But Lesser tried again when in 1937 he sensed that the MGM series was flagging. This time his Tarzan was Glenn Morris, the 1936 Olympic decathlon champion. He signed Morris to a five-picture contract. While waiting for *Tarzan's Revenge* to start shooting Morris played a small supporting role in the college football film *Hold that Coed* (1938). The film *Tarzan's Revenge* (1938), directed by D. Ross Lederman, turned out to be a lifeless, low-budget imitation of MGM's much superior *Tarzan the Apeman*, in which the characters trudge round a studio jungle set for seventy minutes encountering stock footage of African animals. Glenn Morris as Tarzan rescues society girl Eleanor Reed from a lion, a swamp and a lustful Arab potentate and she decides to stay with him in the jungle permanently. An impassive Glenn Morris, athletic enough but restricted to four words of dialogue, was handicapped by the lack of any spark of acting talent and from certain angles a distinct facial resemblance to Harpo Marx. Eleanor Reed was played by the swimming star Eleanor Holm who made an attractive and spirited heroine and actually had more footage than Morris. She subsequently described the film as 'just horrible' and confirmed the total lack of chemistry between herself and Glenn Morris.[22] Two lengthy swimming sequences were included in the film to showcase their talents. Eleanor Holm, who won the 100 metres backstroke gold medal at the 1932 Olympics, was a beautiful party girl who claimed to train on champagne and cigarettes. She was selected for the 1936 Olympics but her heavy drinking and sexual antics on the voyage out to Germany led to her being thrown off the team by the outraged officials. However, she covered the games as a journalist. Neither Holm nor Morris acted again and Lesser quietly dropped the idea of a Morris *Tarzan* series. Leni Riefenstahl's *Olympia*, the film of the 1936 Berlin Olympics, gave a much better account of the athletic prowess of Glenn Morris.

Burroughs eventually lost patience with the failure to screen his Tarzan and decided to make a Tarzan film himself. He became a partner in Burroughs-Tarzan Enterprises, set up to shoot a Tarzan adventure on location in Guatemala. Burroughs personally selected for the role of Tarzan Herman Brix, an All-American football star and the silver medallist in the shot-put at the 1928 Olympics. He ensured that Tarzan would be played for the first time as an articulate English gentleman. The script, provided by Charles Royal and Edwin Blum, was absurdly far-fetched, centring on the adventures of two rival expeditions seeking to obtain the statue of the green goddess, which contains a lost Mayan formula for a secret explosive. The usual routine of chases, captures, fights and escapes, shot on location in Guatemala, was supplemented by stock animal footage, some of it ludicrously incongruous (the elephant, giraffe and rhinoceros footage in particular). *The New Adventures of Tarzan* (1935) was released both as a twelve-episode serial and a seventy-five-minute feature film. It was reissued in a re-edited form as a feature film *Tarzan and the Green Goddess* (1938). In all its incarnations, it remained crude, slapdash and badly acted. MGM intervened to ensure the film did limited business. Burroughs abandoned his personal film-making ambitions and gave MGM a new option for further Tarzan features. Herman Brix changed his name to Bruce Bennett, took acting lessons and re-emerged some years later as a reliable character actor.[23]

Where *Tarzan the Apeman* and *Tarzan and His Mate*, with their violence, semi-nudity and undeniably sexy relationship between Tarzan and Jane were conceived for an adult audience, the third MGM film *Tarzan Escapes* (1936) marked a transition to the family film with particular appeal to children. Originally titled *The Capture of Tarzan*, it was scripted by Cyril Hume as a third reworking of the basic narrative of a safari to the Mutia Escarpment, which enabled MGM to recycle footage from the two previous films. This time Jane's cousins come to bring her back to civilization to claim an inheritance with a villainous white hunter who proposes to capture Tarzan, 'the great white ape' as a circus exhibit.

The film, as directed by James McKay, 2nd Unit director on *Tarzan and His Mate,* emerged as a vivid and violent thriller in which the natives torture their captives and Tarzan and his band, escaping through the swamps, encounter murderous pygmies and hideous vampire bats. However, when it was shown to preview audiences, the children present were terrified and MGM ordered the film reshot. McKay refused to alter the film, was replaced as director by John Farrow who stayed only long enough to marry Maureen O'Sullivan and finally a reliable journeyman, Richard Thorpe, was brought in to sanitize the production and make it more family friendly. The pygmies and the vampire bats were excised and the crocodile fight and elephant stampede footage from *Tarzan and His Mate* reused to provide action highlights. As a result, Thorpe was to direct the three remaining MGM Tarzans. But the reshooting and re-editing and the expense of constructing an elaborate tree house for Tarzan and Jane had pushed up the cost and *Tarzan Escapes*, as the film was renamed, came in at $1,063,000. It netted $1,926,000.

The decision to aim Tarzan at a family audience dictated the nature of the next film, *Tarzan Finds a Son* (1938). Burroughs' Tarzan and Jane were legally married and Jane bore a son, Jack, whose ape name was Korak, and whose adventures were recounted in the novel *Son of Tarzan* (1917). But MGM's Tarzan and Jane never got round to being legally married and the idea of the hero having a child out of wedlock was unthinkable in the censorship conditions of the time. Scriptwriter Cyril Hume came up with the solution in *Tarzan Finds a Son* (1939). Tarzan and Jane adopt and raise a child discovered in the jungle following a plane crash in which his parents are killed. Hume added a nod to Burroughs in making the child's father Richard Lancing, the favourite nephew of Lord Greystoke, so that the child, christened Boy by Tarzan, is actually a Greystoke, unlike his adoptive father. The presence of a son and the footage devoted to his exploits and the antics of Cheeta marked out the series as being firmly aimed at the family market. Hume reworked the narrative of *Tarzan Escapes* by having relatives of Richard Lancing arrive on safari five years after the crash seeking news of the Lancings because of Lord Greystoke's will and its millions. They trick Jane and

Boy into returning to England with them. But the party is captured by the savage Zambeli tribe and Tarzan rides to the rescue with his elephants. The jungle family is reunited. This time along with the familiar safari and elephant stampede footage, the action incorporated Tarzan's fight with a rhino from *Tarzan and His Mate* and for once the crocodile fight was given a rest. One notable feature of the film was underwater swimming sequences of Tarzan and Boy, shot in the clear waters of the Silver Springs in Florida. Weissmuller personally chose five-year-old Johnny Sheffield to play Boy and he took to the role enthusiastically. He was in fact the son of English character actor Reginald Sheffield, who had himself been a child star in England under the name Eric Desmond before emigrating to the United States to become part of the Hollywood British colony. Johnny, born in the United States, had grown up to be an All American boy. The film, like its predecessors, was not free from controversy. Maureen O'Sullivan, tired of her role, wanted to leave the series and the script had her killed in the finale. But when news of this was announced, there were protests from both Burroughs and fans of the series. The end of the film was reshot to have Jane injured but surviving and O'Sullivan, placated by a pay rise, stayed with the series until MGM dropped it. Also finally reconciled was Burroughs who on the eve of the release of the new film wrote 'I am no longer a critic of my own stories on the screen. Johnny Weissmuller is just Tarzan to me'.[24]

Tarzan's Secret Treasure (1941), scripted by Myles Connolly and Paul Gangelin, had members of a scientific expedition discovering gold on the Mutia Escarpment and kidnapping Jane and Boy to force Tarzan to disclose its location and later shooting him to prevent him following them. Hostile natives capture them but Tarzan revives and pursues them. In an exciting finale, Tarzan, swimming underwater, overturns canoes containing the natives and their prisoners. The villains are conveniently eaten by crocodiles and Tarzan is reunited with his family. MGM prudently reused sequences from previous *Tarzan* films, including the crocodile fight, the elephant stampede, Tarzan's tree-swinging and the natives' brutal execution of their prisoners.

The final film in MGM's *Tarzan* series, *Tarzan's New York Adventure* (1942), scripted by Myles Connolly and William Lipman, showed signs of economizing. Its running time at seventy minutes was twenty minutes shorter than the previous films and its budget at $707,000 the lowest of any of the titles in the series. It also recycled footage from the previous films, notably the flight and arrival of the plane lifted from *Tarzan Finds a Son*. It did, however, have the virtue of novelty. A group of animal trappers, landing on the escarpment, kidnap Boy and take him to New York to work in a circus as elephant trainer and performer.

Tarzan and Jane follow and much of the New York footage is comedy based on the unfamiliarity of Tarzan, seen for the first time in a suit, with the ways of civilization and the antics of Cheeta, who contrives to wreck a hotel room and a nightclub. There is also a deeply racist sequence in which Cheeta, who picks up the telephone and gibbers into it to a black caretaker, is mistaken by the caretaker for 'a coloured boy'. The film livens up when Tarzan, on the run from the police, swings across the roofs of New York, dives from the Brooklyn Bridge into the East River and eventually summons the circus elephants to stop the villains making off with Boy. Elmo Lincoln, the first screen Tarzan, had a bit part as a circus roustabout.

Although *Tarzan's New York Adventure* netted $2,719,00 worldwide, making it far more profitable than its predecessors in the series, given its lower budget, MGM decided to terminate the series. This was almost certainly because half of the box-office returns for the series had always come from overseas. *Tarzan* films were popular in the United Kingdom, Continental Europe, Latin America and the Far East: Russia, Egypt, Israel and Korea, among the more unlikely places. The universal appeal is perhaps explained by Tarzan's archetype of independent rugged masculinity, his defence of the oppressed and his status as an eco-warrior. But with the world at war, continental markets were closing, the East was in turmoil and the future of the United Kingdom, Hollywood's biggest overseas market, was uncertain. Interestingly it was at about the same time that the MGM careers of Greta Garbo and Nelson Eddy and Jeanette Macdonald, whose films had similarly depended on overseas box-office returns, were also ended. MGM, however, were to re-release *Tarzan's Secret Treasure* and *Tarzan's New York Adventure* in 1947–48 and *Tarzan the Ape Man* and *Tarzan Escapes* in 1954–55.

The MGM conception of Tarzan resulted in two major changes to Burroughs' concept. Burroughs' books not just on Tarzan but on Mars and Pellucidar are centrally concerned with the question of language. Burroughs invented several new languages with extensive vocabularies for his books. In the first book *Tarzan of the Apes* he shows how Tarzan learned English from books but could not initially speak it. His first spoken language was French, taught him by Lieutenant D'Arnot of the French navy. But he subsequently mastered English, Arabic and Waziri and whenever he encountered one of the many lost races in the Dark Continent he rapidly picked up their language. But MGM's Tarzan never progressed beyond monosyllables and Sol Lesser insisted on retaining this characterisation for the duration of his Tarzan franchise (1943–58).

The original books have a strong charge of eroticism. Tarzan is regularly described as a Greek god, roams about naked except for a loin cloth and inspires loving descriptions of his athletic physique. Similarly the curvaceous beauty of the skimpily-clad white queens Tarzan regularly encounters on his travels is hymned. That erotic charge remains present in the first two MGM films. Tarzan is an object of heterosexual desire. The casting of a succession of athletes in the role also gives the male viewer permission to admire the near-naked male without suspicion of homosexual desire.[25] But with *Tarzan Escapes* the erotic charge begins to be mitigated until Alex Vernon can call the series 'a remarkably asexual oeuvre'.[26] Jane's costume gets longer and more concealing, due to censorial pressure, and the creation of the elaborate tree house with jungle versions of all modern conveniences signals her transformation into the jungle equivalent of a suburban housewife, a characteristic even more marked when she and Tarzan adopt Boy and become the perfect nuclear family. This compounds Tarzan's inarticulacy which gives him a childlike innocence and increases his dependence on Jane to learn 'correct behaviour'.

It was only a matter of time before Burroughs sought to exploit the newest medium – radio – and Tarzan duly made his radio debut in 1932. He was eventually to be heard on the air waves in the United States, Australia, New Zealand, Canada and South Africa, though, curiously, not in the United Kingdom. Frederick Dahlquist of American Radio Features Syndicate acquired the rights to produce a radio version of Tarzan but Burroughs, anxious to avoid the alterations which film producers introduced into his stories, insisted on script approval. From 1932 to 1934 on over sixty radio stations 286 fifteen-minute episodes of *Tarzan of the Apes* were broadcast. They were based directly on Burroughs' novels *Tarzan of the Apes* and *The Return of Tarzan*. The series was scripted by David Taylor, directed by James Knight Carden and narrated by Fred Shields. Burroughs' daughter Joan played Jane Porter and her husband James Pierce played Tarzan. Pierce was the former All-American football player who had starred as Tarzan in the last silent film version of the stories, *Tarzan and the Golden Lion* (1927).[27]

Radio adaptation presented certain problems. The many fights, chases and vine-swinging were purely visual and had to be narrated with accompanying sound effects. Tarzan himself did not speak until well into the serial as in the book he did not learn English until he encountered the French naval officer Lieutenant Paul D'Arnot. On the radio, it is Jane who teaches him English in episode sixteen after Tarzan has rescued her from lions. Until that point his appearances were narrated. It was impossible to dramatize his upbringing among the apes (nine of the book's twenty-eight chapters) – except by narration, interspersed by grunts, so the script cut from the death of his parents and his adoption by the apes to when he was fully grown and encounters American mutineers and their stranded passengers, Professor Porter and his daughter among them. The account of the mutiny was built up as this provided the backstory of the passengers. The comic negro maid Esmeralda was cut. So each programme consisted of passages of narration and acted scenes with a very striking aural tapestry of sound effects. This was something Burroughs approved of, as he wrote to his niece:

> They have injected all of the jungle noises, including the roaring of Numa, the lion, the screaming of Sheeta, the panther, the cries of the bull apes, the laughing of the hyenas, the rustling of the leaves, the screams and shots – you can almost hear the blood gushing out of jugulars.[28]

Despite the limitations outlined above and some over-emphatic acting by certain members of the cast, the surviving episodes constitute an effective enough version of Burroughs' narrative. But as so often with Burroughs, dissatisfaction set in. He began to feel he could do better himself. He complained to Dahlquist that the series had degenerated into 'a series of captures, rescues, recaptures, escapes, more captures and more escapes'.[29] He decided not to renew Dahlquist's contract but to produce two new, thirty-nine episode serials himself through Edgar Rice Burroughs Inc. He chose Rob Thompson as scriptwriter but otherwise engaged many of the production staff and actors from the Dahlquist series. It used to be thought that Thompson had devised the scripts for the serials, *Tarzan and the Diamond of Ashair* and *Tarzan and the Fires of Tohr*, but Robert R. Barrett, the foremost authority on Tarzan on radio, has discovered that Burroughs provided the synopsis for *The Diamond of Ashair* which he later reworked as his novel *Tarzan and the Forbidden City* (1938).[30] James Pierce had decided not to continue in the role of Tarzan – he went on to play Thun, King of the Lion Men, in Universal's *Flash Gordon* film serial. Carlton Kadell took over the role of Tarzan and Fred Shields directed. Both serials explored the theme that dominated Burroughs' later Tarzan novels, the discovery of a lost race with a white queen, in the heart of Africa, an idea borrowed from Rider Haggard (*Allan Quatermain, She*). In the books, Tarzan successively encountered Romans, Crusaders, Midianites, Portuguese navigators, even Atlanteans. In *Tarzan and the Diamond of Ashair* it was ancient Egyptians. Where the MGM films retained the romantic idyll of Tarzan and Jane in the jungle, Burroughs' radio serials dropped Jane, allowing Tarzan to experience romantic encounters with mysterious native queens, whose advances he could chastely resist.

Tarzan and the Diamond of Ashair, broadcast in 1934, boasted a classic Burroughs narrative for which Thompson proved an effective *pasticheur* of the Burroughs style. Supposedly taking place immediately after the events of the previous serial, which are summarized in the new one and which saw Jane returning to the United States, the new serial featured two rival expeditions seeking the fabled city of Ashair, one, guided by Tarzan, is trying to find the lost explorer Brian Gregory and the other headed by the sinister Oriental Atan Thome is after a mythic treasure, the Father of Diamonds. Tarzan saves various characters from attack by lion, crocodile and giant ape. The expedition survives tornado and native attack and eventually reaches the city of Ashair which is built inside an extinct volcano and where members of the ruling family speak seventeenth-century English in the manner of the King James Bible because an ancestor had travelled to 'Anglo-land' in search of famine relief centuries before. The kingdom, called Hesiheria, is home to prehistoric creatures and Tarzan successively tackles a tyrannosaurus rex, a pterodactyl, a giant python and a sabre-toothed tiger. The expedition gets caught up in a power struggle between the King, Sou-Ten, and Queen, Tirah, of Hesiheria, but they eventually escape with the rescued Brian Gregory but return the Father of Diamonds, seized by Atan Thome to the nobleman Hakeru who has helped them escape. They hand over Atan Thome as well for punishment by the Hesiherians.

Tarzan is, as Burroughs intended, articulate and intelligent and in the early episodes referred to as Lord Greystoke. But he displays all the skills he learned while being raised by apes. He deploys the authentic Burroughs calls, the challenge of the great bull ape ('Kreegah') and the victory cry 'Tarmangani', three guttural syllables rising to a high pitched screech, wholly unlike MGM's manufactured ape-call. There are three characters with terrible over-the-top foreign accents, the Frenchman D'Arnot, the Swede Larsen and the German Wolff. But there are two well modulated and subtle radio performances from Cy Kendall as the suavely sinister Atan Thome and Jeanette Nolan as the seductive half-caste Magra. Tarzan was played with authority by Carlton Kadell. Each of the pre-recorded fifteen-minute episodes featured a central dramatic situation and climaxed with a cliffhanging ending.

When Burroughs came to rework the radio narrative for his novel *Tarzan and the Forbidden City*, he retained many of the characters and incidents but also made significant changes. He dropped some characters (Larsen, Sou-Ten and Tirah) and added others (Lt Jacques Lavac who is a rival to D'Arnot for the love of Brian's sister Helen Gregory; sympathetic nobleman Thetan). Various characters met different fates. On the radio, Gregory Sr., Brian's father, and Lal Taask, Atan Thome's henchman, are killed halfway through but in the book they survive until the end. On the radio, Magra, who loves Tarzan, dies interposing her body in the way of a bullet from Atan Thome to save Tarzan; in the book she survives. Atan Thome himself, an Egyptian on the radio, an Indian in the book, is handed over to the Hesiherians for punishment on the radio; goes mad and dies in the book. Wolff, killed by a giant ape on the radio, is killed by Magra in the book. Burroughs elaborated the Ashair episodes considerably from the radio narrative, employing his favourite device of two warring cities (Thobos versus Ashair) and having the temple of the diamond underwater, so that Tarzan instead of the tackling the prehistoric monsters of Thompson's radio script has to fight sea creatures (shark, sea serpent, giant sea horses).

Interestingly there are in Thompson's script some explicitly anti-racist comments which are not carried over into the novel. When Sandra Gregory apologises for assuming that Tarzan was a native, he replied: 'It's no insult to be taken for a native of Africa'. Later Tarzan stops Wolff flogging a native and threatens to flog him if he lays another hand on a native.

Broadcast on thirty-six radio stations in the United States, Canada and Australia, *Tarzan and the Diamond of Ashair* was officially pronounced a success and work began on another thirty-nine-episode serial, *Tarzan and the Fires of Tohr* with much the same production team and cast. Carlton Kadell returned as Tarzan and Cy Kendall as another Oriental villain, this time Chinese, Dr Wong Tai. Rob Thompson provided the script. He opted for a structure similar to that of *The Diamond of Ashair*. Tarzan and Lt D'Arnot, on a mission to suppress the Arab slave trade, encounter a lost expedition searching for the lost city of Tohr and led by Englishman Major Burton-Ashleigh. It includes his American ward Jeanette Burton, Irish adventurer Terry O'Rourke and Oriental scientist Dr Wong Tai. Eventually they are captured by giant yellow Neanderthals, inhabitants of the city of Tohr which is ruled over by a cruel and capricious white queen Ahtea. She demands that Tarzan become her consort and when he refuses imprisons him and his party, planning to sacrifice them in the sacred fires of the god Pantu. Tarzan leads a revolt of the slaves in the jewel pit and his revolt coincides with an attack by the rival city of Ra-Tohr. It all ends with Ahtea, on the point of sacrificing Jeanette, being pulled into the fires by the wounded Wong Tai, and the Ra-Tohrians securing victory.

Each episode was built around a dramatic incident, fights with lions, elephant stampede, slave revolts, native attack, dungeon escape. The narrative also showed the influence of Burroughs' novels. The rivalry of Tohr and Ra-Tohr, the cruel and capricious queen, the arena battle between Tarzan and a giant warrior, the threat from the hunting lions raised by the Tohrians all directly recall Burroughs' *Tarzan and the City of Gold* with its rival cities of Athne and Cathne, beautiful and despotic queen Nemone, arena battle and hunting lions. The idea of a female beauty ruling over male neanderthals comes from *Tarzan and the Jewels of Opar*. Like *The Diamond of Ashair* the radio serial had some awful foreign accents (this time French and Irish), a sinister Oriental in pursuit of Tohrian treasure and a blossoming romance between two of the members of the expedition (Jeanette and Terry recalling the similar romance of Helen and D'Arnot). *Tarzan and the Fires of Thor* was completed in late 1935 and broadcast in 1936 but only over ten radio stations. Too much time had elapsed between the production of the two serials and the radio stations had filled their air time with other offerings. Although *The Fires of Tohr* was as gripping and entertaining as its predecessor it was pronounced a failure and Burroughs abandoned radio production.

When MGM decided to terminate its Tarzan series, independent producer Sol Lesser stepped in and immediately offered contracts to Weissmuller, Sheffield and O'Sullivan. O'Sullivan declined, preferring to end her association with the role of Jane; the other two accepted and Lesser began production of a new Tarzan series with his own Principal Artists productions (later Sol Lesser Productions) releasing through RKO Radio Pictures. Burroughs benefited as he was paid a percentage of the profits from the new films. Tarzan, Boy and Cheeta the chimp featured but the running times were reduced, from MGM's ninety to seventy five minutes and budgets were cut. But the first of Lesser's Tarzans, *Tarzan Triumphs* (1943), scripted by Carroll Young and Roy Chanslor, was to prove his most financially successful production. At the request of the government, Tarzan became involved in the Second World War. When Nazi paratroopers occupy the lost city of Palandria, another Burroughs-type settlement of peace-loving, sun worshipping, light-skinned inhabitants in the middle of black Africa, and enslave the populace in pursuit of valuable raw materials for the war effort, Tarzan abandons his previous isolationist stance ('jungle people only fight to live – civilized people live to fight') for commitment to the war effort ('Now Tarzan make war') and leads an uprising of the Palandrians to wipe out the Nazis. The follow-up, *Tarzan's Desert Mystery* (1943), scripted by Edward T. Lowe, was much less satisfying. Nazi agents seek to dominate an Arab emirate in the Sahara and are tackled by Tarzan. But the political message was diluted, too much footage was devoted to the activities of a travelling female American magician and to Cheeta's comic capers before the film plunged into absurdity when, seeking for a fever cure in the jungle, Tarzan was menaced by prehistoric monsters and a giant spider, which ended up eating the chief Nazi. German emigré director William Thiele directed both films but after Lesser had much of *Desert Mystery* reshot, Thiele was dropped, and associate producer Kurt Neumann directed the next three Tarzan films. Meanwhile Jane was said to be in England, first nursing her sick mother and later nursing injured soldiers.

The remaining four Weissmuller Tarzan films, though not directly based on any of the Burroughs novels, were much closer in spirit to his work than the MGM films. Jane returned to the series in the attractive form of Brenda Joyce. In *Tarzan and the Amazons* (1945), scripted by Hans Jacoby and Marjorie Pfaelzer, Tarzan saves an all-female, sun-worshipping white tribe in the hidden city of Palmyria from the depredations of a multi-national group of archaeologists seeking to steal their treasures. In *Tarzan and the Leopard Woman* (1946), scripted by Carroll Young, Tarzan assisted the British District Commissioner in suppressing a leopard-worshipping cult whose adherents, under their powerful High Priestess and a renegade half-caste doctor are raiding local caravans.

In *Tarzan and the Huntress* (1947), scripted by Jerry Gruskin and Rowland Leigh, Tarzan foils a ruthless gang of trappers, with a female leader, seeking to capture animals for zoos. Tarzan believes animals should remain in the wild. At the end of the film he summons a herd of elephants to destroy the trappers and their camp, freeing all the animals they have captured.

The last of the Weissmuller Tarzans was *Tarzan and the Mermaids* (1948), scripted by Carroll Young. Now forty-four, visibly overweight and ageing, Weissmulller was dropped by Lesser but only because he was demanding a share of the gross profits as part of a new contract. Lesser, however, provided him with a fitting swansong, which was artistically the best of the RKO Tarzans. The story had Tarzan saving a community of native pearl-divers from exploitation by a ruthless white man, posing as their ancestral god Balu. It featured several swimming sequences to play to Weismuller's athletic strengths. But more significantly it was shot entirely in Mexico and Lesser engaged Robert Florey, a director with a strong visual sense and a romantic sensibility (manifested in such films as *Murders in the Rue Morgue*, *The Face Behind the Mask* and *The Desert Song*), composer Dimitri Tiomkin who provided a pulsatingly symphonic score and Mexican cameraman Gabriel Figueroa who shot some wonderfully artistic location sequences utilising spectacular Mexican sea-coast locations and Aztec pyramids. Particularly notable were a balletic cliff-diving sequence (during the shooting of which Weissmuller's double was actually killed), the underwater swimming sequences and a battle with an octopus. The film was flawed only by the tiresome comic relief provided by a singing boatman Benjy, played by popular Mexican musical star John Laurenz, whose presence Sol Lesser had insisted on. A notable absentee from the final Weissmuller Tarzan was Johnny Sheffield as Boy. *Tarzan and the Huntress* had shown that Sheffield was now a strapping teenager, almost as tall as Weissmuller, and so in *Tarzan and the Mermaids* Boy was said to have been sent to school in England. Sheffield, dropped by Lesser, was snapped up by the Poverty Row studio Monogram for a low-budget series of adventures as Bomba the Jungle Boy, a teenage Tarzan imitation created by Roy Rockwood. He starred in twelve Bomba films between 1948 and 1955. A similar jungle career beckoned for Weissmuller. B-picture producer Sam Katzman at Columbia signed him, with a guaranteed share of the grosses, to star in a series of films as Jungle Jim, a fully clothed jungle adventurer and he duly appeared in sixteen of them between 1948 and 1955.

Soon after Burroughs died in 1950, Walter White Jr. of Commodore Productions, which had made a hit with its *Hopalong Cassidy* radio series, acquired the radio rights to Tarzan and eventually produced seventy-five half-hour shows, the vast majority of them scripted by Budd Lesser (no relation to Sol). Lamont Johnson, later a successful film and television director, played Tarzan much in the manner of Carlton Kadell. But the series differed from the books and the 1930s radio serials in certain respects. Tarzan was now based in his sea-coast cabin in West Africa, where his castaway parents had first taken refuge. He often cooperates with British colonial officer Captain Stanley Lawrence 'of the governmental police' in an unnamed British Colony to defeat injustice. As Burroughs would have wanted, Tarzan is an entirely articulate character. Once again Jane is dropped to give Tarzan the freedom to roam. Tarzan spends much time with the Punya tribe and educates and protects a Punya boy, Torgo, who functions as a surrogate son.

Opening with the Tarzan yell, a variation on Weissmuller's version, each episode of *Tarzan, Lord of the Jungle* began with the narrator intoning: 'From the heart of the jungle comes a savage cry of victory. This is Tarzan, Lord of the Jungle. From the black core of dark Africa – land of enchantment, mystery and violence comes one of the most colourful figures of all time. Transcribed from the immortal pen of Edgar Rice Burroughs – Tarzan, the bronzed white son of the jungle'. He adds 'And now in the very words of Mr Burroughs' and introduces the episode. But in fact the episodes were not in the very words of Mr Burroughs though the scriptwriter captured something of his style, particularly in describing struggles between the ape man and various animals.

Tarzan ranged right across Africa in his adventures, episodes taking place in the north (Egypt, Sudan) the south (South Africa), the west (Congo, Nigeria) and east (Kenya). But the scriptwriter had only the vaguest idea of African geography, locating Zulus on the road to Timbuktu (*Adventure on the Road to Timbuktu*) and British military posts in the Congo (*Message to Fort Shabir*). Scriptwriter Bud Lesser also made an elementary error in having Tarzan fight a

tiger in *Hooded Death*. But later in the series he correctly pointed out to a family
of British castaways in *Paradise Island* that there were no tigers in Africa.

There are certain continuing themes in the series. The Arabs are invariably
villainous. Tarzan has to rescue an American girl (*Jungle Heat*), a French girl
(*African Thanksgiving*), an English princess (*Quicksands of Wadehara*) and an
eleven-year-old girl (*Arab Vengeance*) from the lustful attentions of Arab po-
tentates and to protect black tribes from Arab slave raiders (*Black Ivory*, *Strange
Book of Araby*).

But Tarzan also seeks to protect the animals, the natives and the environment
from the depredations of ruthless white men: animal trappers (*The Decoy*, *Hunter's
Fury*), oil prospectors (*Black Gold of Africa*), pirates (*Pirates of Bandeira*), cruel
diamond mine owners (*D is for Diamonds and for Death*). When women turn up
in leading roles, they are more often than not treacherous and ruthless (*The Decoy*,
The Female of the Species, *Jungle Orchids*, *Across a Continent*, *The Lipigor*).

Tarzan frequently engages in detective work: solving the murder of an
American gold prospector (*Congo Murder*), the hijacking of government arms and
supplies (*Jungle Hijackers*), the theft of gold from a train (*Gold Coast Robbery*),
the theft of the sacred emerald of the Karmiki (*The Siren of Omdurmara*), the
theft of the wedding gifts of the Pasha of Omdurmara (*Stolen Jewels*). There is a
Cold War slant in episodes in which Communist agents seek to obtain uranium
(*Jungle Legacy*) and a British secret weapon (*The Rays of Death*). In *Contraband*
Tarzan helps the authorities track down the source of guns being supplied to
Communist-inspired rebels in a British colony.

Tarzan regularly encounters and exposes as falsehoods native superstitions.
As the opening narration of *The Headhunters of Yambesi* puts it: 'Some parts
of Africa have changed little since the days when the first white men crossed
the Dark Continent. Those changes which have occurred may be traced to the
patient missionaries, dedicated colonists and the intrepid pioneers who have
long battled against the aboriginal cruelties of a wild people who inhabit a wild
land'. Among the cruelties Tarzan helps to counter are human sacrifice (*The
Manuema*), the need to put a live boy inside a tribal drum (*Drum Without a
Heart)*, the killing of the surviving twin when a twin dies (*Trouble Comes in Pairs*)
and voodoo (*Congo Magic*).

While generally remaining faithful to Burroughs' version of the Tarzan myth,
with Tarzan being regularly identified as John Clayton, Lord Greystoke, and explaining how he was raised by apes after his parents were cast away on the West
Coast of Africa and subsequently killed, one episode (*Trail of Death*) contrived to
incorporate the MGM version, with Tarzan returning to the Mutia Escarpment

with an unscrupulous white man in search of the elephants' graveyard and there finding his tree-home still intact.

Combining evocative sound effects, vivid narration and tightly plotted, action-packed narratives, these half-hour episodes were invariably gripping and entertaining and took the Tarzan story in new directions while reflecting the attitudes and values of the time in which they were made.

Sol Lesser's search for a new Tarzan ended with the selection of Lex Barker to play the apeman. Barker, unlike previous Tarzans, was actually an actor, an RKO contract player who had been seen in small supporting roles in such films as *Mr Blandings Builds His Dream House*, *Crossfire* and *The Velvet Touch*. Tarzan made him a star. Tall, handsome and athletic, he fitted the part very well. But despite Barker's repeated requests for more dialogue, Lesser insisted on retaining the monosyllabic Weissmuller characterisation. But in the absence of Weissmuller, there was now markedly less swimming.

Barker's first outing in his new role was *Tarzan's Magic Fountain* (1949), scripted by Curt Siodmak and Harry Chandlee and directed by Lee Sholem. The basic plot idea, a hidden valley whose inhabitants remain ever youthful and healthy, thanks to a fountain of youth, was lifted from *Lost Horizon*, a borrowing acknowledged in the name of the Blue Valley, a nod to Shangri-La's Valley of the Blue Moon. The valley with its Egyptian-style white tribe under a beneficent priestly ruler, the High One, is threatened when an English aviatrix who has lived there for twenty years since crashing her plane has to return to civilization to free her wrongly imprisoned fiancé. Aged fifty, but looking twenty-five, she is evidence of the efficacy of the fountain. She wants to return there to live with her new husband but an unscrupulous trader seeks to locate and market the miraculous water. He is foiled and the valley's secret is kept. *Tarzan's Magic Fountain* marked Brenda Joyce's last outing as Jane. After it, she gave up the role and retired from acting to spend more time with her family. As a publicity gimmick, Lesser cast Elmo Lincoln in a bit part as a fisherman and he did promotional interviews with Barker. For purists the downside was the extensive footage devoted to Cheeta, by now virtually a co-star, and his misadventures with bubblegum, pepper and an ant hill.

Tarzan and the Slave Girl (1950), scripted by Hans Jacoby and Arnold Belgard and directed by Lee Sholem, featured yet another lost Egyptian-style white race, this time the kingdom of Lionia, which worships a lion god. Stricken by a mysterious disease, the Lionians start kidnapping women from native tribes in order to ensure the survival of the race. Among their captives are Jane and a flirtatious French nurse, Lola. Tarzan swings to the rescue, bringing a doctor to cure the disease, and securing the release of the women. Lesser was never able to find an adequate replacement for Brenda Joyce as Jane and so each of Barker's films saw him teamed with a new Jane, played by a bevy of more-or-less interchangeable starlets; Vanessa Brown took the role in *Tarzan and the Slave Girl*, to be succeeded in turn by Virginia Huston, Dorothy Hart and Joyce Mackenzie. Burroughs paid a visit to the set of *Tarzan and the Slave Girl* and was photographed with Lex Barker. It was his last visit to a Tarzan set as he died on 19 March 1950.

Burroughs' Tarzan had always played his part in combating the enemies of the United States, fighting against the Germans in the First World War, the Russians in the 1920s and the Japanese in the Second World War. But in the 1950s he became a Cold War warrior. In *Tarzan's Peril* (1951) (UK title: *Tarzan and the Jungle Queen*), Tarzan is battling Communist infiltration in Africa and explicitly supporting British colonial rule as a bulwark against it. Lesser had intended that this would be the first Tarzan film to be shot in Africa and the first to be filmed in colour. But director Phil Brandon, despatched with a crew to British East Africa, hit a series of disasters, including bad weather and the spoiling of much of his colour footage. So the production was withdrawn to Hollywood and although some impressive footage of tribal ceremonies and customs, an attack on a native village and a safari crossing spectacular scenery was included, the bulk of the film, including all the scenes with the principals, was shot on the RKO back lot in black and white, under the direction of Byron Haskin.

The script by Samuel Newman and Francis Swann showed the influence of Edgar Wallace as much as that of Edgar Rice Burroughs. British District Commissioner Peters, attending the coronation of Queen Melmendi of the Ashuba, explains to his successor, Commissioner Connors, that he had devoted his career, like Sanders of the River, to keeping gin and guns out of his territory. Melmendi regrets Peters' impending retirement, declaring, like Bosambo in *Sanders of the River*, 'You are our mother and our father, Lord' and agrees never to accept guns in her village. But Peters and Connors are murdered by gunrunners, led by Radijek, the agent of an unnamed foreign power who is peddling Eastern European weapons to the tribes to stir up inter-tribal warfare and undermine British colonial rule. Tarzan, whose origin as the son of Lord Greystoke is acknowledged for the first time in the series, avenges the murder of the Commissioners, prevents tribal war and eliminates Radijek.

The Communists are still up to no good in *Tarzan's Savage Fury* (1952), directed by Cy Endfield and scripted by Cyril Hume, veteran of the Weissmuller series, Hans Jacoby and Shirley White. This film had direct reference back to Burroughs' novels as the principal villain is Rokoff, a Russian agent, who had been a character in Burroughs' *The Return of Tarzan* (1915) and *The Beasts of Tarzan* (1916). This Rokoff and an English traitor Edwards, who has agreed to pose as Lord Greystoke, Tarzan's cousin, after Rokoff murders the real Greystoke, seek out Tarzan with the diary of Tarzan's father, the previous Lord Greystoke. The diary had told of a native tribe, the Wazuri, who had a fortune in uncut diamonds which, according to the fake Lord Greystoke, is needed by England for military and industrial purposes. Jane urges Tarzan to help them for the sake of England but when their true nature and true mission, to secure the diamonds for Russia, becomes clear, Tarzan foils their plans. Intertwined with this narrative is Lesser's attempt to recreate a family for Tarzan. The character of Joey Martin (Tommy Carlton) is introduced, an American orphan stranded in the jungle and being used by a native tribe as crocodile bait. But he is rescued and taken under the wing of Jane and Tarzan, who teaches him to conquer his fear of lions. However, he never reappears in the series.

Lex Barker's final outing as the apeman was *Tarzan and the She-Devil* (1953), scripted by Karl Kamb and Carroll Young and for which Kurt Neumann returned as director. In this film Tarzan defeats a gang of ivory poachers, headed by a ruthless French woman. He comes to the defence of another of those inexplicably white-skinned and in this case even more inexplicably boomerang-wielding native tribes that feature in Lesser's films when they are enslaved by the ivory hunters to act as bearers and beaters. He also defends the elephants which in the climax he summons to destroy the ivory hunters and their camp. The elephant stampede was lifted from the 1934 jungle film *Wild Cargo*.

Following this film, Lex Barker, his star credentials established, gave up the role of Tarzan and moved on to star mainly in Westerns. The eleventh Tarzan, chosen by Lesser to carry on his series, was an unknown tall and muscular lifeguard Gordon Scott, who was signed to a seven-year contract on a modest salary. Lesser was increasingly concerned about the profitability of the series. He revealed that his first Weissmuller Tarzan *Tarzan Triumphs* made 'more than a quarter of a million dollars' but 'thereafter each one of my Tarzan pictures made less and less money – although they all realised a profit. Sometimes it was because of increasing costs, other times because of world conditions'.[31] The RKO ledger confirms this view. The Weissmullers had made $2,315,000 (*Tarzan's Desert Mystery*), $2,885,000 (*Tarzan and the Amazons*), $2,610,000 (*Tarzan and the Leopard Woman*), $2,535,000 (*Tarzan and the Huntress*) and $2,025,000 (*Tarzan and the Mermaids*). Lex Barker's Tarzans brought in steadily declining profits: $1,850,000 (*Tarzan's Magic Fountain*), $1,725,000 (*Tarzan and the Slave Girl*), $1,675,000 (*Tarzan's Peril*). *Tarzan's Savage Fury* and *Tarzan and the She-Devil* continued the declining curve. In all but one case (*Tarzan and the Mermaids*) more than half of the gross came, as it had in the MGM Weissmuller years, from the overseas markets.

Gordon Scott's first Tarzan film *Tarzan's Secret Jungle* (1955), directed by Harold Schuster and scripted by William Lively, was a cheap and tired rehash, heavily padded with footage from previous productions of *Tarzan and the Huntress* and *Tarzan and the She-Devil* with Tarzan protecting jungle animals from the depredations of white hunters. Perhaps the worst of Sol Lesser's Tarzan films, it was also the last to be released by RKO Radio Pictures. The studio was closed down and sold to Desilu Productions in 1956.

Lesser negotiated a deal with MGM to revive the Tarzan franchise with the old home studio of Tarzan. The first MGM release was a distinct improvement on the last RKO release. *Tarzan and the Lost Safari* (1957), directed by Bruce Humberstone from a screenplay by Montgomery Pittman and Lillie Hayward, was the first Tarzan film to be shot in colour, the first to be made largely on location in Africa (Uganda, Kenya, Tanganyika, Belgian Congo) and the first to be made entirely outside Hollywood, studio scenes being shot in the United Kingdom and the cast and crew being largely British. It emerged as a lively and watchable thriller with Tarzan rescuing the passengers from a crashed airliner and escorting them to safety. At the climax he saves them from the inhabitants of Opar who have captured them and intend sacrificing them to the Lion God.

But it was back to Hollywood for *Tarzan's Fight for Life* (1958), directed by Bruce Humberstone from a screenplay by Thomas Hal Phillips. For this film, Lesser made a final attempt to resurrect Tarzan's family. Jane, who had been absent from Scott's first two films, returned in the person of Eve Brent and they were given an adoptive son, named Tartu but often referred to as Boy (Rickie Sorensen). The plot had Tarzan assisting an American doctor who is developing a fever serum to overcome native superstition, fanned by a malign witch doctor. Although the production was promoted as being 'Filmed Where it Happens', much of it was very obviously shot on the MGM back lot in Hollywood with African location footage lifted from *Tarzan and the Lost Safari*.

After this, Lesser decided to try and break into television and filmed three half-hour episodes of a proposed *Tarzan* TV series, with Gordon Scott, Eve Brent and Rickie Sorensen. Shoddy, low-budget, studio-bound rehashes of old Tarzan plots (ruthless trappers capturing animals, a white hunter hunting Tarzan, treasure-hunters seeking a lost city), they failed to sell to the networks. Eventually spliced together and titled *Tarzan and the Trappers*, they made it to television as a single feature in 1966.

The poor returns on the three Scott films, the failure of the television venture and a heart attack persuaded Lesser to give up his series. Lesser sold his company, the rights to Tarzan and Gordon Scott's contract to two young producers, Sy Weintraub and Harvey Hayutin, who determined to modernize Tarzan's image. They did so with a vengeance in a brace of tough, gritty, contemporary thrillers, *Tarzan's Greatest Adventure* (1959) and *Tarzan the Magnificent* (1960), released by Paramount. Out went Jane, Boy and Cheeta and even, in *Tarzan the Magnificent*, the Tarzan yell. Tarzan became articulate and fluent in English, finally abandoning the monosyllabic characterization Lesser had clung to throughout his franchise. The films were shot on location in Kenya with studio work in England and they were largely in the hands of British technicians and casts. *Tarzan's Greatest Adventure*, directed by John Guillermin and scripted by Guillermin and Berne Giler, had Tarzan hunting down one by one a gang of ruthless diamond hunters, headed by Anthony Quayle, who had wiped out an African village. *Tarzan the Magnificent*, directed by Robert Day and scripted by Day and Berne Giler, refurbished that old Western plot of the criminal being transported over hostile territory by a lawman with the criminal's crazy family in pursuit. In this case when the local police inspector is murdered, Tarzan takes charge of transporting the murderous Coy Banton (Jock Mahoney) to jail. He is accompanied by assorted passengers from a river boat, stranded when the Banton family blow it up, and is pursued by the Banton family. Culminating in a spectacular final fight between Tarzan and Coy, *Tarzan the Magnificent* along with its predecessor decisively re-established the series as cinematic fare for adults. Going out on a high note, with critics and audiences responding enthusiastically to the updated Tarzan, Scott resigned the role and set out for Italy to star in a series of historical muscleman epics.

Weintraub continued to produce Tarzan films through the 1960s but with 'the wind of change' blowing through Africa and the civil rights movement highlighting discrimination in the United States against African-Americans, Africa became something of a difficult property for Hollywood. So during the decade Tarzan was sent to India (*Tarzan Goes to India*), Thailand (*Tarzan's Three Challenges*), Central America (*Tarzan and the Valley of Gold*) and South America (*Tarzan and the Great River*). Weintraub did, however, produce a popular Tarzan television series in 1966–67, set in Africa but filmed in Mexico, starring the personable and articulate Ron Ely. In addition all Burroughs' original novels were issued in paperback in the USA by Ballantine Books and in the UK by New English Library and were eagerly devoured by readers. MGM twice remade their original *Tarzan the Apeman*, both times disastrously. A low-budget colour version of *Tarzan the Apeman* (1959), starring Denny Miller, went so far as to insult the intelligence of its audience by lifting all the big action scenes from the 1932 black and white version and tinting them. The 1981 version was if anything even worse, execrably scripted, fatally lacking in narrative drive or period feel (though the setting is 1910), it was evidently conceived by director John Derek as a vehicle for the bodily charms of his wife Bo Derek, a non-actress who strips off or falls into the water in clinging blouses as often as is feasible. Miles O'Keefe's Tarzan does not appear until halfway through and is called upon neither to speak nor act but merely to rescue Jane from a succession of perils (lion, python, ivory hunters).

In one respect the 1981 *Tarzan the Apeman* conformed to the tendency established since the 1960s with regard to *Tarzan*. Whereas all the Tarzan films up to 1970 were set in the present, those made since (*Greystoke: The Legend of Tarzan*, 1984; *Tarzan and the Lost City*, 1998) have been set firmly in the Edwardian era. This includes the most recent version, the 1999 Disney cartoon version which provided a simplified narrative focusing on the typical Disney themes (family and belonging), featuring cute anthropomorphic animals speaking colloquial twentieth-century American ('Hi, guys'), anodyne pop songs (Phil Collins), and a suave English villain, a big game hunter out to capture the apes. This suggests that the white lord of the African jungle is now consigned safely to history and to the realm of politically correct children's fiction. One wonders what Burroughs would have made of it.

Notes

1 Erling B. Holtsmark, *Tarzan and Tradition,* London: Greenwood Press, p. 83.
2 Holtsmark, *Tarzan and Tradition*, pp. 147–8.
3 Irwin Porges, *Edgar Rice Burroughs: The Man Who Created Tarzan*, New York: Ballantine Books, 1976, p. 221.
4 Porges, *Edgar Rice Burroughs*, p. 213.
5 Porges, *Edgar Rice Burroughs*, p. 219.
6 Porges, *Edgar Rice Burroughs*, p. 219.
7 Holtsmark, *Tarzan and Tradition*, p. 63.
8 Holtsmark, *Tarzan and Tradition*, Appendix 3, p. 168.
9 Holtsmark, *Tarzan and Tradition*, p. 157.
10 Sir Arthur Conan Doyle, *Sherlock Holmes: The Complete Short Stories*, London: John Murray, 1963, p. 68.
11 Robert W. Fenton, *The Big Swingers*, Englewood Cliffs, NJ: Prentice-Hall, 1967, pp. 63–7.
12 Porges, *Edgar Rice Burroughs*, p. 436.
13 Fenton, *The Big Swingers*, p. 87.

14 John Taliaferro, *Tarzan Forever: The Life of Edgar Rice Burroughs*, New York: Scribner, 1999, pp. 167–8.

15 Porges, *Edgar Rice Burroughs*, p. 491.

16 Porges, *Edgar Rice Burroughs*, p. 491.

17 Gabe Essoe, *Tarzan of the Movies*, Secaucus, NJ: Citadel Press, 1972, p. 56; Taliaferro, *Tarzan Forever*. p. 221

18 On the *Tarzan* film grosses at MGM, see H. Mark Glancy, 'MGM film grosses, 1924–1948: The Eddie Mannix ledger', *Historical Journal of Film, Radio and Television* 12 (1992), pp. 127–45; on the *Tarzan* film grosses at RKO, see Richard Jewell, 'RKO film grosses, 1929–1951: The C.J. Tevlin ledger', *Historical Journal of Film, Radio and Television* 14 (1994), pp. 37–49.

19 Rudy Behlmer, 'Tarzan and His Mate', *Behind the Scenes*, Hollywood: Samuel French, 1990, pp. 303–4.

20 Essoe, *Tarzan of the Movies*, p. 62. This is an excellent account of the cinematic Tarzan. See also David Fury, *King of the Jungle: 'Tarzan' on Screen and Television*, Jefferson, NC: McFarland, 1994.

21 Fenton, *The Big Swingers*, p. 173.

22 Mike Chapman, *The Gold and the Glory*, Newton, IA: Culture House, 2003, p. 93

23 Porges, *Edgar Rice Burroughs*, pp. 848–73.

24 Taliaferro, *Tarzan Forever*, p. 309.

25 Walt Morton, 'Tracking the sign of Tarzan: Trans-media representation of a pop-culture icon', in Pat Kirkham and Janet Thumin (eds), *You Tarzan: Masculinity, Movies and Men*, London: Lawrence and Wishart, 1993, pp. 106–25.

26 Alex Vernon, *On Tarzan*, Athens,GA: University of Georgia Press, 2008, p. 96.

27 Essoe, *Tarzan of the Movies*, p. 56.

28 Porges, *Edgar Rice Burroughs*, pp. 770–1.

29 Robert R. Barrett, *Tarzan on Radio*, Schiller Park, IL: Radio Spirits, 1999, p. 24. This is the best account of Tarzan on radio.

30 Author's interview with Robert R. Barrett, 29 January 2002, broadcast on BBC Radio 4.

31 Fenton, *The Big Swingers*, p. 174.

10

The many voices and faces of Sherlock Holmes

Sherlock Holmes has had such enduring appeal because he embodied the strengths, the complexities and the contradictions of the late-Victorian age. For he is not one man but at least three men in one, three different archetypes of masculinity, each vying for dominance, and each capable of being emphasized in performance.

First and most obviously, he is a rational man, the epitome of the Victorian era of scientific discovery and invention, of the railways, the electric light, the steamship and the telephone. He is the embodiment of hard facts and cold logic, remorseless reason, scientific method; unemotional, detached, indifferent to women. There is plenty of textual support from both Holmes and Watson for these conclusions 'I am a brain, Watson, the rest of me is a mere appendix' says Holmes. And 'Women have seldom been an attraction to me, for my brain has always governed my heart'; and 'Love is an emotional thing, and whatever is emotional is opposed to that true cold reason which I place above all things. I should never marry myself lest it bias my judgement' (*Sign of Four*), and 'I have never loved' (*The Devil's Foot*). Watson records:

> All emotions were abhorrent to his cold, precise but admirably balanced mind. He was, as I take it, the most perfect reasoning and observing machine that the world has seen; but as a lover he would have placed himself in a false position. He never spoke of the softer passions, save with a gibe and a sneer (*A Scandal in Bohemia*).

It is this rationality that leads him to reject supernatural explanations for the Sussex Vampire and the Hound of the Baskervilles. The celibacy fits him into that classic paradigm of the detective – the detective as the latterday secular equivalent of the priest, a man who combats evil, hears confessions, brings about redemptions or retributions, who restores the moral equilibrium of society. Some detectives, such as Father Brown and Brother Cadfael, have actually been priests; other detectives (Miss Marple, Hercule Poirot, Inspector Morse) have been celibate. Priestlike, Holmes pardons and frees at least three murderers in *The Abbey Grange, Charles Augustus Milverton* and *The Devil's Foot.*

Holmes's view of his profession leads him to express disapproval of Watson's accounts of his cases. He tells him in *The Sign of Four*: 'I cannot congratulate you on it. Detection is or ought to be, an exact science and should be treated in the same cold and unemotional manner. You have attempted to tinge it with romanticism, which produces the same effect as if you worked a love-story or an elopement into the fifth proposition of Euclid' and in *The Abbey Grange* he declares 'your fatal habit of looking at everything from the point of view of a story instead of a scientific exercise has ruined what might have been an instructive and even classical series of demonstrations. You slur over work of the utmost finesse and delicacy to dwell upon sensational details which may excite but cannot possibly instruct the reader.'

And yet, beneath that much vaunted surface of remorseless logic beats the heart of a true *romantic*, chivalrous, patriotic, imaginative. Holmes is a patriot, a royalist and an imperialist, like his creator. Picking up on Doyle's admission in the preface to the *Casebook* that the Holmes adventures belong in 'the fairy kingdom of romance', Peter MacDonald in his excellent section on Doyle in *British Literary Culture and Publishing Practice* says that the stories could be described as 'modernized fairy tales playfully masquerading as documentary history'. Mary Morstan refers to Holmes and Watson as 'two knight errants to the rescue'. MacDonald writes that the stories are structured around 'the chivalric code of honour which, in the medieval romance, encompassed both the elaborate rules of combat followed by knightly opponents and the conventions of courtship observed by courtly lovers. In Conan Doyle's manly detective romances, both central characters, observe every article of this code, though Holmes, the just opponent of criminals and intellectual rival of the official police, is the principal exemplar of the rules pertaining to combat and Watson, especially in *The Sign*, is the model gallant lover. By extension, male villains are typically identified by their disregard for either set of rules or simply by their failure to reflect the ideals of manliness these rules enshrined'.[1]

Watson in *The Gold Pince Nez* noted of Holmes 'a remarkable gentleness and courtesy in his dealings with women. He disliked and distrusted the sex, but he was always a *chivalrous* opponent' and Holmes himself declared to the traitor Colonel Valentine Walter in *The Bruce-Partington Plans*, 'How an English gentleman could behave in such a manner is beyond my comprehension'. Watson says of their breaking into Charles Augustus Milverton's house: 'The high object of our mission, the consciousness that it was unselfish and chivalrous, the villainous character of our opponent, all added to the sporting interest of the adventure'. MacDonald concludes that Holmes is 'not so much the modern scientific detective he purports to be but … a mythical figure … a beneficent wizard from the world of the medieval romance disguised as a charismatic late-Victorian genius'.[2] It is in that chivalric spirit that Holmes is willing to sacrifice his life to destroy Moriarty at the Reichenbach Falls.

American audiences like the British were enthralled by the lightning feats of ratiocination, the quirky characterisations, the Victorian atmosphere which by the inter-war years came to seem reassuring, and the memorable one-liners: 'This, I think is a three pipe problem'; 'it is a capital error to theorise without data'; 'When you have eliminated the impossible, whatever remains, however improbable, must be the truth'; 'The game's afoot' (a phrase borrowed from Shakespeare's chivalric epic *Henry V*) and of course the apocryphal 'elementary, my dear Watson, elementary'. But there is more to it than that.

The continued and continuing popularity of Holmes and Watson in the United States is part of a wider cultural phenomenon – that shared Anglo-American transatlantic culture which underpinned the so-called 'special relationship', which saw regular traffic in fiction, drama and entertainment between the two countries, and which was linked by a common commitment to chivalry.[3]

Doyle firmly believed in the shared heritage and culture of the United Kingdom and the United States, dedicating his novel *The White Company* 'to the hope of the future reunion of the English-speaking races' and ensuring that his celebrated creation Sherlock Holmes shared his view. As Holmes said to Mr Francis Hay Moulton in *The Noble Bachelor*:

> It is always a joy to me to meet an American, Mr Moulton, for I am one of those who believe that the folly of a monarch and the blundering of a minister in fargone years will not prevent our children from being some day citizens of the same world-wide country under a flag which shall be a quartering of the Union Jack with the Stars and Stripes.

Yet there is a third type of masculinity lurking within Holmes and it is one whose appearance caused a crisis of masculinity at the end of the nineteenth century – the aesthete, who was the product of the Wildean decadent movement. Doyle was acquainted with Wilde and his ideas. For there was in 1889 a dinner party, when the publisher of *Lippincott's Magazine* while visiting London entertained to dinner at the Langham Hotel Conan Doyle and Oscar Wilde and following that dinner, commissioned the one to write *The Sign of Four* and the other *The Picture of Dorian Gray*. Holmes has elements of the aesthete about him: Watson refers to his 'Bohemian' soul (*Sign of Four*). Holmes alternates between periods of languor and hyperactivity, he is a prey to boredom ('My whole life is spent in one long effort to escape the dreary commonplaces of existence' he says (*The Red-Headed League*). He rises late, keeps his cigars in the coal scuttle, his tobacco in a Persian slipper and unanswered correspondence transfixed by a jacknife to the mantelpiece. He takes drugs and speaks in epigrams. Watson declares of Holmes 'Like all great artists he lived for his art's sake', directly quoting the aesthete's prime directive: 'art for art's sake'.

Perhaps an extension of this Bohemianism was Holmes's talent as an actor, something regularly remarked upon. He had an uncanny ability convincingly to assume any character and we know he successfully impersonated a plumber, an elderly bookseller, an Italian priest, a French workman, an old woman, a sailor, a Nonconformist clergyman, a drunken groom and an opium addict, and kept five refuges in different parts of London from which to sally forth. Watson wrote of him: 'His expression, his manner, his very soul seemed to vary with every fresh part he assumed. The stage lost a fine actor when he became a specialist in crime' (*A Scandal in Bohemia*). The three sides of his character are encapsulated in his three principal pastimes: chemical experiments, improvising on his violin and a 7% solution of cocaine.

It was Doyle's genius to provide Holmes with a partner, Dr John H. Watson, who was his polar opposite and perfect foil. Watson is a solid, decent, down-to-earth English gentleman, loyal, brave, reliable, and reveres Holmes as 'the best and wisest man I have ever known'. Although Holmes teases and mystifies Watson and takes him for granted, when Watson is wounded in *The Three Garridebs* he gets the one and only indication ever of the depth of Holmes's affection for him: 'It was worth a wound to know the depth of loyalty and love which lay behind that cold mask' he writes.

Dennis Porter writes: 'Holmes is a class hero before he is a national hero. He embodied the heroic qualities of an ascendant middle-class that had learned to groom itself for an imperial role … His investigative adventures were capable of matching … the exploits of the heroes of the Empire itself'.[4] He is middle-class, a professional consulting detective who earns his living from his work. In his interesting study *The Intellectuals and the Masses*, which explores the contempt of intellectuals for the people and in particular the suburban middle class, John Carey talks of Conan Doyle 'redrawing the English cultural map along anti-intellectual, pro-clerk lines'.[5] Doyle's heroes and heroines are typists, governesses, engineers, stockbrokers' clerks and civil servants, and Holmes praises the Board Schools, which were providing an elementary education for the working and middle classes. There is also barely a decent aristocrat in the entire canon. They are almost invariably cold, cruel, snobbish, selfish, exploitative: the Duke of Hol-derness, Sir George Burnwell, Lord Robert St Simon, Lord Mount James, Lord Cantlemere, and even worse are foreign aristocrats Baron Adelbert Gruner and Count Negretto Sylvius. But he is both a class and a national hero, for Holmes embodies a dominant view of British/English identity which developed in the nineteenth century and comprised a sense of duty, a sense of individuality, a sense of humour, a sense of emotional restraint, a sense of superiority to foreigners – elements of all these can be found in Holmes.

Rosemary Jann argues: 'Significantly the Sherlock Holmes stories for the most part do not focus on what were perceived as the most serious threats to social order in later Victorian and Edwardian society. We catch no glimpses of the white-slavery sensations of the 1880s or of the anarchists or terrorists who disturbed the peace of the closing decades of the century for political reasons … the increasing masses of the unemployed urban slum dwellers, those "dangerous classes" whose revolutionary potential was a persistent source of anxiety in later Victorian London, remain virtually invisible. Instead, wrong-doing tends to be focused inwards; on threats to the security and reputation of individuals and families and to the codes of conduct that underpin middle-class power'.[6]

Doyle was of course operating under certain constraints. He was writing for a middle-class family magazine and this probably dictated why Watson says he chose to lay before the public 'those cases which derive their interest not so much from the brutality of the crime as from the ingenuity and dramatic quality of the solution'.[7] But Doyle seems to have agreed with the element of restraint, as for years he refused to reprint the story *The Cardboard Box* (with its postal delivery of an amputated finger) regarding it as too gruesome. The period when Doyle began writing was a period fraught with anxiety: it was a period of Fenian bomb outrages, trade union unrest culminating in the Trafalgar Square riots, suffragette agitation and the Jack the Ripper murders. Doyle's stories deal with threats to the fabric of society and its structures. On the domestic front, there is the threat to family life in a series of stories about patriarchal tyranny; fathers, stepfathers, employers seeking to prevent young women from marrying in order to gain control of their property or conversely seeking to marry them themselves to gain their property (*The Copper Beeches, The Speckled Band, The Solitary Cyclist, The Greek Interpreter, A Case of Identity*). The threat to public morality and social order from high-society scandals features in: *The Three Gables, Charles Augustus Milverton, A Scandal in Bohemia, The Noble Bachelor, The Beryl Coronet*. Then there is the threat to national security and world order. The United Kingdom, despite having the mightiest empire the world had ever seen, was increasingly anxious about losing its international pre-eminence to Germany and the United States. There are threats from spies and secret agents in *The Bruce-Partington Plans*, *The Second Stain* and *The Naval Treaty* and from secret societies, the Scowrers, the Mormons, the Ku Klux Klan, the Mafia, the Red Circle. The anxiety is embodied in Professor Moriarty, an elemental force of evil, intellect gone bad, he is Holmes's alter ego, tall, thin, brilliant, 'The Napoleon of Crime'. Although Moriarty actually appears in only two stories (*The Final Problem* and *The Valley of Fear*), he has captured the imagination of the public and of film-makers and regularly appears in films as head of a vast unseen criminal network destabilizing society, evidence of growing middle-class concern about the threat to the 'thin crust of civilization'.

Holmes and Watson like Doyle himself were believers in empire and monarchy. Holmes famously amused himself by shooting the initials 'VR' on the walls of the sitting-room of 221B Baker Street and Dr Watson purchased a portrait of the imperial martyr, General Gordon, and installed it in that same sitting-room. Holmes had come to the aid of his country in 1895 by recovering the Bruce-Partington Submarine Plans and spending a day at Windsor where he received an emerald tie-pin from 'a certain gracious lady'. Watson had served in Afghanistan as an army doctor.

Interestingly, a rather less positive view of Empire emerges from the stories, betraying something of an ambivalence towards Empire in the middle-class psyche. Firstly, the Empire is depicted as a source of wealth, licit and illicit. *The Sign of Four* centres on the Agra treasure seized by Jonathan Small and his Sikh associates during the Indian mutiny and subsequently stolen by Colonel Sholto and conveyed to England. *The Solitary Cyclist* hinges on the plot by Woodley and Carruthers to gain control of the fortune made by Ralph Smith in South Africa, depriving his niece Violet of her rightful inheritance. *The Boscombe Valley Mystery* centres on John Turner, better known as bushranger Black Jack of Ballarat, who made his fortune by robbery in Australia and retired to England where he killed the man who had been blackmailing him.

Then there is the Empire as a source of violence, death and horror. Some of Doyle's most memorable villains come from the Empire. Dr Grimesby Roylott of *Speckled Band* fame had practised as a doctor in Calcutta and married the widow of Major-General Stoner of the Bengal Artillery but had been sent to prison for beating his native butler to death and later murders one stepdaughter and tries to murder another. Colonel Sebastian Moran, chief of staff to Professor Moriarty and 'the second most dangerous man in London', was the murderer of the Hon Ronald Adair, second son of the Earl of Maynooth. Moran was the son of the British Minister to Persia, educated at Eton and Oxford and 'once of Her Majesty's Indian Army' (1st Bengalore Pioneers). He was also 'the best heavy game shot in our Eastern Empire' and author of *Heavy Game of the Western Himalayas* and *Three Months in the Jungle*. Holy Peters, the man behind the disappearance of Lady Frances Carfax, was 'one of the most unscrupulous rascals that Australia has ever evolved – and for a young country it has turned out some very finished types'.

Horrors too come out of the Empire: the deadly swamp adder, used by Dr Grimesby Roylott to kill Julia Stoner; the black Formosa corruption and the Tapanuli fever and other hideous Oriental diseases of which the Sumatran plantation owner Culverton Smith is an expert and one of which he uses to kill Victor Savage; the poisoned arrows of the hideous cannibal pygmy from the Andaman Islands in *The Sign of Four*; the Devil's Foot root discovered by Dr Leon Sterndale in Africa and used by Mortimer Tregennis to poison his family and by Sterndale to dispose of Mortimer. But there was a brighter side too – the Empire as a place of redemption. Gilchrist, the student who had surreptitiously examined the Fortescue Scholarship paper at the College of St Luke's in *The Three Students* takes a commission in the Rhodesian Police and goes out to the Empire to redeem himself. James Wilder, illegitimate son of the Duke of Holderness and the man behind the Priory School kidnapping, is sent to Australia 'to seek his fortune'. The Hon Philip Green went to the South African goldfields to escape the consequences of his wildness and there made a fortune, returning in search of Lady Frances Carfax. And Dr Leon Sterndale was allowed by Holmes to bury himself in Central Africa to expiate his sin of murdering Mortimer Tregennis.

Doyle believed firmly in the Anglo-American alliance. He said in 1892: 'I take the greatest possible interest in all things American … There is, or ought to be, so little difference between them and us. … The centre of gravity of the whole race has shifted to the West, and I believe in time that every Saxon will be united under one form of government … America and England, joined in their common Anglo-Saxonhood, with their common blood, will rule the world. We shall be united. And the sooner that day comes the better'. Yet as Joseph Kestner points out, it is possible to read the canon as 'a body of stories warning the United Kingdom about the nature of Americans, who are described variously as deceptive, greedy, violent, untrustworthy, scheming, conniving, ruthless and criminal'.[8] Americans bring violence to the streets of London through a variety of secret societies, the Ku Klux Klan, the Scowrers and the Mormons, and Holmes is unable to save the life of clients John Douglas and John Openshaw from them, such is their diabolical violence and *The Valley of Fear* portrays an American community as a hell of terrorism, violence and viciousness, and Kestner sees the book as evidence of Doyle's 'anxiety at the increasing power of America and concern that its masculine paradigms are dangerous, atavistic and reversionary to a mode of bestiality and lawlessness'.

Every generation since Conan Doyle has had its perfect Holmes. An ideal Holmes exhibition would include for the first two decades of the twentieth century William Gillette, for the 1930s Arthur Wontner, for the 1940s Basil Rathbone, for the 1950s Carleton Hobbs, for the 1960s Peter Cushing and for the 1980s and 1990s Jeremy Brett. Several of the interpreters of Holmes were aficionados of the stories and faced with scriptwriters' inventions, pressed for the inclusion of authentic Doyle dialogue. Among these aficionados were Eille Norwood, Reginald Owen, Arthur Wontner, Carleton Hobbs, Peter Cushing, Douglas Wilmer and Jeremy Brett.

It is impossible to overestimate the importance of William Gillette as an interpreter of Holmes. In him the Anglo-American alliance takes palpable form. For it is a remarkable fact that the first theatrical incarnation of Holmes was by an American actor William Gillette (1856–1937) who in 1899 gained permission from Doyle to create a play out of the stories and for the next twenty years he toured the United Kingdom and the United States in his play, becoming for several generations on both sides of the Atlantic the face and voice of Sherlock Holmes. Having read all the stories and mined them for dialogue, he drew on *A Scandal in Bohemia* and *The Final Problem* for his plot. It was Gillette who popularised the deerstalker and the dressing gown and introduced the meerschaum pipe as an accessory (to avoid his face being obscured by any other kind of pipe), and devised the line 'Elementary, my dear Watson'. Although Gillette and his play were coolly received by the London critics, they were enthusiastically welcomed by the British public. And Doyle's verdict? He wrote in his memoirs that the play 'was written and most wonderfully acted by William Gillette, the famous American. Since he used my characters and to some extent my plots, he naturally gave me a share of the undertaking, which proved very successful. "May I marry Holmes?" was one cable which I received from him when in the throes of composition. "You may marry or murder or do what you like with him" was my heartless reply. I was charmed both with the play, the acting and the pecuniary result'.[9] Doyle graciously acknowledged Gillette's importance in 1921 in a speech when he said: 'If my little creation of Sherlock Holmes has survived longer perhaps than it deserved, I consider that it is largely due to three gentlemen, who have, apart from myself, associated themselves with it' and he singled out Sidney Paget the artist who established the visual image of Holmes,

Greenhough Smith the editor of *The Strand* magazine who brought the character to a mass readership and William Gillette.[10] Not only did Gillette tour in his play for over twenty years, he filmed it in 1916 in a silent version now lost. He was the model for artist Frederick Dorr Steele's illustrations of the stories in *Collier's Magazine*. He was also the first radio Holmes, appearing in an adaptation of *The Speckled Band* on American radio in 1930.

Gillette's play not only served as the basis of his own 1916 film but – according to the credits – as the basis of John Barrymore's 1922 film *Sherlock Holmes*, Clive Brook's 1932 *Sherlock Holmes* and Basil Rathbone's 1939 *Sherlock Holmes*, though there was less and less of the play in each successive version; virtually nothing by 1939. The most faithful surviving film version of Gillette's play is the 1922 *Sherlock Holmes* (UK title: *Moriarty*), directed by Albert Parker and scripted by Marion Fairfax and Earle Brown. John Barrymore, popularly known as 'The Great Profile', leant that profile very successfully to the role of Holmes, making him a commanding figure and finding excellent support in Roland Young's Doctor Watson and Gustav von Seyffertitz' grotesque and menacing Moriarty. The film is enlivened by location shooting in London, Cambridge and Switzerland, opens with the nice conceit of Holmes as an undergraduate at St John's College, Cambridge, solving the theft of the Athletic Club funds, but it is flatly directed, fatally weighed down with explanatory titles and ultimately emerges as dull and plodding.[11]

If William Gillette was the pre-eminent theatrical interpreter of Holmes, the most significant silent screen Holmes was the British actor Eille Norwood (1861–1948). There had already been British film versions of *A Study in Scarlet* (1914) and *The Valley of Fear* (1916). In *A Study in Scarlet* Holmes was played by James Bragington, an accountant who had never acted before and would never do so again. He was chosen for his physical resemblance to the Paget illustrations. But George Pearson the director recalled: 'he looked the part and played it excellently'. Southport Sands and Cheddar Gorge stood in for the Salt Lake Plains and Rocky Mountains of the American section of the story.[12] *The Valley of Fear* starred H.A. Saintsbury, who had already played Holmes on stage in William Gillette's *Sherlock Holmes* and Doyle's own *The Speckled Band* and had also been chosen for his resemblance to the illustrations.

In 1920 the Stoll Film Corporation acquired the rights to the entire corpus of the Holmes stories. They then produced three series of films, each comprising fifteen titles, *The Adventures of Sherlock Holmes* (1921), *The Further Adventures of Sherlock Holmes* (1922) and *The Last Adventures of Sherlock Holmes* (1923). Each film ran for some thirty minutes and was a faithful screen transcription of the original short story. The series comprised all the published stories up to and including *Thor Bridge* with the single exception of *The Five Orange Pips*. There were also two feature-length films, *The Hound of the Baskervilles* (1921) and *The Sign of Four* (1923). The features were directed like the first of the three series by leading British director Maurice Elvey.

The part of Holmes in all the films, forty-seven in total, was taken by Eille Norwood, who became so devoted to the role that when the films ended, he went on stage in 1923 in a newly written play *The Return of Sherlock Holmes* by J.E. Harold-Terry and Arthur Rose. An entertaining and popular production, it was based on elements of *The Disappearance of Lady Frances Carfax*, *The Empty House*, *The Red-Headed League* and *Charles Augustus Milverton*. Opening on 1 October 1923, it ran for a year in London and the provinces. *The Stage* praised the 'finesse, imperturbable lyricism and quiet force' of Norwood's performance as well as his 'skilful production work'.[13] Norwood never appeared in films again.

Norwood took great pains to look like the illustrations, to the extent of shaving back his hair to extend his forehead. He studied the stories in detail, insisting on fidelity to the text and he took great pains over and enjoyed the many disguises he had to assume. Norwood defined his approach:

> My idea of Holmes is that he is absolutely quiet. Nothing ruffles him but he is a man who intuitively seizes on points without revealing that he has done so, and nurses them with complete inaction until the moment when he is called upon to exercise his wonderful detective powers. Then he is like a cat – the person he is after is the only person in all the world, and he is oblivious to everything else till his quarry is run to earth.[14]

His interpretation won the approbation of Doyle who wrote approvingly:

> He has that rare quality which can only be described as glamour, which compels you to watch an actor eagerly even when he is doing nothing. He has the brooding eye which excites expectation and he has also a quite unrivalled power of disguise. My only criticism of the films is that they introduce telephones, motor cars and other luxuries of which the Victorian Holmes never dreamed.[15]

Although Holmes is now indelibly associated with the nineteenth century, the Holmes films of the 1930s, like those of the 1920s, all have contemporary twentieth-century settings. The decade began with the shadow of Gillette still long on the interpretations. After all his final stage appearance in the role of Holmes was in 1929 and he was still playing Holmes on the radio in the 1930s.

The first talkie Holmes was Clive Brook, selected, I believe, because of a certain facial resemblance to Gillette. He starred first in *The Return of Sherlock Holmes* (1929), directed by the British stage producer Basil Dean from a screenplay by

Dean and Garrett Fort. The contract between the Doyle estate and Paramount specified that they not use one of the published cases and Dean's inspiration came from the Crippen case and his flight from England by ocean liner.[16] The film had Holmes brought out of retirement to rescue the fiancé of Dr Watson's grown-up daughter kidnapped by Professor Moriarty and Colonel Sebastian Moran. Dean and Brook fell out and Brook completed the film when Dean resigned. Brook injected a considerable amount of humour into his character- ization, took on several disguises (one as an Austrian musician) and recalled preview audiences rocking with laughter.[17] In 1939 detective story aficionado Graham Greene pronounced *Return* the worst Holmes film he had seen as it had the great detective 'shipped as passenger on the latest transatlantic liner in pursuit of a Professor Moriarty who used electricity, sub-machine guns, the radio in eliminating his enemies'.[18]

Brook returned to the role in 1932 in *Sherlock Holmes* which is in many ways a remarkable film. Allegedly based on Gillette's play, it retained only the most objectionable feature of the play – Holmes's engagement to Alice Faulkner. It virtually eliminated the Holmes–Watson partnership, reducing Watson (Reginald Owen) to a mere walk-on part and giving Holmes as partner Billy the Page, played by Howard Leeds with an atrocious cockney accent. There are distinct elements of parody in Brook's West End drawing-room comedy version of Holmes. But it is genuinely amusing and Brook adds to the fun with his disguise as a deaf old lady. The film is modernized and Americanized, with Holmes inventing a mo- tor-wrecking ray to combat the new menace of automobile crime and Moriarty introducing an American-style protection racket and bomb-throwing as cover for his real plan – to rob Faulkner's Bank, owned by Alice's father. Holmes denounces the threat from American crime: 'We're not used to American rackets; children machine-gunned in the streets … there's only one way to deal with these alien butchers: their own way. Shoot first, Investigate afterwards'. Brook thought the film 'terrible'.[19] But the film has two saving graces: Ernest Torrence's elementally evil Moriarty and the dynamic cinematicity of William K. Howard's direction. Rapid cutting, mobile camerawork and atmospheric photography enhance the key sequences of Moriarty's escape from prison, the gathering of international criminals at a funfair and the attempted bank robbery. It remains visually and cinematically impressive if canonically false.

The modernization of Holmes was carried over into the 1931 British film version of *The Speckled Band*, directed by Jack Raymond. It was adapted by W.P. Lipscomb both from the short story and Conan Doyle's own 1910 stage ver- sion of it. Raymond Massey played an unusually youthful Holmes, at one stage

disguised as a workman. The film, like the play, opens up the story, building in
Oriental menace by the inclusion of an Indian manservant and Eastern music.
Holmes is given an absolutely up-to-date office in Baker Street, with secretaries
and all modern conveniences, typewriters, a tickertape machine and an inter-
com. Massey later wrote 'I could not avoid a sense of guilt at my participation
in this travesty of a classic'.[20] However for the scenes at Stoke Maron there were
expressionist sets, looming close-ups, an overwrought heroine and an over-the-
top melodramatic stage villain, in Lyn Harding who had created the role of Dr
Grimesby Rylott on the stage and revived it for the film. But the film, which
had no background music, fatally lacked narrative drive.

The 1931 British version of *The Hound of the Baskervilles*, directed and written
by V. Gareth Gundrey with dialogue contributed by Edgar Wallace, also had a
modern setting. It had originated in a poll conducted by *Film Weekly* to see what
story audiences would most like to see. *Hound* topped the poll. Gainsborough
produced it by casting Robert Rendel, a stolid character actor who looked nothing like the illustrations of Holmes. *Variety* said that none of the cast looked
anything like the popular visualizations of the characters. Long a lost film, when
it was found and restored and shown in 1999 to the Sherlock Holmes Society of
London, it was received with laughter and pronounced 'preposterous'.[21]

Reginald Owen, marginalized as Watson in Fox's 1932 *Sherlock Holmes*, got
his revenge in 1933 when he assumed the role of the great detective in *A Study
in Scarlet*. The minor Hollywood studio, Tiffany, acquired the rights to Doyle's
novel but then abandoned the plot, perhaps because its anti-Mormon theme
would have gone down badly with part of the American audience. An entire new
plot was devised by the intended director Robert Florey with dialogue provided
by Reginald Owen, who was a Holmes aficionado. However, having completed
the script, Florey left Tiffany for a better-paid job at Warner Brothers and Edwin
L. Marin inherited the project and directed it effectively from the blueprint
provided in Florey's script.

The plot centred on a succession of deaths of members of the Scarlet Ring, a
group of jewel thieves waiting to dispose of their loot. Each death was preceded
by the arrival of a note containing a verse from the music hall song 'Ten Little
Niggers' (tactfully rendered as 'Black Boys' in this version). This was six years
before Agatha Christie adopted the same idea for her novel and later play *Ten
Little Niggers*. Owen was insufficiently aquiline for Holmes but devised some appropriate Holmesian dialogue which he delivered with relish and enjoyed himself
when disguised as an old man. The film boasted some atmospheric Limehouse
sets and a mist-shrouded old manor house at Shoeburyness, a fine villain in Alan

Dinehart's scheming lawyer Thaddeus Merrydew, 'the king of blackmailers' and an elegantly enigmatic oriental woman played by Anna May Wong. Its one major error was to give Holmes's address as 221A Baker Street.

Arthur Wontner (1875–1960) was the most admired Holmes of the 1930s. He looked exactly like the Sidney Paget illustrations, down to the receding hairline, and in the five films in which he starred he was the cerebral Holmes *par excellence*, the ratiocination and deduction delivered with careful deliberation and enlivened by a dry and sardonic sense of humour. The respected American Sherlockian Vincent Starrett said of him: 'No better Sherlock Holmes is likely to be seen and heard in our time. His detective is the veritable fathomer of Baker Street in person'.[22] He regularly garnered favourable reviews. The British magazine *Picturegoer* called him 'the perfect Holmes'.[23] Wontner, who on stage had played Sax Rohmer's detective Paul Harley and Sexton Blake, was once told by Conan Doyle that he should play Holmes (*Film Weekly*, 19 December 1931). In four of the five films, Wontner's Watson was Ian Fleming who played the part as a debonair middle-aged man with an eye for the ladies and Minnie Rayner was a cheerful cockney Mrs Hudson who when Holmes retires to Sussex, goes with him to keep house.

Four of the Holmes films were made for producer Julius Hagen of Twickenham Studios. Despite their obviously limited budgets and tinny background music, they were made with care and dedication and turned out as satisfying entertainments acceptable to the general public and the Holmes fans alike. The first three films were directed by Leslie Hiscott and scripted by H. Fowler Mear and Cyril Twyford. *The Sleeping Cardinal* (1931) (US title: *Sherlock Holmes' Fatal Hour*), based on *The Final Problem* and *The Empty House*, pitted Holmes against Professor Moriarty (Norman McKinnell) who speaks from behind the painting of the title. His latest crime is a counterfeiting operation. Atmospherically lit, it is as a film static and slow-moving but is redeemed by Wontner with his razor-sharp mind, deadpan teasing of Watson and Lestrade and obvious delight in baffling them. *The Missing Rembrandt* (1932), based on *Charles Augustus Milverton*, has Holmes, who disguises as an old woman and a clergyman, exposing the Milverton figure, rechristened Baron von Guntermann (Francis L. Sullivan), a villain who combines blackmail and art theft. *The Triumph of Sherlock Holmes* (1935), based on *The Valley of Fear*, opens with Holmes retiring to keep bees in Sussex and Watson and his wife taking over 221B Baker Street. Moriarty (Lyn Harding) calls to bid him farewell in the famous confrontation scene from *The Final Problem*. But later Moriarty masterminds the plot to eliminate the Pinkerton agent who fell foul of the American Secret Society, the Scowrers. Holmes foils the plot and Moriarty plunges to his death from the top of Birlstone Tower. The central flashback sequence to the activities of the Scowrers in Pennsylvania is cramped, studio-bound and unconvincing.

Wontner's last film, more satisfying than *Triumph*, is *Silver Blaze* (1937) (US title: *Murder at the Baskervilles*) directed by Thomas Bentley from a script by H. Fowler Mear. It fleshed out Doyle's short story by having Moriarty (a gleeful Lyn Harding), operating from a disused Tube station, behind the plot to nobble the favourite for the Barchester Cup, and Holmes and Watson going to stay with Sir Henry Baskerville and his family.

The exception to the Twickenham Holmes films was *The Sign of Four* (1932), made at Ealing Studios for Associated Radio Pictures, scripted by W.P. Lipscomb and directed by Graham Cutts. It was produced by the American Rowland V. Lee, who as a director was a master of film melodrama. He conceived of Holmes as more of an action man than he had previously been portrayed. Lee said:

> Sherlock Holmes is to be a vivid hero, a tiger among men, a fighting detective, superhuman in every way … Was the mighty Sherlock Holmes a man who simply played the violin and drugged himself when seeking inspiration? Not a bit of it. He was a MAN! … Now I am going to make him the man he was … not a dreamy detective who spent his life back-chatting with Watson.[24]

There is plenty of the traditional Holmes in the film: the violin playing, the disguise (as an elderly sea captain), the deductions and analysis. But the film ends with a spectacular speedboat chase down the Thames and a lengthy fist-fight between Holmes and Watson and the villains, one-legged Jonathan Small and tattooed Meade Bailey. Ian Hunter was cast as a youthful Watson, capable both of fisticuffs and romancing the heroine Mary Morstan. Arthur Wontner made a final return to the character of Holmes in 1943 for a BBC radio production of *The Boscombe Valley Mystery*. His Watson was Carleton Hobbs, who was to become *the* British radio Holmes in the 1950s and 1960s.

It was not until 1939 and 20th Century Fox's *The Hound of the Baskervilles* and its splendid sequel *The Adventures of Sherlock Holmes* that the film versions were actually set in the nineteenth century and audiences now got a very different Holmes from Arthur Wontner's reflective figure. Basil Rathbone is best described as dynamic Holmes. He was to become for many people the definitive Holmes, physically perfect and vocally commanding. Not everyone, however, was won over at the time. Graham Greene complained 'the cinema has never yet done justice to Sherlock Holmes' after viewing *Hound*.[25] Greene liked the period atmosphere but thought the producers obsessed with action at the expense of deduction. He also thought Rathbone's reading of the role was wrong with its 'good humour

and general air of brisk good health'. He was similarly critical of *Adventures*, once
again praising the atmosphere, admiring George Zucco's Moriarty ('viciously correct') but saying that Rathbone was 'physically made for the part of Holmes: one
feels that he was really drawn by Paget, but mentally he forgets that he belongs
to the end of a century … one can't imagine this Holmes indolent, mystical or
untidy'.[26] Evidently Greene was looking for the languid fin-de-siècle aesthetic
Holmes but what he got was Holmes as action man, the man he memorably
described as having a 'dark knife-blade face and snapping mouth',[27] the result
undoubtedly of the films' American origin. American cinema always preferred
action over reason. Boldly *Hound* did make a nod in the direction of Holmes's
drug habit with Rathbone's exit line: 'Watson … the needle' but otherwise he is
dynamic, incisive and authoritative. Rathbone also enjoys himself impersonating
an elderly pedlar. Nigel Bruce as Watson had not succumbed to the buffoonery
that alienated many Sherlockian purists in later films. The passage of time has
considerably improved the standing of the film. Many would now agree with
Professor Wallace Robson who in the World's Classics edition of *Hound* called
the 1939 *Hound* the best Holmes film yet made, a view shared by Sherlockian
Michael Pointer. Directed by Sidney Lanfield and scripted by Ernest Pascal, it
is a prime example of Hollywood Gothic, constructed entirely in the studio
and providing a hugely atmospheric mist-wreathed Dartmoor for the chases,
pursuits and dramatic encounters that provide the substance of the action. The
scriptwriter added a seance to enhance the general spookiness of the story. But
another addition to Doyle's original story, a speech by Dr Mortimer at the end
of the film, cast Holmes as a national hero:

> Mr Holmes, we've admired you in the past as does every Englishman. Your record
> as our greatest detective is known throughout the world. But this – seeing you work
> – knowing that there is in England such a man as you gives us all a sense of safety
> and security. God bless you, Mr Holmes.

It is hard to believe that this is not the message from Hollywood's most Anglophile
studio on the eve of the outbreak of war.

The success of *Hound* was such as to prompt Fox to rush a sequel into production. *The Adventures of Sherlock Holmes*, directed by Sidney Lanfield from
a script by Edwin Blum and William Drake, was ostensibly based on William
Gillette's play. But apart from the inclusion of two of the characters prominent
in the play (Bassick, Billy the Page), the film owed nothing to the play. Moriarty,
acquitted in the high court of murder, plans the crime of the century – the theft
of the Crown Jewels from the Tower of London. Staging a murder and an attempted murder (to the strains of an ancient Inca funeral dirge), Moriarty seeks

to distract Holmes while he puts his plan into operation. The foggy Victorian London setting, Rathbone's priceless impersonation of a music hall entertainer singing 'I do like to be beside the seaside', murder by South American bolas and the thrilling climax with Holmes commandeering a hansom cab, racing through the streets and having a shootout and fight with Moriarty who plunges to his death from the top of the Tower all contrive to make this a memorable piece of Sherlockian apocrypha.

20th Century Fox dropped Sherlock Holmes after *The Adventures of Sherlock Holmes* (1939), a decision that has puzzled Holmes fans for many years. The reason for this decision has now been uncovered by Amanda J. Field. 20th Century Fox had inherited the rights to *The Hound of the Baskervilles* and to William Gillette's play *Sherlock Holmes* from the Fox Film Corporation which had acquired them in 1932. But after it had filmed *The Hound* and *The Adventures*, allegedly based on Gillette's play, it entered into negotiations with the Doyle estate for further rights. However, the demands in particular of Denis Conan Doyle led 20th Century Fox to abandon any idea of further Holmes films. Negotiations were begun with MGM and Warner Brothers but similarly came to nothing. It was not until 1942 that a deal was done by the Doyle estate with Universal Pictures. Universal signed a seven-year deal which gave them the right to use any of the short stories and to devise their own fresh stories.[28] Basil Rathbone and Nigel Bruce, who had continued playing the roles on radio in the meantime, were signed to recreate the roles. But there was a significant difference. The Fox films and the radio series were set in the nineteenth century, and the Universal series were set in the present. The films were made on the Universal backlot as B pictures on a seventeen-day shooting schedule and deployed the British acting colony as a permanent repertory company. A foreword to the first film in the Universal series, *Sherlock Holmes and the Voice of Terror* declared that the character of Holmes was 'ageless, invincible and unchanging. In solving significant problems of the present he remains – as ever – the supreme master of deductive reasoning'. The problems in the first three films in the series related to the activities of the Nazis in the Second World War.

Sherlock Holmes and the Voice of Terror, directed by John Rawlins from a script by John Bright and Lynn Riggs, was inspired by though not based on Arthur Conan Doyle's *His Last Bow* in which Holmes unmasked a German masterspy Von Bork in the First World War. The theme of the film was the use of radio by the Nazis and in particular the broadcasts by 'Lord Haw-Haw' aimed at demoralizing the British public. The film opens with a radio mast and a montage of broadcasts by 'the Voice of Terror': 'People of Britain, greetings from the Third Reich. This is the voice you have learned to fear – the Voice of Terror'. He announces a series of disasters; the destruction of factories, shipping and troop trains and assassinations and gives instructions to Nazi agents. His broadcasts punctuate the film. Holmes studies the oscillations of radio waves in a broadcast of Beethoven's Fifth Symphony (with its iconic use of the opening bars to represent V for Victory) and deduces that the broadcasts are gramophone records made in advance and almost certainly made in the United Kingdom. He appeals to the patriotism of the London underworld to help him track down the Nazi agents: 'Our country – England – is at stake. The cut-throats of the world menace us all. You can help stop this savagery.' He eventually unmasks a member of the Intelligence Inner Council, Sir Evan Barham, as 'the Voice of Terror' and foils a planned German invasion. Barham turns out to be the German masterspy Heinrich Von Bork, a Barham lookalike who took his place during the First World War and thus infiltrated the highest echelons of British society. The film ends with Rathbone reciting the memorable last lines of *His Last Bow*: 'There's an east wind coming … such a wind as never blew on England yet. It will be cold and bitter, Watson, and a good many of us may wither before its blast. But it's God's own wind, nonetheless, and a greener, better, stronger land will be in the sunshine when the storm has cleared'. Denis Conan Doyle, Sir Arthur's son, pronounced 'It is incomparably the best Sherlock Holmes film ever made'.[29]

The remaining eleven films in the series were directed by a minor master of the Gothic, Roy William Neill (*Black Moon, The Black Room, Dr. Syn, Frankenstein Meets the Wolfman*). *Sherlock Holmes and the Secret Weapon* (1943), written by Edward T. Lowe, W. Scott Darling and Edmund L. Hartmann and allegedly based on Conan Doyle's *The Dancing Men*, had Holmes spiriting out of Switzerland under the nose of the Nazis a Swiss scientist and his invention, a revolutionary bombsite. However, the scientist is kidnapped in London by Professor Moriarty (Lionel Atwill) who plans to sell him and his invention to the Nazis. The whereabouts of the bombsite is encoded in 'the dancing men' code. Holmes breaks the code and rescues the scientist, reciting at the end several lines from John of Gaunt's 'This England' speech from *Richard II*. The film encapsulates the three aspects of Holmes: his rational deductions, his acting (he disguises as an elderly bookseller, a sailor and a Swiss professor) and his drug habit (alluded to by Moriarty).

Sherlock Holmes in Washington (1943) made no pretence of being based on a Doyle story but was in fact an original story by Bertram Millhauser developed for the screen by Millhauser and Lynn Riggs. It entailed Holmes and Watson flying to the United States to locate a vital microfilmed document which had vanished following the murder of a British secret agent. Holmes locates it, foiling a Nazi spy ring headed by Heinrich Hinkle (George Zucco). Holmes employs his scientific analysis methods and also his acting skills impersonating an eccentric antiques collector and imitating the voice of Hinkle. It ends with Rathbone quoting a speech by Winston Churchill: 'It is not given to us to peer into the mysteries of the future. But in the days to come, the British and American people for their own safety and the good of all will walk together in majesty and justice and peace.' While the film duly emphasized cooperation between the British and Americans in combating enemy espionage, it lacked much of the atmosphere of the earlier productions. A Universal press release later admitted that the stories in which a modern Holmes sought 'to solve problems of the current war … did not meet with the expected response from devotees of the Conan Doyle mysteries. Film fans seem to want their Holmes and Watson in typical Doyle plots and in the English settings where they belong.'[30]

Roy William Neill was in his element in these settings. Rathbone attributed the look and feel of the films directly to him: 'There was a nominal producer and some writers also, but Roy Neill was the master and final hand in all these departments'. [31] There was atmosphere aplenty in the next four entries in the series which constitute the peak of the series' achievement. *Sherlock Holmes Faces Death* (1943) was scripted by Bertram Millhauser and inspired by Doyle's story *The Musgrave Ritual*. Set in the ancestral home of the Musgraves, Hurlstone Towers, now situated in Northumberland and not in Doyle's West Sussex, and serving as a convalescent home for injured officers, this unfolded its tale of a series of murders against a suitably Gothic background of haunted manor, howling wind, secret passages, shadows, a clock striking thirteen and a suit of armour struck by lightning. The cause of the murders is a search for the secret hidden in the Musgrave Ritual, which turns out to be a valuable Tudor land grant and not the Stewart crown jewels of Doyle's original. Sally Musgrave burns the parchment rather than evict people from their land, prompting a peroration from Holmes which reflects the democratic spirit of the war effort: 'The old days of greed and grab are on their way out. We're beginning to think of what we owe the other fellow, not just what we're compelled to give him. The time is coming, Watson, when we cannot fill our bellies in comfort while the other fellow goes hungry, or sleep in warm beds while others shiver in the cold. And we shan't be able to kneel and thank God for blessings before our shining altars while men anywhere are kneeling in either physical or spiritual subjection.'

The horror element was maintained in *The Spider Woman*, also scripted by Bertram Millhauser and said to be based 'on a story by Sir Arthur Conan Doyle'.

Actually it took elements from several stories and wove them into a narrative in which Holmes did battle with a cunning and ruthless female adversary, Adrea Spedding (Gale Sondergaard), the eponymous spider woman. A rash of pyjama suicides occur in which a succession of men kill themselves in the middle of the night. Holmes fakes his own death to be free to investigate and returns to Baker Street in disguise (as a postman), in echoes of *The Empty House*. He discovers that deadly spiders are being introduced into the victims' rooms (like the snake in *The Speckled Band*), their bite causing agonizing pain and leading to suicide. The deliverer of the spiders is an African pygmy (like the pygmy in *The Sign of Four*). Holmes investigates Miss Spedding disguised as a Sikh army officer but when she recognizes him, she tries to poison him and Watson with a deadly powder (the devil's foot poison of the eponymous Doyle story). However, Holmes eventually exposes her scheme (an insurance policy swindle) and has her arrested.

The Scarlet Claw (1944), scripted by Edmund L. Hartmann and Roy William Neill from an original story by Paul Gangelin and Brenda Weisberg, was set in Canada for no obvious reason other than the propagandist opportunity to pay tribute to the North American ally of the United States. The film ends with Rathbone quoting Churchill in praise of the Dominion's 'relations of friendly intimacy with the United States on the one hand and their unswerving fidelity to the British Commonwealth and the motherland on the other. Canada, the link which joins together these great branches of the human family'. Otherwise with its manor house and titled squire, its lonely village and haunted misty marshes it could easily be set in rural England. A legendary monster 'La Mort Rouge' is suspected of a series of murders in which victims have their throats torn out. Holmes, who is in Canada to attend a meeting of the Royal Canadian Occult Society, is properly sceptical and eventually unmasks the 'monster' as a deranged actor exacting vengeance on a series of people he believes to have wronged him. He haunts the marshes coated in phosphorescent paint when he is not assuming one of a series of disguises. The most successful is as the village postman, an idea borrowed from G.K. Chesterton's Father Brown story *The Invisible Man* in which the point is made that no one ever notices the postman. The story is actually referred to in the film by Dr Watson.

The Pearl of Death (1944), scripted by Bertram Millhauser and based on Doyle's *The Six Napoleons*, has Holmes on the track of the Borgia Pearl stolen by master criminal Giles Conover. Conover is assisted by the monstrous 'Hoxton Creeper', a brute who breaks people's spines and is played by Rondo Hatton, a real-life sufferer from the disfiguring disease of acromegaly. Neill builds up his appearances gradually as he is seen in shadow and in outline until a climactic close-up of his hideously ugly face. Holmes shoots him after he has turned on and killed Conover. Holmes disguises as both an elderly clergyman and an elderly doctor and also impersonates Conover on the telephone.

Following the high water mark of the four satisfying Gothic mysteries, the series deteriorated with three pedestrian films in which Holmes performed little in the way of brilliant deduction and assumed no disguises. Each of the films had its compensations but they were on the whole deeply unsatisfying. *The House of Fear*, scripted by Roy Chanslor, took the idea of the five orange pips as a warning of death from Doyle's story *The Five Orange Pips* and inserted it in a narrative whose basic idea was borrowed from Agatha Christie's *Ten Little Indians*. A series of apparently gruesome murders in a lonely Scottish house turns out to be an elaborate insurance swindle as none of the victims is dead. The compensation was 'the old dark house' with which Neill was able to evoke a consistently creepy Gothic atmosphere. *The Woman in Green* (1945) centred on a blackmail plot in which the victims were hypnotized into believing themselves guilty of a series of horrible murders of young women. The compensation here was the performance of Henry Daniell as Moriarty, the brains behind the plot. Rathbone thought Daniell's Moriarty 'masterly', writing: 'There were other Moriartys, but none so delectably dangerous as that of Henry Daniell'. [32] It also included the attempted murder of Holmes from *The Empty House*. But by now all pretence of basing the scripts on Doyle stories had been abandoned.

Pursuit to Algiers (1945), scripted by Leonard Lee, had Holmes escorting to Algiers the heir to the throne of a fictional Balkan country (Rovenia) whose monarch had been assassinated by anti-democratic forces. The steamship setting, Dr Watson reconstructing the story of 'The Giant Rat of Sumatra' and a lively comic cameo by Rosalind Ivan as a tiresome busybody lady passenger were all that could be salvaged from this tired entry.

Terror by Night (1946), scripted by Frank Gruber, represented something of a return to form. It is a neat, tightly plotted, fast-moving train thriller in the classic mould. The fabulous 'Star of Rhodesia' diamond is stolen on the London to Edinburgh express and Holmes, hired to protect it, identifies the culprit from among a colourful range of suspects and a satisfying succession of plot twists – Colonel Sebastian Moran, the second most dangerous man in London (Alan Mowbray).

The series came to an end with *Dressed to Kill* (UK title: *Sherlock Holmes and the Secret Code*). Scripted by Frank Gruber and Leonard Lee, it took its basic idea once again from *The Six Napoleons*. This time it was three musical boxes created by a Dartmoor convict and containing in a musical code the hiding place of the stolen Bank of England banknote plates. Holmes cracks the code, solves the murder of one of the music-box owners and foils the female master criminal, the exquisitely dressed Mrs Hilda Courtney (Patricia Morison).

In 1946 Rathbone's film and radio contracts expired and although a further seven years' contracts were negotiated, he refused to sign them. He had tired of the role and feared irrevocable typecasting. As he wrote in his autobiography:

> Had I made but one Holmes picture, my first, *The Hound of the Baskervilles*, I would probably not be as well known as I am today. But within myself, as an artist, I should have been well content. Of all the 'adventures', *The Hound* is my favourite story, and it was in this picture that I had the stimulating experience of creating, within my own limited framework, a character that has intrigued me as much as any I have ever played. But the continuous repetition of story after story after story left me virtually repeating myself each time in a character I had already conceived and developed. The stories varied but I was always the same character merely repeating myself in different situations. My first picture was, as it were, a negative from which I merely continued to produce endless positives of the same photograph.[33]

Rathbone sold his Hollywood home and returned to New York and the stage, achieving success in *The Heiress*, the dramatization of Henry James' *Washington Square*. His abandonment of the character caused 'severe and recurring shocks' to his longstanding friendship with Nigel Bruce who wanted to continue playing Dr Watson.[34] But Rathbone was adamant about abandoning the character. Roy William Neill died in 1946 and Universal terminated its film series. The radio series continued for another season with Tom Conway taking over the role of Holmes to Nigel Bruce's Dr Watson. After that it switched to New York and a new Holmes (John Stanley) and Watson (Alfred Shirley).

Rathbone did not abandon radio and crime entirely, starring in two short-lived mystery series, *Scotland Yard's Inspector Burke* (1947) and *Tales of Fatima* (1949), both produced in New York. In 1953 he attempted a return to the character of Holmes to give his career a boost. But a half-hour television production *The Adventure of the Black Baronet*, a Holmes pastiche by Adrian Conan Doyle and John Dickson Carr, produced as a possible series pilot and a lavish stage play *Sherlock Holmes*, written by Rathbone's wife Ouida, both failed – the play closed after three days.

Rathbone became for many people the definitive interpreter of the role of Holmes. For Sherlockians, however, his films had a major drawback – Nigel Bruce. As David Stuart Davies points out, in their films together Bruce made Watson an equal partner with Rathbone for the first time.[35] In previous films he had been little better than a cipher, fairly characterless and often way down the cast list. An accomplished comic performer, Bruce had perfected the persona of an upper-class buffoon and played it in film after film. But it was a characterisation at odds with Doyle's depiction of Dr Watson as intelligent and reliable, a good doctor and a successful writer.

The keynote of Bruce's performance as Dr Watson both in film and on radio was a comic obtuseness, which when mixed with a degree of pomposity and self-importance and an eye for the ladies, provided a very obvious comic counterpoint to Rathbone's razorsharp delivery and intelligent observations. In addition, Bruce had a unique line in burbling and chuntering which no one else could manage and which he would carry on under the lines of other characters. But whatever the true aficionados thought of his Watson, the listening and viewing public in the United States genuinely loved Bruce. His importance can be gauged from the fact that when Rathbone left the radio series and was replaced as Holmes by Tom Conway, Bruce received top-billing ahead of the new Holmes.

Rathbone and Bruce were good friends in real life and worked well together, and Rathbone loved Bruce's interpretation, writing in his autobiography:

> There is no question in my mind that Nigel Bruce was the ideal Dr Watson, not only of his time but possibly of and for all time. There was an endearing quality to his performance that to a very large extent, I believe, humanized the relationship between Dr Watson and Mr Holmes. It has always seemed to me to be more than possible that our 'adventures' might have met with a less kindly public acceptance had they been recorded by a less lovable companion to Holmes than was Nigel's Dr Watson, and a less engaging friend to me than was 'Willy' Bruce.[36]

There is no doubt that the personal warmth between them was an asset to the series.

After Rathbone gave up the role of Holmes in 1946, there was a long silence in the cinema. It was broken only in 1958 by Hammer Films' *The Hound of the Baskervilles*, directed by Terence Fisher from a Peter Bryan script. With Holmes now firmly and permanently located in the nineteenth century, this film solved the Watson problem. André Morell was a splendid Watson, sensible, decent, goodhearted, an ordinary (in the best sense of the word), down-to-earth English gentleman. He is the perfect foil to the highly-strung Holmes. Peter Cushing's Holmes with his precise diction and ascetic features is another dynamic, incisive Holmes like Rathbone's and in Hammer's cosmology a bloodbrother to Cushing's Van Helsing. Hammer played up the supernatural and horror film elements, stressing the idea of Holmes combating evil, in what was a free but nonetheless satisfying adaptation. Hammer had envisaged a Holmes film series but the box-office returns were not good enough to justify it and the silence fell again until the 1970s.

Holmes's next cinematic outings saw a third version of the character emerge. If Wontner had been cerebral Holmes and Rathbone and Cushing dynamic Holmes, the 1970s Holmes is best described as neurotic Holmes, a Holmes with a drug habit and psychological problems. This is a classic post-1960s urban man, no longer the self-contained, rational man, the 'pure thinking machine' but the emotional prey to anxieties and inner problems. In this vein came Robert Stephens (*The Private Life of Sherlock Holmes* (1970)), Nicol Williamson (*The Seven Per Cent Solution* (1977)) and Christopher Plummer (*Murder By Decree* (1978)). The films are also characteristic of post-1960s cinema in having Holmes uncover establishment conspiracies and cover-ups, a strange predicament for a man who in his heyday was a staunch supporter of Crown, empire and government.

Holmes was to become an even more familiar figure on television than films where the character has inspired a veritable speckled band or silver blaze of different Holmeses, some of them highly unlikely. By no stretch of the imagination could Roger Moore (*Sherlock Holmes in New York*), Charlton Heston (*The Crucifer of Blood*), Stewart Granger (*The Hound of the Baskervilles*), Tom Baker (*The Hound of the Baskervilles*) or Edward Woodward (*Hands of a Murderer*) be regarded as a convincing Holmes. There were however several notable Holmeses. Douglas Wilmer in a 1965 BBC series was robust, self-possessed, urbane and sardonic and like Ian Richardson's Holmes, cool, controlled and good-humoured in a brace of flawed 1983 films for American television, played to the rational side of the great detective. Cushing revived his incisive and dynamic characterization for a 1968 BBC series. But a new definitive Holmes emerged in Jeremy Brett who played Holmes in a series of films between 1984 and 1994 which aimed at fidelity in every department. Brett created a Holmes as flamboyant actor-manager, the Byronic romanticism fully emphasized with its arrogance, drug-taking, neurotic edge and mercurial temperament. The quick laughs, facial twitches and fluttering hand movements all conveyed perfectly a creature of suppressed nervous energy. Brett's Watsons, David Burke and Edward Hardwicke, characterising the doctor as sensible and supportive, were well-nigh perfect. It is the complexity of the character which has allowed it to be reinterpreted for every generation, a situation likely to continue indefinitely.

Holmes's long film career is comparatively familiar to devotees, thanks to cinematic revivals and television showings, but until recently his equally extensive radio career was largely unknown, particularly his American radio career. The radio programmes were never revived and most were believed lost. But that situation has now altered with the rediscovery and release of a wealth of American radio material, which allows us to fill in a missing dimension of the Holmes saga.

For all the undeniable attractions of the best Holmes film and television adaptations, there is a case for saying that radio was the medium which served Holmes best after the printed page. It is a truism that listening to the radio is a qualitatively different experience from watching television. Television provides pictures ready-made and tends to give the visuals priority over the spoken word. Radio is, as Dr Louis Judd put it in his seminal work, *The Anatomy of Atavism*, 'the kingdom of the imagination'. In the kingdom of the imagination, the words reign supreme and each individual creates his or her own mental pictures to match the words – and there was no better wordspinner than Sir Arthur Conan Doyle. It is not just his stream of Holmesian one-liners which have entered the popular consciousness but his unforgettably evocative descriptions of place, atmosphere and weather that are part of the spell he exerts. It requires on radio only for the narrator to begin: 'In the third week of November, in the year 1895, a dense yellow fog settled down upon London. From the Monday to the Thursday I doubt whether it was ever possible from our windows in Baker Street to see the loom of the opposite houses … ' for the imagination to be immediately activated. Thereafter Sir Arthur's prose had us in its grip, not letting go until the case is solved and Holmes and Watson are able to file the details in their respective records – Holmes's huge cross indexed book of reference and Watson's battered despatch box with the notes on all the cases on which he had assisted. Radio was a particularly effective medium for evoking the Victorian world of Holmes and Watson – the clatter of horses' hooves on cobbled streets, the rattle and hiss of steam trains, the melancholy sirens of the ships on the Thames, the howl of the wind on lonely moors and the sinister creaks and groans of ancient manor houses, steeped in history and crime. With an adroit mixture of sound effects to underscore Doyle's vivid prose and memorable dialogue, the listener is well and truly launched on a voyage of the imagination.

What is remarkable about the radio career of Holmes and Watson is that it flourished in the United States long before it did in the United Kingdom. The radio adventures of Sherlock Holmes were an integral part of US radio culture for virtually the whole of its existence. The mention of Holmes's name conjures up a visual image. As Orson Welles put it introducing his radio adaptation of William Gillette's play *Sherlock Holmes*: 'There are only a few of them – these permanent profiles – everlasting silhouettes on the edge of the world … We'd know them anywhere and call them easily by name'. He lists them as Punch, Charlie Chaplin, Charlie McCarthy, Don Quixote and Sir John Falstaff. He adds to this list the name of a gentleman 'who has never lived and will never die … the gentleman with the hawk's face, the underslung pipe, and the fore and aft cap' – Sherlock Holmes. So the image of Holmes is fixed but what of Holmes's 'voice'. According to Doyle, it was quick, high, 'somewhat strident'. This was evidently the vocal style aimed at by the first great interpreter of Holmes, William Gillette, but subsequent Holmes interpreters did not always follow his lead.

The radio adventures of Holmes and Watson in the United States were the result of the dedication and persistence of a single person – Edith Meiser. In Holmesian radio she was *the* woman. Edith Meiser (1898–1993) was a graduate of Vassar, a Broadway actress and playwright, who in 1927 married the producer-director Tom McKnight. She became convinced that a series of Sherlock Holmes dramatizations would work on the newly-created radio networks in the United States. She began pressing her suggestion in 1927 but it was not until 1930 that she persuaded the NBC network to agree. So on 30 October 1930, the first series of *The Adventures of Sherlock Holmes* was launched on NBC and ran for thirty-five weeks. From then on every year except for 1937–38 until 1950 there was an annual Sherlock Holmes series on American radio, many of them written by Edith Meiser, who eventually contributed 220 complete scripts devoted to the adventures of Sherlock Holmes. From 1930 to 1944 she was the sole scriptwriter for the series. She returned to script the 1947–48 season. Her husband Tom McKnight directed many of the radio productions. *Sherlock Holmes* was the first major network dramatic radio series to be broadcast. It opened the way for others and in particular cemented Holmes and Watson firmly into the American consciousness.

Although Holmes and Watson were played in the initial radio series by Richard Gordon and Leigh Lovell, Edith Meiser pulled off a publicity masterstroke to launch the series. She persuaded her old friend William Gillette to play Holmes in the opening programme *The Speckled Band*, broadcast on Monday 20 October 1930. Edith Meiser herself played Julia Stoner. Then in 1935 at the age of eighty William Gillette recreated his celebrated stage performance for a broadcast of his play *Sherlock Holmes* as part of the *Lux Radio Theatre*. Adapted by the inevitable Edith Meiser and featuring six members of the recent 1929 Broadway revival of the play, it went out on 18 November 1935.

Sadly neither of these broadcasts has survived. Indeed the only surviving record of Gillette's voice was made in 1936. While Gillette was on tour with a production of Austin Strong's comedy *Three Wise Fools*, Professor Frederick Clifton Packard of the Speech Department of Harvard University prevailed on Gillette to make a recording of scenes from *Sherlock Holmes*. A nine-minute recording on a glass disc was made with Packard as Watson and his wife Alice as Alice Faulkner. The nine minutes was rediscovered in 1987 and digitally remastered. It contains passages from Act two Scene two and the end of act four of the play. Gillette's voice is inevitably that of an old man but there is surprisingly little of an American accent, only the telltale short 'a' on the words romance, chance and can't. Otherwise it is smooth and suave though not particularly high or light.

However, a better idea of what Gillette sounded like in his heyday can be found in 1938 when the year after Gillette's death Orson Welles chose to include Gillette's play in his *Mercury Theatre on the Air* radio series broadcast on the CBS network on 25 September 1938. It was much later issued on record and audio cassette. Adapted by Welles himself and featuring themes from Elgar and Eric Coates as incidental music, it is a neat one-hour condensation of the play, with narration provided by Dr Watson as in the stories. Welles, physically quite wrong for the role, was vocally perfect in the sense that he evidently decided to imitate Gillette's voice and his delivery. Welles was an expert mimic (his performance in *Break of Hearts* on the *Lux Radio Theatre* is a precise imitation of the original star of the film, Charles Boyer). In his introduction Welles paid tribute to Gillette:

> As everybody knows that celebrated American inventor of underacting lent his considerable gifts as a playwright to the indestructible legend of the Conan Doyle detective and produced the play that is as much a part of the Holmes literature as any of Sir Arthur's own romances and, as nobody will ever forget, he gave his face to him. For William Gillette was the actual and aquiline embodiment of Holmes himself. It is too little to say that William Gillette resembled Holmes. Sherlock Holmes looks exactly like William Gillette. Sounds like him too.

Comparing the Gillette recording with Welles' performance, it is clear that he had modelled his delivery and intonation precisely on that of Gillette and the voice is quick, light, high and often sardonically drawling, contrasting nicely with Eustace Wyatt's deep growl as Moriarty. Ray Collins provided a crisp and incisive but undeniably, American Watson.

In the United States from 1930 to 1936 except for the 1934–35 season Holmes was played by the American actor Richard Gordon (1882–1967). In 1932 Gordon won the Bosch Radio Star Popularity Poll in the category of dramatic actor. In 1934–35 following a contract dispute with Gordon, Louis Hector, who had previously played Moriarty, took over as Holmes. Gordon returned in 1936. British actor Leigh Lovell played Watson from 1930 to 1935. Following his death, another British actor Harry West took over as Watson. Intriguingly throughout these years the announcer, the person to whom Watson in his study narrates the stories, was Joseph Bell, who shared the name of the Edinburgh professor who was Doyle's original inspiration for the character of Holmes. The programmes were broadcast live and have not therefore survived. They went out on the NBC network until 1936 when the programme moved to the newly organized Mutual Broadcasting Network. Mutual required the programmes to be recorded for future re-broadcast and this enables us to judge Gordon's performance. He evidently went directly for the 'quick, high, somewhat strident' tone described by Doyle and some of the intonations clearly echo William Gillette. But he often sounds merely elderly and querulous. Harry West's Watson comes over as bluff and sturdy.

Edith Meiser adapted every short story and novel for the series except for *The Final Problem* which she was superstitious about broadcasting in case it presaged the end of the series and *The Valley of Fear* which, dealing with labour relations in the Pennsylvania coalfields was thought potentially too political. But given that there were thirty-five to forty Holmes programmes every year, she eventually ran out of the Doyle originals. So she took two of Doyle's non-Holmes stories (*The Jewish Breastplate* and *The Lost Special*) and inserted Holmes into them. She also wrote up several cases alluded to by Doyle but never developed (*The Giant Rat of Sumatra*, *The Singular Affair of the Aluminium Crutch* and *The Case of Vamberry the Wine Merchant*). She then began to contribute her own originals, demonstrating the extent to which she had mastered Doyle's style and structure. They include such intriguing titles as *The Hindoo in the Wicker Basket* and *Her Majesty's Wine Cellar*. She was particular fond of *The Haunted Bagpipes*, which was revived in almost every season of Holmes adventures. It involved Holmes and Watson foiling a plan by Moriarty to unleash bubonic plague on Edinburgh, in revenge for his being driven out of the city when as the young assistant to Dr Knox he was implicated in the Burke and Hare bodysnatching scandal.

After Holmes was off the air in 1937 and 1938, there was a spectacular return to radio in 1939. The success of Basil Rathbone and Nigel Bruce in the film of *The Hound of the Baskervilles* inspired the network to hire them for a new Holmes radio series. It was the continuing success of the radio series that almost certainly inspired Universal Pictures to revive the Holmes film series in 1942. There was direct overlap between the film and radio series as in addition to Rathbone and Bruce, several of the regular supporting actors in the films turned up regularly on the radio, constituting an unofficial repertory company. Mary Gordon, the actress who played Mrs Hudson in the films, could be heard from time to time in the radio programmes. Frederic Worlock, who appeared in five different roles in the Universal films, played Inspector Lestrade on the radio. Rex Evans, who played an assassin in *Pursuit to Algiers*, was heard as Mycroft Holmes on the radio. Carl Harbord, who played Inspector Stanley Hopkins on film, turned up week after week in different roles on the radio. None of the supporting actors on the radio programmes were credited as it was against network policy. Only in the late 1940s did this change.

The Rathbone–Bruce radio series with its Victorian and Edwardian settings and faithful evocations of the atmosphere of the original stories could be considered superior to the Universal film series, with their low budgets and modern settings. The engagement of Rathbone and Bruce was part of a new trend in US radio. Instead of the largely unknown actors used in radio in the 1930s, during the 1940s the networks began to use film stars in series deriving from their screen images. In the United Kingdom these programmes were not heard but in the United States both in the 1940s and 1950s, most of the great stars had their own dramatic series on radio. Rathbone and Bruce pioneered the trend.

Edith Meiser was recalled to script the new *Sherlock Holmes* series, which went out on the NBC network, sponsored by Grove's Bromo Quinine Tablets. She began by returning to the canon and refurbishing her previous dramatizations of all the canonical stories and providing a six-part radio version of *The Hound of the Baskervilles* but not the other three novels. From 2 October 1939 to 17 July 1944 Edith Meiser scripted the series, dropping out when her marriage to Tom McKnight broke up. She handed over scripting duties to Denis Green and Leslie Charteris (writing under the pseudonym Bruce Taylor) who wrote scripts from 24 July 1944 to 19 March 1945. When Charteris decided to give up the job, Green recruited mystery writer Anthony Boucher to collaborate on the scripts and from 26 May 1945 they wrote the series together until it left Hollywood for New York in 1947.

The NBC programmes were performed live and recorded on fragile sixteen-inch disks with fifteen minutes per side. But over the years most of them were broken or lost. A handful survive. One of them is *The Bruce-Partington Plans* (broadcast on 6 November 1939 and years later issued on a gramophone record). Atmospheric and fast-moving, and complete with the dialogue fluffs inevitable in live broadcasts, it showed Rathbone in fine incisive form and Bruce playing Watson far more straight and less comedically than later in the series. In 1943 there was a change of network (from NBC to the Mutual Broadcasting Company) and sponsor (the Petri Wine Company of California), but the cast, writing and production style remained unaltered.

During the years in which they were combining their film and radio careers as Holmes and Watson, Rathbone and Bruce were permitted to leave the Universal Studios at noon each Monday in order to appear in the radio programmes which were broadcast on the Mutual Broadcasting System on Monday evenings. An early evening programme was performed for the East coast with an identical programme three hours later for the West coast. Glenhall Taylor recalled in his autobiography:

> For nearly two years, it was my privilege to direct the radio series 'Adventures of Sherlock Holmes', starring Basil Rathbone and Nigel Bruce. It may come as a surprise to most readers that this turned out to be a madcap experience, for despite the elegant dignity of that splendid actor Basil Rathbone and the bumbling ingenu-ousness exuded by that other excellent performer, Nigel Bruce the atmosphere was not only pleasant but sporadically hilarious. Both men were delightfully humorous and, as their English friends might call it 'frightfully unpredictable' … It was the custom of Rathbone and Bruce to stop at a supermarket on their way from Universal to Mutual studios and purchase snacks which could be consumed during the first read-through of the radio script … Almost invariably they bought cartons of milk and packages of … 'sugar buns'. As a result of their informal repasts, our studio became a sloppy shambles by the time rehearsals were concluded. Left-over milk was often poured into ashtrays to extinguish cigarette stubs … as I sat behind the huge window of the control room engrossed in following the script of making pencilled corrections, the two 'dignified' Britishers would suddenly bombard the glass with their sugar buns. Though caught unaware and, as the sticky missiles came hurtling toward me, I would duck out of sheer reflex as they splattered against the glass. This delighted them no end and they never seemed to tire of it. As the broadcasts were performed before a studio audience, a clean-up crew had to go to work every Monday night before the audience could be admitted.[37]

Long believed lost, recordings of many of the Green-Boucher scripted *Sherlock Holmes* radio shows were rediscovered in 1987 and, packaged by 221A Baker St Associates, were released on audiocassette by Simon and Schuster. They include the whole of the 1945–46 Rathbone–Bruce series, thirty-eight programmes di-rected by British actress Edna Best, which constitute Rathbone's last appearances in the radio role. They reveal that by any criteria you care to employ Green and Boucher must be regarded as major providers of Holmesian apocrypha. They are fine examples of dramatic radio at its best.

Green and Boucher scripts fell into three categories. There was a sprinkling of canonical tales, such as in the 1945–46 season *The Speckled Band, A Scandal in Bohemia, Thor Bridge* and *The Man with the Twisted Lip*. There were versions of the unwritten cases recorded by Dr Watson, such as *Colonel Warburton's Madness, The Notorious Canary Trainer* and *The Tankerville Club Scandal*. Then there were Green and Boucher originals, allegedly based on incidents in the original stories, but sometimes taking no more than a particular locale, such as the opium den in Upper Swandam Lane which features in *The Man with the Twisted Lip* and inspired the Green and Boucher originals *The Eyes of Mr Leyton* and *Queue for Murder*.

Denis Green (1905–54) was British, originally a stage and film actor. He had had an unremarkable film career in Hollywood, appearing for instance in a small role in the 1939 *Hound of the Baskervilles* film. But having written plays in the United Kingdom, he developed a second career as a prolific writer for radio series in the United States. He became head writer on the *Sherlock Holmes* series when Edith Meiser gave up. Boucher was the pen name of William Anthony Parker White (1911–68) who was a reviewer and writer of crime fiction, including the ingenious thriller *The Case of the Baker Street Irregulars* (1940). He had an encyclopaedic knowledge of the Holmes canon. He and Green worked very well together, Boucher devising plots and Green supplying dialogue and atmosphere. Their canonical adaptations were faithful and their pastiches ingenious and hugely entertaining. They extended our knowledge of Holmes and Watson, but always within the bounds of probability. They reveal that Holmes received the land for his Sussex bee farm as fee for settling *The Case of the Out of Date Murder*, that he was fluent in Hindi (*The Unfortunate Tobacconist*, *The Vanishing White Elephant*) and Romany (*The Guileless Gypsy*) and undertook delicate matters on behalf of the Emperor Franz Josef of Austria (*Waltz of Death*) and Edward, Prince of Wales (*The Indiscretion of Mr Edwards*). They take Holmes and Watson to India (*The Vanishing White Elephant*), North Africa (*Murder in the Casbah*), Vienna (*Waltz of Death*, *The Viennese Strangler*) and Rome (*The Terrifying Cats*). Green and Boucher enjoyed private jokes, and several times contrived to have Nigel Bruce pose as an aristocrat called Sir William to allow some young woman to christen him 'Willy', which was Nigel Bruce's nickname. They embellished the saga by creating a case involving Mrs Hudson's sister, a Bayswater landlady (*The Tell-Tale Pigeon Feathers*), a murder in 221B Baker Street (*The Innocent Murderess*), Holmes's temporary marriage (*The Book of Tobit*) and Watson's arrest for murder (*The Indiscretion of Mr Edwards*). Since the stories appeared weekly for 38 weeks of the year, they were also able to devise stories to fit particular annual events, Christmas Eve (*The Night before Christmas*), New Year's Eve (*The Iron Box*), Bonfire Night (*The Gunpowder Plot*), April Fool's Day (*The April Fool's Adventure*).

These rediscovered programmes plus a selection of the earlier Edith Meiser-scripted canonical adaptations that have survived (*The Copper Beeches*, *The Retired Colourman*, *The Bruce-Partington Plans*) reveal that Basil Rathbone is the definitive radio voice of Sherlock Holmes. The crystal clarity of his diction, the urgent, authoritative whiplash delivery, the confidence of the lightning logical deductions, all are quite perfect.

Even in his non-Holmes films, Nigel Bruce was always more or less the same.

But Rathbone was a more versatile actor and revelled in variety in both films and stage plays. His vocal versatility led the writers to include in the radio series numerous occasions when Holmes put on disguise and also disguised his voice. Rathbone evidently enjoyed the occasions when Holmes and Watson posed as cockney workmen: as removal men (*The Uneasy Easy Chair*), grooms (*A Scandal in Bohemia*), gasmen (*The Tell-Tale Pigeon Feathers*) and plumbing inspectors (*The Gunpowder Plot*). But Rathbone also impersonates a Chinese actor (*The Viennese Strangler*), an Arab guide (*Murder in the Casbah*), a French art expert (*The Girl with the Gazelle*), a Spanish nihilist (*The Amateur Mendicant Society*), a German count (*The Manor House Case*) and in one memorable case (*The Murderer in Wax*), Rathbone as Holmes impersonated Nigel Bruce's Watson. Ken Greenwald, who helped to produce audio cassette versions of the Rathbone and Bruce radio shows, recalled the experience of first hearing them when he was ten:

> When I got home from school, I tossed my books and homework on my bed and went right to the radio to catch up with what was happening to Superman and all the other adventure heroes. But what I was really waiting for, as I did every week for thirty-nine weeks a year, was to turn the radio dial to KHJ, the Mutual Radio Network radio station in Los Angeles, so I could listen to *The New Adventures of Sherlock Holmes* … By that time, my mother had gotten me ready for bed … She would give me a kiss, then tuck me under the covers and close the door to my room … I never wanted to go to sleep that early. I wanted to listen to all the adult radio shows, just like my mom and dad were doing. When I was sure my parents were busy in the other room, I would quietly turn on the radio, which was located next to my bed on the desk … I knew exactly where each important radio station was on the dial by touch and position. It was easy for me to find KHJ … And sure enough, there came the familiar theme music, which always sent a chill up my spine. I would pull the covers tight around me and punch my pillow and head as close to the radio as I could to catch every word, every action, every deed that Sherlock Holmes and Doctor Watson went through. I was never disappointed. For some reason, I never remembered the stories for more than a week, each new story taking over when the next Sherlock Holmes show was broadcast. But I never forgot the music or those wonderfully familiar voices of Basil Rathbone and Nigel Bruce.[38]

The Petri Wine Company dropped their sponsorship when Rathbone left but the series was snapped up by Kreml Shampoo, moved to a new network (ABC) but retained the services of Green and Boucher. Nigel Bruce resumed the role of Dr Watson for the 1946–47 season of *Sherlock Holmes*, with a new Holmes, Tom Conway. Tom McKnight returned as producer and Edith Meiser's adaptation of seven canonical tales were remade along with her apocryphal tale *The Haunted Bagpipes*. Denis Green and Anthony Boucher wrote the new adventures, joined towards the end of the run by Leonard Lee, author of two of the Universal Holmes films.

Tom Conway was the brother of actor George Sanders and had succeeded Sanders in the film role of The Falcon, a suave, man-about-town detective created by Michael Arlen. Conway successfully played Tom Lawrence, the Falcon, in ten films between 1942 and 1946. In 1948 he starred as Bulldog Drummond in two B pictures. He was British but his natural voice was a suave, world-weary purr, far from the Rathbone whiplash. Cast as Holmes, he made his voice brisker and more authoritative although he did not entirely eliminate the purr. Nevertheless he made an acceptable Holmes, particularly convincing with an unexpectedly powerful performance in *The Dying Detective*. The stories, however, continued to be excellent, ingenious, atmospheric and wholly engaging. The departure of Rathbone had an effect on Bruce's performance as, perhaps lacking that close friendship with Conway that he enjoyed with Rathbone, he indulged in less bumbling. In *The Devil's Foot*, *The Speckled Band*, *The Dying Detective* and *The Haunted Bagpipes* he played Watson absolutely straight. However, *The Elusive Emerald* had a comically amorous encounter between Watson and the Dowager Duchess of Penfield which saw Bruce in full chuntering mode.

At the end of the 1946–47 season, however, there was a major change. Bruce retired from the role of Watson to concentrate on his film career and Conway gave up the role of Holmes, assuming several years later the rather more suitable role of Simon Templar in the radio series which had previously starred Brian Aherne and Vincent Price.

In 1947 production of the *Sherlock Holmes* series moved from Hollywood to New York, appearing on the same network (Mutual) but with a new sponsor (Clippercraft Clothing Company). For this season which ran from 28 September 1947 to 20 June 1948, Edith Meiser returned as scriptwriter. The roles of Holmes and Watson were assumed by two experienced radio actors. John Stanley (1903–82) played Holmes. Although an American, Stanley had been born, educated (at an English public school) and trained for the stage in England. He returned to the United States aged 21 to begin a career as announcer and radio actor. His Holmes, brisk, clipped, authoritative and impeccably British is excellent. But he sounded so much like Basil Rathbone that many people believed it actually was Rathbone, moonlighting under a pseudonym. Watson was played by the experienced British radio actor Alfred Shirley who made Watson not a buffoon but a bluff, hearty, goodnatured companion to Holmes, who is frequently chaffed by Holmes about his weight. Shirley had played Moriarty's henchman Bassick in Orson Welles' radio production of *Sherlock Holmes*.

Edith Meiser provided thirty-nine scripts. The deal with the Conan Doyle estate specified that every third production should be a canonical story and so

Meiser dusted off, revised and refurbished thirteen of her canonical adaptations. But she also created twenty-nine entirely new adventures, which showed she had lost none of her powers of invention and conjuring of atmosphere. She provided several new stories in which Holmes confronted his arch-enemy Professor Moriarty as Moriarty plans to flood the country with counterfeit sovereigns (*The Cadaver in the Roman Toga*) and blow up Buckingham Palace during Queen Victoria's Diamond Jubilee celebrations (*Professor Moriarty and the Diamond Jubilee*), to nobble the favourite for the Wessex Cup (*A Case of Sudden Senility*), develop a drug to destroy willpower and conscience (*The Sinister Crate of Cabbages*) and foment rebellion in a pro-British Indian princely state (*The Serpent God*).

She provided sequels to canonical stories: *The Cradle that Rocked Itself* in which there was another family murder tragedy back in Poldhu Bay, Cornwall, the scene of *The Devil's Foot*; *The Lucky Shilling* in which the eldest son of the Earl and Countess of Maynooth almost met the same fate as the second son as recounted in *The Empty House*, death following involvement in crooked card games; *A Case of Sudden Senility* in which the son of *Silver Blaze*, Blazing Star, is nobbled like his illustrious parent; *The Case of the Sanguinary Spectre* in which the new wife of Reginald Musgrave of *Musgrave Ritual* fame seeks to save Hurlstone from being sold to Hennessy Plunkett, the pickle king, by inventing a ghost.

There are several stories in the vein of *The Sussex Vampire* in which apparently supernatural happenings prove to have earthly explanations, usually as plots to gain wealth or power or to bring about a death (*The Laughing Lemur of Hightower Heath*, *The Bleeding Chandelier*, *The Ever-Blooming Roses*). Meiser's trademark was to set a case in some famous or historic British location, to allow Holmes to dispense titbits of historical knowledge to the American radio audience, so in this series there were stories set in the Tower of London (*King Philip's Golden Salver*), the Elephant and Castle (*The Wooden Claw*), Albany (*Lady Waverly's Imitation Pearls*), Buckingham Palace (*Professor Moriarty and the Diamond Jubilee*), Charing Cross (*The Avenging Blade*), Eel Pie Island (*The Complicated Poisoning on Eel Pie Island*), the British Museum (*The Missing Heiress*) and Waterloo Station (*The Case of the Accommodating Valise*).

Production by Basil Loughrane was well up to the standard of the Hollywood productions and the rich layering of sound effects along with the accomplished radio acting performances brought Edith Meiser's scripts to vivid life. She sometimes put the sound effects staff to the test as when along with the usual repertoire of hansom cab, train, footsteps, fights, wind and storm effects she required the croaking of the Tower ravens and the sound of a descending portcullis in *King Philip's Golden Salver*. Cy Harrice, the announcer on the 1947–48 season and

Dr Watson's interlocutor, recalled the productions:

> We rehearsed on Wednesdays in the Mutual Network's Studio 3 at 1440 Broadway,
> twenty third floor, just off Times Square. Then, on Sundays, to the famous Longacre
> Theatre we would go, to perform the actual broadcast from 7 to 7.30 p.m. Those
> were the days when radio listeners hungered to see their radio performers. They saw
> them perform rarely … fortunately. I say fortunately because radio was essentially
> 'Theatre of the Mind'. … You provided your own mental images to match the
> voices and sounds you heard on the radio … So, when we occasionally broadcast
> a radio show before a large audience, as we did *The Adventures of Sherlock Holmes*
> at the Longacre theatre, we would caution the audience beforehand not to react
> when they saw the sound effects man reproduce the sound of running horses, for
> example, with a couple of coconut shells and some sand. Or, when he re-created a
> fight between two men by hurtling himself on the floor and thrashing about with
> the accompanying grunts.

Edith Meiser, then acting on the Broadway stage, would attend the rehearsals:

> She exuded quiet confidence and graciousness … And … she was prepared to offer
> suggestions to the cast through our director Basil Loughrane, and alterations to the
> script if necessary. We admired, respected, and loved this woman. The cast assembled
> at a large table. John Stanley was our Sherlock Holmes – aquiline, crisp of speech.
> Alfred Shirley was Dr Watson, always a twinkle in his eye. His voice was husky and
> mellow with experience. Perfectly cast. Then, the actors taking the appropriate parts
> of the week's adventure: perhaps a disgruntled chemist, a jealous husband, the driver
> of a hansom cab, a London bobby, two French peasants, Professor Moriarty. At the
> Wurlitzer organ located in a corner of Studio 3, sat Albert Buhrman, our show's
> musician. His music set the mood for the action that took place in our script. It was
> all business at a Sherlock Holmes rehearsal, none of the banter and light-heartedness
> you would find in the soap-opera rehearsal down the hall. There was suspense and
> tension at our rehearsal, a feeling of wordless anticipation. Then, on Sunday, we
> carried this atmosphere with us to our broadcast location.[39]

Stanley carried on as Holmes in the 1948–49 season with a new Watson (Ian
Martin). But pressed by the advertising agency to make her scripts more action
packed and 'hard-boiled' Edith Meiser ended her association with Holmes
at the end of Stanley's first season and was replaced by a team of writers for
1948–49, who responded to the agency's demands with such scripts as *The
Knife of Vengeance*, *The East End Strangler*, *The Mad Miners of Cardiff* and *The
Blood-Soaked Wagon*.

The final American season of *Sherlock Holmes*, 1949–50, saw a return to Hollywood and transfer to the ABC network, the return of Denis Green as scriptwriter and a new Holmes and Watson in Ben Wright and Eric Snowden, both
British and both experienced radio actors. Ben Wright had appeared in several

of the *Holmes* programmes in the Tom Conway season and on 10 March 1947, when Conway was suffering from a heavy cold and had lost his voice, Wright took over the role of Holmes in *The Egyptian Curse*, giving a neat approximation of Conway's tones. Wright had become a regular on the show after his arrival from England in 1947. Eric Snowden had stood in for Bruce, who had flu, in *The Terrifying Cats* (25 February 1946). His Watson had a measured, acute and intelligent voice. During the 1950s television in the United States effectively killed off dramatic radio and although some radio series transferred to television *Sherlock Holmes* did not.

British radio only belatedly took up the Holmes saga. The first BBC Holmes radio play was *Silver Blaze*, broadcast on 12 April 1938 with F. Wyndham Goldie as Holmes and Hubert Harben as Watson. In 1943 a BBC Home Service production of *The Boscombe Valley Mystery* teamed Arthur Wontner as Holmes and Carleton Hobbs as Watson. Arthur Wontner had in five films become Britain's leading Holmes impersonator in 1930s cinema. His voice was calm, considered, drily humorous but undeniably elderly and by 1943 he was in his late sixties. In 1945 the BBC Home Service broadcast an adaptation of *The Speckled Band* with Sir Cedric Hardwicke as Holmes and Finlay Currie as Watson. Adapted by John Dickson Carr, produced by Martyn C. Webster, it was uncharacteristically pedestrian: Hardwicke settled for suave imperturbability but was nicely contrasted with Currie's distinct Scottish burr. Grizelda Hervey was characteristically over-wrought as Helen Stoner. It was Sir Cedric's son, Edward Hardwicke, who was later to become the much-admired television Watson to Jeremy Brett's Holmes. In the same year, another production of *Silver Blaze* featured two veteran radio actors, the gruff-voiced Laidman Browne as Holmes and the even gruffer voiced Norman Shelley as Watson.

The enterprising independent producer Harry Alan Towers, who had already secured the services of Orson Welles for *The Lives of Harry Lime* and Sir Michael Redgrave for a series of Hornblower adventures, decided the time was ripe to revive the canonical stories and managed to team Sir John Gielgud as Holmes and Sir Ralph Richardson as Watson. The excellent adaptations were by John Keir Cross and Gielgud and Richardson, already friends, worked well together. The familiar fluting cadences of Gielgud had the effect of turning Holmes's utterances into poetry while Richardson, who was known for his definitive performances of the common man, produced a Watson who was the epitome of robust, down-to-earth common sense. In a nice touch, Sir John's real-life brother, radio producer Val Gielgud, was brought in to play Mycroft in *The Bruce-Partington Plans*, and Orson Welles guested as Moriarty in *The Final Problem*. Sixteen stories were adapted, twelve of them being broadcast on the BBC in 1954 and all sixteen on American radio in 1955.

But despite the eminence of these stars, it was two veteran radio actors who became Britain's definitive radio Holmes and Watson, Carleton Hobbs and Norman Shelley. They were first teamed in three series of Holmes adaptations scripted by Felix Felton, for BBC Children's Hour between 1952 and 1957. There was a six-part adaptation of *The Hound of the Baskervilles* in 1958, also scripted by Felton. They also starred in a BBC Home Service broadcast of Gillette's play in 1953. Then between 1959 and 1969 they starred in six successive series of short story adaptations by Michael Hardwick for the BBC Light Programme as well as full-length ninety-minute adaptations for the BBC Home Service of *The Valley of Fear*, *A Study in Scarlet* and *The Sign of Four*, all scripted by Hardwick. Hobbs's Holmes, incisive, amused, authoritative, is the serenely omniscient problem-solver, largely devoid of the intensity and dynamism of Rathbone's Holmes or the theatricality and nervous energy that Jeremy Brett was to bring to the role on television. Norman Shelley's Watson was a splendid foil: the voice redolent of port and cigars, that of the elderly clubman who combines the functions of Horatio and Boswell. But Shelley's performance had none of Bruce's comic obtuseness. The BBC productions in which they starred have all the hallmarks of the best BBC radio drama, neat adaptations, careful characterization and a satisfying aural atmosphere of Victorian England. Enyd Williams, later to produce a complete series of the canonical stories for BBC Radio but then a young studio manager, worked on the Hobbs-Shelley series:

> They were enchanting to work with – delightful. Very different from each other. They were of course already far too old to play the parts. But Hobbo had a wonderful sensitive feeling for Holmes and brought a lot of the intellect to Holmes. Norman went more for the buffoon as Watson – but that was Norman's style. Hobbo was a great actor and a great radio actor. They both understood how to handle the microphone, what they could do to utterly make the audience believe they were somewhere else.[40]

Thanks to audio cassette, we can enjoy a plethora of Holmeses. The short stories leant themselves perfectly to half-hour adaptation and radio provided pictures that no film or television version could ever equal. Everyone will have their own favourites from the many interpretations on offer. But for me, there is no doubt that for American radio, Basil Rathbone and Nigel Bruce and for British radio, Carleton Hobbs and Norman Shelley remain the champions, setting the vocal standards that all other contenders have to beat.

Notes

1 Peter MacDonald, *British Literary Culture and Publishing Practice*, Cambridge: Cambridge University Press, 1997, p. 164.
2 MacDonald, *British Literary Culture*, p. 169.
3 John Fraser, *America and the Patterns of Chivalry*, Cambridge: Cambridge University Press, 1982, p. 12.
4 Quoted in Joseph A. Kestner, *Sherlock's Men: Masculinity, Conan Doyle and Cultural History* Aldershot: Ashgate, 1997, p. 207.
5 John Carey, *The Intellectuals and the Masses*, London: Faber and Faber, 1992, p. 64.
6 Rosemary Jann, *The Adventures of Sherlock Holmes: Detecting Social Order*, New York: Twayne, 1995 p. 50.
7 MacDonald, *British Literary Culture*, p. 162.
8 Kestner, *Sherlock's Men*, p. 8.
9 Arthur Conan Doyle, *Memories and Adventures*, London: John Murray, 1930, p. 121.
10 Michael Pointer, *The Sherlock Holmes File*, New York: Clarkson Potter, 1976, p. 18.
11 On the film versions of Sherlock Holmes see David Stuart Davies, *Starring Sherlock Holmes*, London: Titan, 2001; Alan Barnes, *Sherlock Holmes on Screen*, London: Reynolds and Hearn, 2002; Allen Eyles, *Sherlock Holmes: A Centenary Celebration*, London: John Murray, 1986; Michael Pointer, *The Public Life of Sherlock Holmes*, Newton Abbot: David and Charles, 1975; Michael Pointer, *The Sherlock Holmes File*; Chris Steinbrunner and Norman Michaels, *The Films of Sherlock Holmes*, Secaucus, NJ: Citadel Press, 1978.
12 George Pearson, *Flashback*, London: Allen and Unwin, 1957, pp. 36–8.
13 J.E. Harold-Terry and Arthur Rose, *The Return of Sherlock Holmes*, Romford: Ian Henry, 1993, p. iii.
14 Pointer, *The Public Life of Sherlock Holmes*, p. 49.
15 Doyle, *Memories and Adventures*, p. 126.
16 Basil Dean, *Mind's Eye*, London: Hutchinson, 1973, pp. 96–9.
17 Pointer, *The Sherlock Holmes File*, p. 46.
18 Graham Greene, *The Pleasure Dome: The Collected Film Criticism 1935–40*, ed. John Russell Taylor, London: Secker and Warburg, 1972, p. 231.
19 Davies, *Starring Sherlock Holmes*, p. 28.
20 Raymond Massey, *A Hundred Different Lives*, London: Robson, 1979, p. 114.
21 Davies, *Starring Sherlock Holmes*, p. 26.
22 Steinbrunner and Michaels, *The Films of Sherlock Holmes*, p. 46.
23 Davies, *Starring Sherlock Holmes*, p. 24.
24 Pointer, *The Public Life of Sherlock Holmes*, p. 71.
25 Greene, *The Pleasure Dome*, pp. 231–2.
26 Greene, *The Pleasure Dome*, p. 274.
27 Greene, *The Pleasure Dome*, p. 210.
28 Amanda J. Field, *England's Secret Weapon: The Wartime Films of Sherlock Holmes*,

Hendon: Middlesex University Press, 2009, pp. 102–6.
29 Steinbrunner and Michaels, *The Films of Sherlock Holmes*, p. 87.
30 Steinbrunner and Michaels, *The Films of Sherlock Holmes*, p. 149.
31 Basil Rathbone, *In and Out of Character*, Haslemere: Ianmead, 1989, p. 180.
32 Rathbone, *In and Out of Character*, p. 180.
33 Rathbone, *In and Out of Character*, pp. 181–2.
34 Rathbone, *In and Out of Character*, p. 183.
35 Davies, *Starring Sherlock Holmes*, p. 38.
36 Rathbone, *In and Out of Character*, p. 181.
37 Glenhall Taylor, *Before Television: the Radio Years*, South Brunswick and New York: A.S. Barnes, 1979, pp. 124–6.
38 Ken Greenwald, *The Lost Adventures of Sherlock Holmes*, New York: Mallard Press, 1989, pp. 7–8.
39 Lucy Brusic, James Hubbs and William Nadel, *Edith Meiser and Her Adventures with Sherlock Holmes*, Minneapolis: University of Minnesota Libraries, 1999, Minneapolis, 1999, pp. 10–13.
40 Author's interview with Enyd Williams, *The Radio Detectives*, BBC Radio 4, 27 May 1998.

Index